Foreword

Modern accounting may appear to be a matter of electronic wizardry but a computer can only be as good as the data and programs with which it is supplied. It follows that we need a growing body of accountants who understand industry and commerce in accountancy terms and can turn this knowledge into useful programs, supplied with accurate, up-to-date data.

Success in Management Accounting: An Introduction is an intermediate-level text which will be of benefit to any student whose course covers the study of all the basic elements of cost accounting: job costing, contract costing, process costing, marginal costing, standard costing (variance accounting) and budgetary control. It also covers integrated accounting and computerised systems, introduces such recent developments as just-in-time accounting, activity-based costing, etc., and features some of the costing problems of particular industries.

The book contains detailed questions, each with an answer solution, and a comprehensive index to help students locate the large number of subject areas covered. It will be suitable for students taking BTEC National and Higher National awards, those studying intermediate professional examinations for all the professional bodies (but particularly CIMA students) and those on management degree-level courses or degree-equivalent courses.

In producing this book we have received much help from professional bodies and colleagues and should particularly like to thank Dave Gooch for general advice on the computerisation of cost accounts and Janice Brown, formerly of John Murray (Publishers) Ltd, for her patience and support.

The courtesy of the Chartered Institute of Management Accountants in permitting the use of diagrams and numerous definitions from its handbook *Official Terminology* is gratefully acknowledged. This handbook is essential reading for students of management accounting and may be obtained from the Institute at 63 Portland Place, London W1N 4AB.

We should like to acknowledge permission from Helen Coult to reproduce the table of definitions of computer terms from her book for bankers. We should also like to thank Sue Davey of Thurrock Technical College for the use of some questions, and Micro-Retailer Systems Ltd for material on the computerisation of the accounts of retailers.

Geoffrey Whitehead
Arthur Upson

First published 1992

Some parts of this book were originally published in a similar form in Success in Accounting and Costing *and its associated* Problems and Projects *book* (1982).

Typeset in 9/11pt Times Roman by Colset Private Limited, Singapore
Printed and bound in Great Britain
by Clays Ltd, St Ives plc

A catalogue entry for this title is available from the British Library

ISBN 0-7195-5034-3

Contents

PART ONE

The main text

UNIT 1

Introduction to management accounting

1.1 Relationship between financial and cost accounts

Accounting is a term which refers to the numerous record-keeping activities carried out as a result of business transactions. It deals with the collection and recording of business facts and figures and is an information system reporting to a wide variety of individuals and interested parties.

Accounting is concerned with business transactions and the exchange or transfer of value in respect of goods and services. These transactions involve transfers which are either internal or external and are recorded at *historical cost*. This means that items are valued at what they cost when they were purchased or manufactured internally at some past time. There are many forms of business ownership such as sole traders, partnerships, limited companies and public sector enterprises responsible to the government and public authorities. There are also non-profit-making organisations and co-operative societies. The accounting systems found in these organisations vary considerably, depending on the demands of management and the legal requirements which have to be met.

Many people are confused by the titles given to accountants and systems of accounting. They are familiar with the term *financial accounting*, relating it to book-keeping which produces a profit statement and a Balance Sheet, but are unsure of the functions of *cost accounting* and *management accounting*.

(a) Financial accounting

Book-keeping systems and methods can be adapted to suit a particular form of business enterprise; in the first instance they are concerned with *stewardship* and are designed to comply with the law. Stewardship means that the business must account to the owners for the activities carried out in their names. To a large extent, financial accounts are concerned with external affairs and relationships, that is with individuals and organisations outside the business.

The increasing size of business units and the advent of limited companies and, more recently, of holding companies and multinational corporations have resulted in large and very complex organisations. There is also the effect of economic conditions which have caused rapid inflation and the distortion of profits shown in company accounts. The financial accounts record the results of transactions and transfers carried out, so that at the end of a period, the Trading and Profit and Loss Account, the Appropriation Account and the

Balance Sheet can be produced. The company books show the amount invested in the business and the amount withdrawn by the owners. The accounts are classified as *Real Accounts*, showing the value of the fixed assets; *Personal Accounts*, recording transactions with debtors and creditors connected with the activities of the business; and *Nominal Accounts*, showing the expenses and losses incurred and any gains or profits made. There are also the Cash Account and Bank Account entries to record receipts and payments.

The draft final accounts may, in the first instance, be drawn up for internal use, and after any necessary adjustments have been made they will be prepared (as far as companies are concerned) as published accounts to comply with the legal and taxation requirements of the Companies Acts 1985–9 and various Finance Acts. They will take account of any recommendations by the directors on the payment of dividends and similar matters.

There is no strict borderline between financial, cost and management accounts, and in some organisations integration may take place. Any statistics or other statements prepared depend on the type, size and nature of the business and the requirements of management.

Three organisations or institutions have exerted a great influence on the way in which financial accounts are produced.

(i) The law The accounting requirements for companies are clearly laid down in the Companies Acts 1985–9. Every company Balance Sheet must now give a true and fair view of the state of affairs of the company as at the end of its financial year, and every Profit and Loss Account must give a true and fair view of the profit or loss of the company for the financial year. There are many other matters in the Companies Acts which have to be complied with, including requirements in connection with income and corporation tax, value added tax and so on.

(ii) Professional bodies Accountancy organisations now exert considerable influence on the way in which accounts are laid out. The accountancy bodies issue Statements of Standard Accounting Practice (Accounting Standards, or SSAPs) which describe methods of accounting approved by their various governing councils. Members of these bodies are obliged to observe accounting standards or justify departures from them.

(iii) The Council of the Stock Exchange This organisation is chiefly concerned with the protection of the shareholder, and any company which wishes to make a public issue of its shares must submit financial information covering many years and must comply with the rules issued by the Council.

(b) Cost accounting

Cost accounting is defined in the *Official Terminology* handbook of the Chartered Institute of Management Accounting as 'the establishment of budgets, standard costs and actual costs of operations, processes, activities or products; and the analysis of variances, profitability or the social use of funds'. It is an essential aid to management in establishing selling prices and providing information for the day-to-day control of operations. It helps management in the decision- and policy-making processes and in determining future policies in respect of operations and plans for further capital expenditure. The form of costing used depends on many factors, and in the small business may be merely an estimation using certain details from the financial books. In other organisations the system may be very sophisticated, using standard costing, budgetary control and other modern techniques, which form the subject-matter of this book.

Cost accounting uses basically the same information as is shown in the financial books, but in the process of costing, through the analysis and classification of accounts, it reveals the costs of departments, processes, products and units; it also shows selling, distribution and administrative costs by departments, functions and services. Costing indicates inefficiencies and waste of materials and wages, and analyses losses caused by idle time of machinery and plant. It classifies expenses as direct and indirect costs and charges these at each stage of manufacture to the product. Cost accounting records the actual cost which can be compared with estimates or standard costs. It can provide a perpetual inventory of stores and other materials. In summary, costing uses book-keeping procedures to classify and record expenditure so as to allow accumulation of cost information in order to be able to measure managerial efficiency. All these methods are explained in the units which follow.

(c) Management accounting

Management accountancy provides management with accounting information for the purpose of planning and running a business. It developed because of management's demands for information on past and present operations and future trends. It integrates cost and financial accounting – analysing and interpreting past and present results and providing forecasts for the future. It is also concerned with alternative methods of production and operational procedures and with financial planning. The CIMA handbook *Official Terminology* says that the management accountant participates in management to ensure that there is effective:

- formulation of plans to meet objectives (strategic planning);
- formulation of short-term operation plans (budgeting/profit; planning);
- acquisition and use of finance (financial management) and recording of transactions (financial accounting and cost accounting);
- communication of financial and operating information;
- corrective action to bring plans and results into line (financial control);
- reviewing and reporting on systems and operations (internal audit and management audit).

Thus it can be seen that financial, cost and management accounting are interrelated. Financial accounting has limitations because insufficient information is made available for management to be able to identify and forecast major trends and problems. Financial accounting can only show the results that have been achieved, but this may be too late for events to be controlled or changed. Management must identify the need for change in advance of any emergency and detect problems in time to take corrective action. In this respect, cost and management accounting must supplement the information provided by financial accounting so that management can develop, interpret and achieve overall policies and objectives.

1.2 Elements of cost

The cost of a particular item or service is the amount spent on materials, labour and expenses (Fig. 1.1). These three groups of costs may be divided into direct and indirect costs.

(a) Direct costs

These costs consist of materials, wages and expenses which can easily be identified with a particular unit, a product or a service which a business or organisation sells. For example, if a customer orders a piece of mahogany furniture which is to be made to a special design, the direct costs would include the main material (mahogany), the wages of the cabinet-maker and other workers, and the charge made by the designer. These costs are directly related to the goods being manufactured, and collectively make up what is known as the *prime cost* of the product.

(b) Indirect costs

These are costs which are added to the prime cost in order to obtain the total cost. They are *overhead costs* because they cannot be allocated directly to the unit or service, but have to be apportioned or absorbed by *cost units* (see Unit 1.6) or *cost centres*.

Cost centres Administrative departments are not usually suitable as units for determining production costs, and therefore the organisation is divided into cost centres. Other natural divisions would be groups of similar machines, similar processes or operations to which costs can be charged.

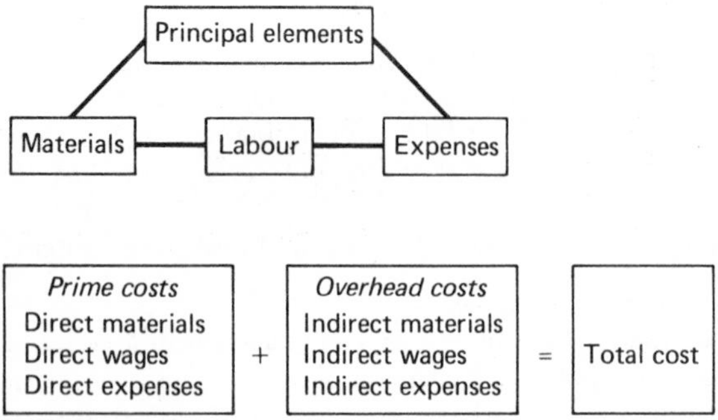

Fig. 1.1 The elements of cost

Using furniture again as an example, the indirect materials could include the glue which could not be measured as a charge to a particular piece of furniture, but would be included in the costs of the department where the furniture was made. The wages of the supervisory staff would have to be charged to the cost of running the department and their wages would be apportioned to the products of that department, so that each product would bear a share of that cost. An example of indirect expense of this type of department would be the maintenance cost of machinery used by the employees.

1.3 Classification of overhead costs

Cost classification is the process of grouping costs according to their common characteristics. This is a very important procedure in respect of overhead expenses as it is essential that each unit of production or service bears its fair share of indirect costs (see Table 1.1, p. 8). There are five major functions of a business to which costs are allocated.

(a) Production

This department produces or prepares the goods or service sold, and its involvement ends when these are complete after the primary packing of the product.

(b) Administration

This is the function of controlling the operations of a business, formulating the policy and directing the activities, but it is not directly related to the functional activities of production, selling, distribution or research. However, the production and marketing divisions need the service of administrators and this is classified separately, although the benefit derived from the administrative service may be charged separately to production and marketing at a later stage.

(c) Selling

This is the operation of the sales department in securing orders and retaining customers and includes the costs incurred in promoting sales.

(d) Distribution

This process begins with making the product ready for dispatch and is completed when it is delivered to the customer and the returned container or empty package is made ready for further use. The selling and distribution functions are sometimes combined and costs applied as a single charge.

(e) Research and development

This function may exist only in large organisations and covers research for new or improved methods and the development of new or improved products. Allocation of the cost is a policy decision made by management, normally including the chief accountant and the managing director.

Table 1.1 Examples of overhead costs

Production department (factory)

Rent and rates
Insurance of premises, plant, employees, etc.
Indirect wages and salaries (i.e. wages and salaries not attributable directly to a particular unit of production)
Heating and lighting
Indirect power (i.e. power not attributable to a particular unit or process of production)
Depreciation
Repairs to plant, buildings, etc.
Indirect materials (i.e. materials not attributable to a particular unit or process of production)
Personnel expenses

All other departments

Note: The costs of all other departments will be overhead costs. These will include many general costs (for example, all departments will have to pay rent, rates, lighting and heating, wages and salaries, etc.). Some of the more specialised departmental costs are shown below.

Administration costs	Selling and distribution costs	Research and development costs
Service (office machinery and equipment)	Advertising and display	Models and prototype
Computer purchase or hire	Commission	Design
Legal	Tendering	Research questionnaire
Company secretarial (issue and transfer of shares)	Motor vehicle	Laboratory, quality control and experimental
Personnel	Showroom	Literature survey
Pension	Exhibition	Purchase and testing of rival products

1.4 How total cost is made up

How do we identify cost? It may be thought that cost is the price paid, the value of the goods, or the outlay. In fact, it is the amount of expenditure incurred on a given item. In cost accounting we use certain procedures *in order to ascertain each outlay incurred on particular items*. Total cost includes several elements which have to be added together. This accumulation can be done after each operation or after each stage of assembly, but for administrative purposes it is usually shown on a cost sheet as direct and indirect expenditure. We start with the prime or direct costs and finish with the indirect costs. For purposes of control, details can be shown by breaking down the cost into classes of direct material and labour and of indirect or overhead costs (Fig. 1.2, p. 10).

1.5 The costing department

The costing department, which is supervised by the chief cost accountant, has the following objectives:

(a) analysis and classification of all expenditure so that the cost of operations, units, processes and products can be ascertained;
(b) where appropriate, developing cost standards, reporting variances and indicating waste of materials, wages and resources;
(c) provision of *actual costs* for comparison with *estimates*, as an aid in price fixing, and for use in the preparation of quotations and tenders;
(d) provision of information to enable Profit and Loss Accounts and Balance Sheets to be prepared at suitable intervals;
(e) maintenance of adequate records so that information can be provided quickly and efficiently to all who may need assistance in the control of the organisation;
(f) operation of a system of perpetual inventory for raw materials, finished parts, components and finished goods;
(g) collection of data for the preparation of *budgets* and for use in cost control accounts and budgetary control procedures;
(h) designing and installing new methods and systems so that effective information can be given promptly to other departments.

1.6 Methods of cost accounting

Various *basic costing methods* have been established to suit the kind of goods manufactured or the type of service provided. For purposes of control there are different ways in which cost information may be given to management. In order to present this information in the most suitable way, superimposed principles and techniques are applied and used in the costing system. The basic costing methods are either *costing for specific orders* or *costing for continuous operations* (Fig. 1.3, p. 11).

(a) Costing for specific orders

This method applies to production which is authorised by a special order or contract and for which the work consists of separate *jobs, batches* or *contracts*. An order number is issued to collect the elements of cost for goods manufactured for stock or to the requirements of a customer, or when the specific order is a contract (usually concerned with constructional or civil engineering activities).

(i) Job costing This applies to goods manufactured for stock or to customers' special requirements. It also applies when capital expenditure is made and the fixed asset is manufactured internally instead of being purchased.

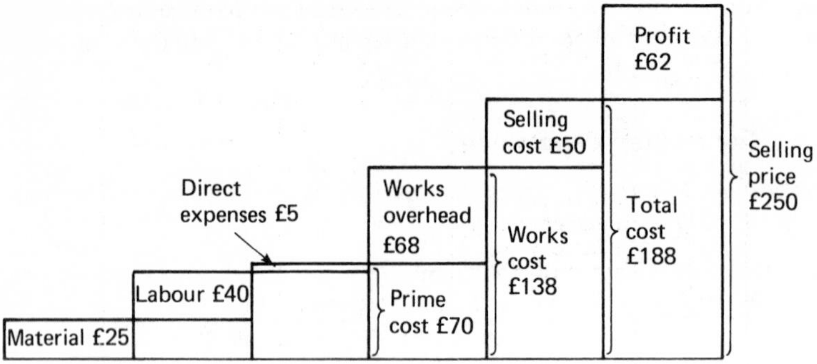

Cost Sheet

	£	£
Materials		
Steel	5	
Brass	20	
		25
Labour		
Machining	30	
Assembly	10	
		40
Direct expenses		
Patterns		5
Prime cost		70
Works overhead		
Machining (200% on labour)	60	
Assembly (80% on labour)	8	
		68
Works cost		138
Selling cost		50
Total cost		188
Profit		62
Selling price		£ 250

Fig. 1.2 How total cost is made up
Note: In this example the cost of administration is included in works overhead and selling costs.

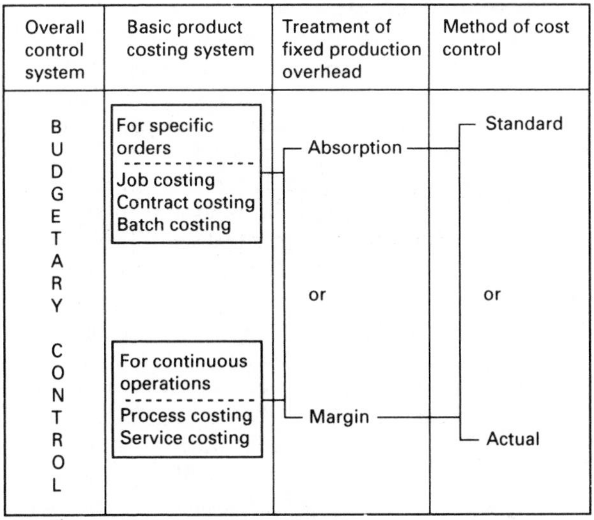

Fig. 1.3 Elements of a product costing system
(*Reproduced by courtesy of the Chartered Institute of Management Accountants*)

When repairs are exceptional and not regarded as normal maintenance, the work is carried out and the costs are charged to a job order number. A characteristic of job costing is that the job moves through the processes or operations as a continuously identifiable unit.

(ii) Contract costing This form of specific order costing is usually applied to work which extends over a long period and, consequently, the cost is considerable. It is work undertaken to customers' special requirements and applies particularly to construction work such as ship-building, bridge-building and civil engineering.

(iii) Batch costing This is similar to job costing and applies when similar articles are manufactured in batches either for sale or for stock or when units from a batch are required for use or assembly on other specific orders. The batch of items is costed as a job and as the parts are identical the *unit cost* is obtained by dividing the batch cost by the quantity produced.

The term *unit cost*, used in (iii) above, is a unit of quantity of product or service, or time, in relation to which costs may be ascertained or expressed. Examples of typical units are:

Industry	*Operation or product*	*Unit used: cost per*
Automotive	Stampings	100 stampings
Brewing	Beer	Kilolitre
Brick-making	Bricks	1 000 bricks
Fertiliser	Acid phosphate	Tonne
Pharmaceutical	Tablets	1 000 tablets
Transport	Heavy goods movements	Tonne/kilometre

(b) Costing for continuous operations

This basic costing method applies to operations of a process or service nature where standardised goods or services result from a sequence of repetitive and more or less continuous operations or processes. The average cost per unit is obtained by taking the total cost which applies and averaging this over the units produced during the period.

(i) Process costing Manufacture which is continuous or where production is on a mass production basis, causing a loss of identity of individual items or materials, uses process costing. It is assumed that similar amounts of material, labour and overhead will be charged to each process. It is an averaging technique where the process cost per unit is obtained by finding the average cost per unit for the period. Production may be of a single process or several processes, where the completed units are transferred from one process to the next. Among the industries using process costing are brewing, paint, cement production and food products.

(ii) Service costing This is operation costing where a standardised service is provided by a service cost centre or an undertaking. Average costs per unit are calculated per period and costs can be ascertained in relation to the standardised unit or measurement. Services using this method include transport, canteens, power, heating, personnel and welfare.

(c) Superimposed principles and techniques

The costing system uses the basic costing method appropriate to the way in which goods are manufactured or the services provided, and it is then adapted by superimposing on the basic costing method certain principles and techniques so that the routine system will supply information which can be presented in a particular manner. The main principles and techniques which may be superimposed consist of:

(i) absorption costing;
(ii) marginal costing;

((i) and (ii) are simply different ways of treating fixed production overhead.)

(iii) standard costing;
(iv) actual cost ascertainment;

((iii) and (iv) enable the costs envisaged before production begins - standard costs - to be compared with the actual costs incurred when production actually takes place. The differences are called *variances* and give rise to a method of cost control called:)

(v) variance accounting.

Superimposed upon the whole costing procedure is a system of:

(vi) budgetary control, which seeks to control every aspect of operations by requiring heads of departments to prepare budgets for their future activities so that over-spending (and under-spending) can be detected and investigated.

The inter-relation of these costing methods is shown diagrammatically in Fig. 1.3. These techniques are described briefly below, and form the major subject-matter of this book. One or two other techniques are also described briefly:

(i) Absorption costing This is a principle whereby *fixed* as well as *variable* costs are allotted to cost units. The object is to ensure that, as far as is possible, all the costs of operating a business are charged to the cost units. The problem is that although variable costs tend to vary in direct proportion to changes in the volume of output or turnover, fixed costs accrue in relation to the passage of time. As the level of activity and the overhead absorption rates are estimated and predetermined, any variation in activity or overhead costs results in an over- or under-absorption of overhead costs. This is more fully explained in Unit 5.9.

(ii) Marginal costing This technique is used in the routine costing system which ascertains the variable (marginal) cost of cost units. The margin or difference between the variable cost and the selling price is known as the *contribution* and the fixed costs for the relevant period are written off in full against the contribution for that period (see Unit 8.1 (v)).

(iii) Standard costing This is the method of costing in which the standard costs (predetermined costs) of products and services are prepared (see Unit 9).

(iv) Budgetary control This is a method which relates to the establishment of budgets for responsibility centres. These centres are the responsibility of executives and their performance is assessed by a continuous comparison of actual with budgeted results (see Unit 10).

(v) Actual cost ascertainment This is the principle whereby the costs of cost centres and cost units are ascertained and, subject to certain approximations, are then assumed to represent actual costs. The term *historical cost* is generally used to indicate actual cost but the term is not recommended because the word historical applies also to other concepts.

(vi) Variance accounting This technique is concerned with standard costing and budgetary control. Standard costs and budgeted cost allowances are established and the difference between these and the actual costs are variances, which are recorded and studied in order to find out why there is a difference between planned and actual performance (see Units 9 and 10).

(d) Other techniques

(i) Uniform costing Trade associations often adopt and recommend this system to their members so that all members of the association can use the same principles and/or practices. This system can also be used by a group of companies so that useful comparisons of detailed costs which have been prepared using the same costing principles and practices can be made within the group.

(ii) Differential costing This refers to the manner in which alternative courses of action are examined. It is a technique which studies the behaviour of costs at different volumes of output and sales and the relationship between contribution and sales value, which is the contribution/sales ratio (see Unit 8.8).

(iii) Incremental costing This is used in the preparation of special information where consideration is given to a range of graduated changes in the level or nature of activity. The additional costs and revenues likely to result from each degree of change are presented.

Costing and pricing are interrelated. Costing is invaluable in the formulation and approval of policies; the information it provides enables expenditures to be controlled and prices to be established.

In general, selling prices are determined by competition and the effect of supply and demand. In this respect operating efficiency is of paramount importance. It is essential to maintain a high level of activity with volumes of output which will result in low unit costs. There are occasions when prices are set below the full cost, in order to retain regular customers, and when new products are introduced. When there is no established price structure, goods are sometimes priced on cost, plus an agreed percentage to cover the profit. When this applies to large contracts, it is sometimes a condition that an auditor's certificate is sent with the invoice stating that the price is correct within the terms of the contract. Contracts on a *cost-plus* basis are not always favourable to the customer because:

the cost tends to be higher than when there is a fixed price;
manufacturers have little incentive to reduce costs as they would receive a smaller return;
dishonest contractors may increase the actual cost by fraudulently including amounts which are not applicable to the contract.

This demonstrates the need for an auditor's certificate which, in some cases, is supplied by the customer's auditor after inspection of the documents and cost sheets.

1.7 Value analysis

This is a management technique for reducing or eliminating items of cost, by questioning the need to use the particular materials, labour or services specified in the original process. *Value engineering* is the application of the value analysis techniques to new products in the development or prototype stage, but often there is insufficient time at this stage to investigate, compare and secure the cost of alternatives as required by the application of value analysis.

This procedure is designed to improve profitability by cutting out unnecessary costs, while maintaining the quality and usefulness of the product. A checklist is used which presents a series of questions with the object of encouraging an individual or members of a team to produce ideas which will lead to a reduction in cost and/or an improvement in design. The following list gives an indication of the kinds of question which can be asked during the value analysis of any component, product, item of equipment or service.

(i) Does it serve a useful purpose?
(ii) Can the design be simplified?
(iii) Does its use justify the expenditure involved?
(iv) Can the item be replaced by something better or less costly?
(v) Can a cheaper or different grade of material be used?
(vi) Can the item be replaced by a standard product?
(vii) Can it be produced more cheaply using a different process?
(viii) Is there another supplier who can provide it for less?

A value analysis team may consist of people from departments such as design, methods, production, sales, purchasing and costing. Considerable savings and improvements can be made by companies using this technique. In particular, savings can be made in raw materials costs, production time taken, and reducing the weight of the product.

1.8 Quality circles

The idea of quality circles came from Japan and they have now spread to many other countries. The aim of the circles is to improve efficiency in an organisation, reduce its costs and increase competitiveness by allowing employees to participate in its running and to help contribute to its success. The procedure is concerned with analysing problems and solving them by using the knowledge and experience of small groups of workers.

The quality circle is a voluntary body which meets fortnightly or monthly. A departmental group may consist of the supervisor, usually the leader, and several workers. Shop-floor workers have a special contribution to make, as they are in daily contact with the products and manufacturing operations and are aware of many problems and uneconomic methods which management may not have noticed. Problems may concern complaints from customers, difficulties arising in the engineering or design department, imperfect processing and planning, excessive scrap, unsuitable tools or equipment, product quality and reliability, and progressing of materials.

In the course of their deliberations, members may have to seek advice from specialists and experts within the organisation. The company appoints a *facilitator* to co-ordinate the affairs and activities of the group and to contact other individuals in the company when information and help is needed. The facilitator must be carefully selected for his or her ability to obtain the respect of others by listening, consulting and communicating, in order to motivate the group and maintain morale.

The leader of the circle may receive training in the organisational aspects of group activities such as how to obtain, select and interpret information, constructive discussion, and how to respond usefully to the contributions of others. There may also be instruction in statistical methods and other problem-solving techniques such as Pareto analysis, which pays attention to key areas and which uses the more or less constant relationship between quantity and value. Graphs may be used to illustrate the items or areas where the greatest losses appear or to indicate the possible causes of failure.

When recommendations are made to management, they must be implemented if possible, but if the suggestions are unacceptable, clear reasons must be given for the rejection; otherwise there is a collapse of confidence in the use of quality circles as an aid to management.

1.9 Personnel

In different organisations, the staff of a costing department varies widely and the duties and responsibilities of individuals depend on those given to the head of the department. The staff may consist of a chief cost accountant or controller with assistants, time clerks, wages clerks and cost clerks. Or it may be organised into separate sections such as timekeeping, wages, costing, stores control accounting and similar activities.

It is the duty of the chief cost accountant to maintain and improve the system at all times, especially when changes are taking place within the organisation or when new techniques become available outside the business. He or she must have close contact with the executives of other departments, determining their needs and presenting information promptly.

1.10 Cost accounting manual

A manual or set of standard practice instructions should be drawn up by the chief cost accountant to outline the system in detail so that misunderstandings can be avoided. This is most useful to new employees, since, among other things, it indicates the forms to be used and the routes they will travel. It will also give detailed information on the various procedures, on the coding and classification of accounts and on the reports to be issued.

1.11 Relationship with other departments

In order to carry out this work, the cost department must co-operate with the other departments in a business. It processes a vast amount of data which is received from the following departments:

Engineering	Progress	Sales
Planning	Inspection	Purchasing
Production control	Storekeeping	Accounts
Work study, method study and rate fixing	Dispatch and packing	

In addition, the cost department gives and receives advice from many individuals in the firm, from general management to superintendents and supervisors.

Transfer pricing

Transfer pricing is a device which seeks to measure departmental performance. Each department is expected to earn a profit, therefore an arbitrary selling price or value is fixed when work is transferred to other departments. The system is not widely used. As an example, in the manufacture of a mixing drum:

Department 1 (the plate department) draws out a steel plate, cuts it to size and trims the material. This cost, material, wages and overhead is collected and a percentage is added for the profit element for the department. This is a notional profit. The plate department transfers this blank plate at the agreed price to :

Department 2 (the press department) which presses the plate in the press, by the use of dies, to the shape of the mixing drum. This department records its costs for power, overheads and notional profit. The total cost, that is the original transfer cost plus the costs of Department 2, decides the new transfer price to Department 3. The process continues through the departments until the drum is a finished good.

Every individual and every process or department contributes towards the performance and profitability of an organisation. If this is to be measured to assess the degree of efficiency of managers or divisions of a business, what method of pricing is to be used as output is transferred? The use of market price is satisfactory in theory, but the transfer of work or units of production at intermediate stages in a manufacturing process generally cannot be related to market prices, since none exist. This is because values have to be assigned to operations on a product which is incomplete or which is special and not produced elsewhere.

Within a group or in one particular factory it is sometimes possible to establish a market price by inviting quotations for the work before deciding where the work is to be carried out. Management needs to be assured that the quality of the work and the rate of delivery are up to company standards.

The *transfer price* is the minimum price quoted, whether internally or by another business. When a market price is unobtainable the usual procedure is to charge cost plus a percentage. Cost must include the full outlay, including any extra costs such as packing and carriage when the work is dispatched to another part of the group. Alternatively, the price can be based on a variable cost plus an addition for fixed cost, and a profit which is related to the overall profit of the organisation. The expected return on capital employed will be known, and if the different segments of the business are allocated their share of this, the profit expected from each segment can be calculated and a percentage established for use in transfer pricing.

1.12 Coding

The costing system needs symbols, codes and account numbers in order to facilitate the collection and processing of a wide variety of data. Coding is essential when computers and other office machines are used, as it aids the sorting and tabulation of data into groups of similar items. It also enables accounts to be located quickly, aids the memory and helps clerical work to be carried out speedily and efficiently.

A coding system should be simple, easily remembered and flexible so that expansion can take place without the need to reorganise the entire system. The following items need codes and account numbers:

Raw material, parts and finished goods	Overhead expenses	Fixed assets
Direct and indirect labour operations	Customers' orders	Tools and equipment
	Stock orders	
	Jobs and processes	

Standing order numbers

Expenses are classified, and each type of expense is given a *standing order number*, or code, to which costs are charged as they occur. These numbers or codes are shown in the manual of accounts, and probably lists of expense orders will be posted up in each department to guide those involved with expense costs. For example, a number could be issued for charging the cost of repairs, which would be used by all departments. It would be followed, however, by additional figures, representing the number of the department where the cost occurred and the type of asset repaired (e.g. desk or machine).

Items in a numerical code can be issued in *sequence*, in *blocks of numbers* or in *groups of related items*, so that a coding system may be drawn up using one or more of the following methods:

(i) Sequence coding On the establishment of a coding system, similar or related items can be grouped together in the classification and given numbers in sequence. However, this does not allow for the introduction at a later date of extra items into a group of related items as each new item has to take the next number in the series. New items have to take a number at the end of the list and to overcome this a *block code* can be used, whereby a block of numbers can be used for similar types of expense with spare numbers for use in the future when new types of expense arise.

(ii) Block coding For example, if the main classification number for 'repairs' is 27 and there are twelve departments, the numbers for repairs will extend from 2701 to 2712 in a sequence coding, but in a block coding the numbers for repairs could range from 2701 to 2720. This allows for expansion as numbers 2713 to 2720 would be reserved for future use.

(iii) Group classification This is a numerical classification where the first figure is the major classification and the succeeding digits are minor classifications. If the major classification for heating is 21, the next digit could represent the type of heating and the next one or two digits would indicate the department.

21 Heating	
211 Gas	2116 (6 representing tool room)
212 Solid fuel	2126 (6 representing tool room)

(iv) Mnemonic codes Letters can be used to designate the various items, such as 'R' for repairs (R27). They can also be used for part numbers or codes to represent the type of material used in the manufacture of a component. For example, 'B' could be brass, 'CS' could be cast steel and 'MS' could be mild steel.
(v) Decimal coding This is a system where important items in a classification can be combined in a code number, for example, 21 heating, 01 gas, 06 tool room, as 21.01.06.

There are other special or proprietary systems in use. One is based on the shape of a component and the class of material used. This groups together all items of a similar shape, size and material and encourages standardisation and the reduction of the variety of stocks held.

Standing orders or codes are appropriate in many cases but for customers' orders, stock orders, jobs and processes, a sequence code is usually adopted as the numbers are assigned at the date of issue.

1.13 Exercises

1. What do you understand by the terms *(a)* financial accounting, *(b)* cost accounting and *(c)* management accounting?

2. What do you consider to be the objects of costing?

3. Write an essay on the methods of cost accounting.

4. Explain what you understand by *(a)* classification of costs and *(b)* coding.

5. Why is it desirable to classify overhead costs?

6. Relocated Ltd have been forced by problems of urban renewal to resite their premises in a development area. This entails the renting of a 'shell' factory built by the Development Authority, and its layout at the firm's expense to suit their whole system of working; this requires the co-ordination of three major processes into an integrated flow-system (with a total of twelve cost centres). There are to be associated office premises in an adjacent building, and a shared computer facility is available on the site. The Authority will provide accommodation for key staff moving to the area; local staff will be recruited from among workers resettled in the town from areas of urban decay. Relocated Ltd's total output is taken by six wholesalers who market it nationally at their own expense.

   Consider the types of cost that may be involved in such a relocation.

7. What is *value analysis*? Taking any room or work area in a business premises with which you are familiar, draw up an analysis of every piece of equipment in it (including furniture, fittings, windows, doors and so on) to assess its value to the business and its effectiveness. (If you are not, or have not been, in a working situation, apply the same process to a room in a college or educational centre where you have studied.)

UNIT 2

Recording material costs

2.1 Types of material

In the process of production the following materials are required:

(a) Direct materials

The term *direct* means materials which are actually embodied in the finished product. Examples are raw materials, manufactured items, components and other purchased items such as steel, timber, castings, nuts and bolts, engines and electric motors.

(b) Indirect materials

There are also indirect materials or consumables which do not enter into the product, but are needed during the course of manufacture. Examples are oil and cleaning materials for machines, fluorescent tubes for lighting the factory, polish and stationery for works' offices, and batteries for electric trucks. When certain direct materials cannot be accurately or economically charged direct to the product because the quantities are small, they are treated as indirect material costs.

2.2 Basic documents

In the process of accounting for cost there are a number of basic documents which are used in the recording procedures, and there are at least three essential forms used for materials.

(a) Specification or bill of materials

The specification or parts list shows the direct materials required in the production process and indicates the quality and quantity of the materials and components to be used. The list shows the code or item number of the parts specified, and these materials will be held in stock until required, or they will be purchased and charged direct to the job or account number. In many industries a large number of the items will be manufactured on the premises and held in stock until required for assembly.

(b) Materials requisition

This is a stores requisition which authorises the stores department to issue the specific items of material written or listed on the requisition form. Various

MATERIALS REQUISITION				No. G.294
Bin no.	Drawing no. 72 491	Code no. 46	Group 6	Order no. X.20 798
	Description	Quantity	Unit price £	Value £
X.284	Crawler Pad	1	30.85	30.85

Authorised by:	Date	Stores Ledger	Cost Ledger	30.85
J. Brown	September 7	I. P.	H. F.	Total

MATERIALS REQUISITION		No. 296	
Stores code	Bin no.	Material group	Account no.
D. 142	A.164	7	JP. 20 496
Quantity	Description		Value
20 litres	Engine Oil		£ 25.00
Authorised by:	Priced by:	Stores Ledger	Cost Ledger
R. Gregg	P.S.	S.C.	R.F.

Fig. 2.1 Examples of materials requisitions

departments or officials may be authorised to requisition materials, but normally requisitions are prepared by the production department. There may be several copies of the same requisition but one of these will be priced by the stores ledger clerk and sent to the cost office. In a modern organisation the stores ledger clerk will probably be the person who operates a stores computer. Examples of materials requisitions are given in Fig. 2.1.

(c) Materials return note

After the items have been issued, it is sometimes discovered that some are faulty or incorrect. For example, if a component such as a water pump is

<table>
<tr><td colspan="3">MATERIALS RETURN NOTE</td><td>Cost code
5</td><td colspan="2">Order no.
B.3.879</td></tr>
<tr><td>Quantity</td><td colspan="3">Description</td><td colspan="2">Condition</td></tr>
<tr><td>1</td><td colspan="3">Water Pump</td><td colspan="2">New</td></tr>
<tr><td>Date of return</td><td colspan="5" rowspan="2">Water pump G.307 was issued instead of G.309. The incorrect item has been examined and is to be taken into stock.
Signature: J. Brown . . . . Date: Sept. 8</td></tr>
<tr><td>Sept. 8</td></tr>
<tr><td>Material code</td><td colspan="2">Description</td><td>Quantity</td><td colspan="2">Value</td></tr>
<tr><td>G.307</td><td colspan="2">Water Pump</td><td>1</td><td>£
18</td><td>38</td></tr>
<tr><td colspan="2">Posted to stock records</td><td>✓</td><td rowspan="2">Total</td><td colspan="2" rowspan="2">18 38</td></tr>
<tr><td colspan="2">Credited to Cost Account</td><td>✓</td></tr>
</table>

Fig. 2.2 A materials return note

found to be of the wrong type, it is returned to the stores with a materials return note, and a materials requisition for the correct type of pump.

If more material is issued than is actually used, as in the case of steel plate, tubes or bricks, which come in stock sizes or large quantities, the excess material is returned to stores, together with a materials return note which is, in effect, a credit note. Three or more copies may be issued, of which one is retained by the factory department, one is sent to the storekeeper and a third is priced by the stores ledger clerk and sent to the cost office. A materials return note is shown in Fig. 2.2.

(d) Materials transfer note

This form records the transfer of material from one store, department or cost centre to another. Double-entry accounting must be applied so that Stores Control Accounts are adjusted, and debited and credited with the value transferred. On receipt of the materials transfer note the cost office will make the necessary entries in the Cost and Stores Accounts. A materials transfer note is shown in Fig. 2.3.

2.3 Purchasing procedure

The purchasing department receives purchase requisitions from various departments and procures raw materials and finished goods of the correct quality and type, and at the lowest possible cost, for delivery on the date required by the department. The purchase requisition may be issued by a

MATERIALS TRANSFER NOTE — No. 708

Date October 6 — To order no. G. 3293 — From order no. G. 1765

From: Fitting department — To: Erecting department — Requisition issued: ✓

Drawing no. 76408	Code no. 32		Material group 9	
Description		Quantity	Unit price	Value
			£	£
Spindle		2	15.00	30.00

Authorised by:	Received by:	Cost Ledger
J. Brown	W. Jones	M. Y.

Fig. 2.3 A materials transfer note

materials controls section from the storekeeper, production controller, supervisor or similar official. The stores ledger clerk is probably authorised to prepare purchase requisitions when the stock of particular items falls to the re-order level, as indicated on the *stock ledger card* (see Unit 3.10 and Fig. 3.5). The purchasing department is aware of prices and delivery times for many of the items required but where this information is not available a request for a quotation is sent to the suppliers. In due course, a *purchase order* is prepared and sent to the supplier. There may be several copies of this order with the original going to the supplier, the second copy retained by the purchasing department for filing and other copies going to the stores department, accounts department, etc.

(a) Receipt of purchases

Procedures vary considerably in different businesses but usually goods are checked for quality and quantity. The arrival of goods is recorded by the issue of a *goods received note* by the receiving department, usually the stores department (Fig. 2.4, p. 24). The supplier sends an advice note in respect of the goods, and after noting the number of this and the number of the purchases order, the goods received note is prepared. Where there is no separate receiving department this note will be made out by the stores department, and copies are needed for:

(i) the purchasing department, to enable their copy of the purchases order to be checked with the goods received note and the invoice, when the copy of the purchases order is transferred to the completed file. If the order is incomplete, a note is made and the order held until final delivery.

(ii) the accounts department, to enable payment to be made after checking with the supplier's invoice. This copy is then passed to the cost department for updating the stock records card, where appropriate.

GOODS RECEIVED NOTE		No. 368 Date Sept. 9
Order no. B. 40 826	Supplier XY Manufacturing Co.	Carrier B.R.

No. of packages	Particulars	Quantity	Unit price		£	
2	Diesel Engines	2	926	00	1852	00

Received by: J. Pells	Approved by: N. Smith	Bin no. E. 28
Stores Ledger B.M.	Cost Ledger J.V.	Invoice no. G. 1 058

Fig. 2.4 A goods received note

(iii) the requisitioning department, as notification that the material has arrived.

When goods are returned to a supplier a debit note is sent and the copy of the note is retained by the accounts department for checking against the credit note which is expected in due course.

(b) Purchases invoices

The procedure for recording invoices and accounting for materials may be comparatively simple where a small quantity of materials is purchased or where only one product is made. Where there are many different products and large amounts of materials, however, the procedure is more complex because of the amount of analysis required. The procedure depends, therefore, on the way in which costs are controlled or recorded, and the reconciliation which may be necessary between the cost and financial accounts. Essential information has to be extracted from the invoices for entry into the financial accounts and the costing system, and this may be entered on a posting slip or on the invoice itself using a rubber stamp. Each posting slip or invoice is given a reference number, and in the process of accounting for purchases it is necessary to record the liability arising from the purchase, and the quantity and value of the materials for the stock records and cost accounts. The stamp on an invoice or the slip may include the following:

(i) date invoice received;
(ii) goods received note number;
(iii) buying office approval;
(iv) extensions and totals checked;
(v) VAT element (if any);

		PURCHASES				
		Debits				
Date	Invoice number	Capital expend-iture	Overhead expenses	Stores department		
				1	2	3
		£	£	£	£	£

ANALYSIS			January 19. .			
						Credits
Customers' orders			Stock orders			Accounts payable
Product group			Product group			
A	B	C	A	B	C	
£	£	£	£	£	£	£

Fig. 2.5 A purchases analysis sheet

(vi) cash discount terms;
(vii) charged to . . . (standing order no., job no., stock, etc.);
(viii) date paid . . .

Invoices for materials and goods supplied are entered in a purchases journal and other items or services are recorded in an expense journal. Suppliers' accounts are credited, and debit is made to a Purchases or Materials Control Account. When separate totals of purchases have to be obtained for different stores, departments or products, a columnar purchases journal can be used, or the invoices can be listed and shown on a purchases analysis sheet (see Fig. 2.5, where the sheet is shown in two halves).

The whole procedure for procuring goods and materials, recording and paying for them is shown diagrammatically in Fig. 2.6 (p. 26).

2.4 Adjusting invoice costs

In arriving at the cost of materials and supplies it is necessary to ensure that the value charged to stock and cost accounts is the total cost of the items at the point of usage. The net amount on the invoice represents the list or catalogue price less the seller's trade discount and, where appropriate, includes value added tax. When we determine the cost we must see that the correct trade discount is given, that the VAT is deducted and that a deduction has been made for any other allowances which are in the terms of the contract.

If a cash discount is allowed for prompt payment, this is usually deducted,

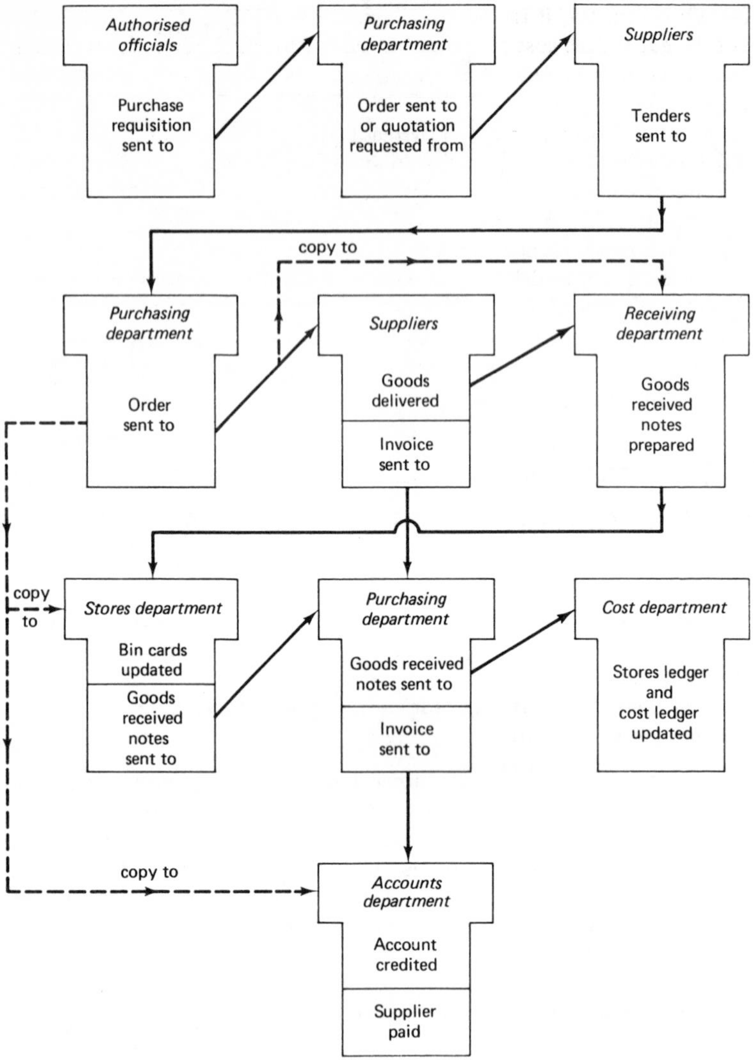

Fig. 2.6 Procedure for procuring goods and materials
Note: For bin cards see Unit 3.3 and Fig. 3.2.

when payment is made, from the net amount on the invoice. Cash discount is generally excluded from the cost accounts as the gain is attributed to good financial management. The cost of transport or carriage inwards is another item which has to be accounted for. Sometimes this is shown on the invoice or sometimes a charge for carriage will follow later, unless the price shown includes the cost of carriage. When the purchaser arranges his own transport by using a contractor, it is important to see that the charge is added to the cost of the goods. The cost of carriage inwards is treated only as an overhead expense when it is inconvenient to charge it to the cost of materials and supplies.

When the cost of unreturnable containers is included on an invoice, it is usually treated as a part cost of the goods. If the containers are returnable, the cost must be deducted from the invoice price and charged to a Returnable Containers Account for eventual credit by the supplier. However, sometimes containers are returnable at a reduced cost and if this is the case, the Containers Account should only be debited with the reduced value, the difference in cost being included in the cost of the goods.

You will see from the foregoing that material costs are collected in various ways but principally from invoices, goods received notes, posting slips, material requisitions and transfer notes.

2.5 The collection of material costs

The following types of cost may be collected.

(a) From invoices, goods received notes and posting slips:

(i) all goods and materials purchased for stores and recorded as stock;

(ii) goods and materials purchased for a special purpose and chargeable to a particular job, cost account or expense account;

(iii) components from outside the business for stock or as a special purchase for a job, cost account or expense account.

(b) From material requisitions and transfer notes:

(i) goods or materials held in stock and required for jobs, cost accounts or expense accounts, and materials already charged to these accounts but needed on another job, or for another account or department;

(ii) components purchased or produced internally and held as stock.

It should be noted that an internally manufactured item or component becomes a material cost when completed and taken into stock. The document for recording this charge to stores may be a special *posting slip* or, in some cases, the *final route slip* which follows the final inspection of the completed item. As there is no invoice, it follows that manufactured stock items have to be costed and entries will be needed between Materials, Labour and Expense Accounts and the total cost in each case transferred to the stores ledger. The various documents used in the system are designed and printed to suit the particular business. In this respect, differently coloured paper or coloured bands at the top of sheets of paper can be used to indicate the different groups or classes of materials.

Cost sheets also vary widely between businesses and industries but it is usually convenient to show material costs in groups or classes as this makes comparison and control of costs much easier. The cost of cast steel, plates and sections, non-ferrous materials, timber, special purchases, etc. can then be checked and compared.

2.6 Exercises

1. What basic documents are used for materials issued from, or returned to, the stores department and for those materials moved between departments? Design one of these documents.

2. Describe the procedure which follows the receipt of a purchases requisition by the purchasing department, up to the time when the invoice is received and passed for payment and the cost of the goods is recorded in the accounts of a business.

3. Purchases invoices have to be posted to creditors' accounts, but they also have to be dealt with in the Cost and Stores Accounts. Describe the routine for dealing with invoices from the time of receipt until they are charged to the Cost or Stores Accounts.

4. Material costs have to be collected and charged to Cost and Stores Accounts. Explain in detail the kinds of material involved and the documents which record the costs to be debited to the Cost or Stores Accounts.

5. In a large manufacturing company it is often necessary to analyse the purchases invoices as they arrive, in order to provide essential information. State why a purchases analysis is essential and show the layout of a purchases analysis sheet.

6. An engineering company manufactures a large number of different machines on a batch production basis and has an extensive general stores department for holding the many items which are purchased for eventual use on the assembly lines. Describe the system and the documents which are used to deal with these materials from the moment it becomes clear that extra stock will be required until the goods are entered in the stock records and the accounts are paid.

7. Indicate the significant features of the following documents, and show the layout of one of them with which you are familiar: *(a)* goods received note, *(b)* materials return note, *(c)* material transfer note, *(d)* materials requisition, *(e)* purchases analysis.

UNIT 3

Stores control and the pricing of requisitions

Note: Before students commence their study of this chapter about stock control the authors wish to draw students' attention to Unit 3.13, which is about *just-in-time activities*. This form of stock control is a new approach to production developed in Japan and to some extent calls into question traditional stock-control attitudes.

3.1 Stock control

It is necessary for a business to hold stocks of materials, whether they are used regularly or infrequently, and, as far as possible, deliveries should be matched with usage. Stockholding is an expensive business. The costs have to be weighed against losses which may occur if the company is unable to supply customers or the operational needs of the factory. Storage costs include the loss of interest, the overhead costs of the stores and possibly loss due to obsolescence or deterioration. The practice of storekeeping varies widely but material control is concerned with the following:

(a) deciding on the items to be held in stock and the requirements to meet planned production;
(b) ensuring that material of the correct quality and quantity is available as and when required;
(c) providing information for the purchasing department on future requirements together with the expected delivery dates;
(d) the provision of records of movements into and out of stores and of materials used for each order;
(e) economy in storage and ordering costs and the effect of price reductions for bulk purchases.

A general stock list should be maintained for the use of stores staff and for production control, purchasing and technical requirements. This list should provide the description, the code numbers, dimensions and units of issue (litres, grams, for example).

3.2 Levels of stock

The fixing of stock levels is difficult and frequent revision is necessary due to changing conditions. Where information and facilities are available, statistical and scientific methods can be used, but these methods are outside the scope of this book. Computerised records will be used which reproduce in electronic form the paper records and card indexes described, particularly in larger firms today.

For most purposes the following system is appropriate. A materials record card should be kept for each item of stock, on which is listed:

(i) location symbol and bin number;
(ii) description and code number of the item;
(iii) maximum, minimum and re-order level and re-order quantity;
(iv) quantity reserved for specific jobs;
(v) quantity on order still awaiting delivery.

There may also be a record of receipts, issues and balance in hand, although this may be recorded on a separate sheet.

(a) Re-order level

The object of this stock level is to prevent stock falling below the minimum. In this calculation it is necessary to assume that there will be maximum consumption and that the supplier will take the maximum period to supply the goods. If the maximum consumption is 250 units per week and the supplier takes two to four weeks to deliver, then the calculation is as follows:

$$\text{Maximum consumption} \times \text{Maximum delivery period}$$
$$= 250 \times 4 = \underline{\underline{1\,000 \text{ units}}}$$

(b) Minimum stock level

This is the lowest level to which the balance can be allowed to fall, and is a danger signal, indicating that action must be taken to avoid a *stock out*. In this calculation it is assumed that there will be normal consumption during the normal waiting period. If consumption is 150 units per week for a period of three weeks the minimum stock level is calculated as follows:

$$\text{Re-order level } \textit{less} \text{ Normal consumption during normal re-order period}$$
$$= 1\,000 \text{ units } \textit{less } (150 \times 3) = \underline{\underline{550 \text{ units}}}$$

(c) Maximum level

This is the highest permitted stock level, and is set with the object of restraining excessive investment in stocks, economising on storage space and avoiding losses in perishable goods.

This method of calculation begins with the quantity at re-order level and expects minimum consumption during the shortest delivery time.

Re-order level *less* (Minimum consumption × Minimum re-order period)
plus Re-order quantity of, say, 250
= 1 000 units *less* (100 units × 2 weeks) *plus* 250
= 800 + 250 = 1 050 units

(d) Re-order quantity

This is the standard quantity to order in normal circumstances. The re-order quantity has to be reviewed from time to time and amended where necessary, and consideration should be given to the rate of consumption and the delivery time.

(e) Economic order quantity (EOQ)

The most favourable ordering quantity can be calculated by using a formula, although applying this to each item held in stock would be quite a task. It is easier to prepare a table based on the formula to show the optimum ordering quantity for various amounts of consumption.

The object of the EOQ is to show in particular circumstances the size of the order which provides the lowest stockholding cost per item purchased. The problems involved in this exercise are connected with:

(i) storage accommodation available;
(ii) the expenses incurred when placing orders;
(iii) the cost of storage.

These problems are difficult to solve because of the many variable factors. Storage accommodation may be adequate, for example, but if the effect of EOQ is to increase stocks considerably, then extra costs may be incurred if extra space has to be acquired or rent has to be paid for storage. The cost of placing an order must also account for items such as the cost of stationery and postage, and the expenses of operating the purchasing department. Records of the transactions will have to be made, the invoices will have to be checked and paid, and the receiving department may incur greater or lesser expenses for storage, stock management, etc.

The cost of storage includes the cost of running the stores department, as well as the cost of transport and insurance, and costs connected with interest on capital invested in stocks. Stocks may, of course, deteriorate or become obsolete, and you have to allow for any reductions in cost which may result from the receipt of quantity discounts. It will be seen that storage costs increase in direct proportion to the quantities ordered, and in proportion to the average level of materials stored, whereas the cost of re-ordering is reduced as the quantities are increased or as a result of a smaller number of orders placed. This is shown diagrammatically in Fig. 3.1 (p. 32).

The recommended formula for finding the economic order quantity is:

$$\text{EOQ} = \sqrt{\frac{2\text{CoD}}{\text{Ch}}}$$

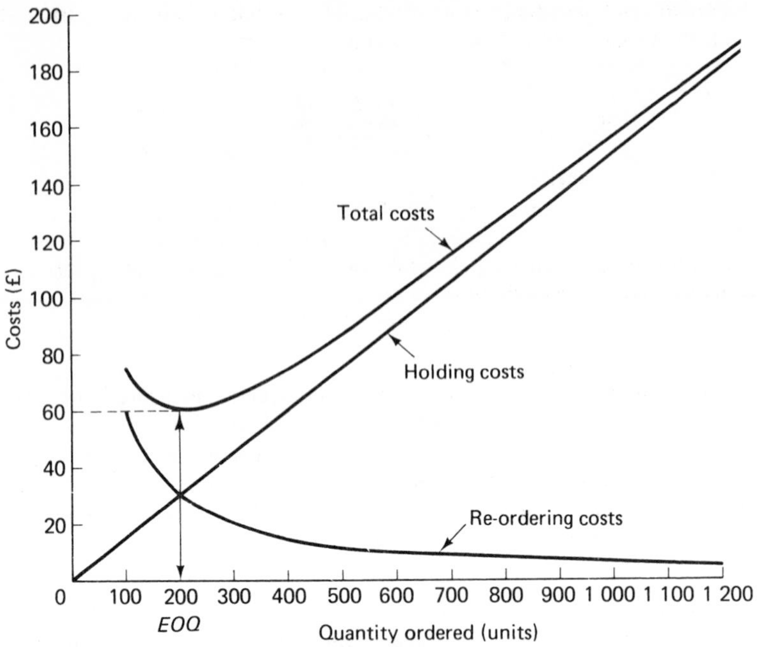

Fig. 3.1 Economic order quantity (EOQ)
Notes:
(i) Holding costs are low when the quantity ordered is small, and high when the quantity ordered is large.
(ii) Re-ordering costs are high when the quantity ordered is small, and low when the quantity ordered is large.
(iii) Total costs are lowest at £60, when the quantity ordered is 200 units. This is therefore the *economic order quantity*.

where EOQ = economic order quantity (basic order quantity, whenever re-ordering is required).
Co = costs per order (i.e. delivery and administrative costs of each order).
D = the annual demand.
Ch = capital and handling (storage) costs per unit per annum (usually expressed as a percentage of the cost per unit).

EXAMPLE 3.1

Imagine an article costing £1.50 per item, the capital and handling charges for which are estimated at 20 per cent on cost. Other details are:

Cost of ordering = £5.00 (Co)
Annual consumption = 1 200 units (D)

Capital and handling (Ch) costs per unit per annum = 20% of £1.50 = £0.30

$$\text{EOQ} = \sqrt{\frac{2\text{CoD}}{\text{Ch}}} = \sqrt{\frac{2 \times £5 \times 1\,200}{£0.30}} = \sqrt{\frac{£12\,000}{£0.30}}$$

$$= \sqrt{40\,000} = \underline{\underline{200}} \text{ units}$$

Since the annual demand is 1 200 units and the EOQ is 200 units this means we shall re-order six times per year.

This can be illustrated further in the following schedule:

Orders placed during the year	1	2	3	4	5	6	10	12
Quantity re-ordered	1 200	600	400	300	240	200	120	100
Average stock	600	300	200	150	120	100	60	50
	£	£	£	£	£	£	£	£
Value of average stock @ £1.50	900	450	300	225	180	150	90	75
Storage and holding cost 20%	180	90	60	45	36	30	18	15
Cost of placing orders	5	10	15	20	25	30	50	60
Total cost per annum	185	100	75	65	61	60	68	75

From the formula, it can be seen that when 1 200 units are ordered annually and consumed, 200 is the size of the order which produces the lowest cost per item purchased. When placing six orders during the year, the total cost is estimated at £60. The cost of ordering has little effect on large-value orders. However, the cost of placing small-value orders is extremely high when compared with the value of the average stock and the cost of storing. See the schedule for twelve orders above. The EOQ formula is easily handled by a computer, or the quantity can be found from EOQ tables.

3.3 Perpetual inventory

In this system, the stores ledger or stock record cards show the quantity and value of receipts, issues and balance in hand. Information about the stock situation is always available, as the balance is known after each receipt or issue. However, perpetual inventory is no substitute for a physical stocktaking which should take place at least once a year. If the stores ledger is kept up to date, it should correspond with the storekeeper's records as shown on the bin cards.

Bin card

This is the storekeeper's record of stocks and it is normally a rough record showing the quantity of stock moved in or out. The card is located at or near the bin, rack or shelf. It shows only essential information such as location and description of material, code number and the unit of issue, although other details can be shown if it helps with the control of stores stock. The receipts, issues and balances on hand are shown in quantities only. Bin cards

BIN CARD

Description . . . . Bin number . . . .

Maximum stock . . . . Code number . . . .

Minimum stock . . . . Re-order qty. . . . .

Re-order level . . . . Unit of issue . . . .

Received			Issued			Balance
Date	Ref.	Quantity	Date	Ref.	Quantity	Quantity

Fig. 3.2 A bin card

should be checked with the stores ledger card when a physical check takes place.

The storekeeper is responsible for the custody and issue of materials and takes note of instructions from the production or materials controller. In this respect, materials may be allocated or reserved for future orders and this information, which can be shown on a bin card, gives the *free balance* or stock available for other purposes (Fig. 3.2).

3.4 Annual stocktaking

Stocktaking involves counting, weighing, measuring, listing and valuing raw materials, work-in-progress and finished goods. It is a physical inventory which takes place annually or at other dates during the year. The annual stocktake fits in with the preparation of the final accounts and Balance Sheet and the requirement that the accounts show a true and fair view. The object is also to verify the accuracy of stock records and to reveal any losses resulting from pilferage, fraud or any other cause. The stocktake shows up any problems or weaknesses in the system or caused by the action of employees. The annual stocktaking usually means that the production departments have to be closed, but this can be avoided if continuous stocktaking is carried out instead.

The plans and procedure for stocktaking should be made in advance by selecting personnel and instructing them in their duties, and arranging for the printing of stock sheets. Information and instructions should also be given to the production and service departments, so that preparations can be made for stocktaking to operate in an orderly manner. If possible, the stock sheets should be written up in advance with the basic information such as description, code number, etc.

Work-in-progress is usually dealt with by taking cost as shown in the cost ledger for each of the unfinished jobs. If the cost is not available through the costing system, a physical check is necessary to determine this, either by a technical estimate or on the basis of a percentage of the materials, labour and other expenses which are relative to the work already carried out. The valuation of work-in-progress will be dealt with in later units but it should be noted that stocks and work-in-progress normally need to be stated at cost, or if lower, at net realisable value, and reference should be made to SSAP 9. The valuation of work-in-progress should include the prime cost plus a fair share of overheads. Fair overheads include production overheads and those incurred in bringing the product to its present location and condition (see Unit 5).

In some branches of the retail trade where the branches are being controlled from a head office the branches are charged with the goods they receive from head office at selling price, and do not know, or need to know, what the head office paid for them. When branches are opened the goods supplied may be charged out on a particular basis according to the nature of the business; for example:

(a) at cost;
(b) at a fixed percentage on cost;
(c) at selling price.

If the goods are charged at selling price the head office will add on to its cost prices a profit margin which reflects the margin of profit required on that particular class of merchandise. As far as the branch is concerned, all stocktaking will be done at selling price. A small team of specialist stocktakers will descend on the branch, probably without notice, to take stock. In theory either the branch should have the stock, or the money for it should have been paid in over the previous period. Of course at head office the 'stock at selling price' produced by the stocktaking will be reduced by the appropriate profit margin to arrive at the cost price.

Any special features (shop-soiled items, etc.) will be allowed for according to any report by the stocktakers. The procedure mentioned above establishes a definite check upon the branches because frequent stocktaking will reveal whether there are leakages or not.

3.5 Stocktaking procedure

(a) A senior member of the staff should be in control. In many companies stocktaking and investigations into discrepancies would be under the supervision of the internal auditor, who is a member of the company staff, and is responsible either to the chief accountant or directly to the management. S/he works in accordance with an audit programme, and also deals with special assignments on behalf of the management. S/he surveys the accounting system, makes investigations, suggests improvements and reports generally.

(b) The stocktake should take place during a slack period and, as far as possible, stores departments and storage sections should be closed to normal operations.

(c) When certain items belong to customers or suppliers the items should be distinctly labelled by attaching labels to parts or complete products with string or wire. Labelled items should be kept in a separate area of the stores.

(d) Strict instructions should be issued to the effect that no records of receipts or issues made after stocktaking begins should be entered until the stocktaking is complete. Receipts should be held in the receiving department or in a special storage area and exceptional issues should be noted on the bin card. To avoid unauthorised entries the stock record cards can be ruled off as the stocktaking begins.

(e) Stocks are counted, weighed or measured and when this is not convenient an estimate will be made by someone qualified to make such calculations. The auditor's permission must be received if it is essential to use an estimate instead of an exact amount.

(f) Before a reconciliation can be made between the value of physical stocks and book figures, certain matters have to be dealt with:

(i) materials may have been recorded but the invoice may not have been received, or vice versa;

(ii) goods may have been drawn from the bins and held in containers ready for assembly but they may not have been charged to the accounts;

(iii) account will have to be taken of materials in service vans, on constructional sites or away from the factory being processed or repaired.

There is a variety of different ways of recording the inventory and the example in Fig. 3.3 shows that it should be possible to write up the first three columns before the beginning of the stocktaking.

3.6 Investigating discrepancies and adjusting the Stock Control Account

The stock discrepancy report shows the difference between the number of items counted in the physical check and the number shown on the bin card and

INVENTORY SHEET

Sheet no. . . . . . .

Department . . . . Date . . . .

Stocks recorded by . . . . Checked by . . . . Priced by . . . .

Bin no.	Description	Code no.	Quantity	Unit	Unit price	Value

Fig. 3.3 An inventory sheet

on the stock record card. It provides information to enable the auditor or selected employees to examine all the records (bin cards, stock record cards, materials requisitions, goods received notes) and to reconcile the quantities indicated, by establishing the causes of the variances (Fig. 3.4, p. 38).

Clerical or arithmetical errors may be responsible for discrepancies, and requisitions may have been lost, mislaid or posted more than once. It may be necessary to check the basic documents connected with the receipt and issue of materials or to seek explanations from the storekeeper and other people. Perhaps the issue or receipt was entered on the wrong card, or the error may date from the last stocktake. If pilferage or fraud is the cause, improved security arrangements will be needed.

When the stocktaking and investigations are complete, there will be a list of two columns, one of items and values which have to be added (stock surpluses and revaluations) and the second column which reduces the quantity and value of stocks (stock deficiencies and items written off as depreciated or obsolete). The Stock Account or Stock Control Account will have to be debited with the surpluses and credited with the deficiencies.

3.7 Obsolete, slow-moving and dormant stocks

Statement of Standard Accounting Practice No. 9 now says that 'if there is no reasonable expectation of sufficient revenue to cover cost incurred (e.g. as a result of deterioration, obsolescence or a change in demand) the irrecoverable cost should be charged to revenue in the year under review. Thus, stocks normally need to be stated at cost, or, if lower, at net realisable value' (SSAP 9, part 1.1). The items should be reviewed in order to deal with deterioration, obsolescence or a change in demand.

INVENTORY
Stock Discrepancy Report

Sheet no . . . .

Date . . . .

Department . . . . Investigated by . . . .

Bin no.	Description	Code no.	Actual quantity	Bin card		Stock record card				Remarks
				Quantity				Value		
				+	−	+	−	+	−	
								£ p	£ p	

Fig. 3.4 A stock discrepancy report

(a) The determination of net realisable value

The initial calculation of provisions to reduce stocks from cost to net realisable value may often be made by the use of formulae based on predetermined criteria. The formulae normally take account of the age, movements in the past, expected future movements and estimated scrap values of the stock, as appropriate. While the use of such formulae establishes a basis for making a provision which can be consistently applied, it is still necessary for the results to be reviewed in the light of any special circumstances which cannot be anticipated in the formulae, such as changes in the state of the order book.

(b) The application of net realisable value

The principal situations in which net realisable value is likely to be less than cost are where there has been:

(i) an increase in costs or a fall in selling price;
(ii) physical deterioration of stocks;
(iii) obsolescence of products;
(iv) a decision as part of a company's marketing strategy to manufacture and sell products at a loss;
(v) errors in production or purchasing.

Obsolescence is the decline in value of an asset as a result of new inventions or improved designs. The slow movement or dormancy of an item may be related to obsolescence, or may be caused by over-stocking, made by mistake, or because of unforeseen changes since the time when the purchases or manufacturing requisition was issued. When it is established that some or all of a particular item is no longer usable or it is doubtful whether it will be required in future, this should be written off or written down (reduced in value).

One method of dealing with the slow movement of stocks is to fix a period when it is considered that their value will be a nil value, and to write off a proportion or percentage of the cost each year. For example, if a five-year period was chosen, and provided the item has not moved during the past year, then 20 per cent of the value is written off. This continues year by year and if the inventory list has five columns, one for each year, to show the value written off at each stage of the non-movement, it provides useful information on the real value of stocks and acts as a signal to the relevant department to investigate the possibility of using the items in some other way. Materials may also be dormant due to deterioration caused by bad storage conditions or faulty handling. Items may be damaged, or rusty, or in a dirty condition, or may be useless because of storage in damp conditions. They should be written down or written off, and steps taken to avoid future losses of this kind.

3.8 Continuous stocktaking

The time between successive annual stocktakings is a long one and it may be advisable to check certain types of materials more frequently. This applies where there is a breaking of bulk causing losses or where there is a large quantity of off-cuts, such as with steel and timber. More frequent checking is required in these circumstances. Continuous stocktaking is a system which proceeds throughout the year, with the object of checking each item at least once during the year. It has the advantage of using experienced stocktakers who check a certain number of items each day. The shutdown of production departments is avoided, while those who might carry out frauds or falsify records can be deterred by changing each day the area where the checking takes place. Continuous stocktaking helps the stores manager to be kept informed more frequently of any problems and discrepancies found by the auditors.

3.9 Stores layout and methods of storage

The stores department should be located somewhere close to, and with easy access to, the production departments. There may be a large central stores or a number of smaller stores. The business may commence with a large central stores but as expansion proceeds it is more difficult to situate the stores close to the production departments.

The stores department may be sectionalised, with a raw material store for primary materials such as iron, steel and timber, and a general store for other purchases and items manufactured by the factory and held for subsequent assembly or for sale as spare parts. There may be sub-stores where it is more convenient to hold certain stock adjacent to a production centre. Sub-stores can be used for partly finished stock and sub-assemblies which are not due for final assembly until a later date. Finished stocks awaiting sale and dispatch may also be held in a separate store.

When materials arrive, they must be identified, labelled and kept in a place where they can easily be found. Goods of particular classes should be stored in their respective sections. Firms need either a good coding system or well-displayed signs, on or over the aisles and at the bins or shelves. In a large store, the floor plan should be posted in various parts of the building and location lists should be prepared to enable staff to find the various types of goods.

The following matters have to be considered when establishing a new store or expanding an existing one:

(a) the size and location of the site and the services available, such as water, gas and electricity;
(b) ease of access to rail, road, inland waterways and possibly sea-borne traffic;
(c) the amount and type of materials to be stored and the handling requirements;
(d) the kind of building needed (single- or multi-storey) or modifications necessary to enable the use of fork-lift trucks, conveyors, hoists, overhead cranes, lifts, etc.;
(e) the type of lighting and amount of heating required;
(f) the space needed for the receiving and issuing sections, and the accommodation necessary for office staff;
(g) the quantity and type of fixtures, fittings and equipment needed, such as bins, racks, shelving, cupboards, pallets, etc., and any special flooring requirements;
(h) the size of doors, aisles and platforms, for easy access;
(i) the storage of any special materials requiring security or safety precautions, including additional ventilation;
(j) the provision of fire-fighting equipment, hydrants, sprinklers, etc.;
(k) the provision of toilet, cloakroom and welfare facilities.

3.10 Recording of receipts and issues

The stores ledger consists of the stock record cards which are basic records in accounting for materials and supplies. The ledger is a perpetual inventory showing the materials received into stock, materials issued and balance on hand, and sometimes includes other information such as material reserved. The cards are also referred to as stores ledger cards or stock control cards. The kind of information shown on the card includes the name of the item, its code or part number and its location in the stores, showing the bin, shelf or rack where the item can be found. The card may also show the unit in which the item is purchased or issued and a record of purchases, with the source of supply and possibly the maximum, minimum and re-order level and re-order quantity. A typical form is shown in Fig. 3.5 (p. 42).

3.11 Material costing

When materials and supplies are issued, the material requisition has to be priced and details of the issue are entered on the stores ledger card. Materials which are purchased for particular orders are kept in a separate section of the stores and are not usually priced from the stores ledger as they are charged direct to the Cost Account when the invoice is received. This method is known as the *specific cost method* and it means that the actual cost of goods purchased specially is charged to a specific Cost Account.

There is no one method of valuing stores issues which can be used under all conditions, but the accountant and the management must select the method(s) which they consider appropriate and must use them consistently when pricing material requisitions.

When goods are perishable or liable to deteriorate, the physical stock should be issued on a first in, first out basis. With non-perishable goods this does not matter, and it is important to appreciate that there is no connection between the order of issue of the physical stock and the method of pricing, which is a book-keeping procedure.

The usual methods adopted for the pricing of issues are as follows:

(a) first in, first out (FIFO);
(b) last in, first out (LIFO);
(c) simple average cost;
(d) weighted average cost (AVCO);
(e) standard cost;
(f) replacement cost;
(g) base stock.

(a) First in, first out

In this method, the price of the oldest stocks is used, regardless of the order in which the goods leave the store. The most recent purchases have to be accumulated until they equal the new quantity balance, then the previous price or prices can be used to calculate the value of the issue.

EXAMPLE 3.2

The stores ledger card shows a stock of 65 items at a total value of £539.50, and a requisition is received for 15 items. The receipts were as follows:

Ref.	*Quantity*	*Price each*	*Value*
		£	£
A	10	7.000	70.000
B	15	8.000	120.000
C	20	8.500	170.000
D	20	8.975	179.500
	65		£539.500

STOCK LEDGER CARD

Location . . . . Unit . . . . Re-order quantity . . . .

Code number . . . . Delivery time . . . . Maximum stock . . . .

Description . . . . Re-order level . . . . Minimum stock . . . .

Receipts					Issues					Balance		
Date	Ref.	Quantity	Price £	Value £	Date	Ref.	Quantity	Price £	Value £	Quantity	Price £	Value £

Fig. 3.5 A stock ledger card

The entries are shown in Fig. 3.6 (p. 44).

The new balance is 50 (65 *less* 15) items. To select the price on a FIFO basis, work backwards using the most recent purchases to accumulate stocks, until 50 is reached. This consists of D 20 + C 20 + 10 of B. The prices to be used for pricing the requisition include the remaining 5 of B at £8.00 each and 10 of A at £7.00 each, which is a total of £110.00.

The advantages are:

(i) prices are based on cost and no profit or loss can arise in the accounts when this method of pricing is used;
(ii) the inventory value which results from the method of pricing is normally a fair representation of current commercial values as the inventory value shown represents the most recent purchases;
(iii) the method is well founded as it assumes that goods are issued in order of receipt;
(iv) it is an easy method to operate.

The disadvantages are:

(i) issue prices may not be equivalent to current values;
(ii) clerical errors may be made because of having to select the appropriate prices for issues and the correct quantities and prices when valuing the stock;
(iii) with changing prices, a comparison of the cost of one job with another can be misleading;
(iv) when prices are increasing, the charge to production will be low, and the replacement cost will probably be much higher. This tends to overstate the profits and reduces the amount of working capital if the profits are paid out as dividends.

(b) Last in, first out

In this method of pricing, issues are priced using the cost of the most recent purchases. When further issues are made, the latest price is taken from the stock which remains, and each time a new batch is received, the price changes to the value of the most recent purchase. This may result in several receipts being only partly issued on the stock card.

The advantages are:

(i) issues are priced at cost and no profits or losses arise;
(ii) the price of issues is fairly close to current values;
(iii) the charge to production is close to current values and replacement costs;
(iv) the information to management is an indication of current costs and is more realistic.

The disadvantages are:

(i) inventory values are based on the oldest stocks and may not correspond to current prices;

STOCK LEDGER CARD (FIFO)

Location A.10 | Unit 1 | Re-order quantity 120

Code number 21c | Delivery time 2-4 weeks | Maximum stock 200

Description Pinion R.H. | Re-order level 100 | Minimum stock 40

Receipts					Issues					Balance		
Date	Ref.	Quantity	Price £	Value £	Date	Ref.	Quantity	Price £	Value £	Quantity	Price £	Value £
19..					19..							
JAN. 1	S.387	10	7.000	70.00						10		70.00
" 7	"	15	8.000	120.00						25		190.00
" 10	"	20	8.500	170.00						45		360.00
" 17	"	20	8.975	179.50						65		539.50
					JAN. 19	21942	15					
							10	7.000	70.00			
							5	8.000	40.00			
										50		429.50

Fig. 3.6 A FIFO stock ledger card

(ii) clerical errors can arise as the records are somewhat involved, with different quantities and prices on a stock card which have to be kept and used when pricing issues or valuing the inventory;
(iii) a comparison of the costs of different jobs may be misleading.

The entries are shown in Fig. 3.7 (p. 46).

(c) Simple average cost

The simple average cost method is easy to operate and may be satisfactory when prices are stable but it often gives ridiculous results and has not much to recommend it. Issues are not based on actual cost, and a profit or loss may arise because of the use of fictitious prices which are calculated by averaging the prices instead of using a weighted average, by taking into account quantities and values. The price is fixed by adding the prices of receipts represented by the stock-in-hand and dividing by the number of receipts. For example, two receipts with unit prices of £7 and £8 are added together and divided by two, giving a simple average of £7.50. This method ignores the quantities, and when these differ, discrepancies arise in the accounts. For general use it cannot be recommended, but an example is given in Fig. 3.8 (p. 47) to illustrate these discrepancies. The simple average prices are shown with the balance on hand: 50 at £8.492 is £424.60, compared with the value of £417.715, giving an error of £6.885.

The advantage is that the system is simple to operate.

The disadvantages are:

(i) profits or losses may arise from its use;
(ii) it gives inaccurate figures when pricing issues or valuing stocks and cost sheets can present misleading information.

(d) Weighted average cost

The weighted average cost method requires a calculation each time an invoice is received for the receipt of goods. The quantity purchased is added to the present stock-in-hand and the invoice value is added to the present value. The new quantity is then divided into the new value to obtain the weighted average. This involves a greater amount of clerical labour, but this method has much to recommend it, especially where the materials are subject to wide price fluctuations, and where they are carried in stores for a relatively long period. When using the weighted average price, the larger the multiplier the greater the error, and it may be necessary to use five places of decimals in the unit prices so as to avoid a discrepancy between the balances on the stores cards and the balance shown in the Stores Control Account.

In costing exercises, whenever materials are returned to stock, they should be valued at the price of issue, in order to cancel out and credit the Cost Account with the original amount charged. When using the weighted average method a new unit price has to be calculated when materials are returned. Unit prices are also calculated each time there is a receipt of materials. The

STOCK LEDGER CARD (LIFO)

Location A.10 | Unit 1 | Re-order quantity 120

Code number 21c | Delivery time 2-4 weeks | Maximum stock 200

Description Pinion R.H. | Re-order level 100 | Minimum stock 40

Receipts					Issues					Balance		
Date	Ref.	Quantity	Price £	Value £	Date	Ref.	Quantity	Price £	Value £	Quantity	Price £	Value £
19..					19..							
JAN. 1	S.387	10	7.000	70.000						10		70.000
" 7	"	15	8.000	120.000						25		190.000
" 10	"	20	8.500	170.000						45		360.000
" 17	"	20	8.975	179.500						65		539.500
					JAN. 19	21 942	15	8.975	134.625	50		404.875

Fig. 3.7 A LIFO stock ledger card

STOCK LEDGER CARD (SIMPLE AVERAGE COST)

Location A.10	Unit 1	Re-order quantity 120
Code number 21c	Delivery time 2-4 weeks	Maximum stock 200
Description Pinion R.H.	Re-order level 100	Minimum stock 40

Receipts					Issues					Balance		
Date	Ref.	Quantity	Price £	Value £	Date	Ref.	Quantity	Price £	Value £	Quantity	Price £	Value £
19..					19..							
JAN. 1	S. 387	10	7.000	70.000						10	7.000	70.000
" 7	"	15	8.000	120.000						25	7.500	190.000
" 10	"	20	8.500	170.000						45	7.833	360.000
" 17	"	20	8.975	179.500						65	8.119	539.500
					JAN. 19	21 942	15	8.119	121.785	50	8.492	417.715

Fig. 3.8 A simple average cost stock ledger card

entries are shown in Fig. 3.9. Of course, such recalculations are no problem in a computerised system, the program ensuring that each time a receipt of materials, or a return of materials to store, occurs the necessary recalculation is made and recorded.

The advantages are:

(i) the price is based on cost, and the method is generally accurate, provided the unit price is carefully set. With this method, no profits or losses arise;
(ii) it is a sensible system which operates on the basis that if parts are identical the prices should also be the same;
(iii) it avoids the involved calculations and records which occur with FIFO and LIFO, and as prices are only fixed on receipts, it simplifies the procedure.

The disadvantage is that there is usually a need to fix unit prices to several decimal places.

(e) Standard cost

This method uses a predetermined cost and can be applied whether or not a system of standard costing is used. A standard cost is not a rough estimate, but a cost fixed after a careful study of all the factors involved in purchasing and producing the goods. As a fixed price is used for issues during the period of account, it is only necessary to keep a record of quantities. The variance which is found when comparing actual cost with standard cost is written off to a Material Price Variance Account, either when the item is taken into stock or at the date of issue.

The advantages are:

(i) there is a reduction in clerical costs, as the continual calculations and recording of unit costs is avoided; it is therefore simple to operate;
(ii) the system eliminates the variations in cost which occur with other methods and makes cost comparisons much easier;
(iii) it indicates to what extent the purchasing department is operating efficiently and securing supplies at the recognised prices.

The disadvantages are:

(i) standard prices have to be set carefully when the system is installed or a new price is fixed and revisions are necessary from period to period;
(ii) profits and losses arise due to the variations in prices;
(iii) when prices change, the issues do not represent current values until the standard prices are revised.

(f) Replacement cost

In this method, the intention is to price issues at the current buying price, with the object of showing product costs at the replacement or current cost. This may be a practical method when the item to be sold is almost entirely made up of raw material, but the maintenance of a list of current prices for

STOCK LEDGER CARD (WEIGHTED AVERAGE COST) AVCO

Location A. 10	Unit 1	Re-order quantity 120
Code number 21C	Delivery time 2-4 weeks	Maximum stock 200
Description Pinion R.H.	Re-order level 100	Minimum stock 40

Receipts					Issues					Balance		
Date	Ref.	Quantity	Price £	Value £	Date	Ref.	Quantity	Price £	Value £	Quantity	Price £	Value £
19..					19..							
JAN. 1	S. 387	10	7.000	70.000						10	7.000	70.000
" 7	"	15	8.000	120.000						25	7.600	190.000
" 10	"	20	8.500	170.000						45	8.000	360.000
" 17	"	20	8.975	179.500						65	8.300	539.500
					JAN. 19	21942	15	8.300	124.500	50	8.300	415.000

Fig. 3.9 A weighted average cost stock ledger card

masses of different items and a large variety of raw materials is a considerable problem. This method involves not only raw materials, but also the cost of labour and expenses for the manufactured items which are held in stock.

The advantages are:

(i) the method used and calculations are comparatively simple;
(ii) the values of the issues are at current prices.

The disadvantage is that when there are frequent price changes, it is difficult to maintain price lists which record the current costs.

(g) Base stock

It is assumed that a minimum amount of raw materials or items should be carried in stock as a reserve or buffer stock in case of emergencies. Such stock is treated in a similar manner to fixed assets, as it is held at the original cost, but stock above the base may be priced on some other basis.

There are one or two other methods. One is the *highest in, first out* (HIFO) where the most costly items are disposed of first, but it is a difficult method to operate. Then there is *next in, first out* (NIFO) which charges the price of materials ordered but not yet received. It too is difficult to administer as future prices may have to be estimated and problems arise when reconciling the stock valuations and the accounts at the end of the period.

The object of material costing is to recover costs and there are certain kinds of materials which are subject to losses, such as evaporation during storage or at the time of issue, when breaking bulk or cutting off. In order to credit the stores ledger with the amount debited, an attempt is made to do this by fixing an *inflated price* which allows for the wastage.

For example, assuming there is an estimated loss of 10 per cent and the material cost is £9 per kilogram, the inflated price is:

$$\frac{100}{90} \times £9 = \underline{\underline{£10 \text{ per kg}}}$$

SSAP 9 allows the following methods for valuation of stocks, but it requires that:

> the method chosen must be one which appears to the directors to be appropriate in the circumstances of the company. The valuation method chosen must give a true and fair view of the affairs of the business.
>
> (a) the method known as 'first in, first out' (FIFO);
> (b) the method known as 'last in, first out' (LIFO);
> (c) a weighted average price; and
> (d) any other method similar to any of the methods mentioned above.

This standard requires the use of a method which provides a fair approximation to the expenditure actually incurred. The use of some of the methods shown above will not necessarily meet this requirement. The use of the LIFO method can result in the reporting of current assets at amounts that bear little relationship to recent costs.

Much of the subject matter of SSAP 9 has been incorporated into Company Law in Schedule 4 of the Companies Act 1985, which requires companies to value their stocks by any method which appears to the directors to be appropriate to the circumstances of the company. It lists the methods to include FIFO, LIFO and weighted average cost (AVCO), or any other similar method. However, to meet the difficulty that these methods do not all give the same value to stocks at the Balance Sheet date, as referred to above, the Act requires that an 'alternative amount' should be calculated according to a formula laid down in the Act. This 'alternative amount' is the cost of replacing the same quantity of stock at the Balance Sheet date. This replacement cost may be determined from the most recent purchase made, or the most recent production cost (where this is more appropriate).

The difference between the stock figure as shown on the Balance Sheet and the replacement cost as found has to be shown as a note to the Balance Sheet. This is a neat way of reconciling the difficulties inherent in the valuation of stock.

See Unit 6.9 for a fuller discussion of SSAP 9.

3.12 Scrap material

In many manufacturing processes a certain amount of scrap such as turnings and borings is anticipated, and there is also scrap consisting of defective items caused by poor work, bad design, faulty tools or equipment or the use of sub-standard materials.

Waste is generally taken as having no value, whereas *scrap* is considered to have some value, although the material cannot be used for its original purpose. It is necessary to place a fair value on scrap, although this may be difficult because of market fluctuations. The value of scrap taken into stock should take account of the market price and should allow for the cost of handling and disposal. Depending on the procedure adopted, the following entries should be made:

Debit Scrap Sales Account
Credit Original Cost Account
or
Overhead Expenses Account

or

Debit Scrap Materials Account
Credit Original Cost Account
or
Overhead Expenses Account

Whenever possible or convenient, the original job or process should be credited with the value of scrap, but if it is impracticable the credit should be set off against the Overhead Expenses Account.

If materials purchased for a specific job prove to be defective, the rectification cost should be charged to that job as a direct expense, and credit should be given for any allowance made by the supplier. In other cases, the cost of rectification should be charged to a Spoilage Account and treated as an overhead expense. The Spoilage Account should be credited with any sales of defective materials.

Scrap may be collected or may be allowed to accumulate in the stores before being sold at a convenient date or at an advantageous price.

If any profits are shown in the accounts for the sale of scrap or defective work, they should be treated as *other income*.

3.13 Just-in-time activities

Just-in-time (JIT) activities are activities where, by careful planning and changes in such activities as ordering procedures, raw materials and components reach the place of manufacture just in time for the operation for which they are required. There are enormous savings to be achieved in both capital expenditure and revenue expenditure if such a system can be developed. For example, the holding of large stocks can be avoided and consequently warehousing and storage space can be saved. Work-in-progress can be reduced and the finished product can be made up into economic delivery loads for onward transit to depots, customer destinations, etc.

The basic consideration in just-in-time activities is that it is always possible to change current practices in order to increase efficiency. The changes must make greater use of the existing available resources, so as to raise output and enhance the productivity of all employees. This need not involve sweated labour or increased belt-speeds but simply a better way of working. In one Japanese factory building railway carriages, where the installation of wiring and circuitry to be hidden in the roofs of the carriages was carried out with workers standing with hands above their heads for much of the day, the carriages were simply rotated in an enormous jig to bring them upside down. The wiring was now very accessible – workers sat down or knelt to get at various components being wired into the system and gravity operated in favour of the layout rather than against it, the cables falling into position where they could be properly secured.

An essential element in just-in-time operations is the way in which supplies are ordered. Instead of worrying about EOQs (economic order quantities) and similar stock procedures we only need to know how many of a particular component, or how much of a certain class of material, we shall need tomorrow. Orders are phoned through or faxed through to suppliers on a day-by-day basis and production is 'to order' rather than for stock. Suppliers are required to deliver to the shop floor where the raw materials or components are actually required. Double-handling (taking goods into stock and then requisitioning them from stock for the various cost centres) is eliminated.

Storage space is greatly reduced, goods going straight from the unloading bay to the production line and finished goods going from the production line to the loading bay and away to the customer.

Layout of the shop floor is carefully thought through so that items move directly from one machine to the next or from one cost centre to another, with appropriate planning to ensure the minimum of material handling. Quality control procedures reduce scrap and reworking costs by discovering faults early, and feedback occurs to correct the errors causing the problems. By reducing the batch sizes the work becomes a flow and costs are collected on a basis similar to that of process costing, being charged to a flow order. Detailed records of costs of materials and labour are not required, costs being calculated from the final output, bearing in mind how much material must have been incorporated in the component and the labour that it must represent. This technique is called 'back-flushing' - working backwards from the finished product rather than cumulatively to a final cost.

The attitude in JIT activities to labour efficiency is interesting. The aim is for work-in-progress to flow through the factory at a steady rate. Where a bottleneck occurs the workers in the bottleneck situation do their utmost to overcome the problem, but those in the cost centres held up do not produce more product - since this will only add to inventory that is not required. The idle time is used on chores such as cleaning up, preventative maintenance, preparatory work for the next set-up activity, etc. Since work is based on team incentives all staff are quality conscious and team productivity is increased by flexibility in training without demarcations. Such training may be developed in idle time, to be abandoned quickly if the work flow resumes. A main aim of JIT is improved quality, to avoid waste and reworking. High rejection rates should be scrutinised to make sure the cause is discovered and eliminated. The investigation can move backwards to suppliers, who are expected to guarantee quality.

Some special points are:

(a) Batch sizes match those of customer orders so there are no finished goods inventories. Unsold stocks mean capital has been wasted ordering and paying for materials, components, etc. before they are needed.

(b) The manufacturing cycle is kept as short as possible to ensure work-in-progress levels are low.

(c) Cost recording is short-circuited to save clerical time and reduce budgeting, variance analysis, etc. Instead the costs are discovered by back-flushing from the finished output and recording it for the whole line by period or flow order.

(d) It takes time to build up JIT systems and establish new attitudes. The systems are introduced a bit at a time and gradually extended across the whole factory.

(e) The manufacturer takes delivery and acquires title to the supplies as they reach the factory gate. Smaller quantities frequently delivered eliminate inventories and raise return on capital invested.

(f) Suppliers, faced with a different approach from the manufacturer, may need to change their own systems so as to guarantee quality and delivery.

(g) There is one criticism of just-in-time activities. One managing director of a brick company, sitting in his vast yard surrounded with a number of brick mountains holding 350 million bricks, said, 'We are as keen as anyone on JIT operations, and if we had our way would not make bricks before they are needed. What can you do when there is a major recession in the whole of industry and no-one is building anything? At such times you must make bricks for stock, or dismiss all your staff and moth-ball the plant.' Just-in-time, it appears, does not meet every situation! Students of economics will recognise the managing director's quandary as the classic dilemma of all industries with specific assets, where it pays to go on producing if there is any prospect of eventual sale.

(h) The following definitions from *Official Terminology* are helpful:

Just-in-time (JIT)
A technique for the organisation of work flows, to allow rapid, high quality, flexible production whilst minimising manufacturing waste and stock levels.

Just-in-time production
A system which is driven by demand for finished products whereby each component on a production line is produced only when needed for the next stage.

Just-in-time purchasing
Matching the receipt of material closely with usage so that raw material inventory is reduced to near-zero levels.

3.14 Exercises

1. Your company operates a large engineering company with a department which is concerned with stock control. What are the functions of the stock controller and why is it essential that this department is operated efficiently?

2. The following information was obtained from the stores records in an engineering company:

Gear wheels – part no. 65892/1
Purchases:

Receipts:	10 Sept.:	180 at £200 each
	17 Sept.:	180 at £240 each
Issues:	14 Sept.:	135
	24 Sept.:	135

You are required to show the stores records in respect of the receipts and issues of gear wheels referred to above. This information should be shown *(a)* under weighted average method, *(b)* under FIFO and *(c)* under LIFO.

3. *(a)* As chief cost accountant to a medium-sized manufacturing company, what considerations would you have in mind when preparing for the annual stocktaking?

   (b) If you should decide to install a system of perpetual inventory and continuous stocktaking, what advantages would you expect the company to receive?

4. A manufacturing company produces an item (part no. B2481) in batches which are transferred to its Finished Stock Account. There were 400 items in stock on 3 June 19.. and these were recorded at a cost price of £8.60 each. Prices were shown in the stock ledger on the weighted average cost basis.

   During the four weeks ended 30 June 19.. the following transactions in this item were recorded:

		Receipts: Quantity in units	Price per unit £	*Issues:* Quantity in units
June	5	–	–	160
	9	240	9.000	–
	12	–	–	300
	17	400	9.090	–
	23	–	–	200
	28	120	9.625	–
	29	–	–	360

   Physical stocktaking was carried out on 30 June 19.. and there were 120 items in stock.

   You are required to *(a)* record the transactions shown above in the Finished Stock Account, part no. B2481, and *(b)* indicate the value of (i) the total issues during the period, (ii) the stock at 30 June 19.. and (iii) the stock losses.

5. The Stores Ledger Account for part no. C2149 shows the following details for the month of July 19..:

			Units	Price per unit £
July	1	Balance b/f	1 100	10.50
	7	Received	4 400	11.80
	16	Issued	3 500	
	23	Received	2 000	12.46
	28	Issued	2 500	
	31	Balance c/f	1 500	

   (a) Write up Stores Ledger Accounts for the above item to show the effect of using (i) the weighted average method, (ii) the first in, first

out method and (iii) the last in, first out method of pricing stores issues.

(b) Write a brief note indicating the distinguishing features of the methods used to evaluate the receipts and issues as shown on the Stores Account.

6. A manufacturing company has a materials control system which includes perpetual inventory records, re-order levels and continuous stocktaking. You are required to:

(a) draft a form for use by the stockcheckers and include on it the following information of stockchecks made in store no. 1 on 10 June 19..:

Item	*Balance per stock card (units)*	*Balance per stores ledger (units)*	*Physical stock in units*	*Cost per unit* £
X	300	300	270	42.00
Y	190	190	195	15.00
Z	680	700	730	1.25

(b) state what action has to be taken and documents raised to adjust discrepancies recorded above.

(c) indicate possible reasons for the shortages and recommend a possible course of action to prevent future losses.

7. The following information relates to purchases and issues of an item of stock which was added to the stock list as from 1 January:

Date	*Ref.*	*Details*
Jan. 14	2078	Purchased 400 at £15.00 each
Feb. 9	2123	Purchased 100 at £15.75 each
Mar. 11	2208	Purchased 200 at £17.50 each
14	9764	Issued 320
Apr. 27	2389	Purchased 200 at £16.50 each
May 14	9945	Issued 320

You are required to write up the stock ledger card for the above item using *(a)* the first in, first out method and *(b)* the last in, first out method.

8. The following receipts and issues were made in respect of swivel pins manufactured on the premises and held in stock for future use in the assembly department:

Swivel pin 70492/3

19..	*Receipts* £	19..	*Issues*
Jan. 11	50 at 3.72 each	Feb. 9	40
23	20 at 4.35 each	18	40
Feb. 7	100 at 3.39 each		
14	20 at 5.40 each		
22	5 at 4.53 each		

Prepare stores ledger cards to show these transactions and the balance in hand. Three record cards are required, showing material requisitions priced on the basis of *(a)* FIFO, *(b)* LIFO and *(c)* AVCO respectively. You are also required to reconcile the balance in hand for methods *(a)* and *(b)* by showing the quantities and prices which make up the value of stock at the end of February.

9. As a stock controller your objective is to ensure that materials are readily available as required and to avoid carrying surplus stocks. How would you deal with the problem of stock levels and the effective control of stores? In your explanation refer to the following: *(a)* maximum level, *(b)* minimum level, *(c)* re-order level, *(d)* re-order quantity.

10. For the six months ended 31 October, an importer and distributor of one type of machine has the following transactions in his records. There was an opening balance of 100 units which had a value of £3 900.

Date	*Bought quantity in units*	*Cost per unit*
		£
May	100	41.000
June	200	50.000
August	400	51.875

The price of £51.875 each for the August receipt was £6.125 per unit less than the normal price because of the large quantity ordered.

Date	*Sold quantity in units*	*Price each*
		£
July	250	64
September	350	70
October	100	74

From the information given above and using the FIFO, LIFO and weighted average methods for pricing issues, you are required for each method to:

(a) show the stores ledger records including the closing stock balance and stock valuation;

(b) prepare, in columnar format, Trading Accounts for the period to show the gross profit using each of the three methods of pricing issues;

(c) comment on which method, in the situation depicted, is regarded as the best measure of profit, and why.

(*CIMA*)

11. Johnson (Camside) Ltd produce an article costing £12.50 per item and estimate the capital and handling charges at 40 per cent on cost. They also believe that ordering costs come to £12.00 per order placed, on average. The annual demand for this product is 3 000 units. Using the formula for EOQ find *(a)* the economic order quantity and *(b)* the number of orders that will be placed per annum.

12. *(a)* Explain what is meant by the term *economic order quantity*. Your explanation should be supported by a sketch or graph, which need not be on graph paper.

(b) Using the information stated below, you are required to prepare a schedule showing the associated costs if one, two, three, four, five or six orders were placed during a year for a single product. From your schedule, state the number of orders to be placed each year and the economic order quantity.

Annual usage of product	600 units
Unit cost of product	£2.40
Cost of placing an order	£6.00
Stockholding cost (as a percentage of average stock value)	20%

(c) Comment briefly on three problems met in determining the economic order quantity.

(*CIMA*)

13. *(a)* What are just-in-time activities?

(b) Outline the sort of savings that might be achieved in (i) capital expenditure and (ii) revenue expenditure if just-in-time methods were adopted.

(c) Explain the term *back-flushing* for calculating the cost of a batch of product turned out by JIT methods.

14. *(a)* What are the advantages of just-in-time activities?

(b) What changes are necessary to operate in this way throughout industry?

UNIT 4

Accounting for labour costs

4.1 Direct and indirect labour

(a) Direct labour

Labour cost may be *direct* or *indirect*. Direct labour cost is the wages paid to employees who are working directly on the material and altering its form or construction. *Conversion costs* in the manufacturing departments include direct labour costs and direct expenses as well as absorbed production overheads (see Unit 5.3). Direct wages are the cost of time spent in actual production or the (wages) cost of performing the main task or service which can be measured and charged to a cost unit. The employee on direct labour produces for stock or for a particular customer, and his or her wages are charged direct to a *stock order number* or *code*, or to the customer's order number.

(b) Diverted hours

It sometimes happens that direct labour is diverted to indirect labour such as cleaning machines, redecorating or other temporary work due to disruption of supplies or some similar reason. In such situations the hours would not be charged directly to a stock order number or customer's order number but would be diverted and treated as indirect labour.

(c) Indirect labour

Indirect labour cost is the wages cost of employees whose time cannot be measured or identified with specific items or products. The indirect worker does not change the form or construction of a product or perform a main service chargeable to a cost unit. The salary of a superintendent or inspector and the wages paid to a maintenance engineer or truck driver in a factory are examples of indirect labour costs. The employee on indirect labour earns a salary or wage which is classed as an *overhead expense* and is chargeable to a *standing order number* or *code*. These expenses are then analysed and shown as either departmental overhead expenses or service department expenses.

With the advance of technology, it is becoming more difficult to identify labour as direct or indirect, and when there are difficulties it is necessary to apply the *test of convenience*. If it is possible to measure the time spent, labour can be classified as direct. For example, it may be very inconvenient to measure and record short operations: in this case it would be easier to treat the wages for such workers as indirect costs and charge them to an Overhead Expense Account. The spray-painting of a large number of small, but different, items every hour of the working day is an example of this problem.

4.2 Methods of labour remuneration

There are many different methods of paying for work, based broadly on time or production, and the elaborate nature of some schemes makes the subject a complicated one. Wages calculated on time tend to be independent of production, whereas wages based on production usually involve some form of incentive scheme, and tend to be independent of time.

Remuneration is the reward for labour and service, and *incentive* is the stimulation of effort and effectiveness by offering monetary inducement or enhanced facilities. We shall consider labour remuneration and incentive systems under the following headings:

(a) time rates;
(b) piece rates;
(c) bonus systems.

(a) Time rates

(i) Time rates at ordinary wage levels This system operates by paying labour for the time spent rather than the work produced. The employee is paid on a time rate, generally referred to as a *day rate*, and payment is by the hour, day or week. Wages are calculated by taking the rate per hour and multiplying this by the total hours worked as shown on the clock card or time sheet. Any premium due for overtime or any allowance for shiftwork is added on.

Some occupations are unsuitable for payment on the basis of output produced, especially those requiring a high degree of skill or when the output or degree of efficiency is difficult to measure. Examples are work in process industries, such as chemical and oil refining, where the operator has little or no control over the rate of production. The day rate method is also favoured where a worker is learning a job or trade.

(ii) Time rates at high wage levels This method provides a high day rate payment for a continuously high standard of performance and productivity. Because payments are well above the normal rates paid to workers elsewhere, labour is attracted to the firm. This factor enables the firm to select good employees, but supervision has to be carefully organised in order to maintain output at a high level. Like the time rates at ordinary wage levels this system is simple to operate, but in return for a much higher day rate it demands a much higher standard of performance and output from workers. This method can result in lower unit costs and a reduction in fixed overhead cost per unit as against the time rate at ordinary wage levels because of the possibility of greater production.

(iii) Measured day-work During the last forty years, schemes have been introduced which pay employees above the time rate at ordinary wage levels by measuring their output over a period of time, say three months, and paying them on the basis of their efficiency and performance during that time. An assessment is therefore made of each employee's performance during the previous period and the payment made is related to the level of performance. This system replaces the piece-work systems described below. The main reason for the introduction of this method of remuneration was that workers found their earnings fluctuated widely from week to week because of incorrect estimates or bad rate fixing. Arguments and disputes frequently arose as new piece-work prices were fixed and new work was issued. At the end of each period, the worker's efficiency is reviewed and, if necessary, the rate is adjusted for payment during the next quarter.

This system benefits an organisation because it reduces paperwork, saves clerical work and means less time will be spent in calculating wages. Calculating the payment for each job or operation under piece-work conditions is a costly business, especially for machining jobs where the time spent on each item is very short. Furthermore there is a better atmosphere on the shop floor because no time is lost disputing who will do which job, and what time should be allowed. Although payment is based on the output of a previous period the system is referred to as day-work because the employee receives a regular rate per hour for a fairly long period.

(b) Piece rates

This method of remuneration is related to effort, and varies with the rate of production, so payment depends on results, and inducements are offered to the worker to increase output. The aim is to reduce the works cost per article by spreading the total overhead cost of the factory over a greater number of articles.

Monetary incentives for extra output are either *individual*, when a worker receives a reward for personal effort, or *collective*, when the employees share a bonus earned in a group scheme.

Collective schemes should be:

(i) fair to both employer and employee;
(ii) simple for clerical staff and employees to operate and understand;
(iii) in conformity with any national, local or trade agreements;
(iv) clearly defined, with worthwhile and attainable objectives, and with regulations which cannot be misunderstood;
(v) carefully prepared, with allowances being set only after the job or work has been properly assessed. The piece rates or time allowance per job, once fixed, should remain unchanged unless methods or conditions change.

The piece rate system of payment can be considered under three headings:

(i) straight piece rate;
(ii) piece rates with guaranteed day rates;
(iii) differential piece rates.

(i) Straight piece rate A straight piece rate is the payment of a fixed sum per fixed unit produced, regardless of the time taken. Piece-work conditions provide for payment on the basis of jobs completed, units produced or operations performed, and the straight piece rate enables a worker to receive a wage in direct relation to the amount of work completed. Under ordinary day-rate methods of payment, a fast worker receives only the rate of pay of a slow worker, so there is little incentive for workers to do more than is necessary. A variation of the straight piece rate is the standard time system based on the *standard hour*, which allows a worker a fixed time for each operation: it is a hypothetical unit, to represent the amount of work which should be performed in one hour at standard performance.

EXAMPLE 4.1

Piece rate	10 pieces at 20 p per piece = £2
Standard time rate	Standard time for 10 pieces = 1 hour
	Standard rate for 1 hour = £2

If ten pieces are made in 45 minutes, instead of one hour, the worker would earn £2.

The advantages of a straight piece rate are:

(i) it is simple to understand and to calculate;
(ii) there is a direct incentive to increase output;
(iii) individual output can be easily and quickly determined;
(iv) unit costs are reduced.

The disadvantages are:

(i) no payment or allowance is normally made for unsuitable materials, variations in the efficiency of tools and machinery, or production delays, which are matters outside the control of the worker;
(ii) varying rates of output between different workers may result in labour troubles.

(ii) Piece rates with guaranteed day rates Incentive schemes should not be affected by matters outside the employees' control, but there are a number of factors which restrict the output and earnings of those on piece rates. These include shortage of materials, unsuitable materials, power failures, machine breakdowns and delays caused by inefficient planning and progressing. It was, in fact, the loss of earnings of those on straight piece rates that led to the introduction of piece rates with guaranteed day rate.

Straight piece rates have mainly been superseded by piece rates with guaranteed day or guaranteed weekly wages. The following examples illustrate the working of piece rates with guaranteed weekly wage and the standard time rate system.

EXAMPLE 4.2

Day rate and guaranteed weekly wage of £4 per hour for 40 hours gives £160 per week;
piece rate of £2.50 per unit, with guaranteed weekly wage of £160;
standard time rate of an allowance of $37\frac{1}{2}$ minutes per piece with guaranteed weekly wage of £160;
the rate of £2.50 per piece and $37\frac{1}{2}$ minutes per piece are equivalent allowances, but in the following examples the rate paid is £2.50 per piece.

Worker A	Produces 80 pieces in 40 hours	
	Earnings = 80 × £2.50 =	£200 (paid)
	Less Day rate wages	£160
	Bonus earned	£ 40
Worker B	Produces 70 pieces in 40 hours	
	Earnings = 70 × £2.50 =	£175 (paid)
	Less Day rate wages	£160
	Bonus earned	£ 15
Worker C	Produces 55 pieces in 40 hours	
	Earnings = 55 × £2.50 =	£137.50
	Day rate wages	£160 (paid)
	Addition to earnings to reach £160	£22.50 (deficit)

Incentive schemes are introduced for two main reasons:

(i) to enable employees to earn extra wages for increased output;
(ii) to increase the level of output, thereby reducing unit costs.

Table 4.1 (p. 64) shows how unit cost is reduced as the level of output rises.

(iii) Differential piece rates This is the *Taylor* system, introduced as long ago as 1880, which fixes a standard price or time for doing a job, but with two piece rates, a *low rate* for output below standard and a *high rate* for production above standard. This incentive method was later modified by Gantt and Merrick.

The advantages of the differential piece rate system are:

(i) it provides a very strong incentive to fast workers;
(ii) it is simple to understand and work;
(iii) only the best workers are attracted to the firm.

The disadvantages are:

(i) the beginner or slow learner is penalised;
(ii) the quality of the work may suffer as workers strive to reach high output.

Table 4.1 The effect of fixed overhead on the cost per unit

Worker	Units produced	Price per unit	Time taken	Direct material cost (£1.00 per unit)	Direct labour cost	Variable overhead cost	Fixed overhead cost	Total cost	Cost per unit
		£	Hours	£	£	£	£	£	£
A	80	2.00	40	80.00	160.00	120.00	360.00	720.00	9.00
B	64	2.00	40	64.00	128.00	96.00	360.00	648.00	10.12
C	53	2.00	40	53.00	120.00	79.50	360.00	612.50	11.56

Notes:

(i) Workers are on straight piece-work with a guaranteed weekly wage of £120.

(ii) A earns £160, B earns £128 and C earns £106 but receives an extra £14 to reach the guaranteed wage of £120.

(iii) Fixed costs included in the cost per unit are A £4.50, B £5.62 and C £6.79, an increase of £1.12 between A and B and £1.17 between B and C.

(iv) The difference in *cost per unit* is the extra share of fixed cost of £1.12 between A and B, and between B and C it is an extra share of fixed cost of £1.17 per unit, plus 26p, which is the addition (£14 ÷ 53) for guaranteed wage. This gives a total of £11.55, not the figure of £11.56 shown in the table. The small difference is a rounding error.

(c) Bonus systems

(i) Premium bonus schemes (individual bonus systems) These are incentive systems which allow for the payment of day rate plus a proportion of the time saved when the worker performs the task in less than the time allowed. Thus any gain from increased output is shared between the employee and the employer. The employer is protected against high rate-fixing and has the advantage of diminishing labour cost. Premium bonus schemes also have the following features:

(i) basic time rate is usually guaranteed;
(ii) the hourly rate of workers increases but not in proportion to output;
(iii) as a result of the above, rate-fixing which is set too high does not have the same effect as it would with piece rates;
(iv) the employer is given an incentive to improve methods and equipment in order to encourage increased output.

Examples of premium bonus systems are:
Halsey and Halsey–Weir system The percentage of time saved which is paid varies from 30 per cent to 70 per cent, with 50 per cent being the most popular. Although the harder the employees work the less they get per piece, it is possible for them to more than double their earnings. However, an exceptional amount of time saved may indicate bad rate-fixing. With 50–50 sharing, the employee is paid for the time taken plus 50 per cent of the time

saved. The time rate is then multiplied by the total hours in order to arrive at the wages to be paid.

EXAMPLE 4.3

Time allowed, 60 hours; time taken, 40 hours

(40 hours + 50% of 20 hours) × £4.00 = (40 hours + 10 hours) × £4.00

Wages paid = 50 hours × £4.00 = £200

Rowan system This is similar to the Halsey–Weir system with a standard time and a bonus for time saved. The bonus is a percentage or proportion of the time rate. This is calculated by relating the *time saved* to the standard time allowed and working this as a percentage of the time rate.

EXAMPLE 4.4

Time rate £4.00 per hour; time allowed (TA), 30 hours; time taken (TT), 21 hours; time saved (TS), 9 hours.

$$\text{Bonus as a } \textit{percentage} \text{ of the time rate} = \frac{TS}{TA} \text{ per cent}$$

$$= \frac{9}{30} \times 100\% = 30 \text{ per cent}$$

30 per cent of £4.00 = £1.20

Rate for time taken = £5.20 per hour

21 hours @ £5.20 = £109.20

or

21 hours @ £4.00 plus 30% = £84.00 + £25.20 = £109.20

$$\text{Bonus as a } \textit{fraction} \text{ of the time rate} = \frac{TS}{TA} \times £4.00$$

$$= \frac{9}{30} \times £4.00 = £1.20$$

With the Rowan system, the earnings are better than with Halsey 50–50 until the time saved is 50 per cent of the time allowed. After this point, however, the earnings rate declines, and the Rowan system gives a smaller return than Halsey. Earnings can never be doubled under this scheme.

Barth variable sharing plan This method was introduced to encourage people learning a job and slow workers. It does not guarantee a time rate, but earnings are higher than under a straight piece-work system.

(ii) Group or collective bonus systems Sometimes it is easier to measure the output of a group of workers, instead of the output of individuals, or there may simply be a preference for a group system. In order to provide an incentive to a group, a collective payment is made on an agreed basis for any savings in cost, or for output above an agreed minimum. This collective payment is then shared among the group in an agreed way.

4.3 Costs and earnings under different systems

Incentive schemes are introduced with the object of increasing the rate of production, reducing labour costs per unit of output where possible, and minimising fixed overhead cost per unit. Fig. 4.1 shows the earnings and labour cost curves under various systems to illustrate the effect of increased output on remuneration and costs. Table 4.2 (p. 68) shows costs and earnings under different systems.

4.4 The personnel department

Co-operation between the wages department and the personnel department is essential as new employees arrive and others leave. The personnel office should inform the wages office of matters such as dismissals, retirement and changes in rates of pay caused by promotion or demotion. Sometimes wages are related to age, and increments may be awarded on birthdays. The wages office should be told about special deductions from pay and of changes in local or national rates of pay. For its part the wages office provides information and prepares reports for the personnel office on matters such as timekeeping, absenteeism, sickness, earnings in respect of claims for compensation and similar matters.

Labour costs can be expensive if there is a high labour turnover which results in high cost of recruitment, retraining costs and heavy costs of spoilage.

Losses may also occur as a result of inexperience in the handling of tools, equipment and machinery. Delays, machine damage and injury to workers may occur.

The *percentage rate of labour turnover* can be measured as follows:

$$\frac{\text{Total number of people leaving in the year}}{\text{Average number of people employed in the year}} \times 100$$

Notes to Fig. 4.1:

(i) With a time rate, cost per unit falls as output rises. The problem is to keep output high since there is no incentive to raise it.

(ii) Straight piece-work provides a constant rate of pay and constant cost per unit of output.

(iii) The guaranteed wage reduces the power of the incentive. Up to the point where the employee starts to earn a bonus, any gains or losses arising from variations in output are taken by the employer.

(iv) Labour cost falls sharply as output increases up to standard, and above this standard, labour costs continue to fall at a reducing rate.

(v) Labour cost decreases as output increases up to task level.

(vi) Labour cost decreases rapidly for low production but not so rapidly when production increases.

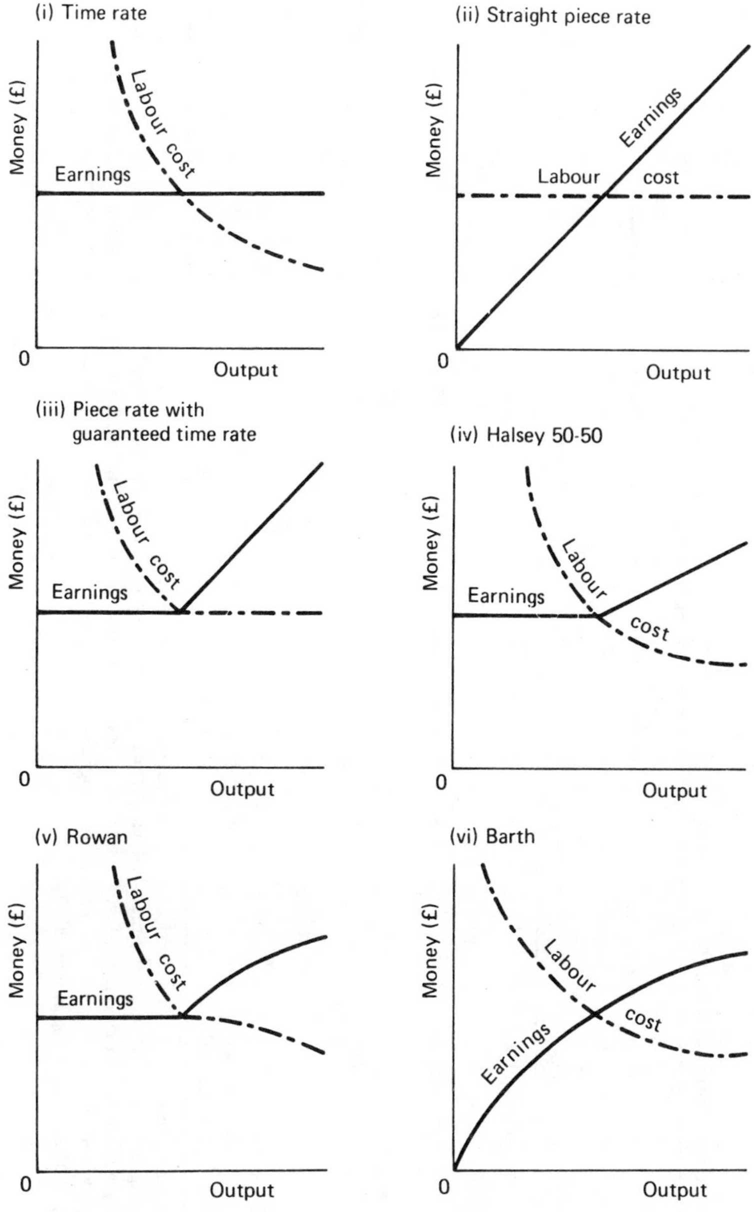

Fig. 4.1 Labour costs and earnings under various systems

Table 4.2 Comparison of costs and earnings under various systems

	Time rate Hour £ (*a*)	Time rate Week £ (*b*)	Time allowed per unit (hours) (*c*)	Units produced (*d*)	Total time allowed (*e*) (*c* × *d*)	Time taken (hours) (*f*)	Time saved (hours) (*g*) (*e* − *f*)	Bonus hours paid (*h*)	Total hours paid (*i*) (*f* + *h*)	Gross wage £ (*j*) (*a* × *i*)	Labour cost per hour £ (*k*) (*j* ÷ *f*)	Labour cost per unit £ (*l*) (*j* ÷ *d*)
Day rate	3.00	120.00	–	15	–	40	–	–	40	120.00	3.00	8.00
Piece rate with guaranteed weekly rate	3.00	120.00	2	18	36	40	–	–	40	120.00	3.00	6.67
Straight piece-work rate	3.00	120.00	2	30	60	40	20	20	60	180.00	4.50	6.00
Halsey 50–50	3.00	120.00	2	30	60	40	20	10	50	150.00	3.75	5.00
Rowan	3.00	120.00	2	30	60	40	20	$13\frac{1}{3}$	$53\frac{1}{3}$	160.00	4.00	5.33
High rate of efficiency:												
Halsey 50–50	3.00	120.00	2	50	100	40	60	30	70	210.00	5.25	4.20
Rowan	3.00	120.00	2	50	100	40	60	24	64	192.00	4.80	3.84

Note: The table shows that the day-worker costs an employer most, followed by the piece-worker with guaranteed weekly rate, but they both receive the same gross wage of £120. With straight piece-work, labour cost per unit is lower than the day rate or the piece rate with guaranteed weekly rate, and the gross wage is the highest among the first five examples. Halsey 50–50 shows a lower unit cost and labour cost per hour than Rowan, but the relationship changes as efficiency improves and output increases. At higher levels of output, the labour cost per unit is reduced considerably and the Rowan cost falls below the Halsey 50–50 cost.

Thus if 100 staff out of 500 leave in the year, the rate of labour turnover is:

$$\frac{100}{500} \times 100 = \underline{\underline{20\% \text{ per annum}}}$$

4.5 Time recording

Most organisations use some form of timekeeping to provide a record of time spent in the factory or department and to record the time spent on a job or operation. Methods of recording attendance and time spent on jobs include the following.

(a) Time sheets or attendance books

Time sheets are usually for the week, although daily sheets are issued where it is more convenient. In wages and costing offices the use of coloured paper or coloured bands is a convenient device for indicating occupations, classes of materials or whether a job is a piece-work or day-work job. This system can be used with time sheets where, for example, a red band across the top of a job card could indicate a day-work job, and a blue one a piece-work job. Time sheets are not entirely satisfactory because of the time spent recording the information and the illegibility of some of these records. Some firms use attendance books for employees to sign in and out as a way of recording attendance and absence.

(b) Time recorders for attendance time

Dial time recorders or card time recorders are situated at the gate or outside the departmental office. In the dial recorder, a radial arm is pressed into holes on a clock face to register the time against the employee's number on a paper roll. Card time recorders are more common but they need *in* and *out* racks to contain the cards. The employee takes the card from the out rack and inserts it in the recorder to register the time, and then places it in the in rack. The cards which remain in the out rack are evidence of absentees.

Sophisticated electronic devices are also available for recording attendance time. Units placed at various access points enable an employee who is arriving to turn a key which immediately *(a)* notifies reception through an indicator light that the employee is in the building and *(b)* starts to record the individual's attendance time. These devices are widely used in such arrangements as flexitime.

(c) Time recorders for process time

These record operation or activity time on the back of job cards or tickets. The time taken, *elapsed time*, has to be calculated from the start and finish times. This method is useful when workers are paid by results. At the end of the week the total time shown on the individual tickets or cards has to be reconciled with the attendance time. A typical job card is shown in Fig. 4.2 (p. 70).

Description: 20 Gear wheels			Charge to : Order no. X.71492		
Drg. no. 50719	Code no. 01C746		M/c sect. 3	Payroll no. 608	
Dept. no. 5	Oper. no. 4	Machine casting	Time allowed		
			Each 2 hrs.	*Total* 40 hrs.	
Send to Dept. no 8	Oper. no. 5		Time taken	Time saved	
			30 hrs.	10 hrs.	
Replaced: Nil			Wages cost		
Qty scrapped Nil	Qty passed 20	Initials AN	Hrs 40	Rate £3.00	Total

Fig. 4.2 Job card

Note: This job card illustrates the fourth operation in the production of a gear wheel. It has to be machined in department 5 and then sent to department 8 for the next operation. The complete sequence of operations will be shown on an operation layout sheet.

(d) Monitel time systems

A recent development (devised by Shaw & Sons Ltd in collaboration with Monitel Ltd) enables costs to be allocated to particular jobs or account numbers without any tedious calculation. Using a special punched card an electric clock can be programmed with an employee's time cost. When starting a job, the hourly rate key on the Monitel unit is depressed, followed by a start–stop button. The digital clock ceases to show the time, and, instead, displays the cost of the employee's time being used on a client's business. This cost is not just the employee's wage, but includes overheads; it is better to use an hourly rate. This system also has applications in the professions. Thus a solicitor's time at £16.00 per hour might be increased to £36.00 per hour when all overheads and so forth have been built into the hourly rate. A ten-minute period spent reviewing a client's problem would therefore be charged to the client's account as £6.00. One added advantage of such a system to accountants, solicitors and professional consultants is that the system offers a package of costing sheets.

4.6 The wages department

The functions of the wages department are as follows:

(i) to calculate the day rate wages and all bonuses earned;
(ii) to calculate overtime and shift premiums;
(iii) to reconcile the clock card total or electronic clock records with the total of hours shown on the job tickets for each employee;

(iv) to check the wage rates and total computation on job tickets, and enter gross wages;
(v) to deal with payroll deductions, including PAYE, and calculate net pay;
(vi) to record details of individual earnings and deductions on personal record cards;
(vii) to arrange for payment by cash, cheque or credit transfer.

4.7 Preparation of wages

(a) Calculation of wages

Time sheets, clock cards and job tickets have to be sent to the wages office at the end of each week, although finished job tickets can be sent daily. This enables the clerks to calculate earnings as each finished job ticket is received. Duplicate job tickets are written out by the time-keepers for unfinished jobs at the end of the week, and the wages office has to keep a record of time taken to date, for use in calculating the bonus earned when the job is completed.

When calculations are complete, a reconciliation is made between the total hours shown on each employee's clock cards and the total hours shown on his or her job tickets. Next, the overtime premium or shift time allowances have to be calculated. The final computation may be as follows:

Total clock hours 48 (Monday to Friday 40 hours; Sunday 8 hours)
Day rate £180 per week (£4.50 per hour)
Double time for Sunday work

	Hours	*Wages earned*	
		£	
Day-work	7	31.50	(7 × £4.50)
Piece-work	41	225.00	(Time allowed 50 hours 50 × £4.50)
Overtime premium	8	36.00	(Allowance for Sunday work, paid at day rate)
	56	£292.50	

(b) Preparation of payroll

Once the job tickets have been collected and calculated, in order to find the gross wages for each worker, it is necessary to refer to the schedule or list of deductions. There are *standard* deductions and *variable* or *special* deductions in respect of PAYE, National Insurance contributions and so on, and these must be recorded in order to find the net pay. The payroll can then be prepared and if necessary a cash analysis made, but in most cases payment is by cheque or credit transfer.

One of the most important documents in a wages office is the earnings record or personal record card of each employee. At the same time as the wages are tabulated, the details of earnings and deductions can be entered on the personal record cards. At the end of the year these records will provide information about total wages paid, tax deducted and superannuation contributions.

(c) Book-keeping entries for wages and deductions

The cost of employing labour consists of gross wages plus employer's contributions to social security payments, pensions schemes and holiday pay. Large manufacturing companies usually have a separate payroll for each manufacturing unit. Total wages paid to employees are called *gross wages* but the total expense incurred by a firm on the Wages Account includes other expenses such as employer's National Insurance contributions.

The entries in the financial books might appear as given below:

Gross wages £40 000; Deductions: PAYE £9 700; National Insurance £4 000; Recreation club £300. Employer's National Insurance contribution £5 000; Employer's recreation club contribution £2 500.

	Debit £	*Credit* £
Wages Account (£40 000 + £5 000 + £2 500)	47 500	
Social Security Account (National Insurance: Employees' £4 000 Employer's £5 000)		9 000
Income Tax Account (PAYE)		9 700
Recreation Club Account (Employees' contributions)		300
Recreation Club Account (Employer's contribution)		2 500
Wages Payable Account (Cash required)		26 000 (net pay)
	£47 500	£47 500

The payroll is one of the easiest parts of the accounting system to computerise, and there are dozens of payroll packages on offer. Many employees will be paid by a computerised system of credit transfers, which credits each employee's personal bank account with the wages due, while at the same time the computer makes the accounting entries shown above to bring the financial books up to date.

(d) Wages analysis

After the completion of the payroll, the next step in costing is to analyse the wages in order to arrive at the labour cost chargeable to each of the Cost Accounts. The way in which the analysis is carried out varies between different organisations because of the method of costing used and the size of the business. For example, a company manufacturing machinery and equipment may be producing five different product groups. It manufactures both for stock and to customers' requirements and has ten production departments and three service departments. It also produces a large proportion of the components for fitting and setting up the products.

The gross wages of the employees are recorded on a large number of job cards, each of which shows a number representing a standing order, a stock order or a customer's order. These cards are sorted into numerical order for each department, and the stock and customers' numbers are sorted into product groups. They are then listed to provide a total for each of the service departments and other departments in respect of indirect labour. For direct labour, totals are provided for the stock and customers' orders under each of the five product groups.

The next step is to calculate, for each department, the overhead chargeable to each cost account, by using the appropriate recovery rate (see Unit 5). The wages analysis provides the figures which are debited to the Work-in-progress Control Account and the various Overhead Accounts and credited to the Wages and Salaries Control Account. A Control Account in the cost ledger, as in the financial accounts, is an account which controls a subsidiary ledger. The transactions which are recorded in detail in individual accounts within the subsidiary ledger are entered in summary form in the Control Account. The balance of the account should always equal the total of the balances on the individual accounts in the subsidiary ledger.

Each department has its own overhead rate and this is used to calculate the overhead expenses chargeable to each cost account. The total expense charged against the department or cost centre will have to be reconciled with the total of the individual calculations. The layout of a wages analysis is indicated in Fig. 4.3.

Unit 12 gives more details about the computerisation of various aspects of management accounting.

Wages analysis and overhead recovery
Department no. 1

Order no.	Wages	Overhead
	£	£
58742	121.50	243.00
58903	64.38	128.76
	etc.	*etc.*
	£5 602.00	£11 204.00

Fig. 4.3 Wages analysis and overhead recovery
Note: This indicates that the direct wages charged to stock orders in department 1 is £5 602. It also shows that the overhead recovery rate for this department is 200 per cent on direct wages, giving £11 204.

4.8 Exercises

1. The managing director of a group of companies requested the group personnel manager to prepare a report on the labour situation in each of its factories. This report indicated that the situation within the group was satisfactory with the exception of one factory where a considerable amount of time was spent in advertising for and recruiting labour. The managing director has now written to you, as chief cost accountant, asking for information which will enable him to become acquainted with the problem of high labour turnover in this factory and to take effective action to correct the situation. You are required to send him a report which:

(a) gives details of the effect of high labour turnover on costs;
(b) shows the steps that could be taken in an effort to reduce costs;
(c) explains how the rate of labour turnover is calculated.

2. Calculate the labour cost chargeable to order no. 2075 in respect of an employee machining a casting, under *(a)* the Halsey 50–50 scheme and *(b)* the Rowan scheme.

Rate of pay:	£4.50 per hour
Time taken:	9 hours 30 minutes
Time allowed:	12 hours 30 minutes

3. A company manufactures three products X, Y and Z. It has thirty direct employees who are paid under a group bonus scheme. There are three grades of employees who are paid a bonus of the excess of time allowed over time taken. The bonus is paid on the employee's base rate less £1.50, and is shared among the direct workers in proportion to the time spent on the work. The production details for the period in question were as follows:

Product	Units produced	Time allowed per unit (minutes)
X	80	63
Y	160	120
Z	300	100

Grade of employee	Number of direct employees	Base rate £	Hours worked per employee
L	10	4.00	15
M	4	3.60	32
N	16	3.70	25

From the above information you are required to calculate (*a*) the percentage of hours saved to hours taken, (*b*) the total bonus payable to the group of direct employees and (*c*) the total wages payable to the group of direct employees.

4. A company manufactures three products P, Q and R. It has forty direct employees who are paid under a group bonus scheme. There are three grades of employee who are paid a bonus of the excess of time allowed over time taken. The bonus is paid on the employee's base rate less £1.00, and is shared among the direct workers in proportion to the time spent on the work. The production details for the period in question were as follows:

Product	Units produced	Time allowed per unit (minutes)
P	60	58
Q	120	140
R	400	150

Employee grade	Number of direct employees	Base rate £	Hours worked by each employee
S	20	3.00	20
T	8	4.00	24
U	12	3.60	30

From the above information you are required to calculate (*a*) the percentage of hours saved to hours taken, (*b*) the total bonus payable to the group of direct employees and (*c*) the total wages payable to the group of direct employees. (Any calculation which does not work out exactly is to be taken correct to one decimal place, or in the case of money correct to the nearest penny.)

5. A factory issues a job to employee A to produce 35 articles with a time allowance of 2 standard hours each, and another job to employee B for 60 articles with a standard time allowance of $1\frac{1}{2}$ hours each. For every hour saved a bonus is paid at 50 per cent of the base rate, which is £4.00 per hour. The factory works a 40-hour week and overtime is paid at time plus a third. At the end of the week A's clock card shows 49 hours and B's 46 hours and the work is complete; three of A's articles failed to pass inspection, however, and the same applied to four of B's. This was due to defective materials and in view of this all the units produced were paid for, although as scrap they have no sales value.

Calculate for A and B: (*a*) the bonus payable, (*b*) the total gross wage payable and (*c*) the wages cost per unit of goods passing inspection.

6. The Balken Manufacturing Company employs 1 500 people in its works and offices. Day-work and piece-work methods of remuneration are used in the works and all the employees use some form of record to show their attendance time. A large percentage of the manual workers spend two hours or less on each job or operation.

Describe the various methods which could be employed in this factory to record attendance time and the time spent on individual jobs. State the advantages or disadvantages of any of the methods you describe.

7. The following details have been gathered from the wages office records for week ending 30 September 19..:

	£
Value of cheque drawn for net wages	10 380
PAYE deductions	1 792
Subscriptions to recreation club	58
Employer's contribution to club	342
National Insurance: employees'	947
National Insurance: employer's	984

Write up the Journal entry to record this information.

UNIT 5

Accounting for overhead costs

5.1 Introduction: accumulation of expenses

Indirect costs are expenses incurred in the performance of a service, not as a result of changing the form of the product. In the process of identifying and classifying these costs and services, standing expense orders and codes are used. The symbols or codes which may be used are in the form of numbers, decimals and letters, to assist memory. The standing order number or code is a permanent feature of the costing system, and exists for a long time, so that new orders do not have to be issued each time an expense is incurred.

The collection of overhead expenses takes place under the standing order code numbers and these expenses consist of:

(i) materials as shown on stores requisitions;
(ii) wages as analysed and charged to expense codes;
(iii) invoices for materials and services chargeable as expenses;
(iv) chargeable expenses made by journal entry for costs incurred internally, and those requiring allocation for a particular period of account, e.g. depreciation and insurance.

An analysis of standing order costs is made in order to assemble the expenses under the various production departments, service departments and cost centres.

(a) Cost centres

A cost centre may be a department, a group of machines, a method, a process or an operation for which costs may be ascertained. A power plant, a steam plant, a machine shop, material store or repair and maintenance department, and hand labour are examples which may be classified as either *production cost centres, process cost centres* or *service cost centres*.

(b) Overhead groups

There are four distinct groups of overhead costs, each of which is usually dealt with separately when collecting the expenses and computing the product costs, as goods are taken into stock or dispatched to the customer. These groups form an important part of the cost control procedures:

(i) factory or works expenses;
(ii) administrative and office expenses;

(iii) selling and distribution expenses (marketing expenses);
(iv) research and development expenses.

Statement of Standard Accounting Practice no. 9 refers particularly to *production overhead*, which it defines as:

> overheads incurred in respect of materials, labour or services for production, based on the normal level of activity, taking one year with another. For this purpose each overhead should be classified according to functions (e.g., production, selling, or administration) so as to ensure the inclusion in cost of conversion, of those overheads (including depreciation) which relate to production, notwithstanding that these may accrue wholly or partly on a time basis . . .
>
> All abnormal conversion costs (such as exceptional spoilage, idle capacity and other losses) which are avoidable under normal operating conditions need, for the same reason, to be excluded . . .
>
> Where firm sales contracts have been entered into for the provision of goods or services to customer's specification, overheads relating to design, and marketing and selling costs incurred before manufacture, may be included in arriving at cost . . .
>
> The costs of general management, as distinct from functional management, are not directly related to current production and are, therefore, excluded from cost of conversion and, hence, from the cost of stocks and long-term contracts . . .
>
> In small organisations whose management are involved in the daily administration of each of the various functions, the cost of management may fairly be allocated on suitable bases to the function of production, marketing, selling and administration . . .
>
> The allocation of costs of the central service departments will depend on the function or functions that the department is serving . . .
>
> Only those costs of the accounts department that can be reasonably be allocated to the production function fall to be included in the cost of conversion.

For example, the accounts department will normally support the following functions:

(a) production – by paying direct and indirect production wages and salaries, by controlling purchases and by preparing periodic financial statements for the production units;
(b) marketing and distribution – by analysing sales and by controlling the sales ledger;
(c) general administration – by preparing management accounts and annual financial statements and budgets, by controlling cash resources and by planning investments.

Overhead costs have to be established for each type of expense and as they are indirect costs they have to be *absorbed* by production and sales. The costs of overhead expenses are kept and recorded in a manufacturing expense, or overhead expense, ledger, where the standing orders and their costs are shown.

(c) Budget centres

For the purposes of budgetary control, the organisation is divided into units known as *budget centres*. These are natural divisions of the organisation to which costs are charged and, for control purposes, they are the responsibility of an individual such as a supervisor or works manager who is, therefore, responsible for organising and controlling the expenditure which relates to his or her own department or budget centre.

5.2 Types of overhead expense

(a) Fixed costs

These remain unchanged within the short term and are not related to the volume of production. They are constant costs over a period of time and include rent, rates, depreciation, insurance and salaries.

(b) Variable costs

These are directly related to the volume of output and consist of items such as fuel, lubricants, power, spoilage, royalties, compressed air and small tools.

(c) Semi-variable costs

These are partly fixed and partly variable. They change as production facilities are utilised above or below normal levels. Examples are the cost of supervision, clerical labour, telephone charges, electricity and gas.

5.3 Allocation, apportionment and absorption

A service department

This is one which provides services and facilities which are ancillary to the production departments and other service or administrative departments. Indirect costs occur within production and service departments and a considerable amount of overhead costs occurs where the actual or specific expenditure is charged direct to the department. Each industry has its own problems of selecting an appropriate basis for apportionment. This may be by man or machine hour, or on the basis of labour costs, mileage run and other methods as mentioned later in this unit.

It is comparatively simple to apportion fixed costs, but complications arise with variable costs which result from activities within a department, such as overtime and shiftworking which changes from time to time. Technical experts generally use activity or operating time when making their estimates. Each of the production and service departments has its own set of standing orders to which indirect costs are charged. For example, the cost of operating and running the overhead cranes in a machine department would be charged to the standing order number of that department. Charging the wages of the crane-driver is a simple matter but other costs such as power are more difficult to allocate and may have to be shared out and apportioned on some appropriate basis. The following terms are used in the process of charging and distributing overhead expenses to departments, cost centres, cost units, jobs and processes.

Allocation is the allotment of whole items of cost to cost centres or cost units.

Apportionment is the allotment to two or more cost centres of proportions of common items of cost on the estimated basis of benefit received.

Absorption is the allotment of overhead to cost units by means of rates separately calculated for each cost centre. In most cases the rates are predetermined.

5.4 Bases for apportioning indirect expenditure to production and service departments

Special principles have to be followed in determining the method of sharing indirect expenditure items, incurred for the benefit of more than one department. Alternative bases are:

(a) **Effective floor area.** Expenses shared include rent, rates, building expense, fire precautions.

(b) **Effective cubic capacity.** Space or volume costs apply for heating and sometimes for building depreciation, industrial cleaning and decorating costs.

(c) **Capital value of buildings and plant.** The book value can be used for insurance and depreciation.

(d) **Volume or weight of materials.** In some industries, storekeeping and material handling costs can be charged out on this basis.

(e) **Number of employees.** Some expenses can be shared pro rata on the basis of the number of employees in each department, or on the number who benefit from the expenditure. This basis applies to personnel and welfare costs, such as canteen costs, first aid costs, wages of gatekeepers and administration costs.

(f) **Metered consumption.** This includes items such as electricity, gas, compressed air, steam and water.

(g) **Average inventory values.** This includes fire protection and insurance.

(h) **Points wired.** This is for telephones.

(i) **Technical estimate.** This is used where it is impossible to apply more exact methods. This may be necessary in the case of electricity, gas, compressed air, steam, hydraulic power, laboratory and telephone costs.

Apportionment rates

Records are kept so that expenses can be shared out on the appropriate basis. These include the area and cubic capacity of each centre, the number of employees in each department, the number of items or weight of materials handled and the capital value of buildings and plant, and so on. This enables percentages to be fixed for each department. A simple example is given below, using the area of five departments for the apportionment of rent. Having calculated the area used by each department as well as the total area, percentages can be fixed. One per cent is represented by £50.

	%	*Rent* £
Machine shop	45	2 250
Welding shop	21	1 050
Assembly department	24½	1 225
Tool room	4½	225
Power and general services department	5	250
	100	£5 000

5.5 Factory or works expenses

The costs recorded in a manufacturing organisation relate to:

(a) materials, wages and expenses in respect of jobs and products;
(b) similar costs in respect of all other work.

The costs under *(b)* may consist of:

(i) expenditure on capital goods or extensions;
(ii) expenditure on research and development;
(iii) the overhead costs of the organisation.

The costs as divided in *(a)* and *(b)* above can be classified as:

(i) direct costs relating to jobs and products [in *(a)*];
(ii) indirect costs relating to all other work [in *(b)*].

The capital expenditure of materials, wages and direct expenses, plus a fair share of overheads, will be transferred and debited to the appropriate Asset Account. If the cost of research and development is fairly stable from year to year it will be written off by a transfer to the Profit and Loss Account. If the cost is exceptionally large in a particular year, and benefit from the research will accrue later, some of the costs may be carried forward and written off at a later date. In some cases it may be possible to recover these costs by a direct allocation to the products identified with the research. The indirect costs of the organisation mentioned in (iii) above are those charged to the standing order numbers of the manufacturing, service and administration departments. They are the overhead expenses of the organisation as charged to budget centres.

Procedures for allocating and apportioning overhead costs

Indirect costs are charged to budget and cost centres by allocation or apportionment. The *allocation* is a straightforward procedure because charging the cost to a standing order number identifies it with a particular budget centre. For example, the salary of a machine shop superintendent is allocated from the staff payroll to the machine shop by charging it to the standing order number for that particular expense. Such costs are peculiar or exclusive to a particular budget centre, but where these costs are closely related to other budget or cost centres, they are known as common costs.

Common costs are distributed by *apportioning* them so that other budget or cost centres are charged a sum equivalent to the benefit received. For example, in an organisation where there are no separate meters the invoice for electricity would be charged by allocating it to a budget centre. As it is a common cost, it is then apportioned and charged to other budget and cost centres. The salary of a production controller would likewise be allocated to the service department where he or she works and then the amount would be apportioned by charging other budget and cost centres with the amounts attributable to them. This apportionment is known as a *primary distribution*. This is followed by a *secondary distribution* when the costs of the service departments are charged to the production departments.

In some systems the service department costs are charged entirely to the production departments, but in others, some of these costs are charged to the production departments and other service departments before a final distribution is made to the production departments.

There are therefore two stages in the distribution of expenses. They are explained more fully in the next section.

5.6 Overhead distribution

Overheads have to be distributed in two stages, a primary distribution and a secondary distribution. The first distributes the costs collected under various standing order headings (electricity, telephone expenses, etc.) on some fair basis to *all* departments and service departments. Then, since all overheads must in the end be borne by the units of production and included in the charges made to the customer, the total costs of the service departments have to be distributed among the production departments in some fair proportion. This is the second stage of distributing overheads.

(a) Primary distribution

This method allocates or apportions expenses to the standing orders of the production and service departments. Primary distribution takes place when it is possible to allocate, measure exactly or apportion a fair amount. A typical distribution is shown in Table 5.1.

(b) Secondary distribution

The costs of a *service department*, such as the tool room, have to be distributed among the production departments and other user/service departments. This is done successively with the various service department costs, in some

Table 5.1 Primary distribution

		Factory overhead analysis				
		Production departments			*Service departments*	
Expense	Basis	Machine shop	Welding shop	Assembly department	Tool room	Power and general services
		£	£	£	£	£
Rent	Area	2 250	1 050	1 225	225	250
Rates	Area	1 125	525	613	112	125
Heat	Cubic capacity	1 400	1 050	1 225	225	200
Light	Area	450	210	245	45	50
Indirect labour	Allocation	670	250	780	90	210
Indirect material	Allocation	110	90	80	700	900
Insurance	Book value	170	100	80	50	200
Canteen	Employees	270	150	180	60	90
etc.	etc.	etc.	etc.	etc.	etc.	etc.
Totals		£8 000	£9 400	£12 600	£4 000	£7 000

cases reactivating the costs of a department which have already been written off. Thus the tool room department costs already written off may be reactivated because the power and general service department costs, when apportioned, mean that the tool room has to bear its fair share of general service costs. These reactivated costs will then have to be re-apportioned. This is illustrated in Table 5.3 later in this unit.

To make the final distribution on the basis of services received, the proportion chargeable to each department is reduced to a percentage of the total. For example, the services of the maintenance department could be shared out on the basis of man hours of service rendered, with the man hours of each department being reduced to percentages. The cost of a stores department could be distributed by using the number of requisitions or the value of the requisitions and fixing percentages for each department using the service.

An example is given below of apportionment percentages used to eliminate the service department costs of a tool room and a power and general services department. The first service department, the tool room, is to be closed off, first, by apportioning the tool room costs to the other service department and to the manufacturing departments as follows:

> 30 per cent to power and general services; 20 per cent to machine shop; 10 per cent to welding shop; and 40 per cent to the assembly department.

Thus the tool room costs can be eliminated by being transferred to the other departments, both service and manufacturing. Although there are now no tool room costs, the costs of the power and general services department have increased by the 30 per cent of the tool room costs which were charged to that department. The cost of the power and general services department (the original cost plus the 30 per cent) are now apportioned to the first service department, the tool room and the manufacturing departments by charging: 20 per cent to tool room; 40 per cent to machine shop; 30 per cent to welding shop; and 10 per cent to the assembly department. This process is continued until all the service department costs have been eliminated by transferring them to the manufacturing departments.

Apportionment percentages of reciprocal services and manufacturing departments

	Manufacturing departments			*Service departments*	
	Machine shop	Welding shop	Assembly department	Tool room	Power and general services
	%	%	%	%	%
Tool room costs shared as:	20	10	40	—	30
Power and general services costs shared as:	40	30	10	20	—

Reciprocal service The easiest method is to charge service department costs direct to the producing departments, but this ignores the fact that generally services rendered by service departments apply to both producing and other service departments, because the services are reciprocal.

There are three usual methods of secondary distribution.

(i) Distribution on a non-repetitive basis When using this method of transferring expenses there is only one distribution of the expenses of each service department. All the expenses of a service department are spread over the producing and other service departments, and from then on, no further expenses are received or distributed by that service centre. The distribution should be carried out in a specific order by first taking the service department which carries out work for the greatest number of other service departments. Where two or more departments service the same number of departments, you should commence with the department with the largest cost. In Table 5.2 this means that the power and general services costs must be distributed first.

(ii) Repeated or continuous distribution This is the reciprocal basis of allotment whereby the Service Department Account is closed, and is reopened and closed again as successive distributions take place. There may be several apportionments until finally all the service costs are distributed. Under this method there is no particular arrangement or order of distribution. A typical distribution is shown in Table 5.3 (p. 86).

Table 5.2 Overhead distribution on a non-repetitive basis

	Production departments			*Service departments*		
	Machine shop	Welding shop	Assembly department	Tool room	Power and general services	Total
	£	£	£	£	£	£
Primary distribution	8 000	9 400	12 600	4 000	7 000	41 000
Service department distributions:						
Power and general services	2 800	2 100	700	1 400	(7 000)	
Tool room	1 543	771	3 086	(5 400)	–	
Totals	£12 343	£12 271	£16 386	–	–	£41 000

Notes:
(i) It wil be seen that the power and general service costs are distributed in the normal way using 40 per cent, 30 per cent, 10 per cent and 20 per cent.
(ii) The tool room cost of £5 400 is distributed only to the producing departments in the proportion of 2:1:4.

(iii) Algebraic method using simultaneous equations This method uses simultaneous equations to solve the problem of distributions. However, the solutions by this method become difficult with a large number of service departments, and a computer may be needed to arrive at the correct answers. The calculations are given below.

Using the same data as in Tables 5.2 and 5.3:

Let £x be the total overhead of the tool room after apportioning y.

Let £y be the total overhead of the power and general services department after apportioning x:

$$x = 4\,000 + 0.2y \quad (20\%)$$
$$y = 7\,000 + 0.3x \quad (30\%)$$

Multiply by 10 to eliminate decimals:

$$10x = 40\,000 + 2y$$
$$10y = 70\,000 + 3x$$

Rearrange

$$10x - 2y = 40\,000 \quad (1)$$
$$-3x + 10y = 70\,000 \quad (2)$$

Multiply (1) by 5 and add (2) to eliminate y:

Table 5.3 Repeated distribution of reciprocal services

	Production departments			*Service departments*		
	Machine shop	Welding shop	Assembly department	Tool room	Power and general services	Total
	£	£	£	£	£	£
Direct expenses	8 000	9 400	12 600	4 000	7 000	41 000
Service department distributions:						
Tool room	800	400	1 600	(4 000)	1 200	
Power and general services	3 280	2 460	820	1 640	(8 200)	
Tool room	328	164	656	(1 640)	492	
Power and general services	197	148	49	98	(492)	
Tool room	20	10	39	(98)	29	
Power and general services	11	9	3	6	(29)	
Tool room	2	1	3	(6)	–	
Totals	£12 638	£12 592	£15 770	–	–	£41 000

Notes:
(i) The tool room costs are distributed among the other departments 2:1:4:3.
(ii) The increased power and general services charges are then distributed 4:3:1:2, thus reopening the Tool Room Account.
(iii) The tool room share of the power and general distribution is then reallocated 2:1:4:3, thus reopening the Power and General Account, which is then redistributed, and so on.
(iv) Finally, the residue is allocated from the tool room to the producing departments, in the ratio 2:1:4.

$$50x - 10y = 200\,000$$
$$-3x + 10y = 70\,000$$

Total $\quad 47x = 270\,000$

Divide by 47 $\quad x = \text{£}5\,744.68$

Substituting 5 744.68 for x in (1):

$$57\,447 - 2y = 40\,000$$

Rearrange $\quad 57\,447 - 40\,000 = 2y$

$$y = \text{£}8\,723.50$$

The total overhead of the power and general services department is £8 723.50. When this is distributed it gives the results shown in Table 5.4.

Table 5.4 Apportionment of repeated distribution totals obtained by algebraic methods

	Repeat distribution total	Amount apportioned		*Production departments* Machine shop		Welding shop		Assembly department		Total
	£	%	£	%	£	%	£	%	£	£
Original overhead cost					8 000		9 400		12 600	30 000
Value of x (tool room)	5 745	70	4 021	20	1 149	10	574	40	2 298	4 021
Value of y (power and general services)	8 724	80	6 979	40	3 490	30	2 617	10	872	6 979
Totals					£12 639		£12 591		£15 770	£41 000

5.7 Recovery of factory or works expenses

Production costs comprise *prime cost plus production overhead*, but as overhead expenses cannot be specifically related to any particular item of output they have to be spread over production. The expenses are *absorbed* by production, and rates for recovering these costs have to be established. It is inconvenient to charge actual costs because you have to wait until the end of an accounting period. So before the actual costs are ascertained, an estimate is made of future costs and *predetermined rates* are fixed. To decide on the method of recovering costs, the production, the raw materials used and the type of labour employed have to be examined. Other factors to take into account are seasonal working, shiftwork, etc.

5.8 Application of overhead to production

The methods used include the following:

(i) percentage of prime cost;
(ii) percentage of direct material cost;
(iii) percentage of direct labour cost;
(iv) rate per direct labour hour;
(v) rate per machine hour;
(vi) rate per unit of product.

The rate of absorption is found by using the following formula:

$$\frac{\text{Estimated overhead expenses of the cost centre}}{\text{Estimated total production in terms of units or value}}$$

This is multiplied by 100 to obtain the percentage for (i), (ii) and (iii).
(i) Percentage of prime cost

$$= \frac{\text{Overhead expenses}}{\text{Direct material + Direct wages + Direct expenses}} \times 100$$

This is a simple method to apply, but as many overhead costs are related to time, and because materials usually form a large part of the total prime cost, it has no logical basis. It can only be used satisfactorily where one standard product is made which uses a fixed quantity of material at a constant price, and where the time taken in production is constant. An example illustrates the problem:

	Product A	*Product B*
	£	£
Direct materials	5.00	15.00
Direct wages	10.00	10.00
Direct expenses	1.00	1.00
Prime cost	16.00	26.00
Works overhead 100%	16.00	26.00
Total cost	£32.00	£52.00

For the same period of time both products use the facilities of the factory, including lighting, heating, and the cost of supervision and administration. Product B, however, is expected to contribute an extra £10 towards overhead costs. In a competitive market where other producers are using a more scientific method of absorbing overheads, orders might be lost for product B because it costs more. Product A may be underpriced but lack of orders for B might require a higher rate of overhead for A which would increase its cost.

(ii) Percentage of direct material cost $= \dfrac{\text{Overhead expenses}}{\text{Total direct material cost}} \times 100$

This method is also simple to compute but has no logical basis. The costs of materials may fluctuate from one supplier to another and at different periods of the year. Some materials are cheap and others expensive. This method ignores all such problems and is therefore unlikely to produce accurate production costs.

(iii) Percentage of direct labour cost $= \dfrac{\text{Overhead expenses}}{\text{Total direct labour cost}} \times 100$

Overheads can be absorbed by using a single rate for the whole factory or by having separate rates for each department. The single or blanket rate is not usually suitable as the time spent on each operation varies within the different departments. It is usually necessary to have separate rates for each department.

The percentage on direct labour is a simple method to use and the details required are usually available without having to keep extra records. The direct labour cost of each department is found in the wages analysis. Although it is more accurate than the other methods mentioned, it ignores the fact that expensive machinery may be contributing considerably towards the value of the output. Also, goods produced by highly skilled and highly paid workers carry more of the burden. Another example would be where a low earner occupies a large floor area for a considerable time on a process or job which requires a large amount of supervision. The space and other overhead costs will be high for the area used, yet the overhead recovery will be small because of the low wages.

(iv) Rate per direct labour hour $= \dfrac{\text{Overhead expenses}}{\text{Total direct labour hours}}$

This method is considered fair where cost centres are not extensively mechanised and where most of the overhead expense is incurred on a time basis. Records of direct labour hours have to be kept. This method overcomes the main objection of the direct labour cost, as jobs taking the same time are charged with the same amount of overhead, whereas with direct labour cost the high rate wages carry a disproportionate amount of overhead.

(v) Rate per machine hour

$$= \frac{\text{Total overhead expenses applicable to the machine}}{\text{Total operating hours for the period}}$$

This is more difficult to compute but is a very accurate and logical method of allocating overhead expenses to each job. It is suitable for a department which is extensively mechanised, but care will be needed when fixing the rates. Details of the effective floor space occupied have to be recorded, in order to charge rent (or the cost of space) and rates, and reference has to be made to the plant register to obtain the amount of depreciation. The estimated cost of power and sundry materials such as oil and cleaning materials used in the previous period must be calculated. A charge is usually made for the cost of supervision and any other salaries which may be applicable. Repairs and maintenance, lighting, insurance and other relevant items must be included in the total cost.

An example of computing the costs to establish a machine hour rate is given below.

Machine no. 273
Costs for a period of 48 weeks

	£
Rent, rates and insurance	467.10
Lighting	48.00
Heating	42.00
Power (metered consumption)	570.10
Consumable materials based on past records	120.20
Repairs and maintenance estimated by manager	466.10
Service department charge	124.00
Supervision	338.70
Indirect labour	314.00
Depreciation	1 340.20
	£3 830.40

Total hours for 48 weeks at 38 hours per week = 38 × 48 = 1 824

$$\text{Rate per hour} = \frac{£3\ 830.40}{1\ 824} = £2.10$$

(vi) Rate per unit of product $= \dfrac{\text{Overhead expenses}}{\text{Number of units of product}}$

This is a simple, direct and equitable method for uniform products where weight or size of product can be used to calculate the rate of charge for overhead expenses.

There is another method but it is seldom used. A *blanket rate* is a single rate which is used for all the production departments. To be of any value at arriving at the correct cost, it would be used where one product is made in a continuous process or where several products pass through all departments, spending the same time in each.

5.9 Over- and under-absorbed overhead

Overhead absorption rates are calculated using either actual or predetermined rates. The use of predetermined rates will avoid the large variation in unit costs which occurs when actual costs are used.

If the rates are established on actual expenses incurred, no costs can be completed until the close of the accounting period, and this delay is very unsatisfactory. By using actual costs, the total cost of overheads is charged to production and there is no balance on the Overhead Accounts. During the year, however, this generally results in a large variation in the unit costs because of holidays, seasonal activity and other factors which affect the use of capacity. The absorption rates change considerably from one month to the next, but if these rates are estimated in advance, costing can proceed as work is completed and a uniform rate can be used which is an estimate of actual costs for the year.

Because of the variation in activity caused by seasonal factors and for other reasons, there is likely to be a difference between the cost of overheads and the total amount absorbed at the end of each period of account. However, if the rates are reasonably accurate the costs and absorptions level out over the year. In some months there may be a large amount of overhead cost under-absorbed and in others there may be an over-absorption. When an overhead cost absorbed by production is greater than the actual cost, it is called *over-absorbed overhead*, but if it is less, it is called *under-absorbed overhead*. Many factors are responsible for this situation, but the main causes are the following:

(a) **Over-absorption**

(i) an increase in activity resulting in greater use of factory capacity – for example, increase in overtime, extra shifts, additional employees on direct labour – means that more overhead will be absorbed than planned;

(ii) an increase in direct wage rates – when overhead is absorbed on a basis of direct wages.

(b) **Under-absorption**

(i) a decrease in activity caused by less overtime, reduced shifts or short-time working as a result of lack of orders, strikes, etc. The decrease in activity means that less overhead will be absorbed than planned;

(ii) a reduction in the number of direct workers;
(iii) the introduction of machines or improved factory services when predetermined rates of absorption are being used and before absorption rates have been adjusted to meet the new conditions.

There are several ways of disposing of the balance on the overhead accounts:

write off to Profit and Loss Account;
transfer to a Reserve Account;
adjust the cost of sales and inventories.

Normal capacity

This is the capacity to manufacture and sell, based on anticipated sales and allowing for limiting factors and normal problems which occur from time to time. Normal capacity is used as a basis for fixing overhead rates and stock levels and also in the planning of production and sales, including price fixing. When overheads are over- or under-absorbed, normal capacity has to be kept in mind, because the way it was determined may be the cause of the variances. The fixed, variable and semi-variable overheads must be examined and the apportionments and calculations must be checked carefully. If the differences are not variable overheads but fixed costs or expenditure variances then they should be written off to Costing Profit and Loss Account.

EXAMPLE 5.1 (Absorption of overhead)

A manufacturing company has four production departments engaged on the production of three groups of products. The methods used for the absorption of overhead expenses are as follows:

Department 1: rate per direct labour hour;
Department 2: rate per machine hour;
Department 3: rate per direct labour hour;
Department 4: percentage on direct wages.

Additional information is as follows:

Dept.	Direct wages	Direct labour or machine hours	Percentage on direct labour	Rate per direct labour or machine hour
	£		%	£
1	2 400	980	—	2.20
2	5 750	2 390	—	6.00
3	17 920	6 800	—	3.20
4	12 568	4 880	150	—
	£38 638	15 050		

Production overhead costs are as follows:

Indirect materials		*Indirect wages*		*Expenses*	
	£		£		£
Purchases	2 496	Wages	22 198	Expense creditors	8 270
Stores Ledger	19 212			Fixed costs	5 946

Absorption of production overheads

Dept.	Direct labour	Rate of absorption	Direct labour/ machine hours	Overhead absorbed
	£			£
1	2 400	£2.20 per hour	980	2 156
2	5 750	£6.00 per hour	2 390	14 340
3	17 920	£3.20 per hour	6 800	21 760
4	12 568	150 per cent	4 880	18 852
				£57 108

The Factory Production Overhead Account is as shown below:

Factory Production Overhead Account

	£		£
Indirect materials			
Purchases	2 496	Transfer to Work-in-progress Account	57 108
Stores Ledger	19 212		
Indirect wages	22 198	Production overhead under-absorbed (Profit and Loss Account)	1 014
Expenses			
Expense creditors	8 270		
Fixed costs	5 946		
	£58 122		£58 122

A diagrammatic display of the collection, distribution and absorption of overhead costs is given in Fig. 5.1 (p. 94).

5.10 Administration overhead

This is the cost of formulating the policy, directing the organisation and controlling the operation. It is incurred for the business as a whole and is not directly related to production, selling or distribution. The cost is usually absorbed by *apportioning* the total over other departments, or sections of the business. Each item should be carefully examined and apportioned on a basis which ensures, as far as possible, a charge which is commensurate with the service received. It may be an arbitrary percentage figure, or an amount based on a sliding scale related to productive output, and it can also be calculated using the total of direct and indirect wages and salaries, or the number of people working in other departments. There are other bases

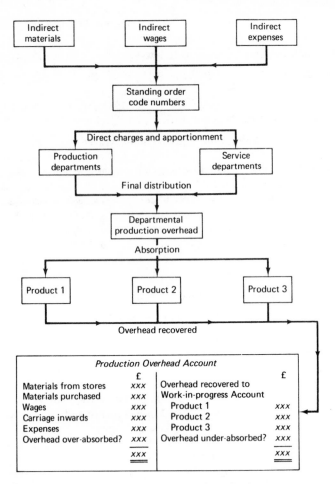

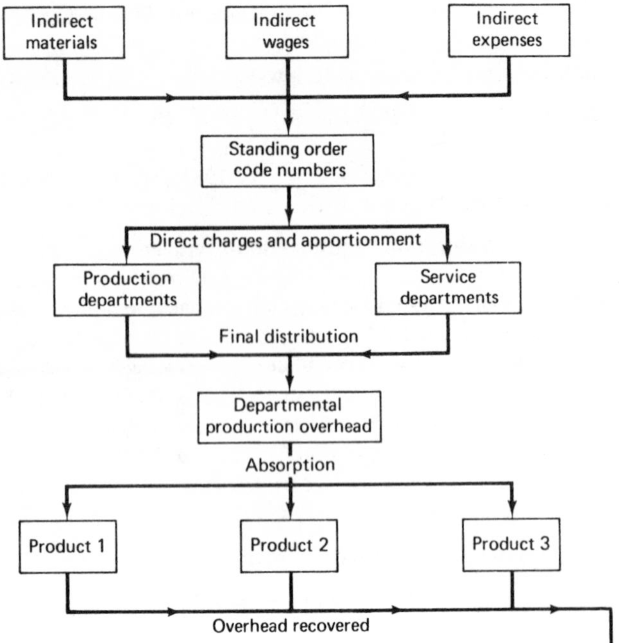

Production Overhead Account

	£		£
Materials from stores	xxx	Overhead recovered to	
Materials purchased	xxx	Work-in-progress Account	
Wages	xxx	Product 1	xxx
Carriage inwards	xxx	Product 2	xxx
Expenses	xxx	Product 3	xxx
Overhead over-absorbed?	xxx	Overhead under-absorbed?	xxx
	xxx		xxx

Fig. 5.1 Collection, distribution and absorption of overheads

Notes:

(i) Overhead (indirect) costs are collected under appropriate headings, using the standing order code numbers, to which are charged the costs and expenses incurred.

(ii) These indirect manufacturing expenses are accumulated on a functional basis for costs charged direct or allocated to the producing and service cost centres. When certain expenses have to be shared, they are apportioned, by transferring proportions of the cost to those departments or cost centres using the service.

(iii) The next stage is the distribution on some fair basis of the cost of each service department, either directly to the production departments or to both producing and servicing departments, until all the service department costs have been transferred.

(iv) The departmental production overheads are then absorbed by the various products by charging these overheads to the products on the most appropriate basis, using predetermined rates of absorption. For example, they could be based on a percentage of direct wages, a rate per direct labour hour or machine hour, or some similar method.

(v) At the end of each cost period a balance is struck between the actual cost of overhead in each department and the amount of overheads absorbed by production. This indicates over- or under-absorption on the Production Overhead Account.

on which to calculate administrative overhead, such as capital employed or the time spent by executives in the various departments of the business.

5.11 Selling and distribution overhead

Selling overhead expenditure is incurred in advertising and publicity and the soliciting and securing of orders; it includes the office costs of the sales department. The *distribution* costs are those incurred after the product has been manufactured when the goods are packed for transport. This expenditure includes the cost of cases, collapsible containers and similar items, and storage costs of finished goods at the works and depots. Also included are the carriage charges and repair costs on returnable containers. Carriage outwards is a distribution expense, but if these costs vary considerably on individual customers' orders, it is more equitable to treat such costs as direct expenses chargeable to the job or to the customer's order.

Examples of selling overheads are:

rent of sales department; advertising; cost of samples; catalogues; royalties; salaries and commissions; market research; bad debts if incurred regularly during the year.

Costs may be recovered as follows:

(a) Costs varying directly with the value of the articles or the quantity sold may be recovered as a direct charge to the works or production cost.

(b) Costs which are not related to particular items sold, and which can be classified as fixed costs, may be recovered by:

  (i) *Percentage of invoice value.* The selling price of each item is a suitable method where standard selling prices are used and where the sale of each type of product is fairly constant during the year.

  (ii) *Rate per article.* The estimated fixed expenses are apportioned fairly to each product group. The total charged to each product group is then divided by the estimated sale of each type to give the rate chargeable.

  (iii) *Percentage on works cost.* This is sometimes used because of its simplicity, but generally it is an inaccurate method except in cases where only one type of product is made. Works cost does not usually reflect the proportion of selling costs which should be chargeable.

The rates of absorption in respect of selling and distribution costs are predetermined in a similar manner to those relating to works' expenses by using past records and taking into account future activities and estimated costs.

5.12 Activity-based costing (ABC)

Activity-based costing is a new approach to costing advocated by leading management accountants from the Harvard Business School. The essence of their approach is to change traditional attitudes to the absorption of overhead costs by relating the system used to the more sophisticated production systems of the computerised age. They hold that many overhead costs today are not volume related and consequently absorption of costs by reference to direct labour hours, machine hours or direct material costs is inappropriate for many overhead costs today. The danger is that if we allow products to absorb costs in inappropriate ways we must distort prices, with some products bearing costs they should not carry and others being underpriced because they have not been loaded with a fair share of overhead. We shall of course find some overheads which are volume related and these should be absorbed in the traditional way, but other overheads which are related not to volume but to other activities should be absorbed in a more appropriate manner. For example, where products have limited production runs, setting up costs for a run may occur more often, while a long production run will not need setting up so frequently. If costs are absorbed on a volume basis the high-volume run will absorb most of the cost when it truly should bear only a small percentage. The low-volume run will absorb little of the cost, but it has actually generated most of the activity. Hence the need for activity-based costing, in which we seek to discover what activities are generating costs, and an appropriate system for absorbing such costs.

The method of approach is as follows:

(a) Identify costs which are arising in non-volume-related ways. They may be such costs as setting-up costs for changes in production runs, ordering cost for just-in-time operations, delivery costs on wholesalers' rounds or estimating cost in connection with marketing campaigns to increase market share. Any activity which generates costs is called a cost-driver.

(b) Find what is the cost-driver which is calling for these expenditures and is driving the cost on and on and up and up. We shall find that the cost is being incurred to provide an activity which is called for by the cost-driver, and which results directly from the cost-driver's attempts to achieve its objective. This is a perfectly legitimate state of affairs, but the cost must be absorbed by the cost-driver if management is to know whether the activity is profitable and justified.

(c) Derive an appropriate measure for absorbing these costs so that the cost-driver carries the burden of the costs it is generating. The method would be to establish a cost centre for each cost-driver in an activity-based system. For example, all delivery expenditures would be allocated to a delivery cost centre and when this was divided by the total number of deliveries made we would have a 'charging-out' rate for each delivery. The number of deliveries made to any particular customer would result in a charge to the customer based on the charging-out rate. If delivery was free to the customer the charging-out rate per delivery would have

to be absorbed by the department generating the business which called for a free delivery, and would let management see the true profitability of the department.

Complexity and costs

A significant contributor to overhead costs is the complexity of the activities being carried on. Complex activities usually call for larger staffs in support departments, with a wide variety of specialist skills. There are scheduling problems; stocks and inventories to be ordered, recorded, maintained and allocated; inspection activities, setting-up activities, design costs, programming costs, etc.

Kaplan and Cooper from the Harvard Business School argue that overhead costs should really be divided into short-term and long-term overheads. The short-term overheads are the volume-related overheads which follow fairly quickly and directly from the production activities and can be absorbed in the traditional way. The long-term overheads are the overheads generated by support departments made necessary by cost-driver activities. If we establish what these costs are, and what they are per unit of activity (for example, per inspection, or per quality-control check-up, or per delivery), we are in a better position to know the true costs. Cost-driver rates can be monitored from time to time to obtain more efficient operations, and can be used in estimating and budgeting. They may also influence decision-making procedures for evaluating new products or life-cycle evaluations for older products. A truer evaluation of diversification proposals can be made if the costs involved in the new activities are quantified more carefully.

5.13 Exercises

1. State what you understand by the following terms used in a costing system: *(a)* allocation; *(b)* apportionment; *(c)* absorption.

2. *(a)* What are the main groups of overhead expenses?
   (b) What bases can be used for apportioning indirect expenses to production and service departments?

3. What is meant by primary and secondary distribution? Explain fully and indicate in your answer how secondary distribution can be carried out.

4. Describe absorption costing, and write about the various methods which can be used in this costing procedure.

5. A company plans to manufacture two products, 800 of A and 1 500 of B, in the next period of account. The total cost of factory overhead is estimated at £91 700. The unit cost of direct materials amounts to £3.35 for A and £3.70 for B, and direct labour cost is expected to be £8.40 for A and £7.50 for B. Direct labour hours for each product have been calculated as 7 hours for A and 5 hours for B, and these times include machining time of 5 hours and 3 hours respectively.

For each product, you are required to calculate the factory cost per unit, by using three different methods of absorbing factory overheads.

6. The budget for a factory with three production departments (X, Y and Z) and two service departments (A and B) is as follows for the year 19. . .

Budget for year

Production departments:	X	Y	Z
	£	£	£
Direct wages	—	—	275 250
Overhead	200 000	211 900	95 000
Hours:			
Machine hours	206 000		—
Labour hours		147 625	—
Service departments:		A	B
		£	£
Overhead		116 000	95 000
Apportioned to production departments:		%	%
	X	25	30
	Y	35	45
	Z	40	25

Record of operations for month of June 19. .:		
Production department:		
Hours: Machine hours	X	18 000
Labour hours	Y	12 000
Wages: Direct wages	Z	£22 000
Total cost of overhead:		£61 000

(a) Calculate the budgeted overhead rates for the production departments as follows:
  (i) Department X: machine hour rate;
  (ii) Department Y: direct labour hour rate;
  (iii) Department Z: percentage of direct wages.

(b) From the above information and the rates calculated, ascertain the amount of overhead under- or over-absorbed for the month of June.

7. A department which produces one product shows the following production and costs for October, November and December 19. .:

19. .	Production (units)	Direct material	Direct labour	Prime cost	Overhead	Total factory cost
		£	£	£	£	£
October	6 200	43 400	34 100	77 500	77 200	154 700
November	8 600	60 200	47 300	107 500	91 600	199 100
December	5 000	35 000	27 500	62 500	70 000	132 500
	19 800	138 600	108 900	247 500	238 800	486 300

(a) Examine the different levels of activity and analyse the above costs according to their behaviour.
(b) Prepare a cost statement for the month of September, when 7 500 units were produced under conditions similar to those prevailing in October to December.

8. The Digby Manufacturing Company has made plans to produce 3 000 small mechanical units in the next twelve months. It has two service departments (Tool room and General services) and three production departments (Machining, Fitting, and Painting and packing). The following estimates have been made:

Material issues: Machining £240 000; Fitting £160 000; Painting and packing £45 000; Tool room £4 500.
Labour: Machining: 11 000 hours at £2.70 per hour; 9 000 hours at £2.60 per hour; 2 500 hours at £2 40 per hour.
Fitting: 6 600 hours at £2.60 per hour; 4 476 hours at £2.50 per hour.
Painting and packing: 5 500 hours at £2.55 per hour; 2 500 hours at £2.45 per hour.
Tool room: £8 000. General services £11 000.
Other costs: Machining £90 050; Fitting £29 000; Painting and packing £18 010; Tool room £18 000; General services £5 000.
The estimated percentages for services rendered are as follows:
Tool room: Machining 50%; Fitting 40%; Painting and packing 10%:
General services: Machining 40%; Fitting 30%; Painting and packing 20%; Tool Room 10%.

(a) Prepare a statement showing the overhead to be absorbed and recovered by the production departments.
(b) Calculate absorption rates using the following bases:
(i) direct labour hour for machining;
(ii) percentage on direct wages for fitting;
(iii) rate per unit of production for painting and packing.

9. The machine shop of a manufacturing company has five different groups of machines. It has been decided to introduce machine hour rates in order to produce more accurate costs. A budget for the department for next year provides the following information:

	£	£
Rent and rates		86 400
Insurance of buildings		7 200
Insurance of machinery		18 000
Depreciation of machinery		145 000
Power		25 200
Heat and light		14 400

		£	£
General expenses			21 600
Supervision			172 800
Maintenance: Machine group	1	12 600	
	2	14 400	
	3	21 600	
	4	30 600	
	5	18 000	
			97 200
Consumable supplies: Machine group	1	5 400	
	2	10 800	
	3	18 000	
	4	21 600	
	5	34 200	
			90 000
			£677 800

Additional information from the operating and accounting records:

Machine group	Power (kilowatts)	Area occupied (m^2)	Book value of machinery £	Operating machine hours
1	15	1 000	45 000	25 000
2	$22\frac{1}{2}$	2 000	225 000	40 000
3	15	500	90 000	15 000
4	$37\frac{1}{2}$	1 000	360 000	20 000
5	60	500	180 000	50 000
	150	5 000	900 000	150 000

You are required to calculate a machine hour rate, showing the bases of apportionment that you use for each class of expense.

10. *(a)* Explain what is meant by *normal capacity* and state what investigation you would make if there were large under- or over-absorbed overhead expenses. Also indicate how you would deal with these variances.

(b) A company is finding it difficult to maintain full production and to keep to the production programme. The average activity of three departments during the first three months of the year was as follows:

Department A: 80 per cent of normal capacity
Department B: 100 per cent of normal capacity
Department C: 50 per cent of normal capacity

During the same period the cost ledger showed the following details:

	Overhead incurred	Overhead absorbed
	£	£
Department A	33 000	30 800
Department B	44 000	47 000
Department C	54 000	50 000

Draw up a statement to show the budgeted overhead, the overhead incurred and the expenditure variance, on the assumption that no variable overheads are included in the figures shown.

11. A factory with three departments uses a single production overhead absorption rate expressed as a percentage of direct wages cost. It has been suggested that using departmental overhead absorption rates would result in more accurate job costs. Set out below are the budgeted and actual data for the previous period, together with information relating to job no. 657.

	Direct wages (£000s)	Direct labour hours (000s)	Machine hours (000s)	Production overhead (£000s)
Budget:				
Department A	25	10	40	120
B	100	50	10	30
C	25	25	–	75
Total:	150	85	50	225
Actual:				
Department A	30	12	45	130
B	80	45	14	28
C	30	30	–	80
Total:	140	87	59	238

During this period job no. 657 incurred the actual costs and actual times in the departments as shown below:

	Direct material	Direct wages	Direct labour	Machine
	£	£	hours	hours
Department A	120	100	20	40
B	60	60	40	10
C	10	10	10	–

After adding production overhead to prime cost, one third is added to production cost for gross profit. This assumes that a reasonable profit is earned after deducting administration, selling and distribution costs. You are required to:

(a) calculate the current overhead absorption rate;

(b) using the rate obtained in *(a)* above, calculate the production overhead charged to job no. 657 and state the production cost and expected gross profit on this job;

(c) (i) comment on the suggestion that departmental overhead absorption rates would result in more accurate job costs and (ii) compute such rates, briefly explaining your reason for each rate;

(d) using the rates calculated in *(c)* (ii) above, show the overhead, by department and in total, that would apply to job no. 657;

(e) show the over/under-absorption, by department and in total, for the period using: (i) the current rate in your answer to *(a)* above, and (ii) your suggested rates in your answer to *(c)* (ii) above.

(*CIMA*)

12. *(a)* What is activity-based costing? In your answer refer to the types of activity generated by complex products.

(b) Suppose that two products have the following characteristics:

No. 1 – a short setting-up time followed by a very long production run

No. 2 – a difficult and complex setting-up procedure, followed by a relatively short production run.

Costs are allocated on the basis of total volume of turnover.

Appraise this method of allocating costs to the two products.

13. *(a)* What is meant by the term *cost-driver?*

(b) What is the importance of cost-drivers in management accounting?

UNIT 6

Job and contract costing

6.1 Main characteristics

Manufacturing is initiated by:

(a) receipt of a customer's order;
(b) issue of an internal production order.

The costs are recorded on a *job cost sheet* (discussed in Unit 6.3) which is designed to record the factual information of all items of expenditure and charges incurred, in order to ascertain the total cost. The job cost sheet is prepared in order to find the amount of profit, and to be used when comparing costs with estimates. It is also used as a comparison with previous costs of similar work and when the contract or order is placed on a *cost plus* basis.

When orders are received for standard products, they are normally taken from stock, but when an order is for a standard product modified to a customer's requirements, then the job cost sheet is charged with the cost of the standard product plus the cost of modifications carried out. In other cases, the work is for whatever the customer has ordered and a manufacturing or job order number will be issued to collect the costs. Internal orders may be issued for individual items, batches of components and units for eventual assembly into finished products. *Job costing* is concerned with the costing of individual orders or contracts. The *contract* may be for items such as the construction of an hotel, a bridge or an oil rig, whereas jobs include the production of tractors, truck mixers, furniture, castings and repair work. With either jobs or contract work, it is possible to follow the work through the factory or on the site from the raw material to the completion of the job or contract.

Conversion costs

Statement of Standard Accounting Practice no. 9 now defines 'Cost' as being 'that expenditure which has been incurred in the normal course of business in bringing the product or service to its present location and condition. This expenditure should include, in addition to cost of purchase, such costs of conversion as are appropriate to that location and condition.'

The cost of purchase:

> comprises purchase price including import duties, transport and handling costs and any other directly attributable costs, less trade discounts, rebates and subsidies . . .

Cost of conversion comprises:

(a) costs which are specifically attributable to units of production, e.g., direct labour, direct expenses, and sub-contracted work;
(b) production overheads;
(c) other overheads, if any, attributable in the particular circumstances of the business to bringing the product or service to its present location and condition.

6.2 Estimating

This relates to forecasting the cost of contracts, jobs, standard products and repair work. The function of the estimating department is to estimate, for the purpose of fixing selling prices, for setting standards and for providing information which can be used for comparison with actual costs. The information is also used to determine whether or not to quote or tender for certain kinds of work.

When an order or an inquiry is received there will probably be a preliminary meeting of the sales department and the design department to suggest improvements or modifications to the order where they consider it necessary. The cost estimator needs to be a person with experience and with a knowledge of plant layout, production methods, machines, equipment and tools. When dealing with tenders and quotations, the estimator must establish the expected factory cost, and allow for selling costs and other factors such as royalties, transport, special packing, value added tax (always treated separately since it may be recoverable) and terms of payment, which may increase the total outlay. S/he often works from preliminary designs or plans as there may not be sufficient time to prepare detailed drawings. The estimate may consist of a series of estimates based on different rates for different classes of work, such as drilling, machining or welding, rather than fixing the cost of many different items, which may not be a feasible proposition because of a shortage of time.

A material schedule is then prepared by the drawing office to show the total weight of each type of raw material. This office also lists the purchased components which will be priced by the purchasing department. In many cases it will be necessary to refer to the chief engineer or drawing office manager for the drawing office costs.

It is necessary to establish the requirements and the grades of labour, with the current rates of pay in each case.

Direct expenses such as transport, insurance and possibly the cost of outside erection have to be allowed for, and charges have to be made for the cost of works overhead, administration costs and selling expenses.

6.3 Job cost sheets

These are designed to supply the information required and are tailor-made to suit the particular organisation. There may be one cost sheet for all the details or a master sheet or summary with supporting sheets for each department.

The cost sheet may include a section which lists the main items of cost as estimated by the estimating department, so that comparisons can be made when the work is completed.

Information shown on cost sheets

The details must be properly arranged and tabulated so that management and others can grasp the important facts quickly. The following information can be provided:

(a) the job order number for internal or customers' orders;
(b) name of customer;
(c) the general description of the product to be supplied or the work to be carried out;
(d) price quoted;
(e) delivery date;
(f) weight of goods dispatched;
(g) terms or conditions of sale;
(h) selling price;
(i) commission payable;
(j) sub-contractors;
(k) direct materials classified as required;
(l) direct labour cost in each department or cost centre;
(m) direct expenses classified for each type of expense;
(n) works overhead for each department;
(o) administration overhead;
(p) selling and distribution overhead;
(q) outside erection costs;
(r) profit and loss;
(s) retention percentage.

Figures 6.1, 6.2, 6.3 and 6.4 (pp. 106–9) are examples of job cost sheets. Many jobs extend over a long period and the value of the work-in-progress accumulates over many months. If the job is incomplete at the end of the first month, the various classes of costs have to be accumulated at the end of the second month, and so on, until the work is complete. This is shown on the intermediate cost sheet in Figs 6.1 and 6.2. When the job is complete the costs can be summarised by transferring the figures to the final cost sheet, shown in Figs 6.3 and 6.4.

Whether computers are used or the work is carried out manually, this information is needed in order to control and report on the progress of job orders. Another type of cost sheet is shown in Figs 6.5 and 6.6 (pp. 110–11).

6.4 Work-in-progress

Many factors determine how the costs are entered on the cost sheets. The costs may be posted weekly or monthly and the sheets may be filed in one ledger, or there may be several ledgers representing different product groups for customers' orders and work-in-progress. At the end of each cost period, the

Order no. INTERMEDIATE COST SHEET							Front
	GROUP	MATERIALS	Month £ p	Month £ p	Total £ p	Month £ p	Total £ p
	1	General stores					
	2	Bolts and nuts					
	3	Iron castings					
	4	Steel castings					
	5	Non-ferrous castings					
	6	Plates and sections					
	7	Welding					
	8	Tubes and pipes					
	9	Paint					
	10	Timber					
	11	Packing					
	12	Direct purchases					
	1	Drawing office					
	2	Carriage					
	3	Freight and insurance					
	4	Outside erection					
	5	Outside erection overhead					
	6	Travelling					
		Carried forward					

Fig. 6.1 Intermediate cost sheet (front)

Order no. INTERMEDIATE COST SHEET											Back
	DEPT.	Month		Month		Total		Month		Total	
		Hours	£ p	Hours	£ p	Hours	£ p	Hours	£ p	Hours	£ p
	b/f	–		–		–		–		–	
	Wages 1 2 3 4 5 6 7 8 9 10 11 12 13										
	Totals										
	Works o/h	%		%		%		%		%	
	1 2 3 4 5 6 7 8 9 10 11 12 13										
	Totals										
	Admin. o/h										
	Totals										

Fig. 6.2 Intermediate cost sheet (back)

Order no.						Front
			FINAL COST SHEET			
Date order booked			Customer		Order no.	
Delivery date			Details			
Date begun			Price		Terms	
Date dispatched			Remarks			
Estimate			Materials			
Weight	£ p	Group			Weight	£ p
		1	General stores			
		2	Bolts and nuts			
		3	Iron castings			
		4	Steel castings			
		5	Non-ferrous castings			
		6	Plates and sections			
		7	Welding			
		8	Tubes and pipes			
		9	Paint			
		10	Timber			
		11	Packing			
		12	Direct purchases			
		Allocations:		From order no.		
		1	Parts common			
		2	Parts peculiar			
		3	Engine unit			
		4	Wheel unit			
		5	Jib			
		6	Jib extension			
		7	Erection			
			Direct expenses			
		1	Drawing office			
		2	Carriage			
		3	Freight and insurance			
		4	Outside erection			
		5	Outside erection overhead			
		6	Travelling			
—			Total carried forward		—	

Fig. 6.3 Final cost sheet (front)

Order no.		FINAL COST SHEET	Cost brought forward		Back
Estimate					£ p
Hours	Wages		Hours	£ p	
	£ p	Wages			
		1 Foundry			
		2 Pattern makers			
		3 Girder and platework			
		4 Forging			
		5 Turning and machining			
		6 Welding			
		7 Fitting			
		8 Erection			
		9 Tooling			
		10 Painting			
		11 Packing			
		12 Maintenance			
		13 Carpenters			
		Works overhead	%		
		1 Foundry			
		2 Pattern makers			
		3 Girder and platework			
		4 Forging			
		5 Turning and machining			
		6 Welding			
		7 Fitting			
		8 Erection			
		9 Tooling			
		10 Painting			
		11 Packing			
		12 Maintenance			
		13 Carpenters			
		ADMINISTRATION OVERHEAD			
		SELLING AND DISTRIBUTION OVERHEAD			
		Invoice price £		Cost £	
				Profit £	
				Loss £	

Fig. 6.4 Final cost sheet (back)

Front

Order no . . . .

MATERIALS

Estimate		Date	Cast iron	Cast steel	Plates and sections	Non-ferrous	Timber	General stores	Direct purchases	Weight	Total
Weight	Cost £ p		£ p	£ p	£ p	£ p	£ p	£ p	£ p		£ p

Fig. 6.5 Job cost sheet (front)

JOB COST SHEET | Back

Customer . . . . Order no. . . . . Date . . . .

Particulars of order . . . . Estimated weight . . . .

Week ending	DIRECT WAGES AND OVERHEADS Departments												Weekly totals		Cumulative cost	
	Foundry		Platework		Welding		Machine		Erection		Painting					
	Wages	O/h	Wages	O/h	Wages	O/h	Wages	O/h	Wages	O/h	Wages	O/h	Wages	O/h	Wages	O/h
	£ p	£ p	£ p	£ p	£ p	£ p	£ p	£ p	£ p	£ p	£ p	£ p	£ p	£ p	£ p	£ p
															—	—

DIRECT EXPENSES					
Drawing office		Outside erection		Carriage	Freight and insurance
Salary	O/h	Wages	O/h	£ p	£ p
£ p	£ p	£ p	£ p		

ESTIMATE	
Weight	£ p

SUMMARY	COST
	£ p
Materials	
Wages	
Manufacturing overhead	
Direct expenses	
Administration overhead	
Selling and distribution overhead	
Total cost	

Invoice price £ | Profit / Loss

Fig. 6.6 Job cost sheet (back)

accumulated costs represent the value of work-in-progress, which is really a book inventory of work that is incomplete and of orders that have not yet been invoiced to the customer.

For example, a manufacturing company may have five product groups, and in each group machines may be produced in a variety of sizes. The company is engaged on the batch production of these machines and in the manufacture of components and spare parts which are taken into stock as they are completed. There will be five job ledgers containing the work-in-progress for the internal production orders and five job ledgers containing the work-in-progress in respect of customers' orders.

Production orders are issued for the manufacture of parts which are common to the machines of a particular group and for parts which are peculiar to different sizes and types of machine. There are also erection orders for the batches of machines. As the work is completed, transfers are made to the Stores Ledger and Finished Stock Ledger and allocations are made to customers' orders in the Job Ledger (Customers'). The sales analysis, dispatch reports and similar documents indicate the customers' orders which are complete, and transfers are made from the Finished Stock Ledger to the Job Ledger (Customers'). If production is continuous, with machines being allocated direct from the Job Ledger (Stock) to the Job Ledger (Customers'), then reference is made to erection or assembly sheets to find the orders which have to be allocated. The cost department costs the parts and components which are taken into stock, and transfers are made in total at the end of each month.

In batch production it frequently happens that some machines are completed and sold before the batch is complete. In this case an estimate is made of the eventual cost per machine when allocating costs to the Customers' Ledger, and this amount is adjusted when the batch order is complete. After all the postings, transfers and allocations have been made, the value on the cost sheets, after deducting the cost of goods already sold, represents the work-in-progress. The value shown on cost sheets in the Job Ledger (Stock) represents the work-in-progress on internal jobs and production orders, and the Job Ledger (Customers') shows the invoice values, the cost of any items and work-in-progress at the end of the month.

In order to ensure that postings, transfers and allocations agree with the original records, and as a reconciliation with the figures posted to the cost ledger, a summary is prepared for each of the job ledgers. This is necessary and is a check on the correctness of the value of work-in-progress carried forward at the end of each month. Examples are given in Figs 6.7 and 6.8 (pp. 114 and 115).

6.5 Special job costs

Many jobs incur special costs which are essential expenses in the manufacture of the product and in the successful completion of the order to the satisfaction of the customer. Some of these special costs are described below, with an explanation of their treatment in the costing process.

(i) Patterns Patterns produced specially for a particular job are chargeable to that job and may be retained for repeat orders or dispatched to the customer when the job is completed. Any repairs during the progress of the job should be charged to the job rather than to overheads.

(ii) Jigs, tools and dies A similar procedure applies to these items when specially produced.

(iii) Estimating costs These costs should be examined carefully and if they apply to both the production and selling functions, they can be apportioned and recovered in works overhead and selling overhead. Only where these costs are exceptionally high should they be considered as a direct expense. If the estimating function comes under the control of the sales manager and the expenses are incurred with the object of acquiring orders, it is a selling overhead.

(iv) Consultant's fees and inspection costs These costs are direct expenses for outside charges for advice and special inspection.

(v) Overtime premium When this is requested by the customer, it can be treated as a direct expense; otherwise it is treated as an overhead expense.

(vi) Hire of special machinery and equipment The cost is a direct expense chargeable to the job.

(vii) Defective work The treatment of waste and scrap has already been mentioned under stores control (see Unit 3.12), but it is important to take into account the difference between the terms scrap, waste and spoilage. Waste usually refers to material which has no value, whereas items spoiled or scrapped may have some value which can be recovered by sale or by use in some other form. Spoilage generally refers to damage resulting from manufacturing operations which may be of such a nature that the work and material has to be scrapped.

Defective work, however, is faulty work or material which does not meet the standard of work or quality desired, but which can be brought up to the standard desired by the use of additional materials or labour. The cost of the additional materials or labour is known as *re-operation cost*.

When the selling price of spoiled and scrapped work is significant, the value can be credited to the job or process. A similar procedure can be used if defective work is sold as scrap or re-used in some other way. If re-operation takes place with defective work, the extra costs can be charged to a standing order as production overhead, since they cannot be charged a second time to the job or contract. This applies to the cost of materials and labour up to the point or operation where the work became defective. If the defective work was caused by another department, then it can be charged to that department. A typical report is given in Fig. 6.9 (p. 116).

(viii) Direct interest Where the job extends over a considerable period there may be a justifiable case for charging the cost of interest. This may apply when there is no agreement for payments on account, and where the value of work-in-progress during the period of the job is of great value. The selling price will allow for this special cost, and if cash is borrowed to finance the contract, the expense can be charged as a direct expense. (See (x) below for notional interest.)

WORK-IN-PROGRESS (STOCK ORDERS) Month . . . . 19 . . .

Order no.	Description	Materials	Direct expenses	Wages	Works overhead	Administration overhead	Allocations	Work-in-progress
	Totals							

Fig. 6.7 Work-in-progress (stock orders)
Note: This is a summary of the balances and final costs on the job cost sheets for stock orders.

WORK-IN-PROGRESS (CUSTOMERS' ORDERS) Month . . . . 19 . . .

Order no.	Description	Materials	Allocation	Direct expenses	Wages	Works overhead	Administration overhead	Selling expenses	Cost of sales	Work-in-progress
	Totals									

Fig. 6.8 Work-in-progress (customers' orders)
Note: This is a summary of the balances and final costs on customers' orders.

INSPECTION DEPARTMENT

SPOILAGE AND DEFECTIVE WORK REPORT

No. 206

Cost Office copy

Date Jan 2 19..

Drawing no.	Part no.	Qty.	DESCRIPTION	Order no.
39798	3	10	PINS	B. 10274

Quantity				Responsible for rejection		
Passed	Scrapped	To be replaced	Re-operation	Personnel no.	Dept.	Supplier
7	3	3	–	179	5	–

Reason for rejection:
UNDER SIZE
Signed H.J. Inspector

Work to be carried out
PRODUCE 3 PINS FROM OPERATION 1 TO 5

DESCRIPTION	Department	Operation no.	Cost			
			Material	Wages	Overhead	Total cost
SAW PIN 9cm × 30cm	7	1	2·50	1·00	1·00	4·50
CENTRE AND SPOT FACE	4	2		1·50	2·25	3·75
TURN, GROOVE AND FINISH TAPER	4	3		4·00	6·00	10·00
SCREW	4	4		1·25	1·87	3·12
DRILL AND TAP	5	5		2·80	3·50	6·30
Chargeable to: Defective Work Account	Totals		2·50	10·55	14·62	27·67

Fig. 6.9 A spoilage and defective work report
Note: The cost of these items has already been charged to the job order number and the excess costs of replacement are treated as overhead expenses.

(ix) Travelling expenses If expenditure on visits to site is heavy and relates to a particular job, then it is chargeable as a direct expense.

(x) Notional rent and notional interest on capital Notional rent and notional interest on capital are two items that can be referred to as 'controversial expenses'. A difference of opinion exists among accountants, managers and others with respect to the inclusion of these items in costs. It is argued that they are arbitrary figures which inflate the cost of production, and give an incorrect profit figure for a given period.

There are those who state that capital tied up in materials and similar assets should return interest on capital before the determination of profit. SSAP 9 provides for the inclusion of interest if it can be justified. It is argued that where the premises are owned notional rent should be charged as cost, but SSAP 12 allows for freehold buildings to be depreciated and the only valid reason or suggestion that rent should be charged is if the rent on similar buildings is largely different from the depreciation charge. SSAP 9 also indicates that only true costs should be included and therefore interest on the valuation of stocks is not justified. The only way that such interest can be included in costs is to charge it, but to eliminate if from the accounts at the end of the period.

Notional rent and notional interest on capital are hypothetical costs charged so that the figures produced are comparable with those of other organisations where these expenses are actual costs. Another argument is that these costs should be included because capital should return an income. With respect to interest on capital the view is put forward that there should be a return on capital invested on contracts of long duration, and on those where no progress payments are received. It is also stated that whether the cash comes from company funds or other sources it should earn interest, and furthermore interest is payable when there is a loan or overdraft which is related to the expenditure on a contract. It is borrowed or used on behalf of the customer. When materials are held in stock until they mature (timber, tobacco, wine and spirits) costs are incurred for storage space and interest on the capital invested. A further point made is that when different methods of production are used or production is financed in different ways, it is necessary to include interest, otherwise a proper comparison cannot be made between such methods or procedures. In economic terms interest is the reward of capital and profit is not truly calculated until interest is included in costs.

There may also be a difference in profit when making inter-firm comparisons, if one organisation includes depreciation on the premises and another charges the rent payable.

6.6 Job costing for parts and components

The following is an example of a cost sheet for parts manufactured for stock, and on completion debited to the account in the stores ledger. For instance, the production department of a manufacturing company issues an order (no. 29374) for the manufacture of ten pulley wheels, part no. 72948/3. The job cost is prepared from the following information:

Material requisition no. 547 shows that ten castings (material group 1) were issued from the stores at £5.75 each.

The job cards received by the cost department recorded the following details:

Cost centre	*Hours worked*	*Wages paid*
		£
1	8	11.80
2	10	18.45
3	4	6.30
4	3	5.25

The works overhead rates are as follows:

Cost centre	*Percentages on direct wages*
1	110
2	160
3	200
4	180

Administration costs are applied to total direct wages as the rate of 200 per cent. As this is a new part, produced to meet customers' requirements for spare parts, it is necessary to fix the selling price, which allows for a profit of 40 per cent on selling price, in accordance with the company's normal policy.

The 40 per cent margin is needed in order to cover the cost of packing and carriage charges, the incidental expenses of operating the spares and sales department, and the net profit which is required.

The selling price of the spare part is based on the estimated cost so that customers can be quoted a firm price. Should the estimated cost vary considerably from the actual cost, then the spares price on future orders will have to be revised.

The estimating department stated that the estimated unit cost of these pulley wheels was as follows:

Materials £5.75

Cost centre	*Wages*	*Works overhead*	*Administration overhead*
	£	£	£
1	1.19	1.31	
2	1.83	2.93	
3	0.63	1.26	
4	0.50	0.90	
1–4			8.30

The cost sheet is shown in Fig. 6.10.

6.7 Job costing of batch production and customers' orders

The next example concerns a cost sheet for the sale of a product composed of parts and units manufactured under job costing methods. The details of these

Cost sheet

Description 10 pulley wheels — Order no.: 29374
Part no. 72948/3 — Date: 23 January 19..

Unit cost *Estimated cost*	*Actual cost*	*Direct materials*			*Total cost*
£	£				£
5.75	5.750	Group 1			57.50
		Direct wages			
			Hours	£	
1.19	1.180	Cost centre 1	8	11.80	
1.83	1.845	Cost centre 2	10	18.45	
0.63	0.630	Cost centre 3	4	6.30	
0.50	0.525	Cost centre 4	3	5.25	
£4.15	£4.180				41.80
		Works overhead	%		
1.31	1.298	Cost centre 1	110	12.98	
2.93	2.952	Cost centre 2	160	29.52	
1.26	1.260	Cost centre 3	200	12.60	
0.90	0.945	Cost centre 4	180	9.45	
6.40	6.455				64.55
		Administration	%		
8.30	8.360	*overhead:*	200		83.60
£24.60	£24.745	*Total cost*			£247.45

Selling price of pulley wheel, 72948/3

Selling price = 100%
Profit margin = 40% of Selling price
Cost price = 60% of Selling price

$$\text{Selling price} = \frac{\text{Estimated cost}}{\text{Cost price\%}} \times \text{Selling price\%}$$

$$= \frac{£24.60}{60} \times 100$$

$$= £41.00$$

Fig. 6.10 Example of a cost sheet

Note: When these items are sold there will be further costs for packing, carriage, etc., as well as a charge for selling and distribution overheads.

costs are shown in the job ledger (stock and work-in-progress), and on the sale of machines a transfer is made of the value of the units which make up a complete machine.

EXAMPLE 6.1

The sales department of a manufacturing company issued an order (no. 3126) for the preparation and dispatch of a machine ordered by a customer, XY Contracting Co. Ltd. The machine is to be modified and painted to the customer's requirements, the production department has already issued various orders to manufacture, for stock, parts and units for these machines, and instructions have been given for the erection of a batch of twelve standard machines. These are still in the process of being erected and the first machine has been completed, modified, dispatched and invoiced to the customer at £10 150 plus £100 for the cost of modifications. The following information enables the cost sheet (see Fig. 6.11) to be prepared:

Units and orders allocated from the job ledger (stock and work-in-progress) to the customer's ledger:

		£
Order no. 30562	One set of parts common	3 483
Order no. 30563	One set of parts peculiar	2 987
Order no. 29578	One petrol unit	1 298
Order no. 31123	Erection	432

Modification costs and other expenses charged to the customer's order:

	£
Materials	
Mild steel	15.88
General stores	10.76
Timber	15.04
Packing materials	12.49
Paint	23.06
Wages paid	
Fitting shop 17 hours	26.98
Painting shop 8 hours	14.63
Packing shop 4 hours	6.38
Works overhead Rate per direct labour hour	
Fitting shop	2.25
Painting shop	1.50
Packing shop	1.45

Direct expenses are as follows:

	£
Drawing office	15
Carriage outwards	174
Royalty	100
Cost of travelling and expenses of operating instructor	35

Administration costs are included in works overhead and selling expenses. Sales expenses are applied at 6 per cent of invoice value.

6.8 Contract costing

Companies engaged in the building, civil engineering and heavy engineering industries use job costing in the form of contract accounts, because the

Cost sheet

Customer: XY Contracting Co. Ltd — Order no.: 3126

Date: 10 June 19..

Description of order: One machine, modified and painted to requirements

		£	£
Materials			
Mild steel		15.88	
General stores		10.76	
Timber		15.04	
Packing materials		12.49	
Paint		23.06	
			77.23
Allocations			
One set parts common	Order no. 30562	3 483.00	
One set parts peculiar	Order no. 30563	2 987.00	
One petrol unit	Order no. 29578	1 298.00	
Erection	Order no. 31123	432.00	
			8 200.00
Direct expenses			
Drawing office		15.00	
Carriage outwards		174.00	
Royalty		100.00	
Travelling costs and expenses of operating instructor		35.00	
			324.00
Direct labour	*Hours*		
Fitting shop	17	26.98	
Painting shop	8	14.63	
Packing shop	4	6.38	
			47.99
Works overhead	*Per direct labour hour*		
Fitting shop	2.25	38.25	
Painting shop	1.50	12.00	
Packing shop	1.45	5.80	
			56.05
Selling expenses: 6% of £10 250			615.00
		Total cost:	£9 320.27
Invoice price:			10 250.00
		Profit/(Loss)	£ 929.73

Fig. 6.11 Cost sheet for machine ordered by XY Contracting Co. Ltd

contracts tend to last for a fairly long time. The terms of the contract therefore usually allow for progress payments to be made during the course of the construction. At the end of the financial year, an assessment is made of the amount of work completed, and when it is clear that a profit is being made, credit can be taken for ascertainable profit while the contract is in progress, subject to certain limitations.

If the outcome cannot reasonably be assessed before the conclusion of the contract, then it is not prudent to take any profit at that stage. When a loss is expected, then provision should be made for the whole of the loss as soon as it is recognised, and this reduces the value of the work done to date to its net realisable value.

(a) Interest on borrowed money

It is not normally appropriate to include interest; however, where sums borrowed can be identified as financing long-term contracts, interest can be included, but the facts should be clearly stated.

(b) Attributable profit

When the outcome of the contract can be assessed with reasonable certainty then it may be possible to calculate that part of the total profit currently estimated to arise over the duration of the contract. But the likely increases in cost so far not recoverable under the terms of the contract, which fairly reflect the profit attributable to that part of the work performed at the accounting date, must be allowed for.

SSAP 9 defines attributable profit as:

> that part of the total profit currently estimated to arise over the duration of the contract (after allowing for likely increases in costs so far as not recoverable under the terms of the contract) which fairly reflects the profit attributable to that part of the work performed at the accounting date. (There can be no attributable profit until the outcome of the contract can be assessed with reasonable certainty.) (SSAP 9, part 2, para. 23)

(c) Foreseeable losses

An estimate of foreseeable losses has to be made, irrespective of whether or not the work has started, or of what proportion of the work has been carried out, or of whether profits are expected to arise on other contracts. SSAP 9 defines foreseeable losses as:

> losses which are currently estimated to arise over the duration of the contract (after allowing for estimated remedial and maintenance costs, and increases in costs so far as not recoverable under the terms of the contract). This estimate is required irrespective of:
>
> (a) whether or not the work has yet commenced on such contracts;
> (b) the proportion of work carried out at the accounting date;

(c) the amount of profits expected to arise on other contracts. (SSAP 9, part 2, para. 24)

(d) Disclosure in accounts

SSAP 9 provides as follows in sections 13 and 14:

13 In the case of long-term contracts:

(a) long-term contract balances classified under the Balance Sheet heading of 'Stocks' are stated at total costs incurred, net of amounts transferred to the Profit and Loss Account in respect of work carried out to date, less foreseeable losses and applicable payments on account. A suitable description in the financial statements would be 'at net cost, less foreseeable losses and payments on account'.

(b) cumulative turnover (i.e., the total turnover recorded in respect of the contract in the Profit and Loss Accounts of all accounting periods since inception of the contract) is compared with total payments on account. If turnover exceeds payments on account an 'amount recoverable on contracts' is established and separately disclosed within debtors. If payments on account are greater than turnover to date, the excess is classified as a deduction from any balance on that contract in stocks, with any residual balance in excess of cost being classified with creditors.

14 In order to give an adequate explanation of the affairs of the company, the accounting policies followed in arriving at the amount at which stocks and long-term contracts are stated in the financial statements should be set out in a note. Where differing bases have been adopted for different types of stocks and long-term contracts, the amount included in the financial statements in respect of each type will need to be stated.

(e) Items included in Contract Accounts

(i) Materials These are sent to site by the stores department or they may be ordered as direct purchases and delivered to site by the supplier. At the end of the year, unused materials are credited to the Contract Account and carried down as a debit in this account on the first day of the following period. During the year, materials are sometimes returned to suppliers or to stores and may also be transferred to, or received from, other sites.

(ii) Wages and salaries These are prepared at the company's head office or, on large contracts, by the site accountant or cashier. When wages are outstanding at the end of the year, the accrued amount should be debited to the Contract Account and carried down as a credit on the first day of the next period.

(iii) Plant and equipment The value of fixed assets sent to site can be charged to the Contract Account or retained on the books at head office. If the book value is charged to the Contract Account, at the year end this must be depreciated in the normal way and the new book value carried down. The account is credited with the written down value of the asset on the last day of the year, and the same figure is debited to the account when brought down on the first day of the new year.

Contract Account

19..		£	19..		£	£
Feb. 7	Plant sent to site	20 000	Dec. 31	Plant	20 000	
				less		
				depreciation	2 000	
				Amount carried down		18 000

If plant is purchased specially for the contract, it should be registered in the plant register in the usual way but posted to the Contract Account, not to the Plant Account. If plant is sold when the work is finished, the value of the sale should then be credited to the Contract Account and no posting is needed in the Plant Account. The wear and tear on plant used on contracts is often very great, and at the end of each accounting period the plant is valued. This amount is credited to the Contract Account and carried down to the next period. The fall in value is therefore taken in as depreciation for the year. Any charges for transport, erection, dismantling and repairs and maintenance are charged to the Contract Account. Plant is frequently hired, and in this case the cost is a direct charge to the account.

When a large company has a number of contracts proceeding at the same time, with plant being used on several jobs, then it may be possible to use an hourly, daily or weekly rate for the use of the plant. A Plant Repairs and Maintenance Account is used for collecting the costs and the appropriate amounts are credited to this account and charged to the Contract Accounts.

(iv) Head office overheads This expense is debited to the Contract Account, but the method used for charging depends on the circumstances. The costs are mainly estimating and administration which should be charged in proportion to the services provided by the headquarters staff.

(v) Sub-contracts This expense may form a substantial part of the total cost and is a direct charge to the account. At each stage of the contract, as the value of the completed work is certified, it is essential to include an amount to cover the cost of sub-contract work completed but not yet invoiced.

(vi) Retention money The method of payment is set out in the contract and normally allows for progress payments at suitable intervals. These payments are made on the authority of certificates issued by the customer's engineer, architect or surveyor stating what s/he considers to be the value of work completed to the standard required. To ensure that the work is completed on time, so called *penalty clauses* are often included in contracts. These set agreed *liquidated damages* which are payable by the contractors if they fail to complete on time, and entitle the customer to retain part of the payment, the *retention money*, to cover the so-called penalty, or the correction of the faulty work. This is a percentage of the value of the work certified or of the contract price. Usually, the full value of the order is invoiced on completion of the work but a certain amount will not be due for payment until a specified date.

(vii) Profit taken during the progress of the contract As already explained under attributable profit earlier in this section, it may be possible to take a reasonable proportion of the profit during the process of the contract. To allow for contingencies and to take a fair amount of profit it is necessary to examine the contract in respect of the proportion of the work which has been completed and the time which has elapsed since the work began, as well as the value of the work certified, the amount of cash received and the total value of the contract. SSAP 9 makes some suggestions about work-in-progress in this type of situation.

We have to arrive at the notional or apparent profit and then to take a proportion of this to the Profit and Loss Account and to reserve or hold in suspense the remainder of the notional profit. The profit taken and the profit reserved are debited to the Contract Account and the amount reserved is carried down as a credit to the next period. After taking into account the above factors it is usual to apply an arbitrary fraction of, say, two thirds or three-quarters when calculating the amount of profit to take to the Profit and Loss Account.

EXAMPLE 6.2

(a)	Cost of work certified	£250 000	
(b)	Value of work certified	£400 000	
(c)	Notional profit (*b* – *a*)	£150 000	(estimated or apparent profit)
(d)	Invoiced to customer (85% of *b*)	£340 000	(allowing for 15% retention money)
(e)	Debited to Retention Money Account	£60 000	
(f)	Cash received	£300 000	
(g)	Total costs to date	£325 000	

Notes:

(i) The general principle is that a long-term contract is one which extends over a period of more than one year, or, if it takes less than a year to complete, is still split across two financial years. If the activity concerned is such that to leave the contract unaccounted for in any year would distort the accounts to such an extent that they did not give a true and fair view, then it is permissible to take an appropriate element of profit at the end of each financial year.

(ii) This may be done in the following ways:
Turnover is ascertained in a manner appropriate to the stage of

completion. 'Turnover' in this context means the value of the work actually done by the date the final accounts are prepared. This turnover will be credited in the Profit and Loss Account and will be used in calculating the profit on the contract. In Example 6.2 the value of the work certified is £400 000. £400 000 is therefore the turnover achieved to date. *The costs incurred are matched with the turnover*. For example, it might be that three-quarters of the contract is completed but we have purchased all the materials we shall need to complete the contract. We would obviously not set the total material against that turnover figure, but only the correct proportion of it. Similarly all the planning costs may have been incurred already, while the labour costs so far incurred might all have been expended on the part completed. When we have matched the costs to the proportion of the work completed these will be transferred to the Profit and Loss Account as cost of sales.

In Example 6.2 the cost of the work certified is £250 000, and this would be the figure to be taken to the Profit and Loss Account as cost of sales. *The difference between the turnover figure and the cost of sales figure is the profit on the contract so far*. In Example 6.2 this is called the 'notional profit' and it is £150 000. However, this would not necessarily be the 'attributable profit' for the period, because we have to assess the profit *prudently*. This involves holding back any part of the profit which for some reason we feel it is prudent not to recognise in the Profit and Loss Account. For example:

(1) If, even at this early stage, it is obvious that we have made a loss on the contract, the whole of the loss should be recognised and charged to cost of sales at once. For example, suppose in another case that in the current year work certified is £200 000 and costs to date are £240 000. Those figures will show a loss of £40 000 on the contract. But if we can already see that the contract cannot be completed without further losses of £25 000 these losses should be recognised at once. This £25 000 would be debited to cost of sales and credited to the provision for Foreseeable Losses Account. No such future loss is envisaged in Example 6.2.

(2) If a customer is behind with his or her payments we should not take the profit on any unpaid portion because we might not ever get paid. For this reason the best thing to do is to regard any unpaid portion as a possible loss that must be provided for and that reduces the turnover. This is usually provided for by using a formula which is explained in (3) below.

(3) Finally, it is usual as part of the general principle of prudence in accounting to take only a fraction of the notional profit. Usually two thirds only of the profit earned is taken, the other third being kept back as a reserve and carried forward to the next year. If the contract is very near completion this two thirds may be increased to three-quarters. The formula used to take account of (2) and (3) above is:

$$\text{Profit taken} = \tfrac{2}{3} \times \text{Notional profit} \times \frac{\text{Cash received}}{\text{Work certified}}$$

$$= \tfrac{2}{3} \times £150\,000 \times \frac{£300\,000}{£400\,000}$$

$$= £100\,000 \times \tfrac{3}{4}$$

$$= £75\,000$$

This means that the profit reserved is £150 000 − £75 000 = £75 000. This figure would be debited to the Profit and Loss Account and credited to the Profit Reserved Account or an account with some similar name.

If we now adopt the display form used in SSAP 9, appendix (appendix no. 3), for our Example 6.2, we have:

EXAMPLE 6.2 (contd.)

	Contract 6.2 (£'000)	Profit and Loss Account (£'000)	Balance Sheet entries (£'000)
Turnover (work certified)	400	400	
Cash received	(300)		
Amounts recoverable on contract	100		40 debtors (asset) 60 retention money (asset)
Total costs incurred	325		
Cost of work certified and transferred as cost of sales to Profit and Loss A/c	250	(250)	
Balance on Contract A/c (Work-in-progress)	75		75 Work-in-progress (Contract A/c) (Asset)
Provision for prudent reserves debited to Profit and Loss A/c		(75)	75 Profit Reserved A/c (liability)
Gross profit on contract (attributable profit for year)		75	

Notes:

(i) On this contract the turnover is £400 000 but only £300 000 has been received. The balance is known as an *amount recoverable on contract*. In another contract it is conceivable that the amount paid in advance by the customer would exceed the work certified (that is, exceed the turnover) and there would be a balance in hand (a payment in advance). (See contract no. 2 in Example 6.3, pp. 130–1.)

(ii) The amount recoverable on contract is shown separately on the Balance Sheet, partly as debtors (£40 000) and partly as retention money (£60 000).

(iii) The long-term Contract Account has a balance of £75 000 which will be designated on the Balance Sheet as Work-in-progress.

(iv) The profit set aside (£75 000) would appear on the Balance Sheet as 'Profit Reserved A/c'.

A multiplicity of contracts Where a company is engaged on a number of contracts the situation on each contract will be different. The SSAP requires the management accountant to appraise each contract separately and feed the final result of all contracts into the Profit and Loss Account. This is illustrated in Example 6.3. The five contracts referred to there are as follows:

1. A contract which has been completed in the year, but on which some money is still receivable.
2. A contract where the amounts paid by the customer in advance exceed the work certified to date, and where there are costs paid in advance which cannot yet be charged against the work completed to date.
3. A contract similar to (2) above, but where the amounts paid in advance are less than the costs incurred on the unfinished work.
4. A contract where it is obvious that an overall loss will be suffered, which has to be recognised in the accounts.
5. A contract where the excess payments in advance by the customer are partly used to offset costs already met on the uncompleted work, and where an expected loss on the contract has had to be recognised in the current year.

Readers should note the way the various contracts amalgamate to give the figures for the Profit and Loss Account and also the relevant items to be included in the Balance Sheet. An explanation of each account is given below.

Contract no. 1 The work done has been invoiced to the customer but only £150 000 has actually been paid. Therefore £45 000 is shown as recoverable on contract and will appear on the Balance Sheet as debtors.

The costs incurred are transferred in full to cost of sales, and when set against the turnover of £195 000 leave a profit on the completed contract of £75 000.

Contract no. 2 In this contract the customer has already paid £600 000 although only £420 000 has been invoiced to the customer as completed to date.

The result is there is an excess of payments on account of £180 000. However, most of the costs involved on the contract have already been paid. These amount to £520 000, of which only £350 000 match up with the turnover and can be carried to cost of sales. This leaves £170 000 on the Contract Account as costs of work-in-progress. If we use £170 000 of the £180 000 payments in advance to offset these costs on the Contract Account (the customer has already reimbursed us), it leaves only £10 000 as payments in advance by the customer (a liability on the Balance Sheet).

The profit on the contract is

$$£420\,000 - £350\,000 = \underline{\underline{£70\,000}}$$

Contract no. 3 Here the customer has again paid more than the value of the work certified and there is a £20 000 excess of payments in advance. However, this time the costs incurred already for the unfinished part of the contract are very large, so the £20 000 is simply set off against these losses, and there is no residual balance of payments in advance.

The profit on this contract is

Turnover (£580 000) − Cost of sales (£350 000) = Profit (£230 000)

There is a balance of costs on the Contract Account of £280 000. This is shown on the Balance Sheet as work-in-progress.

Contract no. 4 This contract is one where a big loss is expected. The contract to date has been certified as to the work done at £300 000, of which the customer has paid £150 000, so that £150 000 is recoverable to date on the contract.

From the profitability point of view the work done (£300 000) has already cost us £350 000, so there is a £50 000 loss already. Since it appears that we estimate further losses of £140 000 these are taken into account at once. The 'prudence' concept requires us to recognise losses as soon as it is obvious they will occur, and this has to be provided for by charging the loss to cost and sales. It will appear as provision for foreseeable losses on the Balance Sheet. The total losses amount to £190 000 on this contract.

Contract no. 5 Here the work completed is £155 000 and the client has already paid £180 000, so there is an excess of £25 000 paid in advance.

Costs to date are £200 000 of which £155 000 can be matched to the work done to date, and are transferred to cost of sales. This means that no profit has been made at all on the contract so far (turnover £155 000 set against costs £155 000). We also estimate that completing the work will mean a further loss of £40 000, which is recognised and written off as part of the cost of sales. Writing off this loss removes £40 000 of the costs still left on the Contract Account. This means that in effect there is £5 000 of costs on the Contract Account not yet written off. However, we can set off £5 000 of the money paid in advance against this, leaving effectively no balance on the long-term Contract Account, and only £20 000 as a payment in advance by customers. The

EXAMPLE 6.3

	Contract number					Profit and Loss Account	Balance Sheet Total
	1	2	3	4	5		
	£'000	£'000	£'000	£'000	£'000	£'000	£'000
Recorded as turnover - being sales value of work done *(a)*	195	420	580	300	155	1650	
Cumulative payments on account *(b)*	(150)	(600)	(600)	(150)	(180)		
Classified as amounts recoverable on contracts $(a) - (b)$	45			150			195Dr
Balance (excess) of payments on account $(b) - (a)$		(180)	(20)		(25)		
Applied as an off-set against long-term contract balances - see below *(c)*		170	20		5		
Residue classified as payments by customers on account *(d)*		(10)	–		(20)		30Cr
Total costs incurred *(e)*	120	520	650	350	200		
Transferred to cost of sales *(f)*	(120)	(350)	(350)	(350)	(155)	(1325)	
Balance on Contract A/c $(e) - (f)$	–	170	300	–	45		
Provision/accrual for foreseeable losses charged to cost of sales *(g)*	–	–	–	(140)	(40)	(180)	

	Contract number					Profit and Loss Account	Balance Sheet Total
	1	2	3	4	5		
	£'000	£'000	£'000	£'000	£'000	£'000	£'000
Classified as provision/accrual for losses *(h)*				(140)			(140)Cr
Balance (excess) of payments on account applied as offset against long-term contract balances *(c)*		(170)	(20)		(5)		
Classified as long-term contract balances *(i)*		–	280		–		(280)Dr
Gross profit or loss on long-term contracts $(a) - (f + g)$	75	70	230	(190)	(40)	145	

(*With acknowledgements to SSAP 9, appendix 3*)

Note: Retention money and reservation of profits have been ignored in this example.

total loss on the contract is £40 000 for the year, made up of no loss on the current year's workings but £40 000 estimated loss taken into account at once under the 'prudency' rules. When these turnover figures are added together they give a total turnover in the Profit and Loss Account of £1 650 000. Total costs of £1 325 000 and expected losses of £180 000 leave a gross profit finally of £145 000.

(viii) Work-in-progress The new method of keeping Contract Accounts required by the procedures in the revised SSAP 9 now means that the Contract Account is reduced in the process to a mere residue to work-in-progress. The various costs which have been debited in the Contract Account as the year proceeds are matched up with the work certified as complete. That proportion of the costs which applies to the work completed is credited in the Contract Account and debited as cost of sales in the Profit and Loss Account. The other costs, which relate to the part of the contract yet to be performed, are left as a residue of work-in-progress. The correct way, according to SSAP 9 paragraph 30, for these balances to be shown on the Balance Sheet is as follows:

> The amount of long-term contracts, at costs incurred, net of amounts transferred to cost of sales, after deducting foreseeable losses and payments on account not matched with turnover, should be classified as 'long-term contract balances' and separately disclosed within the Balance Sheet heading 'Stocks'. The Balance Sheet note should disclose separately the balances of:
>
> (i) net cost less foreseeable losses; and
> (ii) applicable payments on account.

Before proceeding to look at examples of Contract Accounts the reader might like to study the notes on SSAP 9 given in the next section.

6.9 Some notes on SSAP 9

Statement of Standing Accounting Practice no. 9 is the definitive statement on stock valuation. The full text is available in the handbook *Accounting Standards*, published by the Institute of Chartered Accountants in England and Wales, P.O. Box 433, London EC2 2BJ.

The basic accounting concepts are also laid down in IAS 1, the International Accounting Standard, Disclosure of Accounting Policies, which applies to international financial statements issued on or after 1 January 1975.

Stocks are of many types, including:

(a) goods or other assets purchased for resale - for example, tyres sold as spares;
(b) consumable stores like oil, petrol and other items which are not part of the end product;
(c) raw materials and components purchased for incorporation into products for sale - for example, pig iron, gear boxes;
(d) products and services in intermediate stages of completion - for example, work-in-progress and units awaiting incorporation into the finished product;
(e) finished goods.

The essential statement in SSAP 9 is: 'Stocks and work-in-progress normally need to be stated at cost, or, if lower, at net realizable value.' Although at first sight this appears to be a clear definition, we soon find ourselves asking what exactly the cost of this item of stock was. Was it the purchase price? Or should we add the transport charges for delivery, the warehousing costs while it was in stock, the equitable proportion of overheads incurred?

In accounting, the aim is to discover as accurately as possible the profit earned during any particular trading period, and at the same time to establish the value of the assets and their relationship to the owner(s) of the business at the closing date. This is not easy to do, because sometimes an acceptable system of valuing the assets from the profit measuring point of view results in a distorted valuation of the asset on the Balance Sheet, and vice versa. The value that should be placed upon stock is always a debatable question to some extent, and if we consider work-in-progress as an example, it is clear that such valuation is not easy.

Let us imagine a plant producing finished goods as a result of a continuous-belt system. Raw materials (valued at cost price) come in at one end and finished goods leave at the other. At closing time on the last day of the financial year, the work-in-progress (or partly finished goods) consists of work in every stage of production from raw materials (on which work has hardly started) to goods which are almost finished and about to leave the plant. Not only has value been added to the extent of direct wages and other direct costs embodied in the work to date, but a fair share of the overhead costs must also be charged to each unit. If we average out the costs across all units passing through the factory, assuming that the flow is even, we can place a value on work-in-progress, but it is only an estimate. Similar considerations apply to the stock of finished goods, except that these will all be valued at such a figure that the value includes the entire costs of manufacture, both direct and indirect (overheads). Since finished goods incur further costs in distribution, marketing and selling, it could be argued that even finished goods should be valued at a figure which takes into account the distance to the final retail outlet.

SSAP 9 defines cost as *the expense incurred in obtaining the stock and bringing it to its present location and condition*. Net realisable value is defined as *the actual or estimated selling price net of trade discounts and less all costs to completion (of partly finished goods) and all selling and marketing expenses*.

(a) Cost of purchase

This comprises purchase price including import duties, transport and handling costs and any other directly attributable costs, less trade discounts, rebates and subsidies.

(b) Conversion costs

These apply to the activities which bring the product or service to its present location and condition. They are costs attributable to units of production, such as direct labour, direct expenses, sub-contracted work, production overheads, and other overheads attributable in the particular circumstances of the business.

(c) Attributable profit

This is that part of the total profit currently estimated to arise over the duration of the contract, after allowing for remedial and maintenance costs and increases in costs so far as not recoverable under the terms of the contract. It is profit attributable to that part of the work performed at the accounting date. No attributable profit arises until the profitable outcome of the contract can be assessed with reasonable certainty.

(d) Long-term contracts

SSAP 9 states that the prudently attributed profit of a long-term contract should be disclosed in the Balance Sheet as follows:

(a) 'the amount by which recorded turnover is in excess of payments on account should be classified as "amounts recoverable on contracts" and separately disclosed within debtors';

(b) 'the balance of payments on account (in excess of amounts (i) matched with turnover; and (ii) offset against long-term contract balances) should be classified as payments on account and separately disclosed within creditors';

(c) 'the amount of long-term contracts, at costs incurred, net of amounts transferred to cost of sales, after deducting foreseeable losses and payments on account not matched with turnover, should be classified as "long-term contract balances" and separately disclosed within the Balance Sheet heading 'Stocks'. The Balance Sheet note should disclose separately the balances of:
   (i) net cost less foreseeable losses; and
   (ii) applicable payments on account';

(d) 'the amount by which the provision or accrual for foreseeable losses exceeds the costs incurred (after transfers to cost of sales) should be included within either provisions for liabilities and charges or creditors as appropriate'.

6.10 Three examples of Contract Accounts

In order to follow Contract Accounts fully it is necessary to look at three cases, one where the contract is completed with a profit being earned in the year, another which appears to be a profitable contract but is as yet incomplete, and a third where future losses seem inevitable. In each case the contract details are followed by the actual accounts, and then the three are amalgamated to show the Profit and Loss Account and the Balance Sheet extracts (a full Balance Sheet cannot of course be provided).

EXAMPLE 6.4A

A building company is working on a contract for the renovation of school buildings. The contract with Pensthorpe Council is valued at £525 000, of which £250 000 was certified in July. The contract began on 1 February 19 . 7. The contract is finished on 12 December, and invoiced at the agreed price.

Other accounts and details relevant to the contract are as follows:

	£
Materials issued to site	69 504
Wages paid	136 254
Plant sent to site during the year at cost	186 320
Materials returned to headquarters	5 250
Head office overheads	27 250
Sub-contractor's charges	850
Plant returned to head office at valuation	153 250
Plant hire	1 522

	£
Cash received	212 500
Retention money £37 500 + £41 250	78 750
Balance certified in December	275 000

In view of the fact that the contract has been completed and the retention money is deemed adequate to cover any eventuality, the full profit apart from an amount equivalent to the retention money is to be taken. A penalty clause in the contract of £100 per day for late delivery (12 days) is to be charged to the Contract Account.

The various accounts are shown in Fig. 6.12 (pp. 135–6), but the Profit and Loss Account is shown here only in extract form, the full figures being given later when the three contracts are amalgamated.

Contract no. 1 for Renovation of School Premises Account

19.7		£	19.7		£
Feb./Dec.	Materials issued to site	69 504	Feb./Dec.	Materials returned to head office	5 250
Feb./Dec.	Wages paid	136 254	Dec.	Plant returned to head office	153 250
Feb./Dec.	Plant sent to site at cost	186 320			
Feb./Dec.	Head office overheads	27 250			158 500
Feb./Dec.	Sub-contractor's charges	850	Dec.	Cost of work completed, transferred to Profit and Loss A/c as cost of sales	264 400
Feb./Dec.	Plant hire	1 522			
Dec.	Penalty	1 200			
		422 900			
		£422 900			£422 900
19.8					
1 Jan.	Contract balance b/d	264 400			

Profit and Loss Account (extract)

19.7	£	19.7	£
Contract no. 1		Contract no. 1	
Cost of sales	264 400	Turnover at full agreed price	525 000
Profit reserved	78 750		
Profit available on contract	181 850		

(continued overleaf)

Work Certified Account

19 . 7		£	19 . 7		£
31 Dec.	Profit and Loss A/c	525 000	July	Pensthorpe Council/ Retention Money A/c	250 000
			Dec.	Pensthorpe Council/ Retention Money A/c	275 000
		£525 000			£525 000

Pensthorpe Council Account

19 . 7		£	19 . 7		£
July	Work Certified A/c	212 500	Aug.	Cash by cheque	212 500
			Dec.	Penalty	1 200
Dec.	Work Certified A/c	233 750	Dec.	Balance c/d	232 550
		£446 250			£446 250
19 . 8					
1 Jan.	Balance b/d	232 550			

Retention Money Account

19 . 7		£			
July	Work Certified A/c	37 500			
Dec.	Work Certified A/c	41 250			

Profit Reserved Account

			19 . 8		£
				Contract no. 1 A/c	78 750

Fig. 6.12 A completed Contract Account and related accounts

EXAMPLE 6.4B

A building company is working on Contract no. 2 for extensions to factory buildings. The contract with F. and C. Construction Co. Ltd is valued at £720 000, and began on 1 September 19 . 6. The balances shown at 1 January 19 . 7 were as follows:

Debit balances	£
Work-in-progress at cost	70 000
Materials on site	32 000
Plant at cost	33 000

Other accounts and details relevant to the contract for the year 19 . 7 are as follows:

	£
Materials issued to site	134 000
Wages paid	129 000
Plant sent to site during year at cost	95 000
Plant hire	8 000

	£
Materials returned to headquarters	6 000
Head office overheads	24 000
Sub-contractor's charges not yet received	90 000
Accrued wages	3 000
Cash received	468 000
Cost of work not yet certified	73 000
Value of work certified as complete	480 000
Materials on site at 31 December 19 . 7	29 000
Plant on site at 31 December 19 . 7 at valuation	114 000

The Contract Account and other related accounts are shown in Figs 6.13 and 6.14.

Contract no. 2 for Extension of Factory Buildings Account

19 . 7		£	19 . 7		£
1 Jan.	Work-in-progress at cost b/d	70000	Jan./Dec.	Materials returned to stores	6 000
1 Jan.	Materials on site b/d	32 000		Materials on site c/d	29 000
1 Jan.	Plant at site at cost b/d	33 000		Plant at valuation c/d	114 000
Jan./Dec.	Materials issued to site	134 000		Cost of work not yet certified c/d	73 000
Jan./Dec.	Wages paid	129 000			222 000
Jan./Dec.	Plant sent to site at cost	95 000		Cost of work certified, transferred to Profit and Loss A/c as cost of sales	396 000
Jan./Dec.	Plant hire	8 000			
Jan./Dec.	Head office overheads	24 000			
Jan./Dec.	Sub-contractor's charges not yet received c/d	90 000			
31 Dec.	Wages accrued c/d	3 000			
		618 000			
		£618 000			£618 000
19 . 8			19 . 8		
1 Jan.	Materials on site b/d	29 000	1 Jan.	Sub-contractor's charges b/d	90 000
1 Jan.	Plant at valuation b/d	114 000	1 Jan.	Wages accrued b/d	3 000
1 Jan.	Cost of work not yet certified b/d	73 000			

Fig. 6.13 Example of a partially completed Contract Account

Notes:

(i) The account in Fig. 6.13 shows that the total expenditure to 31 December 19 . 7, as represented by the debits, is £618 000, and the credits, including the cost of work not yet certified, is £222 000. This enables a figure to be obtained which provides the cost of work certified:

Cost of work certified = £618 000 *less* £222 000 = £396 000

This figure is taken to the Profit and Loss Account as the cost of sales, in a similar way to that in contract no. 1, Fig. 6.12

(ii) The Work Certified Account would be credited with £480 000, in the same way as with contract no. 1, the debit entries being in the Customer's Account (see below) and Retention Money Account, again in a way similar to that in contract no. 1 (see Fig. 6.12), at 15 per cent of the work certified.

(iii) The Work Certified Account would be debited with the £480 000 as this was carried (as turnover) to the credit side of the Profit and Loss Account.

(iv) Since this is a profitable contract and no future foreseeable losses are apparent, the usual rule of prudent behaviour will be used to decide how much profit to put into reserve.

$$\begin{aligned}\text{Notional profit} &= \text{Value of work certified } \textit{less} \text{ Cost of work certified}\\ &= £480\,000 \textit{ less } £396\,000\\ &= £84\,000\end{aligned}$$

$$\begin{aligned}\text{Profit reserved} &= \tfrac{2}{3} \times \text{Notional profit} \times \frac{\text{Cash received}}{\text{Work certified}}\\ &= \tfrac{2}{3} \times £84\,000 \times \frac{£468\,000}{£480\,000}\\ &= £54\,600\end{aligned}$$

The entries in the accounts related to this contract are shown in Fig. 6.14. Of course in reality the Profit and Loss Account, Retention Money Account and Profit Reserved Account would have entries referring to other contracts.

EXAMPLE 6.4C

The company is working on a contract for Southern Hotels (Cambanks) PLC, renovating a hotel's buildings. The contract is a fixed price contract valued at £850 000 and began on 1 July 19 . 6. The balances shown at 1 January 19 . 7 were as follows:

Debit balances	£
Work-in-progress at cost	170 000
Materials on site	132 000
Plant at cost	138 000

F. and C. Construction Co. Ltd Account

19.7	£	19.7	£
Value of work certified	408 000	Cash	468 000
Balance (in advance)	60 000		
	£468 000		£468 000
		19.8 Balance in advance	60 000

Retention Money Account

19.7	£
Work certified A/c	72 000

Work Certified Account

19.7	£	19.7	£
Turnover to Profit and Loss A/c	480 000	E. and C. Construction Co./Retention Money A/c	480 000

Profit and Loss Account (extract)

19.7	£	19.7	£
Cost of sales	396 000	Contract no. 2 turnover	480 000
Profit reserved	29 400		
Profit on contract for year	54 600		

Profit Reserved Account

		19.8	£
		Profit and Loss A/c contract no. 2	29 400

Fig. 6.14 Other accounts affected by contract no. 2

Other accounts and details relevant to the contract for the year 19.7 are as follows:

Materials issued to site	48 000
Wages paid	256 000
Plant sent to site (at cost)	58 000
Plant hire	26 000
Materials returned to headquarters	3 000
Head office overheads	48 000

Sub-contractor's charges not yet received	65 000
Accrued wages	14 000
Cash received	420 000
Value of work certified as complete (at contract rate)	520 000
Materials on site at 31 December 19 . 7	48 000
Plant on site at 31 December 19 . 7 at valuation	64 000
Cost of work not yet certified	218 000

Retention money is at the 15 per cent level. It is estimated that the work will take a further £125 000 to complete.

The Contract Account and other accounts affected are shown in Fig. 6.15.

Contract no. 3 for Hotel Refurbishment Account

19 . 7		£	19 . 7		£
1 Jan.	Work-in-progress at cost b/d	170 000	Jan./Dec.	Materials returned to stores	3 000
1 Jan.	Materials on site b/d	132 000		Materials on site (Dec.) c/d	48 000
1 Jan.	Plant at site at cost b/d	138 000		Plant at Dec. valuation c/d	64 000
Jan./Dec.	Materials issued to site	48 000		Cost of work not yet certified c/d	218 000
					333 000
Jan./Dec.	Wages paid	256 000			
Jan./Dec.	Plant sent to site at cost	58 000		Cost of work completed, to Profit and Loss A/c as cost of sales	622 000
Jan./Dec.	Plant hire	26 000			
Jan./Dec.	Head office overheads	48 000			
Jan./Dec.	Sub-contractor's charges not yet received c/d	65 000			
31 Dec.	Wages accrued c/d	14 000			
		£955 000			£955 000
19 . 8		£	19 . 8		£
1 Jan.	Materials on site b/d	48 000	1 Jan.	Sub-contractor's charges due b/d	65 000
	Plant on site b/d	64 000		Wages due b/d	14 000
	Cost of work not yet certified b/d	218 000			

Work Certified Account

19.7		£	19.7		£
31 Dec.	Profit and Loss A/c turnover	520 000	31 Dec.	Southern Hotels/ Retention Money A/c	520 000

Southern Hotels (Cambanks) PLC

19.7			£	19.7			£
31 Dec.	Work certified		442 000	31 Dec.	Cash received		420 000
					Balance	c/d	22 000
			£442 000				£442 000
31 Dec.	Balance	b/d	22 000				

Retention Money Account

19.7		£
31 Dec.	Work certified	78 000

Profit and Loss Account

19.7		£	19.7		£
31 Dec.	Cost of sales	622 000	31 Dec.	Contract no. 3 turnover	520 000
	Foreseeable losses	13 000		Loss on contract no. 3 for year	115 000

Note:
Since the uncompleted work has already cost £218 000 and it is estimated that a further £125 000 will be needed to complete the work, the total costs for completion are £343 000. As the contract is fixed at a price of £850 000, of which £520 000 has been claimed (or is retained for claiming later), only £330 000 can still be claimed. We must therefore provide now for foreseeable losses of £13 000.

Provision for Foreseeable Losses Account

			19.8		£
			1 Jan.	Profit and Loss A/c	13 000

Fig. 6.15 Contract no. 3 and other accounts affected

Amalgamating the three Contract Accounts

If we now use the format suggested in SSAP 9 for our three contracts we have the results shown in Fig. 6.16.

	Contract no. 1	Contract no. 2	Contract no. 3	Profit and Loss A/c	Balance Sheet	Notes
	(£'000)	(£'000)	(£'000)	(£'000)	(£'000)	
Recorded as turnover – being value of work done	525	480	520	1525		Turnover
Of which retention money =	(78.75)	(72)	(78)		228.75	Amount recoverable on contract in due course (assets)
and Invoiced to customers	446.25	408	442			
Cumulative payments on account	(212.5)	(468)	(420)			
Classified as amounts recoverable on contracts	232.55		22		254.55	Amount recoverable on contract – debtors (assets)
Balance (excess) of payments on account		(60)				
Applied as an offset against long-term contract balances – see below		60				
Residue classified as payments on account in advance		–	–		–	

	Contract no. 1	Contract no. 2	Contract no. 3	Profit and Loss A/c	Balance Sheet	Notes
	(£'000)	(£'000)	(£'000)	(£'000)	(£'000)	
Total costs incurred	264.4	612	952			
Transferred to cost of sales	(264.4)	(396)	(622)	(1282.4)		Cost of sales
	–	216	330			
Provision/ accrual for foreseeable losses charged to cost of sales			(13)	(13)	13	Provision for foreseeable losses (liability)
		216	317			
Balance (excess) of payments on account applied as offset against long-term contract balances		(60)				
Classified as long-term contract balances		156	317		473	Work-in-progress (balances on long-term contracts)
Gross profit or loss on long-term contracts for year	260.6	84	(115)	229.6	229.6	Profit for year (liability)
Of which profit reserved is	78.75	29.4	–		108.15	Reserve of profits (liability)

Fig. 6.16 Amalgamating the results of various Contract Accounts

6.11 Exercises

1. Arthur Smith has set up business as a painter and decorator. He is in the process of quoting a price for his first job. He has estimated the following requirements for the job of painting and decorating a large lounge in the house of his first customer, Ms Jones:

Materials	
10 rolls of paper at £6 per roll	
2 litres of white paint at £4 per litre	
1 litre of undercoat at £3	
2½ litres of emulsion at £3 per litre	
Wallpaper paste £2	
Estimated time for job	
Stripping old paper	5 hours
Hanging new paper	8 hours
Painting	10 hours
Rubbing down paintwork and filling in	6 hours
Direct expenses	
Hire of steamer for paint stripping	£10

Arthur expects to work 40 hours per week for 48 weeks. However, he expects to work only 30 hours per week directly on jobs and to spend the rest of his time on office work, quoting for jobs, travelling, etc. He expects to earn a basic 'wage' of £5 per hour (£200 per week) plus other profits. (As a self-employed person Arthur cannot actually call any part of his earnings a 'wage'.) Arthur will also employ two part-time staff as direct labour for 2 000 hours in total during the year.

In addition to the costs of his own indirect labour Arthur estimates that he will incur overhead costs as listed below:

	£
Rent and rates	500
Office expenses	440
Van running expenses	600
Sundry materials – fillers, etc.	100
Light and heat	180
Insurance	420
Advertising	220
Depreciation:	
Equipment	100
Van	200

You are required to:

(a) calculate the overhead rate based on the labour hours Arthur will have to charge to jobs in order to recover all his indirect costs. Indicate how Arthur will need to take into account his experiences in his first year of business when he prepares quotations during his second year in business (assuming he completes the first year successfully). Present the information to Arthur in an informal letter.

(b) prepare a quotation to Ms Jones for the job which will be carried out by Arthur himself. He wishes to earn a 10 per cent profit above the cost of the job.

Write notes on how you arrive at the final price. Include these in your letter to Arthur.

2. The cost department in a manufacturing company has just received information to the effect that job no. 30724 has been completed. The job was undertaken on a cost-plus basis with 12½ per cent being specified as the profit to be added to cost. From the following details draw up the cost sheet, showing *(a)* the total cost, *(b)* the profit required and *(c)* the invoice price.

Materials	£36.00
Wages (direct)	Department A 54 hours at £4.00 per hour.
	Department B 96 hours at £3.50 per hour.

Budgeted overhead for the current year, calculated on normal capacity

Variable overhead:

Department A	£216 000 for 27 000 direct labour hours
Department B	£224 000 for 32 000 direct labour hours

Fixed overhead:
The direct labour hours for the factory as budgeted amount to 67 000 hours for a budgeted expenditure of £670 000

3. A component used on a prototype machine and produced for the first few batches of a standard product failed, so it became necessary to redesign this item. An estimate was made of the unit cost and an order issued to manufacture 100 of these components, which are required as spare parts.
   (a) From the following information, prepare a cost sheet showing the estimated and actual cost of one of these components and the total cost of 100, assuming that they all passed inspection.
   (b) Calculate the selling price of the spare part by using the actual cost and allowing a margin of profit which is equal to 45 per cent of selling price.

Unit cost as forecast by the estimating department		*Cost department record of actual costs:*		
	£			£
Cost of materials	6.50	Cost of materials (group 2)		650.00
Direct wages:		Direct wages:	Hours	
Department A	1.54	Department A	107	155.00
B	2.40	B	130	250.00
C	0.92	C	50	85.00
D	0.67	D	40	72.00
Works overhead:		Works overhead:		
		Rate per direct labour hour	£	
Department A	1.60	Department A	1.50	
B	3.42	B	2.75	

C	1.62	C	3.00
D	1.16	D	3.10
Administration overhead	8.30	Administration overhead: 150% on total direct wages	

4. A small company carries out fabrication work in a department where certain employees set up the work before the main operation is completed by other employees. The cost of labour engaged on setting up is charged to overhead expenses and during a particular period 1 250 hours were spent on this work at a cost of £3 750. During this period the following costs were incurred on three jobs (job A, job B and job C):

	£
Direct materials	8 250
Direct labour	11 250
Overhead expenses	18 000
	37 500

Other information which applies to these jobs includes:

	Job A	Job B	Job C
Setting-up (hours)	375	250	625
Direct labour (hours), excluding setting-up time	2 400	300	1 800
Direct material costs	£4 540	£525	£3 185

Job costing is carried out by the use of hourly rates for direct labour and for overheads, but a new system is proposed whereby there are hourly rates for direct labour, for setting labour and for overheads excluding the cost of setting-up time.

(a) Calculate the hourly rates under the old and the new systems and prepare costs as compiled under the existing costing system and also costs under the proposed system.

(b) Indicate which method of costing in your opinion provides the most accurate costs.

5. A building company has recently completed an extension to a private house. This work was carried out in accordance with the contract which was made, when £3 050 was quoted for the extension to the property. The quotation was based on an estimated cost as follows:

		£
Materials:	Direct purchases	910
	Issues from store	218
Wages		939
Overhead (50% on wages)		470
		£2 537

The order department issued job no. PH 279 for this work and the costs incurred were charged to this account number, as shown below:

Materials:	£
Direct purchases (ref. C2037)	710
Direct purchases (ref. C2084)	220
Stores requisition (G1458)	148
Stores requisition (G1563)	75

Labour:	Hours	Rate per hour £
Bricklayers	185	3.00
Carpenters	45	2.40
Plumbers	40	2.50
Electricians	20	3.10
Decorators	60	2.20

Overheads: 50% on direct labour

(a) Draw up a cost sheet which is suitable to record the details of work of this nature.

(b) Write up the cost sheet with the costs incurred and the estimated costs, so that a comparison can be made between them.

6. The export sales department of an engineering company has sold a machine through their agents in France. The invoice price is £2 700, including cost, insurance and freight, and the agent's commission is £100.

The machines are manufactured in batches of ten and are allocated to customers' orders as they are received. The sales office order abstract shows that the order number issued for this machine is B5586. The order was received on 1 June 19 . 9 and the machine was dispatched to Recreo Limited on 10 June 19 . 9. Direct expenses are: carriage £112; freight and insurance £208.

The following information is provided in respect of the batch order for ten machines which have been completed:

Order no. B29342 10 standard machines

Materials:	£	*Direct wages:*	Hours	£
Group 1	597.54	Department		
		A	220	492.54
2	358.39	B	174	304.27
3	146.18	C	306	574.16
4	262.89	D	142	249.68
5	8 283.00	E	110	198.35

Note: All department B's hours are machine hours.

Work overhead rates:

		£	
Department	A	2.25	per direct labour hour
	B	3.60	per machine hour
	C	125%	on direct wages
	D	2.85	per direct labour hour
	E	3.00	per direct labour hour

The administration overhead is included in the works overhead rates and the charge for selling expenses. The overhead rate for selling expenses is 8 per cent of invoice value.

The following charges were made to order no. B5586 when preparing the machine for dispatch to the customer:

Materials:		*Direct wages:*		
	£		Hours	£
Group 3	28.32	Department C	26	39.80
6	37.84	D	28	46.64

You are required to prepare a cost sheet under order no. B5586 incorporating the detailed costs of one machine taken from the batch order.

7. A company in the electronics industry manufactured 120 000 calculators in the year ended 31 December 19 . 8, and sold all of these at £18 each. They plan to increase production by 25 per cent and to reduce the selling price by £1 per calculator. The trading results for the year ended 31 December 19 . 8 were as follows:

	£	£
Sales: 120 000 at £18 each		2 160 000
Less Costs:		
Materials	780 000	
Direct labour	360 000	
Indirect labour	135 000	
Other costs	380 000	
		1 655 000
Profit		£505 000

The increase in production is expected to need changes in the operating activities, and arrangements have been made to ensure that improved trading results are obtained:

(a) As an incentive to increase output the employees on direct labour are to receive a special bonus of 3 per cent on their earnings, provided the target of 25 per cent is met.

(b) No increase is anticipated in the cost of indirect labour.

(c) Other costs include £50 000 which is fixed, and the new arrangements will add a further £15 000 to this item.

(d) The entire output as planned is expected to be sold in the financial year and it is to be assumed that there will be no stocks or work-in-progress.

(e) Negotiations have been concluded with the suppliers of materials, and prices are to be reduced by 6 per cent in view of the increase in the quantities of materials.

Prepare an estimate in the form of a cost statement, setting out the results to be expected should production be increased as planned.

8. A. Subcontractor produces small assemblies on a cost-plus basis for a large manufacturer. Work has recently been completed on three items (A, B and C) and you are required to prepare a cost statement for these showing the jobs costs and the profit or loss. The relevant information is given below:

	A	B	C
Units produced	10	25	50
	£	£	£
Direct purchases per unit	36	–	57
Stores materials per unit	74	54	19
Direct labour hours per unit:			
Machining	16	20	25
Fitting	8	12	6
Painting and polishing	4	6	5

Wages per 40-hour week:		*Works overhead rates per direct labour hour:*	
Machining	£80	Machining	£10
Fitting	£70	Fitting	£4
Painting and polishing	£60	Painting and polishing	£7
Administration costs:		*Profit:*	
50 per cent of prime cost		20 per cent of selling price	

9. On 3 January 19 . 8 B. Construction Ltd started work on the construction of an office block for a contracted price of £750 000, with completion promised by 31 March 19 . 9. Budgeted cost of the contract was £600 000. The construction company's financial year-end was 31 October 19 . 8 and on that date the accounts appropriate to the contract contained the following balances:

	(£'000)
Materials issued to site	161
Materials returned from site	14
Wages paid	68
Own plant in use on site, at cost	96
Hire of plant and scaffolding	72

	(£'000)
Supervisory staff: direct	11
indirect	12
Head office charges	63
Value of work certified to 31 October 19 . 8	400
Cost of work not yet completed	40
Cash received related to work certified	330

(i) Depreciation on own plant is to be provided at the rate of 12½ per cent per annum on cost.
(ii) £2 000 is owing for wages.
(iii) Estimated value of materials on site is £24 000.
(iv) No difficulties are envisaged during the remaining time to complete the contract.

You are required to:

(a) prepare the Contract Account for the period ended 31 October 19 . 8 showing the costs to be included in the construction company's Profit and Loss Account, complying with SSAP 9.
(b) show the Profit and Loss Account so far as this Contract Account is concerned.
(c) show extracts from the construction company's Balance Sheet at 31 October 19 . 8 so far as the information provided will allow.

(CIMA – adapted to comply with SSAP 9)

10. The following particulars at 30 September 19 . 7 relate to a contract (agreed price £330 000) started in February of that year. The contractor's financial year ends on 30 September and you are required to prepare the Contract Account for the period from the commencement of the contract to 30 September 19 . 7. Submit your calculation of the amount of profit which the contract has made, and the amount of that profit that should be reserved.

	£
Materials ordered for the contract and delivered to the site	67 620
Wages paid	48 180
Plant issued to the site (at valuation)	27 000
Materials issued from stores	10 200
Materials transferred to other contract sites	1 320
Cash received on account (being 80% of the value of work certified by the architect)	153 600
Direct expenses	3 360
Plant returned to yard (at valuation)	5 700
Plant transferred to other sites (at valuation)	3 600
Proportion of overhead expenses applicable to the contract	7 800
Payments made to sub-contractors	17 100
Materials transferred to this contract from other sites	3 900

	£
At 30 September 19 . 7:	
Valuation of plant on site	16 200
Materials on site	5 700
Wages accrued on this contract	840
Sub-contract work done but not paid for	720
Cost of work done but not yet certified	7 200

11. A company signed a contract to build an underground car park at a contract price of £845 000. It was to be completed in two years and to commence on 1 August 19 . 8. No profit was taken in 19 . 8, the work not being far enough advanced. The company's financial year ends at 31 December, and in the year following the commencement at 31 December 19 . 9 the state of affairs was as follows:

	£
Cash received	531 000
Retention	59 000
Extra work as certified on 1 December 19 . 9	10 000
Value of work certified at 30 November 19 . 9	590 000

At 31 December 19 . 9 the value of the materials on site amounted to £3 750 and the plant was valued at £40 000. During the year plant valued at £43 750 was transferred to another site. No profit had been taken in the first five months of the contract. At the end of the financial year which closed on 31 December 19 . 9 the cost of work completed but not yet certified amounted to £12 500. The following expenditure has been recorded:

	£
Plant sent to site	111 250
Materials sent by stores department	1 875
Direct purchases sent by suppliers	260 000
Wages paid	125 000
Site general expenses	4 750
Transport charges	3 000
Head office overhead expenses chargeable to the contract	37 875

The contract specified that charges should be made for work outside the terms and conditions of the contract and that payment was to be made in full within one month of certification. Wages due to employees at 31 December amounted to £6 250.

You are required to:

(a) write up the Contract Account as it would appear in the Costing

Ledger, showing the amount to be taken to the Profit and Loss Account as 'cost of sales'.

(b) draw up the Profit and Loss Account, the Retention Money Account and the Profit Reserved Account based on the fact that the profit attributable to the contract at this date is to be represented by two thirds of the notional profit reduced in the proportion that the cash received from the client bears to the value of the work certified to date.

(c) show the relevant Balance Sheet items.

UNIT 7

Process costing

7.1 A comparison of job order costing and process costing

The production or manufacture of specific orders is known as the job order system. In order to find the production cost, each of the elements of cost for the operations to be carried out and for the components of the finished product is accumulated separately. There is a continuous collection of different manufacturing costs and each part of the order can be identified as production proceeds. The cost of the job is found when the order is complete. In comparison, production which is evaluated by using process costing is a continuous flow of the same kinds of unit passing through one or more processes, and the accumulation of the elements of cost is collected from process to process. This continues until instructions are given to stop or reduce production. The cost of each department or process is found at the end of each cost period, and costs accumulate as they are transferred from process to process, or the processes themselves are operations which are added together to find the total cost.

7.2 Equivalent production

With production by processes, costing is carried out at the end of each cost period, and usually some unfinished units remain in process when the costs are taken. It is therefore necessary to have a report on the stage of completion and to calculate what is known as *equivalent units. Equivalent production* represents fully completed units and, when dealing with work in process, information is needed on the degree of completeness so that a correct valuation can be made in the Process Accounts. An estimate of the degree of completion is made on a percentage basis. For example, 100 units which are 50 per cent complete are equivalent to 50 complete units. This type of information is needed so that the correct values can be applied to units transferred to other processes, to the finished units and to the units still in process.

7.3 Process costing procedure

Job costing usually incurs a lot of detail, and costs are computed from day to day, whereas process costs tend to be computed at the end of the month. Process costing is carried out, to a large extent, on the basis of average costs and overall this leads to less work and smaller clerical expenses, although average costs often provide misleading results.

When there is more than one process, costs flow from one process to the next until production is complete. The units are then transferred to a Finished Goods Account. Between processes, the finished output of each process becomes the raw material of the next process in the production programme.

The costing procedure is as follows:

(a) direct and indirect costs are collected in accounts and at the end of the cost period they are charged to processes;
(b) daily and weekly records are made of quantities of production such as units, kilograms, etc. The monthly figures of each process are drawn up and recorded in the form of a report;
(c) the average cost per unit is obtained for each process by dividing the total cost of each process by the normal output of each process;
(d) at the end of the period, a calculation is made to obtain the equivalent production for each process;
(e) the cost of units normally lost is borne by the units completed;
(f) where joint products are manufactured, the process costs should be apportioned on a fair and acceptable basis (see Unit 7.6);
(g) when costs are computed, it is necessary to deal with normal losses, abnormal losses, spoilage and by-products.

On the assumption that all finished products are transferred at the end of a period, the following information is needed for each process.

(i) the quantity of units in process at the beginning of the period and their stage of completion in the form of a percentage;
(ii) the quantity received from the preceding process;
(iii) the quantity transferred to the next process;
(iv) the quantity of finished units at the end of the period;
(v) the units still in process and their stage of completion at the end of the period.

EXAMPLE 7.1 (Equivalent units, unit costs and a Process Account)

(a) Process costs

Process A	£	£	
Opening stock (950 units 40% complete)		1 292	*Opening stock and costs in the current period*
Material	9 143		
Wages	4 600		
Overheads	6 900		
Debited to Process Account		20 643	
		£21 935	

(b) Details of production in current period

	Actual units	Equivalent units
Opening stock (40% complete)	950	380
Units introduced	6 000	
Units transferred to process B	5 900	
Closing stock (36% complete)	1 050	378

(c) Equivalent production

	Units
Incomplete units at beginning of period (60% of 950)	570
Units introduced	6 000
Incomplete units in process	6 570
Less Closing stock (incomplete 64% of 1 050	672
Equivalent production	5 898

Proof:	*Units*
Units introduced and completed (6 000 − 1 050)	4 950
Opening stock completed (60% of 950)	570
Closing stock (equivalent units = 36% of 1 050)	378
	5 898

(d) Unit cost in current period

$$\frac{\text{Current cost}}{\text{Equivalent production}} = \frac{\text{Materials + Wages + Overheads}}{5\,898}$$

$$= \frac{£9\,143 + £4\,600 + £6\,900}{5\,898} = \frac{£20\,643}{5\,898} = £3.50$$

(e) Transfer value of completed units

	£
Process costs (£1 292 + £9 143 + £4 600 + £6 900)	21 935
Less Value of closing stock (36% of 1 050 × £3.50) = 378 × £3.50	1 323
Value of units transferred to process B	£20 612

Proof:

Units		£
950	Cost charged in previous period	1 292
	Cost charged in current period (570 × £3.50)	1 995
4 950	Introduced and completed in current period (4 950 × £3.50)	17 325
5 900	Units transferred	£20 612

(f)

Process A Account

	Units	£		Units	£
Opening stock (40% complete)	950	1 292	Transfer to process B	5 900	20 612
Materials	6 000	9 143	Closing stock (36% complete) balance carried down	1 050	1 323
Wages		4 600			
Overheads		6 900			
	6 950	£21 935		6 950	£21 935
Balance b/d (36% complete)	1 050	1 323			

7.4 Normal losses and abnormal losses or gains

The nature of operations in the process industries usually includes wastage of materials as a result of evaporation, spillage, handling and other causes. The loss or wastage may be perceptible, but frequently it is invisible and unavoidable. In most factories, conditions and circumstances are seldom ideal and a measure of loss has to be accepted as normal. The materials which emerge from a process can be subjected to a quantity and a quality control. Under normal conditions the input of materials will be expected to produce a certain yield. Operating efficiency can be measured by calculating a yield percentage, and comparing this with a percentage which indicates the output expected. The estimated output may be fixed by the use of a formula or based on expert judgement. It is often fixed following tests carried out over a short period when the plant is operating under normal conditions. It is useful to remind ourselves of the terminology used for losses and gains (see Unit 6.5):

- *Waste* is discarded substances having no value.
- *Scrap* is discarded material having some recovery value.
- *Spoilage* is units of output which fail to reach the required standard of quality or specification. Such faulty units may be capable of rectification, and this can be done if the cost of doing so is less than the loss in value from allowing the fault to remain uncorrected. When it is uneconomic to rectify a fault, the article may be sold as sub-standard if it is still functionally sound; otherwise it may be disposed of as scrap.
- *By-product* is a product which is recovered incidentally from the material used in the manufacture of recognised main products. A by-product might have either a net realisable value or a usable value, such value being relatively unimportant in comparison with the saleable value of the main products.

EXAMPLE 7.2

A new process is to receive 1 000 units of material, and it is estimated that there will be a process loss of 5 per cent, and an output of 950 units. During the first period of production the actual output amounted to 945 units. Calculate the yield on output expected and the yield from actual output.

Output expected

$$\text{Yield} = \frac{\text{Estimated output}}{\text{Weight or units entering process}} \times 100$$

$$= \frac{950}{1\,000} \times 100 = \underline{\underline{95\%}}$$

Actual output

$$\text{Yield} = \frac{\text{Actual output}}{\text{Weight or units charged to process}} \times 100$$

$$= \frac{945}{1\,000} \times 100 = \underline{\underline{94.5\%}}$$

In job costing, it is usually easy to trace the source of the loss, but when material goes through a process it is much more difficult, as wastage may occur throughout the process or at the beginning or end of it. If it occurs throughout the process, one might assume that all the units or materials should bear the loss, but general practice is to make the completed units only bear the loss. A loss which is visible and accumulates during the process may be in the form of waste, which has no value, or scrap material, which can be used in future processes or may be sold. If it has a value, the normal loss which is borne by the good units will be smaller by that amount.

Abnormal loss is the loss caused by inefficiency, unsuitable and low standard material, and any conditions which arise during the process which are not acceptable in normal circumstances. An abnormal loss should not be charged to production but credited to the Process Account and debited to an Abnormal Loss Account, before being charged to the Profit and Loss Account.

7.5 Treatment in the accounts of normal and abnormal output

(*a*) Normal output

Producers will want to know the cost per unit of normal output, which is the yield expected from a given quantity of material or units of input. If no loss is expected during processing, the normal output is the quantity of material or units introduced. In other cases, a calculation has to be made by using the yield percentage to find the units of normal output and normal loss.

EXAMPLE 7.3

Yield expected 95%
Costs of materials and conversion costs £9 500
Units of materials introduced 1 000

$$\text{Normal output} = \frac{95}{100} \times 1\,000 = 950 \text{ units}$$

$$\text{Normal loss } (1\,000 - 950) = 50 \text{ units}$$

$$\text{Cost per unit} = \frac{£9\,500}{950} = \underline{\underline{£10}} \left(\frac{\text{Processing costs}}{\text{Normal output}} \right)$$

In this example it is assumed that the normal loss has no scrap value, and therefore the good units bear the whole of the cost, including the normal loss. When the scrap has a value, the cost per unit is reduced by taking the scrap value into account. Suppose, for example, scrap is sold at £0.95 per unit.

$$\text{Cost of processing} = £9\,500 - (50 \times £0.95) = £9\,500 - £47.50$$
$$= \underline{\underline{£9\,452.50}}$$

$$\text{Cost per unit} = \frac{£9\,452.50}{950} = \underline{\underline{£9.95}} \left(\frac{\text{Net processing cost}}{\text{Normal output}} \right)$$

(*b*) Abnormal loss and abnormal gain

When there is a difference between the actual output and the normal (estimated) output there is either an abnormal gain or an abnormal loss. Provided the abnormal units pass through the complete process, thereby incurring the same materials and conversion costs as the other units, then the cost per unit is the same for both normal and abnormal units. The following accounts may be required:

(i) Normal Loss Account

(ii) Abnormal Loss Account This is required when the actual number of units lost is greater than the normal (estimated) loss in units. The loss in abnormal units is found when, after allowing for incomplete units, the units of input exceed the good units produced *plus* the units of normal loss.

(iii) Abnormal Gain Account This is required when, after allowing for incomplete units, the good units produced *plus* the loss in normal units is greater than the units of input.

When an abnormal gain occurs, the real loss in units is the difference between the number of units of normal loss and the number of abnormal units, as the abnormal gain appears on the debit side of the Process Account and the normal loss is shown on the credit side.

When the normal loss is sold as scrap, the amount recovered is shown with the units of normal loss on the credit side of the Process Account. There is a confused situation when an abnormal gain occurs, because the normal loss in units and the scrap value of those units appears on the credit side of the Process Account in the usual way, but an adjustment is made in the Normal Loss Account to reduce the units to the actual number lost. This procedure is necessary in order to record the correct unit cost in the Process

Account and the actual amount recovered for scrap is shown in the Normal Loss Account.

The balance on the Abnormal Gain Account or on an Abnormal Loss Account is transferred to the Profit and Loss Account.

The book-keeping entries are as follows.

Normal loss

Debit Normal Loss A/c	*Credit* Process A/c (with units and scrap value)
Debit Debtor's A/c	*Credit* Normal Loss A/c (with sale of scrap)

Abnormal gain

Debit Process A/c	*Credit* Abnormal Gain A/c (with units and production cost of units)

Reduce the credit amount in the Abnormal Gain A/c by transferring the units at the scrap value to the Normal Loss A/c. This reduces the units in the Normal Loss A/c, to the actual number sold.

Debit Abnormal Gain A/c	*Credit* Normal Loss A/c (with units at scrap value)

Abnormal loss

Debit Abnormal Loss A/c	*Credit* Process A/c (with units and production cost of units)
Debit Debtor's A/c	*Credit* Abnormal Loss A/c (with sale of scrap)

These entries are illustrated in Example 7.4.

EXAMPLE 7.4 (Entries for an abnormal gain)

Units produced	4 850	
Units of normal loss (5% of input)	250	(5% of 5 000)
	5 100	
Less		
Units introduced into process	5 000	@ £1.00 each
Units of abnormal gain	100	
Normal loss: sold as scrap at £0.10 per unit		
Normal recovery 250 @ £0.10	£25	
Less		
Reduction in scrap units sold due to 100 units of abnormal gain	£10	
Value of scrap sold	£15	
Direct labour	£1 900	
Overheads	£3 100	

Process Account 1

	Units	Per unit £	Value £		Units	Per unit £	Value £
Materials	5 000	1.00	5 000	Normal loss	250	0.10	25
Direct labour			1 900	Process 2	4 850	2.10	10 185
Overheads			3 100				
Abnormal gain	100	2.10	210				
	5 100		£10 210		5 100		£10 210

The cost per unit is calculated as follows:

Normal output = 95% of 5 000	=	4 750	units
Actual output	=	4 850	units
Abnormal gain	=	100	units

Normal loss = 5 000 units − 4 750 units = 250 units
Scrap value of normal loss = 250 × £0.10 = £25
Process cost = Total cost − Cost of normal loss
= (Materials + Direct labour + Overheads) − Normal loss
= (£5 000 + £1 900 + £3 100) − £25
= £10 000 − £25 = £9 975

$$\text{Cost per unit} = \frac{\text{Process cost}}{\text{Normal output}} = \frac{£9\,975}{4\,750} = £2.10$$

The 4 850 units transferred to the next process and the *debit* for 100 units of abnormal gain are priced at £2.10 per unit and these entries close the Process Account.

Normal Loss Account

	Units	Per unit £	Value £		Units	Per unit £	Value £
Process 1 A/c	250	0.10	25	Abnormal Gain A/c	100	0.10	10
				Debtor's A/c	150	0.10	15
	250		£25		250		£25

The real loss in units equals 250 units of normal loss *less* 100 units of abnormal gain, and these 150 units are sold for £15. Under normal conditions, £25 is received and the loss of £10 is chargeable against the abnormal gain (*debit* Abnormal Gain A/c, *credit* Normal Loss A/c).

Abnormal Gain Account

	Units	Per unit £	Value £		Units	Per unit £	Value £
Normal Loss A/c	100	0.10	10	Process 1 A/c	100	2.10	210
Profit and Loss A/c			200				
	100		£210		100		£210

The actual gain resulting from the abnormal units is £200.

Journal entries for these transfers would appear as follows:

Journal

		£	£
Normal Loss A/c	Dr.	25	
Process 1 A/c			25
Transfer of normal loss of (5% of 5 000 units) 250 units at £0.10 per unit			
Process 2 A/c	Dr.	10 185	
Process 1 A/c			10 185
Transfer of 4 850 units at £2.10 per unit to the next process			
Process 1 A/c	Dr.	210	
Abnormal Gain A/c			210
Transfer of a gain of 100 units at £2.10 per unit			
Abnormal Gain A/c	Dr.	10	
Normal Loss A/c			10
Adjustment of normal loss (250 units at £0.10) to actual loss of 150 units at £0.10			
Debtor's A/c	Dr.	15	
Normal Loss A/c			15
Sale as scrap of 150 units at £0.10 per unit			
Abnormal Gain A/c	Dr.	200	
Profit and Loss A/c			200
Transfer of gain during process after adjusting for a reduction of 100 normal loss units at £0.10 per unit			

7.6 Joint products

(a) Examples of joint products

The term *joint products* refers to two or more products which are the result of processing operations. The items produced are separated during the process but they may need further processing before they are in a saleable condition. Joint products occur in such industries as oil refining (petrol and fuel oils), agriculture (wool and mutton) and chemical processing. Applying or assigning costs to joint products is a difficult problem.

(b) By-products

A product regarded as a by-product in one factory may be termed as a joint product or scrap in another. The term applied is less important than the use of common sense in valuing the item and in treating it in the accounts. The CIMA publication *Official Terminology* defines a by-product as: 'output of some value produced incidentally in manufacturing something else'. It is a product which is recovered incidentally from the material used in the manufacture of recognised main products, such a by-product having either a net realisable value or a usable value which is relatively low in comparison with the saleable value of the main products. By-products may be further processed to increase their realisable value.

(c) Valuation of joint products

It is essential to make a profit on the processing and to obtain an adequate amount of cash for each joint product, and a method has to be found which can be used in apportioning and allocating costs to them. Management has to make this policy decision, but because of the many changes which take place in demand, technology and marketing, there is no question of methods being fixed, and modifications to the accounting procedures have to take place whenever conditions change.

(d) Apportionment of joint costs

The costs up to the point of separation or split-off are common costs, and after this point expenses arise which are peculiar to each of the joint products. These extra costs may have an important influence on the method adopted for apportioning the common costs. Common costs can be dealt with in the following ways:

(i) Average unit cost When the output of a process emerges at the split-off point in units which are similar and which can be expressed in units of the same type, then the average cost per unit can be calculated for the entire output. When the units are not similar, it may be possible to convert them to other, common units which are, for example, litres, kilograms or metres. But the type, grade or quality of the product may be different.

This method is not particularly good as it is usually difficult to establish whether the cost of production is the same for each of the products.

(ii) Apportionment by using physical units At the separation point, proportions of the total cost are given to each product on the basis of physical output. The proportion may be in the form of percentages or in volume, weight, etc. of the raw material contained in each product.

(iii) Apportionment by market price This is an apportionment on the basis of sales value and is a popular method of arriving at costs, although selling prices are not necessarily based on cost, but are often determined by market forces. The sales value at the separation point is used if the selling prices of joint products are available for production up to this point, but as this is seldom the case the apportionment has to be based on the selling prices of the completed product (final sales value), or on what is referred to as the *net sales* *value*, which is the sales value less the costs after separation. Examples are given below:

Cost of production of joint products A and B before separation: £54 000
Costs after separation: Product A: £6 000
Product B: £9 000
Units produced and selling prices:
Product A: 6 000 units at £5.00 each = £30 000
Product B: 8 000 units at £7.50 each = £60 000

(iv) Apportionment on final sales value

$$\text{Apportionment} = \frac{\text{Product sales value}}{\text{Total sales value}} \times \text{Joint cost}$$

Product A

$$\frac{£30\,000}{£90\,000} \times £54\,000 = £18\,000 \text{ (60\% of sales value)}$$

Product B

$$\frac{£60\,000}{£90\,000} \times £54\,000 = £36\,000 \text{ (60\% of sales value)}$$

$$£54\,000$$

Product	*A*		*B*	
	£	% of sales value	£	% of sales value
Joint cost	18 000	60	36 000	60
Cost after separation	6 000	20	9 000	15
Total cost	24 000	80	45 000	75
Profit	6 000	20	15 000	25
Sales value	£30 000	100	£60 000	100

The above example shows that if an apportionment is made on sales value and the additional costs are ignored, A and B each show a margin of 40 per cent of sales value. The variation of 5 per cent in profit to sales (A 20 per cent, B 25 per cent) is caused by the additional costs which bear more heavily on A at 20 per cent of sales value than on B at 15 per cent of sales value or selling price, and indicates that post-separation costs must be taken into account when apportioning joint cost.

(v) Apportionment on net sales value

Net sales value = Sales value − Further costs
Product A: £30 000 − £6 000 = £24 000
Product B: £60 000 − £9 000 = £51 000

Total net sales value £75 000

$$\text{Apportionment} = \frac{\text{Product net sales value}}{\text{Total net sales value}} \times \text{Joint costs}$$

Product A

$$\frac{£24\,000}{£75\,000} \times £54\,000 = £17\,280$$

Product B

$$\frac{£51\,000}{£75\,000} \times £54\,000 = £36\,720$$

£54 000

Product	A £	A % of selling price	B £	B % of selling price
Joint cost	17 280	57.6	36 720	61.2
Cost after separation	6 000	20.0	9 000	15.0
Total cost	23 280	77.6	45 720	76.2
Profit	6 720	22.4	14 280	23.8
Selling prices	£30 000	100	£60 000	100

For product A, a comparison of the two methods shows that the amount of the joint cost when using the sales value method is £18 000, and this is reduced to £17 280 when applying the net sales value, increasing the profit by £720. The post-separation cost of A is greater in proportion to cost and sales than that of B, and by extracting the separation costs from the sales value we arrive at a more accurate proportion of the joint costs chargeable to each product.

(e) Valuation of by-products

When the value of the by-product is relatively small, the revenue obtained from its sale is treated as other income and the sales value is credited to the Profit and Loss Account, but no cost is transferred to this account from the Process Account. In this method, the major or joint products bear the full cost of the process, and the Profit and Loss Account is debited with any disposal costs. If a large number of transactions occur from by-product sales, it may be convenient to open a By-product Account in order to record these sales and attributable costs incurred after separation, and at the end of the period to transfer the profit or loss to the Profit and Loss Account.

When by-products are given a value, one of the following methods may be used:

(i) Sales revenue or market value The estimated cost is based on the sales value less any costs incurred up to the time of delivery, and this is the net realisable value mentioned earlier in this unit (see Unit 7.4).

(ii) Standard cost As the selling prices of by-products often fluctuate considerably, a standard value may be established. This is a convenient way of avoiding the continual changes in the price set for the by-product and the effect these have on the main product. The standard cost may be fixed by calculating an average of the prices obtained over a short period of time, or an arbitrary figure may be used.

(iii) Transfer value By-products are sometimes used internally in manufacturing or servicing and the market value or standard cost method can be used.

(iv) Accounting for a by-product When a value is given to a by-product, the cost is credited to the Process Account and debited either to a By-product Account or direct to the Profit and Loss Account. In the case of internal usage, it is credited to the Process Account and debited to a Manufacturing or Service Account.

It is necessary to charge against the revenue received any appropriate administrative costs and the cost of packing and carriage.

7.7 Conversion costs

Conversion costs include all production costs of converting the raw materials (or other materials which are direct) into the finished or partly finished product, but the cost of direct material is excluded. In process costing conversion costs refer to the cost of direct labour and production overhead charged to the Process Account.

7.8 Process Accounts

EXAMPLE 7.5

On 1 January, a company starts to make a new product which has to be processed three times before it can be transferred to the Finished Stock Account. The production and costing records at 31 January disclosed the following information for process 1. Show the Process 1 Account.

Materials issued	1 500 @ £3.60 per unit
Direct wages	£2 250
Production overhead	£3 750
Normal loss is set at 5%	
Actual output = 1 400 units	(no work-in-progress)

The normal loss and abnormal units have no scrap value.
The actual output is transferred to process 2.

Workings (see p. 166 for Process 1 Account)

Normal loss = 5% of 1 500 = 75 units

Normal output = 1 500 − 75 = 1 425 units

Actual output	= 1 400 units
Abnormal loss 1 500 − (1 400 + 75) =	25 units
	1 425 units

$$\text{Cost of normal output} = \frac{\text{Cost of processing}}{\text{Normal output}} = \frac{£11\,400}{1\,425} = £8.00 \text{ per unit}$$

Process 1 Account

19..		*Units*	*Per unit* £	*Amount* £	19..		*Units*	*Per unit* £	*Amount* £
31 Jan.	Materials	1 500	3.60	5 400	31 Jan.	Normal loss	75	–	–
31 Jan.	Direct wages			2 250	31 Jan.	Abnormal Loss or Yield Account	25	8.00	200
31 Jan.	Production overhead			3 750	31 Jan.	Output transferred to second process	1 400	8.00	11 200
		1 500		£11 400			1 500		£11 400

Note: Normal loss only has a value when it can be sold as scrap.

EXAMPLE 7.6

Example 7.5 shows a Process Account with an abnormal loss. Occasionally an abnormal gain may occur. Assuming that the actual output transferred was 1 435 units, the account would appear as follows:

Process 1 Account

19..		*Units*	*Per unit* £	*Amount* £	19..		*Units*	*Per unit* £	*Amount* £
31 Jan.	Materials	1 500	3.60	5 400	31 Jan.	Normal loss	75	–	–
31 Jan.	Direct wages			2 250	31 Jan.	Output transferred to second process	1 435	8.00	11 480
31 Jan.	Production overhead			3 750					
31 Jan.	Abnormal Loss or Yield A/c	10	8.00	80					
		1 510		£11 480			1 510		£11 480

Workings

$$\text{Cost per unit} = \frac{\text{Cost of processing}}{\text{Normal output}} = \frac{£11\,400}{1\,425} = £8.00 \text{ per unit}$$

Output transferred = 1 435 @ £8.00 per unit = £11 480
Abnormal gain = 10 @ £8.00 per unit = £80
The normal loss is set at 75 units but as 10 are gained only 65 are actually lost.

EXAMPLE 7.7

In Examples 7.5 and 7.6 the value per unit is the same for both the units transferred and units of abnormal loss and abnormal gain. In this example the units of normal loss are sold at a scrap price of £0.95 per unit.

Process 1 Account

	Units	*Per unit* £	*Amount* £		*Units*	*Per unit* £	*Amount* £
31 Jan. Materials	1 500	3.60	5 400	31 Jan. Normal loss	75	0.95	71.25
31 Jan. Direct wages			2 250	31 Jan. Abnormal loss or yield	25	7.95	198.75
31 Jan. Production overhead			3 750	31 Jan. Output transferred to second process	1 400	7.95	11 130.00
	1 500		£11 400		1 500		£11 400.00

Workings

Cost of processing = £11 400 *less* Value of scrap sold
= £11 400 − 75 units @ £0.95 = £11 400 − £71.25
= £11 328.75

$$\text{Cost of normal output} = \frac{\text{Cost of processing}}{\text{Normal output}} = \frac{£11\,328.75}{1\,425} = £7.95 \text{ per unit}$$

Value of output transferred and abnormal loss charged at £7.95 per unit.

EXAMPLE 7.8

The previous examples have assumed that there is no work-in-progress at the beginning or end of the manufacturing period. To take a simple example where work in process is involved, let us assume that production takes place in two processes.

Process 1

Manufacturing cost	£12 600	
2 400 units in process		
Units completed and transferred to process 2	1 800	units
600 units 50% complete	300	units
Equivalent production	2 100	units

$$\text{Cost of each completed unit} = \frac{\text{Cost of processing}}{\text{Equivalent production}} = \frac{£12\,600}{2\,100}$$

$$= £6.00 \text{ per unit}$$

1 800 units transferred to process 2, at £6.00 per unit	= £10 800
600 units (50% complete = 300 at £6.00 each) work in process	= £ 1 800
	£12 600

Process 2

1 800 units received from process 1, at £6.00			= £10 800
Manufacturing cost:	Direct materials	£600	
	Direct labour	£2 100	
	Works overhead	£3 300	
			= £ 6 000
			£16 800

Units completed and transferred to Finished Stock A/c	1 560	units
240 units 50% complete	120	units
Equivalent production	1 680	units

$$\text{Cost of each completed unit} = \frac{\text{Cost of processing}}{\text{Equivalent production}} = \frac{£16\,800}{1\,680}$$

$$= £10.00 \text{ per unit}$$

1 560 units transferred to Finished Stock A/c at £10.00 per unit	= £15 600
240 units (50% complete = 120 at £10.00 per unit) work in process	= £ 1 200
	£16 800

Process 2 Account

	Units	*Per unit* £	*Amount* £		*Units*	*Per unit* £	*Amount* £
Transfer from process 1	1 800	6.00	10 800	Transfer to Finished Stock A/c	1 560	10.00	15 600
Direct materials			600	Balance (work in process) c/d	240		1 200
Direct labour			2 100				
Works overhead			3 300				
	1 800		£16 800		1 800		£16 800
Balance b/d	240		1 200				

This example is a simplification because it has been assumed that production has proceeded evenly with the application of materials and labour, with work in process at the 50 per cent completion stage. In practice, this does not apply and there are variations in the stage of completion of materials, labour and overheads, and therefore each element has to be dealt with separately.

Calculations will be needed to establish the equivalent production and value for units of materials, labour and overhead, and these may be worked out on the basis of the average cost method or the FIFO method.

(a) Average cost method

In this system, average unit costs are calculated by adding the opening work in process cost to the process costs of the current period and dividing this total cost by the equivalent production for the period. In many process industries production tends to proceed at a steady pace, with similar stocks and volumes of production from one period to the next. There is little variation and generally costs do not change to any great extent. The system is easy to understand and to operate and if prices and costs fluctuate, the calculation of an average evens out the fluctuations. The objections to this method of unit cost valuation are that exceptional changes in operating costs may be hidden by a system that damps down the fluctuations, and cost control may not be as effective as it is intended to be. Average unit costs for materials can be calculated as shown below.

$$\text{Unit cost} = \frac{\text{Opening work-in-progress + Process costs for period}}{\text{Completed units transferred + Equivalent units at close of period}}$$

Process 1

Materials
Unit costs in January

1 January	Opening work-in-progress (100% completed) 200 units	£200
1–31 January	Materials charged	£2 100
31 January	Units transferred	1 500
31 January	Closing work-in-progress (100% completed)	700 units

Calculation of equivalent production

	Units
Units transferred 31 January	1 500
Closing work-in-progress	700
	2 200

Cost of equivalent production

	£
Opening work-in-progress on 1 January	200
Materials charged in January	2 100
	£2 300

$$\text{Average unit cost of material} = \frac{£2\,300}{2\,200} = £1.045\,45$$

A calculation would also be made to find the average unit cost of conversion, i.e. wages and overhead. The average unit costs would then be used to calculate the transfer values which are required in order to close the Process Account. Materials included in the transfer values would be as follows:

		£
Units of material transferred to process 2	1 500 × £1.045 45 =	1 568
Work-in-progress carried down in process 1 on 1 February	700 units at £1.045 45 =	732
		£2 300

(b) FIFO method

This method enables cost control to be exercised because costs of the current period are disclosed and a comparison can be made with the cost in the previous period. The calculations are necessary to find the unit cost in each period, but variations in unit cost are not overlooked as may happen when an average is obtained.

Calculation of equivalent production
Materials

	Units
Units completed and transferred 31 January	1 500
Less Opening work-in-progress completed	200
Unit completed and processed entirely in January	1 300
Add Units of closing work-in-progress	700
	2 000

For purposes of valuation on a FIFO basis, unit costs are calculated as follows:

Materials

$$\frac{\text{Closing work-in-progress in December}}{\text{Equivalent units}} = \frac{£200}{200} = £1.00 \text{ per unit}$$

$$\frac{\text{Material cost in January}}{\text{Units charged and completed in January}} = \frac{£2\,100}{2\,000} = £1.05 \text{ per unit}$$

Cost of equivalent production

		£
December	200 units @ £1.00	200
January	1 300 units @ £1.05	1 365
	1 500 units transferred	1 565
January	700 units @ £1.05	735
	2 200 units	£2 300

The following illustration shows how the three elements of cost are dealt with on a FIFO basis in process costing.

EXAMPLE 7.9

The Process Account on 1 January shows that the balance brought down consists of 200 units at various stages of completion, the value of which is £1 100.

Work in process brought forward

		£
Materials	100% completed	200
Wages	50% completed	500
Works overhead	50% completed	400

At 31 January the situation is as follows:

Work in process carried forward 700 units

Materials	100% completed
Wages	50% completed
Works overhead	50% completed

During January, 1 500 units were completed and transferred to the next process. The costs charged to the process were as given below:

	£
Materials	2 100
Wages	8 925
Works overhead	7 210

Units of output and unit cost are as shown in Table 7.1 (p. 172).

Table 7.1 Calculating for the current period the units produced and unit costs on a FIFO basis

	Units transferred *(a)*	Equivalent units carried down *(b)*	Units completed *(c)* *(a + b)*	Deduct equivalent units brought down *(d)*	Units produced this period *(e)* *(c − d)*	Period costs *(f)* £	Unit cost *(g)* *(f ÷ e)* £
Materials	1 500	700	2 200	200	2 000	2 100	1.05
Wages	1 500	350	1 850	100	1 750	8 925	5.10
Overheads	1 500	350	1 850	100	1 750	7 210	4.12

Workings
Equivalent production (Work in process)

Brought forward

Materials 200 × 100% = 200 for £200 = £1 per unit
Labour 200 × 50% = 100 for £500 = £5 per unit
Overhead 200 × 50% = 100 for £400 = £4 per unit

Carried forward

	£
Materials 700 × 100% = 700 at £1.05 per unit =	735
Labour 700 × 50% = 350 at £5.10 per unit =	1 785
Overhead 700 × 50% = 350 at £4.12 per unit =	1 442
	£3 962

Value of units transferred

			£	£	£
Materials:	200	@ £1.00 per unit	200		
	1 300	@ £1.05 per unit	1 365		
	1 500			1 565	
Labour:	100	@ £5.00 per unit	500		
	1 400	@ £5.10 per unit	7 140		
	1 500			7 640	
Overhead:	100	@ £4.00 per unit	400		
	1 400	@ £4.12 per unit	5 768		
	1 500			6 168	
					15 373
Add Work in process carried forward					3 962
Total charged to Process Account					£19 335

Process 1 Account

19..		Units	£	19..		Units	£
1 Jan.	Balance b/f	200	1 100	31 Jan.	Transfer to process 2	1 500	15 373
31 Jan.	Materials	2 000	2 100	31 Jan.	Balance c/d	700	3 962
31 Jan.	Labour		8 925				
31 Jan.	Overhead		7 210				
		2 200	£19 335			2 200	£19 335
1 Feb.	Balance b/d	700	3 962				

7.9 Exercises

1. Explain how by-products should be dealt with in process costing (*a*) where they are very small in total value, (*b*) where they are of substantial value and (*c*) if they need further processing before they can be sold.

2. J. Boulter and Son (Camside) Ltd manufacture a product which for completion has to pass through process 1 and process 2.
   The cost of the material at the beginning of process 1 is £24 441.
   Labour and overheads: process 1, £23 500; process 2, £51 000.
   The good units amount to: process 1, 2 505; process 2, 2 009.
   The units scrapped amount to: process 1, 390; process 2, 496.
   Scrap value amounts to: process 1, £2.30 per unit; process 2, £3.25 per unit.
   You are required to calculate the cost of the product per unit.

3. Two thousand units of material at £15.50 per unit were charged to a Process Account in respect of the production of joint products A and B. Other common costs consisted of £4 500 for wages and £4 500 for overheads. There is a normal loss up to the point of separation of 5 per cent and this is sold at £7.00 per unit. At this stage there is a by-product which is sold for £190, but this incurs expenses of £30 for packing and carriage. The company uses the market value method less any applicable expenses when assessing the value which is to be charged to the Process Account for the by-product. At the point of separation 55 per cent of the units are apportioned to product A and 45 per cent to product B. After further processing the chargeable costs are: materials £2 625 (A £1 434, B £1 191); wages £3 200 (A £2 000, B £1 200); and overheads £3 200 (A £2 000, B £1 200). There is no closing stock and the completed units are transferred to the Finished Stock Account.

   You are required *(a)* to draw up the Process Account, showing the value transferred to the Finished Stock Account, and *(b)* to show your workings and to indicate the cost per unit of product A and product B.

4. 3 800 units of material which cost £4.75 per unit were charged to a process in which the expected yield was 95 per cent. The discarded material is sold as scrap at £0.95 per unit. Direct wages cost of the process amounted to

£5 054, and works overhead is charged at 150 per cent on direct wages. 3 630 units were produced and transferred to Finished Stock Account. Write up the Process Account, the Normal Loss Account and the Abnormal Gain Account.

5. *(a)* Explain the fundamental differences between job costing and process costing and state three industries, other than the food industry, which use process costing.

(b) A company within the food industry mixes powered ingredients in two different processes to produce one product. The output of process 1 becomes the input of process 2 and the output of process 2 is transferred to the packing department. From the information given below, you are required to open accounts for process 1, process 2, abnormal scrap and packing department and to record the transactions for the week ended 11 November, 19...

Process 1

Input: Material A	6 000 kg at £1.00 per kg
Material B	4 000 kg at £2.00 per kg
Mixing labour	430 hours at £4.00 per hour
Normal scrap	5% of weight input
Scrap was sold for	£0.32 per kg
Output was	9 200 kg

There was no work in process at the beginning or end of the week.

Process 2

Input: Material C	6 600 kg at £2.50 per kg
Material D	4 200 kg at £1.50 per kg
Flavouring essence	£600.00
Mixing labour	370 hours at £4.00 per hour
Normal waste	5% of weight input
Output was	18 000 kg

There was no work in process at the beginning of the week but 1 000 kg were in process at the end of the week and were estimated to be only 50 per cent complete so far as labour and overhead were concerned.

Overhead of £6 400 incurred by the two processes was absorbed on the basis of mixing labour hours.

Within process 1, abnormal scrap arose because some batches failed to pass the quality control check at the end of each mix. However, no loss in weight occurred and all scrap was sold for cash on the last day of the week. Any resultant balance on the Abnormal Scrap Account was transferred to Profit and Loss Account.

(CIMA, adapted)

6. *(a)* Explain briefly the distinction between joint products and by-products.

(b) Discuss briefly the problems involved in calculating the cost of

manufacture of joint products, with particular reference to the apportionment of pre-separation point costs. A common method of apportioning these pre-separation point costs is by physical measurement; outline two other methods.

(c) In a process line of the JP Manufacturing Company Ltd, three joint products are produced. For the month of October the following data were available:

Product	X	Y	Z
Sales price per kilogram	£5	£10	£20
Post-separation point costs	£10 000	£5 000	£15 000
Output	2 500 kg	1 000 kg	1 500 kg

Pre-separation point costs amounted to £20 000.

The joint products are manufactured in one common process, after which they are separated and may undergo further individual processing. The pre-separation point costs are apportioned to joint products, according to weight.

You are required:

(i) to prepare a statement showing the estimated profit or loss for each product and in total;

(ii) as an alternative to the costing system used in (i) above, to present a statement which will determine the maximum profit from the production of these joint products.

The sales value of each product at separation point is as follows: X = £3; Y = £4; Z = £6.

(CIMA)

7. A company operates a department producing a component which passes through two processes. During November, materials for 40 000 components were put into process. There was no opening process stock. 30 000 were finished and passed to the next process. Those not passed forward were calculated to be one-half finished as regards wages and overhead. The costs incurred were as follows:

	£
Direct material	10 000
Factory overhead	12 000
Direct wages	8 000

Of those passed to the second process, 28 000 were completed and passed to the finished stores. 200 were scrapped, which was not abnormal. 1 800 remained unfinished in process, one-quarter finished as regards wages and overhead. No further process material costs occur, after introduction at the first process, until the end of the second process, when protective packing is applied to the completed components. The process and packaging costs incurred at the end of the second process were:

	£
Direct material	4 000
Factory overhead	4 500
Direct wages	3 500

Prepare a cost analysis statement for November, accounting for total costs incurred, analysed into elements of costs for each process, covering finished and part-finished items.

(CIMA)

8. A foundry produces brass castings consisting of 70 per cent copper, costing £450 per tonne, and zinc, costing £120 per tonne. 10 per cent of the metal charged is lost in melting, i.e. before pouring. Melting costs, other than materials, amount to £50 per tonne of metal poured.

Good castings produced vary, according to product type, from 50 per cent to 70 per cent of metal poured. The balance, consisting of runners, heads and scrap, is returned to stock for subsequent use, being valued at cost of metal content only.

(a) Prepare costs of metal and melting for products with (i) 50 per cent, (ii) 60 per cent and (iii) 70 per cent yields.

(b) What difference (if any) is made to these figures when the charge of metals in the ratio 70:30 is supplemented by 40 per cent addition of scrap metal of this mixture?

(CIMA, adapted)

9. A company operates a process to produce product A, as a result of which process by-products Y and Z are also produced. During a normal period costs are as follows:

	£
Direct materials	21 000
Direct wages	8 000
Process overheads	12 000

Production was:

Product A	500 tonnes sold at £100 per tonne
By-product Y	70 tonnes sold at £20 per tonne
By-product Z	80 tonnes which is unsaleable, but it is cleared by a contractor at a charge of £5 per tonne

The process overheads include £8 000 of a fixed nature, the balance (50% of direct wages) being regarded as variable).

Both by-products can be further treated, using existing facilities, and sold. By the addition of extra materials costing £600 and direct labour of £800 to the 70 tonnes of Y, 100 tonnes of product M can be produced and sold at £40 per tonne. By the addition of extra materials costing £800 and direct labour of £600 to the 80 tonnes of Z, 100 tonnes of product P can be produced and sold at £24 per tonne.

Present figures to management and offer advice on the action to be taken.

(CIMA, adapted)

10. A company manufactures and sells two products, X and Y, whose selling prices are £100 and £300 respectively, and each product passes through two manufacturing processes, A and B. In process A, product X takes 2 hours per unit and product Y takes 4 hours. In process B, product X takes 1 hour per unit and product Y takes 3 hours. Labour in process A is paid £4 per hour, and in process B £5 per hour. The two products are made out of materials P, Q and R, and the quantities of each material used in making one unit of each product are:

Product	X	Y
Material P	37 lb	93 lb
Material Q	10	240
Material R	20 sq. ft	75 sq. ft

Material prices are £1 per lb for P, £2.40 per dozen for Q and £0.20 per sq. ft for R.

Sales staff are paid a commission of 5 per cent of sales. The packing materials are £1 for X and £4 for Y. Advertising costs are allocated in the ratio of the total sales revenue earned by the two products. Costs of transporting the goods to the customer are £2 for X and £5 for Y.

Other annual costs are:

		£	£
Indirect wages:	Process A	25 000	
	Process B	40 000	
	Stores	20 000	
	Canteen	10 000	
			95 000
Indirect materials:	Process A	51 510	
	Process B	58 505	
	Stores	1 310	
	Canteen	8 425	
			119 750
Rent and rates			450 000
Depreciation of plant and machinery			140 000
Power			50 000
Insurance:	Fire (on buildings)		3 750
	Workmen's compensation at 2% of wages		12 000
Heating and lighting			4 500
Advertising			90 000

A royalty of £1 per unit is payable on product X. The annual quantities sold are 15 000 units of X and 10 000 units of Y.

Other relevant information is:

	Area	*Book value of plant and machinery*	*Horsepower of machinery*	*Direct labour*	*Number of employees*	*Number of stores issue notes*
	sq. ft	£	%	hours		
Process A	100 000	1 000 000	80	70 000	40	10 000
Process B	50 000	200 000	20	45 000	30	5 000
Stores	100 000	150 000			10	
Canteen	50 000	50 000			5	
	300 000	1 400 000	100	115 000	85	15 000

You are required to:

(a) prepare a production overhead analysis and apportionment sheet, showing clearly the bases of apportionment used;

(b) calculate appropriate rates of overhead recovery for processes A and B;

(c) calculate the full (absorption) cost of making and selling one unit of each product;

(d) calculate the unit profit or loss for each product.

(CIMA)

UNIT 8

Marginal costing

8.1 Marginal costing technique

Marginal costing is the ascertainment of costs by differentiating between *fixed costs* and *variable costs* and bringing out clearly the effect on profit of changes in volume or type of output. This is a technique of management accountancy which recognises the nature of cost and its behaviour under varying conditions. The Chartered Institute of Management Accountants, in its publication *Official Terminology*, defines *marginal costing* as 'the accounting system in which variable costs are charged to cost units and fixed costs of the period are written off in full against the aggregate contribution. Its special value is in decision-making' (for example, deciding whether a particular order will be profitable, or whether we should make or buy a particular component).

Marginal costing is concerned with the effect of *fluctuating volumes* on costs, and assesses the change in profitability which may occur under certain conditions. Although volume is significant in the improvement of profitability, capacity must also be taken into account. There are different definitions of normal capacity, but it usually means the capacity *both to make and to sell* for a reasonable period in the future. Profitability can be affected by a change in normal capacity, as well as by a change in the type of product being made and sold. Efficient management searches for ways of improving the return on capital employed, and an understanding of marginal costing enables them to achieve greater effectiveness because they are aware of the contribution which their products are making or can make towards the fixed costs and profits of their organisation. The following terms are used in connection with this technique:

(i) Marginal cost This is the variable cost of one unit, or the amount at any given volume of output by which aggregate costs are changed if the volume of output is increased or decreased by one unit. In *Official Terminology* the definition given is: 'The cost of one unit of product or service which would be avoided if that unit were not produced or provided'.

(ii) Fixed costs These costs tend to be unaffected by variations in volume of output. They are costs such as rent, rates, insurance, executive salaries, etc. which have no relationship to volume, but accumulate over a period of time.

(iii) Variable costs These costs tend to change directly with variations in the volume of output. Examples are raw materials, direct wages, electrical power, fuel, spoilage and so forth.

(iv) Semi-variable costs These costs contain a fixed element and a variable element, and apply to expenses where there is a fixed charge and a cost per unit such as gas, electricity and telephone charges.

Within certain limits, variable costs alter in accordance with activity but fixed costs remain the same. There are circumstances when fixed costs have to be reduced or increased at various stages of expansion, but in the short term they remain constant. Even when fixed costs change they are not *variable* in the costing sense of *variable with output*. For example, a factory manager's salary does not vary with output, but if the firm grows, s/he may need an assistant. When presented with overhead costs at different levels of activity, the variable element can be separated and the fixed cost determined by deducting the cost at one rate of activity from the cost at a higher level of activity.

EXAMPLE 8.1

	Activity 60%	*Activity* 70%	*Activity* 80%
	£	£	£
	64 000	70 500	77 000
Less 60% Activity		64 000	
Variable cost		6 500	
Less 70% Activity			70 500
Variable cost			6 500

A 10 per cent change in activity costs £6 500 in variable cost. The fixed cost is found by taking the total cost and deducting the variable cost for the level of activity.

	£	
Cost at 60%	64 000	
Less Variable cost	39 000	(6 × £6 500)
Fixed cost	£25 000	

At a level of 80 per cent activity £77 000 *less* (8 × £6 500) = £25 000 fixed cost. Some typical cost graphs are shown in Fig. 8.1 (pp. 181–2), and described in the notes below the diagrams.

(v) Contribution This term is used in profit planning and refers to the difference between sales revenue and variable cost. The variable cost here is also known as the *marginal cost* and consists of the prime cost plus the variable overheads.

Imagine a case where goods costing £2 000 for direct wages, direct materials and variable overheads are sold for £3 000. The difference between this sales revenue and the variable costs is £1 000. This is the *contribution*. To what does it contribute? It contributes to the only part of the costs of the enterprise not yet covered – the fixed costs (fixed overheads). Once these have been totally

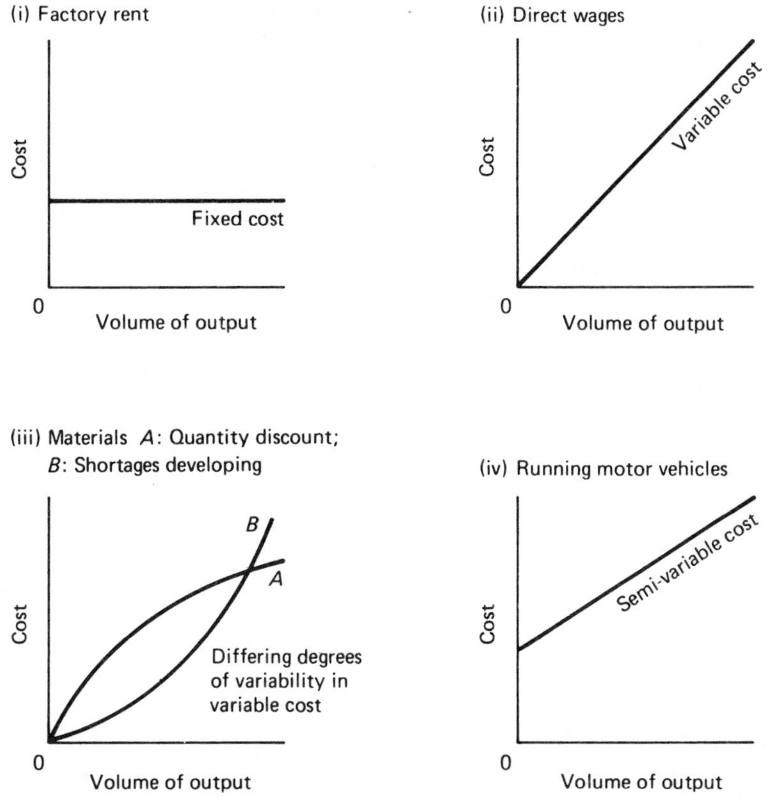

Fig. 8.1 Behaviour of costs (i–iv)

Notes:

(i) The first graph shows a fixed cost (rent) which is fixed over a given period of time. There is a wide range of activity shown as the volume of output. The cost of rent remains the same whatever the volume of output during the set period of time.

(ii) A variable cost (direct wages) is shown on this graph. It illutrates that the cost varies in direct proportion to the volume of output. At zero output, direct wages are zero. As the volume of output increases, so does the cost of direct wages.

(iii) This diagram shows two curves each representing a different variable cost. Costs sometimes behave differently as volume changes and, if the cost of a particular item is plotted on a chart, it may rise steeply at low volume whereas another item may rise less steeply. Graph (ii) is a linear situation (cost varying in direct proportion to output). Curve *A* in graph (iii) illustrates a reduction in unit cost as the output increases as a result of quantity discounts. Curve *B* illustrates an increase in material costs as the demand for material grows and shortages develop.

(iv) This graph shows a semi-variable cost (of running motor vehicles) which consists of a fixed cost (the purchase of the vehicle) and variable costs (petrol, oil, etc.) incurred in running the vehicles.

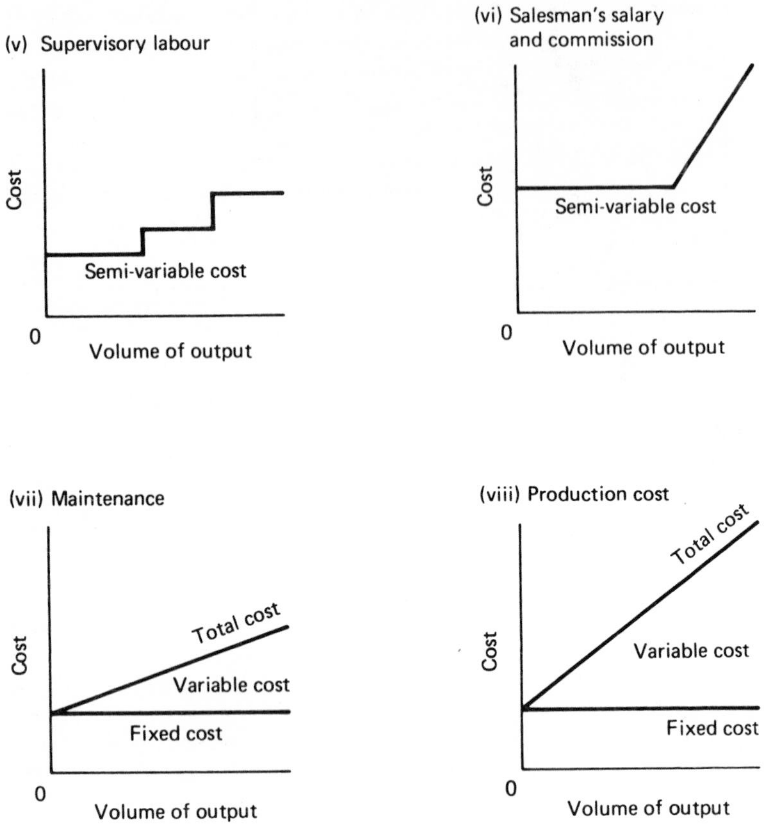

Fig. 8.1 Behaviour of costs (v–viii)

Notes:

(v) This is a stepped graph for semi-variable costs which shows the cost behaviour pattern for supervisors' wages. There is a fixed cost and as the output increases there may be overtime payments and perhaps an increase in supervisory staff as extra workers are taken on.

(vi) This graph illustrates another example of fixed and variable costs where a salesperson receives a fixed salary and commission once s/he has achieved a particular volume of sales.

(vii) This is a semi-variable chart which shows the planned cost of maintenance as fixed cost (preventive maintenance) and a variable cost arising from changes in output.

(viii) This is similar in design to the previous graph but shows the total cost of products (fixed costs plus variable costs) at each level of activity. For example, if a factory with a fixed cost of £4 000 per month produces 250 chairs, with a variable cost of £48 each (£12 000 total), the total cost is £16 000. This represents a cost of £64 per chair, if production and costs proceed according to plan.

covered the firm has *broken even* and will, from this point, make a profit. If, in the example chosen, fixed overheads were £800 then the contribution covers all the fixed costs and contributes £200 to the profits of the business. Had the fixed overheads been £1 300 the firm would not have broken even and an overall loss of £300 would have been sustained.

When marginal costs are truly variable, the marginal cost per unit and the contribution per unit remain unchanged regardless of the level of activity. Under such circumstances marginal costing can be used with advantage as long as it is used after carefully considering all the factors involved.

The contribution per unit of output and sales accumulates as sales are made, and this provides a fund which pays for the fixed expenses and then gives a profit. The point at which total contribution equals total fixed cost is known as the *break-even point*. The different levels of activity have an effect on unit costs because of the burden of fixed costs which, in the short term, are the same at any volume of output. The charts in Fig. 8.2 (p. 184) illustrate the effect of volume.

8.2 Marginal costing and absorption costing compared

Total costing is the traditional way of arriving at and presenting the cost of jobs. Another name for it is absorption costing. As its name implies, an attempt is made to absorb and recover all the costs of the enterprise, including the fixed overheads. The conventional way of showing the cost of a product is to take the marginal costs and to add an on-cost for fixed expenses (that is, an additional cost allocated to each unit in some fair way, in order to recover the overheads of the business from the customer). This enables us to discover the likely unit costs and to present unit or product costs in such a way that the degree of potential profitability can be seen. The charge for fixed expenses, however, is set at the beginning of the trading period when the fixed costs and the volume of production can only be based on estimates. There may be errors in estimating the costs, incorrect methods of apportionment and mistakes made in arriving at the expected volume of output. In these circumstances, the costs and results shown by total costing can be misleading. The fixed expenses are incurred over a period of time and have no connection with volume, and to include an amount for fixed expenses in the cost of a product is considered by the advocates of marginal costing to be incorrect, as the effect of volume changes the amount of fixed cost per unit, as shown in Fig. 8.3 (p. 186).

The marginal costing technique is of special importance to the price estimator who, while remaining conscious of the burden of fixed costs, can use *contribution* when deciding on the level of prices. Initially contribution pays for the fixed costs and once these are accounted for profits can occur. It may be necessary to increase turnover in order to reach the production target set by normal capacity decisions and the estimator may have scope for varying the prices so that the overall profit is improved.

When marginal cost statements are presented, management is assisted in its decision-making as it now knows which products provide the greatest

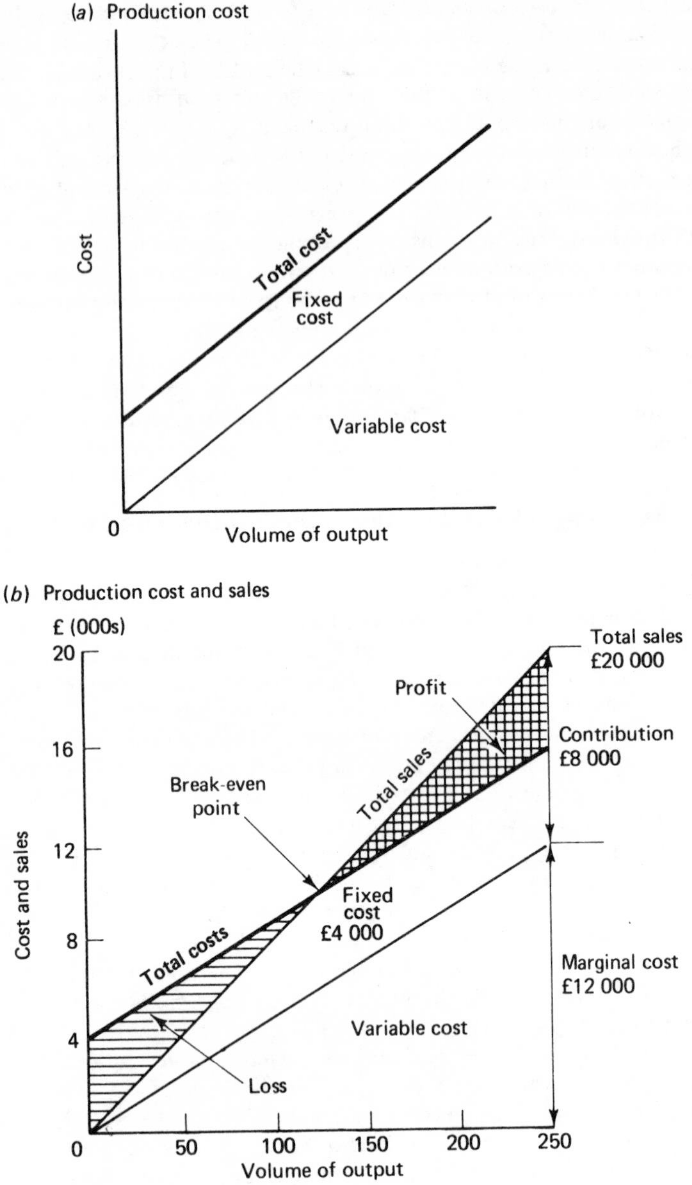

Fig. 8.2 Contribution, total cost, break-even and profit

contribution. Management is therefore in a better position to decide how surplus capacity can be utilised, where expansion is possible, which factories are to manufacture which products and whether expenditure on advertising should be concentrated on selected products.

The measurement of profit is the same under total and marginal costing, although the presentation of the cost information may be displayed differently. As far as the accounts are concerned, it is merely a question of when the profit is taken. At the end of the trading period there will normally be work-in-progress and finished stocks which are carried forward, and in absorption costing these are valued at full cost of production, whereas in

---

Notes to Fig. 8.2:

(i) These graphs show the same information as Fig. 8.1(viii) but the fixed cost and variable cost are shown in reverse order with fixed cost above the variable cost. In addition, the second graph shows the line of total sales, from which can be read the total sales income at any volume of output, assuming all goods are sold. It is also possible to find, at any volume of output, the total variable cost, total fixed cost and total cost. The purpose of showing graph *(b)* in this form is to illustrate the marginal cost area and the components of contribution. The variable item of cost is the marginal cost and the contribution consists of fixed cost recovered plus profit beyond the break-even point. The profit area is the shaded section between total cost and total sales, beyond break-even point.

(ii) Fig. 8.2*(b)* uses the information already given in Fig. 8.1(viii) for the production of 250 chairs. It is planned to sell the chairs at £80 each (total £20 000). It can be seen that the total profit is £4 000 (£20 000 *less* £16 000) giving a profit of £16 per chair. The profit of £16 only applies if the whole of the production is sold and the costs are as planned for that production period. The contribution is that part of the sales income which recovers the fixed costs and produces the profit. For example, at an output of 200 chairs, the income of £16 000 (200 chairs at £80 each) covers variable costs of £48 per chair (£9 600), leaving a contribution of £6 400 (£16 000 *less* £9 600). This covers fixed costs of £4 000 and a profit of only £2 400.

	Sales of 250 chairs		Sales of 200 chairs	
	Total	Per chair	Total	Per chair
	£	£	£	£
Variable cost	12 000	48	9 600	48
Fixed cost	4 000	16	4 000	20
Total cost	16 000	64	13 600	68
Profit	4 000	16	2 400	12
Sales	20 000	80	16 000	80
Contribution:				
Fixed cost	4 000		4 000	
Profit	4 000		2 400	
Total	8 000		6 400	
Contribution per chair	£32		£32	

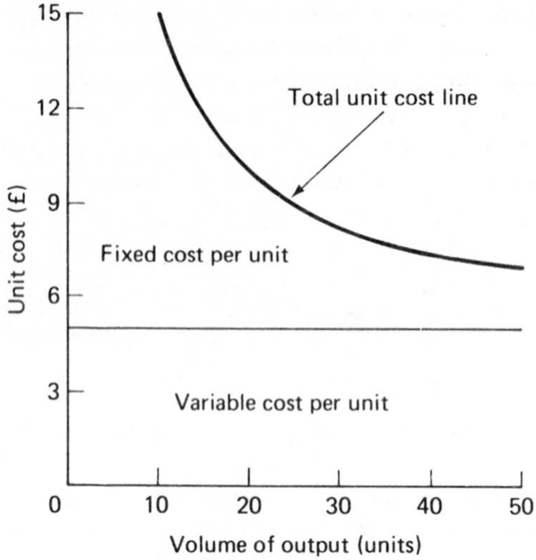

Fig. 8.3 The effect which volume of output has on fixed cost per unit and total unit cost

Notes:

(i) The values below indicate how unit costs are reduced when the volume of output increases as shown in Fig. 8.3. Fixed cost is taken as £100 and the cost of one unit amounts to £105 (which cannot be shown on the graph).

Volume of output	*Variable cost per unit*	*Fixed cost per unit*	*Total unit cost*
	£	£	£
1	5.00	100.00	105.00
10	5.00	10.00	15.00
20	5.00	5.00	10.00
30	5.00	3.33	8.33
40	5.00	2.50	7.50
50	5.00	2.00	7.00

(ii) You can see that while variable cost per unit remains constant at £5.00, the fixed cost per unit is reduced from £100 to £2.

(iii) This not only illustrates how volume affects unit costs, but also shows that volume affects the overhead expenses because absorption rates are predetermined and this results in the under- or over-absorption of overheads, which do not arise under marginal costing.

---

marginal costing they are priced at variable cost. This affects the profits, as, under marginal costing, the fixed cost element is written off in the period when it is incurred, while in total costing some of the fixed cost of the period is carried forward.

8.3 Marginal cost statements

In order for management to measure the performance, statements which show the contribution provided by different products are very important. The following statements show how costs are provided which indicate the total cost and the marginal cost. Note that the overheads are deemed to be made up of £16 000 fixed overhead and £14 000 variable overhead in the first set of figures.

Total cost	£	%	*Marginal cost*	£	%
Direct material	30 000	30	Direct material	30 000	30
Direct wages	20 000	20	Direct wages	20 000	20
Overheads	30 000	30	Variable overhead	14 000	14
Total cost	80 000	80	*Marginal cost*	64 000	64
Profit (net)	20 000	20	Contribution	36 000	36
Sales	£100 000	100		£100 000	100

The marginal cost statement shows that 36 per cent of sales value is *contribution* and this fund pays the fixed costs; the balance is profit.

Cost statement

	£	%
Contribution	36 000	36
Less Fixed cost	16 000	16
Profit (net)	£20 000	20

On the assumption that marginal cost has been correctly assessed, the contribution percentage can be used to estimate future profits, provided fixed costs remain unchanged and there are facilities and capacity to expand sales.

For example, if sales can be increased without increasing fixed costs to a sales turnover of £130 000, the contribution at 36 per cent would be £46 800. As fixed cost has already been covered, the extra contribution would be further profit of £10 800.

Marginal cost statement

	£	%
Direct material	39 000	30
Direct wages	26 000	20
Variable overhead	18 200	14
Marginal cost	83 200	64
Contribution	46 800	36
Sales	£130 000	100
Contribution	46 800	36.0%
Less Fixed cost	16 000	12.3%
Profit	£30 800	23.7%

This indicates that fixed cost as a percentage of sales is reduced from 16 per cent to 12.3 per cent and profit is increased from 20 per cent to 23.7 per cent of sales.

Profit and Loss Statements

The marginal costing technique is a good investigatory procedure as it provides information on the behaviour of costs and greatly helps marketing. Trading results are normally presented in the form of total costs, but if marginal accounts are drawn up, the final figures could be shown as in the example below:

Opening stock	1 800 units at £35 each
Closing stock	1 500 units at £40 each
Production	
Direct material	8 700 units at £25 each
Direct labour	8 700 units at £10 each
Variable overhead	8 700 units at £5 each
Fixed expenses	£137 000
Selling expenses	
Variable	10% of selling price
Fixed	£25 000
Administration expenses	
Fixed	£45 000
Sales	9 000 units at £80 each

The Profit and Loss Account would be as shown below.

Trading and Profit and Loss Account

	£	£	£
Sales (9 000 units @ £80)			720 000
Less Variable costs			
Direct materials (8 700 @ £25)		217 500	
Direct labour (8 700 @ £10)		87 000	
Variable overhead (8 700 @ £5)		43 500	
		348 000	
Add Opening stock (1 800 @ £35)	63 000		
Less Closing stock (1 500 @ £40)	60 000		
		3 000	
		351 000	
Add Variable selling expenses (10% of £720 000)		72 000	
Marginal cost			423 000
Contribution 41.2%		c/d	297 000

	£	£	£
		b/d	297 000
Less Fixed cost			
Fixed production cost		137 000	
Fixed administration expense		45 000	
Fixed selling expense		25 000	
			207 000
Net profit 12.5%			£ 90 000

8.4 Contribution/sales ratio (C/S ratio)

This ratio shows the relationship between contribution and sales value and is usually expressed as a percentage. It is reached by a calculation similar to the one in the last section where the contribution as a percentage of sales is 36 per cent. Using the figures given in Unit 8.3, the calculation is as follows:

$$\text{C/S ratio} = \frac{\text{Contribution}}{\text{Sales}} \times 100 = \frac{£46\,800}{£130\,000} \times 100 = 36\%$$

This ratio used to be called the profit/volume ratio, but as profit only begins when the break-even point has been reached, this term tends to be misleading because it refers to the volume of sales above the break-even point where a percentage of the sales revenue represents profit.

The ratio applies to the sales revenue below, as well as above, the break-even point. It is really a *contribution/sales ratio*, which indicates the proportion of sales revenue which contributes to fixed costs and to profit.

The sales and contribution are in direct proportion to each other, whatever the sales value, and an increase in sales value results in an increase in the value of the contribution by the same percentage that applied to the percentage increase in sales value. The ratio can be used in profit planning to calculate the contribution provided at any level of sales.

The ratio applies if fixed costs remain the same and there are no limiting factors to restrict expansion of production or sales, or to increase marginal costs. This can be shown by using the figures in the above statements.

Sales of £100 000 were increased to £130 000, which is equivalent to a *30 per cent increase*. Contribution of £36 000 was increased to £46 800, which is equivalent to a *30 per cent increase*.

(a) Variable cost ratio

The C/S ratio shows the relationship between contribution and sales, whereas the *variable cost ratio* (VC ratio) shows the relationship between variable cost and sales. It follows that if variable cost plus contribution equals sales value then the two ratios added together always equal 100 per cent. For example, if the C/S ratio is 36 per cent the VC ratio must be 64 per cent.

$$\text{Variable cost ratio} = \frac{\text{Variable cost}}{\text{Sales}} \times 100 = \frac{£83\,200}{£130\,000} \times 100$$

$$= 64\%$$

(Variable cost = Sales − Contribution = £130 000 − £46 800)

(b) Contribution per unit

It is useful to know the value of the contribution per unit as this figure can be used to work out how many extra units need to be sold to provide extra profits. If the selling price of one unit is £10, the volumes of sales shown in the examples above are 10 000 units and 13 000 units and the unit cost is:

Unit cost

	£
Direct material	3.00
Direct wages	2.00
Variable overhead	1.40
Marginal cost	6.40
Contribution	3.60
Selling price	£10.00

The contribution per unit can be used in the following way:

If fixed costs are £16 000 and the profit required is £30 800, the contribution required is £46 800 (£16 000 + £30 800) and the number of units to be sold is as follows:

$$\frac{\text{Total contribution}}{\text{Contribution per unit}} = \frac{£46\,800}{£3.60} = 13\,000 \text{ units}$$

The type of information given above can be shown on a contribution chart or profit graph (Fig. 8.4).

This is the marginal cost statement for the information shown in Fig. 8.4.

Marginal cost statement

Output (units)	4 000		4 445		8 000		10 000	
	£	%	£	%	£	%	£	%
Sales	40 000	100	44 450	100	80 000	100	100 000	100
	£		£		£		£	
Direct material	12 000		13 335		24 000		30 000	
Direct wages	8 000		8 890		16 000		20 000	
Overheads	5 600		6 223		11 200		14 000	
Marginal cost	25 600	64	28 448	64	51 200	64	64 000	64

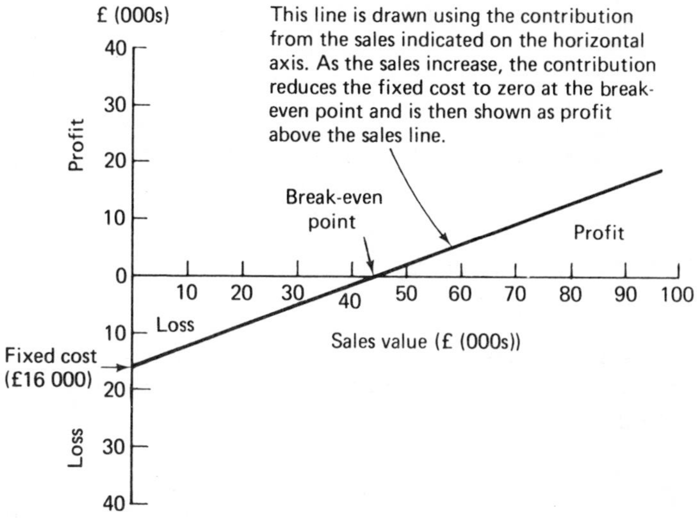

Fig. 8.4 Profit graph

Notes:

(i) The horizontal axis of a profit shows either the volume of output or the sales value, and the vertical axis shows the profit or loss position, with break-even at the zero position.

(ii) The diagonal line is plotted to show the affect of the contribution on both the fixed costs (below the horizontal axis) and the profits (above the horizontal axis).

(iii) It begins at the value of total fixed costs below the horizontal axis and finishes at the value of total contribution above the axis, corresponding to an output of 10 000 units, which has a sales value of £100 000. A loss is shown below the horizontal axis and a profit is shown above.

(iv) Contribution is needed to provide the revenue to pay the fixed expenses, and if there is no production and no sales, the business will make a loss of £16 000. The point at which the diagonal line crosses the horizontal is the *break-even point* or position where the contribution from a certain volume of output and sales equals the fixed cost. The marginal cost statement on p. 190 and below shows the results at various levels of activity.

Marginal cost statement (continued)

	£	%	£	%	£	%	£	%
Contribution	14 400	36	16 002	36	28 800	36	36 000	36
Less Fixed cost	16 000	40	16 000	36	16 000	20	16 000	16
Profit	(£ 1 600)	(4)	£ 2	B/E*	£12 800	16	£20 000	20

* Break-even point.

This statement shows that the break-even point is at approximately 4 445 units. Alternatively, this result can be obtained from the graph by interpolation, as shown in Fig. 8.4.

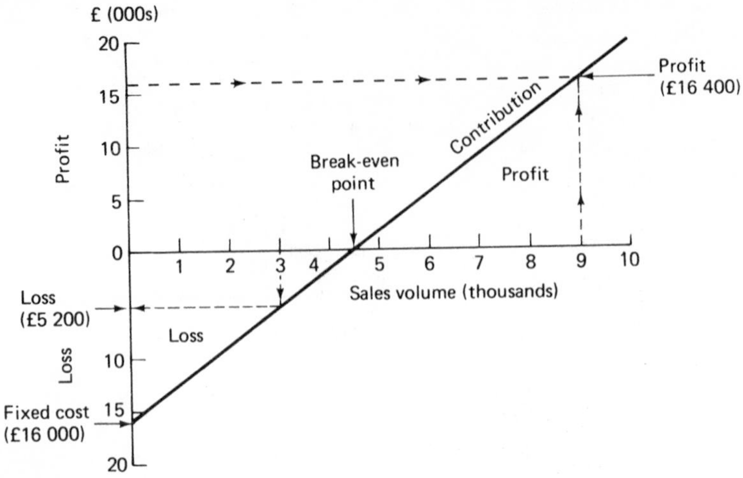

Fig. 8.5 How contribution reaches break-even point and goes into profit
Note: At various levels of output (assuming all output is sold) we can see what the profit or loss situation will be, by drawing in perpendiculars from the horizontal axis to the graph. Thus, at sales of 3 000 units the loss is seen to be £5 200 and at sales of 9 000 units the profit will be £16 400. The point where the graph crosses the horizontal line is the break-even point. At this output - just below 4 500 units - the contribution achieved by the output is sufficient to cover all the fixed costs and we are about to move into a profitable situation. From now on the contribution from further sales will be a contribution to profits.

The break-even point is also the stage where the income from sales exactly equals the total costs or expenditure, and is the point where the contribution from sales equals the fixed cost and where there is neither a profit nor a loss. This is illustrated in Fig. 8.5.

8.5 Break-even analysis

Profit can be measured by analysing costs into fixed and variable categories, and determining profit or loss at varying levels of activity. Break-even analysis operates by furnishing details of the contribution which the various products or processes are making to the profitability of the enterprise. Such analysis helps management to formulate its policy in deciding what products to manufacture and the prices at which they should be sold. It helps in 'make or buy' decisions, in problems connected with conditions of slump and seasonal trading and when closure is under consideration.

Margin of safety

This is illustrated in Fig. 8.6. It is the amount by which sales exceed the break-even point of sales. If there is excess capacity, it could represent the maximum

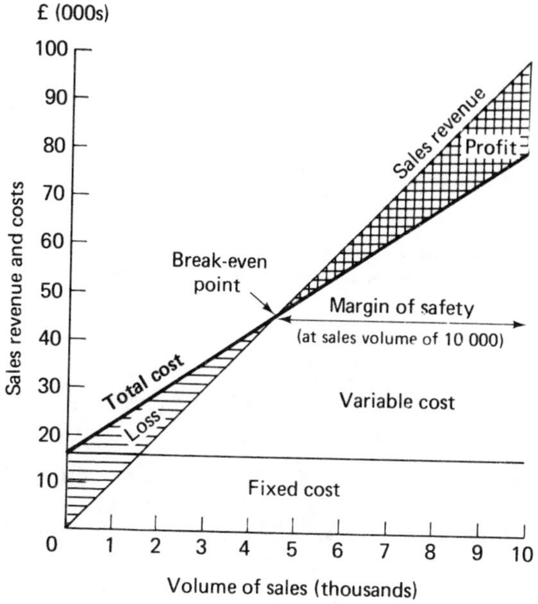

Fig. 8.6 A break-even chart

Notes:

(i) The variable costs do not begin at the origin of the graph, since fixed costs have already been incurred.

(ii) The variable costs, therefore, start above the fixed costs, and rise uniformly with the volume of sales, an extra unit of variable cost being incurred with each extra unit of output.

(iii) The sales revenue graph shows the income from sales. It starts at 0 on both scales, since there is no income when there are no sales, and rises uniformly as the volume of sales rises.

(iv) The total cost line (i.e. the fixed costs and variable costs together) will eventually be crossed by the sales revenue line, provided the goods have been correctly priced to yield a profit. The point where this crossing occurs is the break-even point (where sales revenue is covering total costs). From this point on we shall move into profit.

(v) The chart shows the profit, loss, break-even point and margin of safety. Losses are of course only made if sales are less than the break-even volume. At sales levels above the break-even volume, profits are made.

---

degree of security which the business could provide if the full capacity was utilised. A fairly wide margin is needed in order to cope with competition and changes in demand, and the extent of the margin indicates the amount of turnover which, if lost, would place the business in an insecure position.

The width of the margin depends on the amount of fixed cost and contribution, and the turnover achieved. Each of these factors can affect the degree of safety. For example, an increase in selling price increases the contribution and improves the margin of safety, whereas a reduction in selling price has the opposite effect, by reducing the contribution/sales ratio and requiring additional volume or a reduction in costs to maintain the margin of safety. If fixed costs are increased while contribution and sales volume remain stable, the break-even point moves to the right and reduces the margin of safety.

8.6 Break-even point

At break-even point we are interested in three aspects: (i) sales value; (ii) sales volume; (iii) the margin of safety.

(i) Sales value at break-even point (BEP) This can be expressed as being equal to:

$$\frac{\text{Fixed cost}}{1 - \dfrac{\text{Variable cost (Marginal cost)}}{\text{Total sales value}}}$$

Taking total sales at £100 000, for 10 000 units, marginal cost at £64 000 (made up of direct material £30 000, direct wages £20 000 and variable overhead £14 000), and fixed cost at £16 000, we find:

$$\text{Sales value at BEP} = \frac{£16\,000}{1 - \dfrac{£64\,000}{£100\,000}} = \frac{£16\,000 \times £100\,000}{£36\,000}$$

$$= \underline{\underline{£44\,444}}$$

An alternative formula derived from the above is:

$$\text{Sales at BEP} = \text{Fixed cost} \times \frac{\text{Total sales}}{\text{Contribution}}$$

$$= £16\,000 \times \frac{£100\,000}{£36\,000} \quad \left(\begin{aligned}\text{Contribution} &= £100\,000 - £64\,000\\ &= \underline{\underline{£36\,000}}\end{aligned}\right)$$

$$= \underline{\underline{£44\,444}}$$

The sales value at break-even point can also be found by using the contribution/sales ratio.

$$\text{Sales at BEP} = \frac{\text{Fixed cost}}{\text{C/S ratio}} \quad \left(\text{C/S ratio} = \frac{£36\,000}{£100\,000} \times 100 = \underline{\underline{36\%}}\right)$$

$$= \frac{£16\,000}{36} \times 100 = \underline{\underline{£44\,444}}$$

or, taking 36% as 0.36:

$$\frac{£16\,000}{0.36} = \underline{\underline{£44\,444}}$$

(ii) The number of units sold at break-even point This can be calculated by dividing the fixed cost by the contribution per unit.

The contribution per unit is $\frac{\text{Contribution}}{\text{Units sold}} = \frac{£36\,000}{10\,000} = \underline{\underline{£3.60}}$

Therefore:

$$\text{Number of units sold at break-even point} = \frac{\text{Fixed cost}}{\text{Contribution per unit}}$$

$$= \frac{£16\,000}{£3.60} = \underline{\underline{4\,444 \text{ units at } £10 \text{ each}}}$$

(iii) The margin of safety This can be calculated by dividing the profit by the contribution/sales ratio.

$$\frac{\text{Profit}}{\text{C/S ratio}} = \frac{£20\,000}{0.36}\left(\frac{£20\,000}{36} \times 100\right)$$

= Sales value of $\underline{\underline{£55\,556}}$ (Sales *less* Sales at break-even point)

Another type of break-even chart is one which has the variable cost at the base, showing more clearly the marginal cost and the contribution (see Fig. 8.7, p. 196).

8.7 Marginal costing and break-even analysis

In the break-even charts shown in Figs. 8.6 and 8.7 the graphs of costs and revenues have been shown as straight lines for simplicity. In real life the graphs of costs and revenues might be curved slightly because, for example, discounts may be offered to customers placing bulk orders, or discounts may be obtained from suppliers by ordering raw materials in bulk.

(a) The limitations of break-even charts

Cost behaviour is the response of cost to a variety of influences. Therefore when working out a cost–contribution–sales analysis, we must take into account any factors which may have an effect on the results, and realise that the break-even graph is only a pictorial expression which relates costs and profit to activity. The graph tends to over-simplify the real situation as there are other effects besides volume.

(a) Costs and revenues are shown as straight lines, but selling prices are not necessarily fixed, and the revenue may change depending on the quantities of goods sold direct, sold through agents and sold at a discount. The slope of the graph will not be constant but will vary according to the circumstances.

(b) Variable costs may not be proportional to volume because of overtime working, because of reductions in the price of materials when bulk

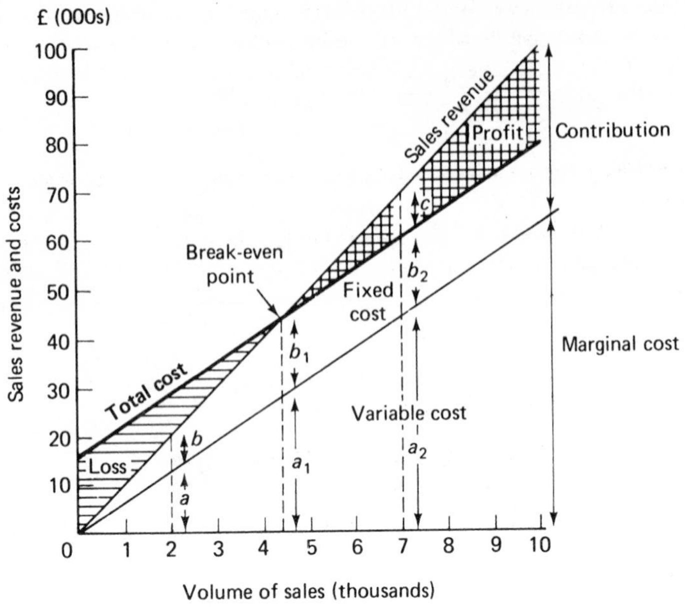

Fig. 8.7 A contribution (break-even) chart

Notes:

(i) At any volume of sales a vertical line from the sales axis to the sales revenue line shows:

(*a*) the recovery of the marginal cost, and

(*b*) the contribution.

(ii) Thus, for a sales volume of 2 000 units, the vertical line shows (*a*) the recovery of the marginal cost and (*b*) part recovery of fixed costs.

(iii) At break-even point the vertical line shows (a_1) the recovery of the marginal cost and (b_1) contribution towards the whole of the fixed costs.

(iv) At a sales volume of 7 000 units the vertical line shows (a_2) the recovery of variable costs, (b_2) the recovery of fixed costs and (*c*) a contribution towards profit.

discounts are negotiated, or because of an increase in the price of materials when demand outstrips supply. If sales are made over a wider area, distribution costs tend to rise considerably.

(c) Fixed costs do not always remain constant during the period of activity.

(d) The efficiency of production or a change in production methods has an effect on variable costs.

(e) The various quantities of different goods sold (the *sales mix*) may not change the total sales value to any great extent but they may alter the amount of profit depending on the proportion of low- and high-margin goods sold.

A graph can, therefore, be drawn from the available information and may be based on assumptions which are well-founded, but manufacturing and business conditions are continually changing and a reappraisal is necessary from time to time.

(b) High fixed/low variable cost compared with low fixed/high variable cost

It has been shown in Fig. 8.5 and the calculations in Unit 8.6 that the margin of safety is approximately 56 per cent of sales value in the case under discussion.

	£	
Sales	100 000	
Sales at BEP	44 444	
Safety margin	£ 55 556	= 55.556%

This has been achieved in a situation where the fixed cost is relatively low and where the variable cost is fairly high. This is now compared with production where the fixed cost is much higher and there is a smaller segment of variable cost. The following costs are used in this example:

	£	%	
Sales	100 000	100	
Direct materials	20 000	20	
Direct wages	10 000	10	
Variable overhead	10 000	10	
Marginal cost	40 000	40	
Contribution	60 000	60	(C/S ratio)
Fixed cost	40 000	40	
Profit	£20 000	20	

$$\text{Sales at break-even point} = \frac{\text{Fixed cost}}{\text{C/S ratio}} = \frac{£40\,000}{60} \times 100$$

$$= £66\,667$$

The sales at break-even point are 66.667 per cent of sales volume, which indicates that the margin of safety is approximately 33 per cent compared with 56 per cent in the previous example, and the C/S ratio is 60 per cent compared with 36 per cent. Profit is the same at £20 000. If it is assumed that production and sales increase by 10 per cent the details are as follows:

Cost statement

	Low fixed cost			*High fixed cost*		
	£	£	%	£	£	%
Sales		110 000	100.0		110 000	100.0
Direct material	33 000		30.0	22 000		20.0
Direct wages	22 000		20.0	11 000		10.0
Variable overhead	15 400		14.0	11 000		10.0
Marginal cost		70 400	64.0		44 000	40.0
Contribution		39 600	36.0		66 000	60.0
Less Fixed cost		16 000	14.5		40 000	36.4
Profit		£23 600	21.5		£26 000	23.6

Reduction in fixed cost as a percentage of sales
16% to 14.5% = 1.5%   40% to 36.4% = 3.6%

Increase in profit   £3 600   £6 000

These figures show that for an increase of 10 per cent in turnover, the profit in the business with high fixed costs is growing faster than in the business with low fixed costs. The effect on profit in high and low fixed cost situations is shown in Fig. 8.8.

(c) The multi-product graph or sequential profit graph

Profit graphs tend to show the contribution as a straight line, and at one particular angle. When several products are manufactured this type of graph obscures the fact that there is a product mix, with different sales levels and different amounts of contribution earned by each of the products. The *multi-product graph* takes account of this situation and shows the contribution line as contribution accumulates for each of the products or product groups. It illustrates the amount of sales and contribution provided by each product, and as it extends from one product to the other it is a cumulative figure, but the individual sales and contribution can be read off the chart.

The slope of the product contribution line indicates the contribution/sales ratio and the graph is constructed by beginning with the highest ratio and finishing with any product which shows a negative contribution. This choice of sequence gives the graph its alternative name of *sequential profit graph*. A profit graph is shown in Fig. 8.9 (p. 200) based on the following information:

Product	Sales	C/S ratio	Contribution
	£	%	£
A	300 000	45	135 000
B	240 000	60	144 000
C	60 000	(15)	(9 000)
D	150 000	20	30 000

[( ) indicates a negative value.]

(continued on p. 200)

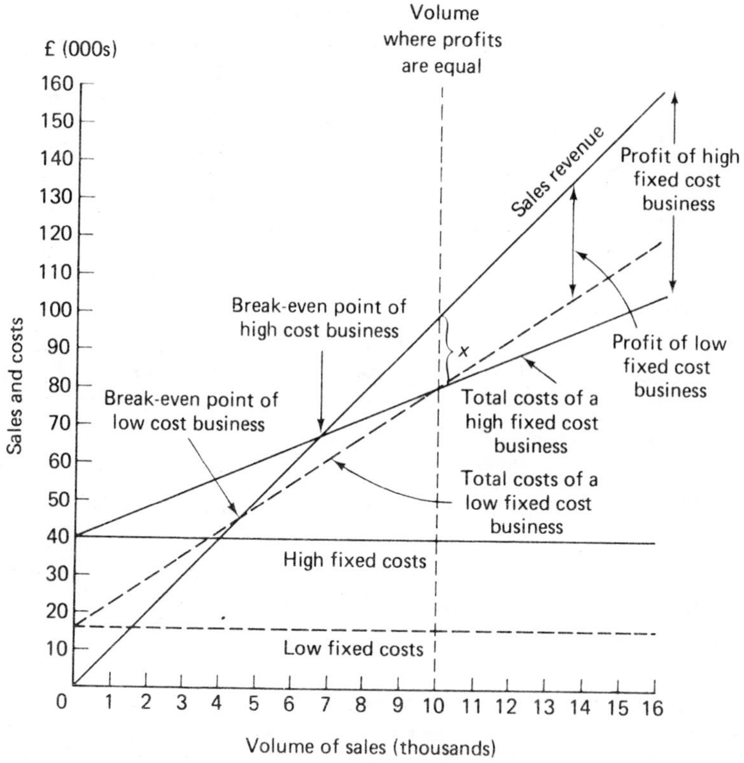

Fig. 8.8 A break-even chart – effects of high and low fixed costs

Notes:

(i) The fixed costs and total costs of a firm with low fixed costs are shown by a dotted line.

(ii) The fixed costs and total costs of a firm with high fixed costs are shown by a continuous line.

(iii) The sales revenue is deemed to be the same for both firms.

(iv) Normal sales are shown as a vertical dotted line at a figure of 10 000 units. At this level both firms are making the same profit (x), and have the same total costs. Note that the two total cost lines intersect at this point.

(v) As turnover increases, the profits of the high fixed costs firm draw quickly away from those of the other business. In boom conditions this firm does well, but in a recession it is vulnerable. Its break-even point is not reached until after that of the low fixed cost firm, and it has a smaller margin of safety.

(vi) As turnover increases, the profits of the low fixed cost firm are less buoyant than those of the high fixed cost firm, but in a recession it is less vulnerable. It has a greater margin of safety since its break-even point is reached early, at a lower level of activity. This gives it greater flexibility as it can stand a recession better than the high fixed cost firm.

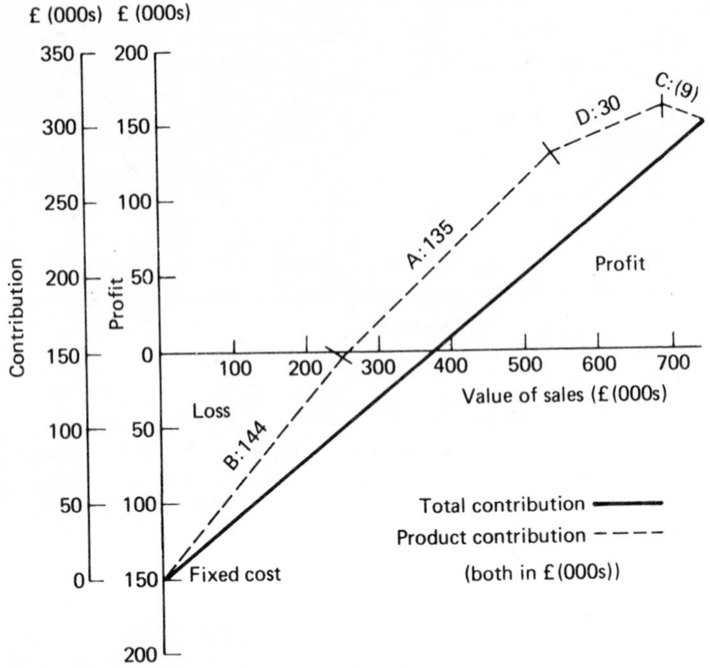

Fig. 8.9 A multi-product graph or sequential profit graph

Notes:

(i) The graph starts below the zero profit point, where losses of £150 000 fixed costs are being suffered. At this point the contribution is at zero on the contribution scale.

(ii) Total contribution is shown by the solid black line, but our sequential profit graph is the dotted line. It begins with the graph of B's contribution, which is the highest of the four, and therefore shows the steepest gradient.

(iii) This brings the graph almost to break-even point, but it does not quite reach the horizontal axis where profits could begin.

(iv) There then follows A's contribution, which is almost as good, and the graph moves into profit. This is then followed by D's contribution, at a smaller gradient, while C's contribution is negative, and actually reduces the profits.

(v) Naturally the final part of the sequential graph must meet the total contribution graph as they are both recording the same total.

Product	Sales	C/S ratio	Contribution
	£	%	£
	750 000	40	300 000
Less Fixed cost			150 000
Profit			£150 000

Contribution accumulates as follows:

Product	Sales	C/S ratio	Contribution	Sales	Cumulative contribution
	£	%	£	£	£
B	240 000	60	£144 000	240 000	144 000
A	300 000	45	135 000	540 000	279 000
D	150 000	20	30 000	690 000	309 000
C	60 000	(15)	(9 000)	750 000	300 000
	£750 000	40	300 000		
Less Fixed cost			150 000		
Profit			£150 000		

8.8 Opportunity cost in management accounting

Those who are familiar with economics will know what is meant by opportunity cost. Any company or firm only has so many resources at its command, and the question arises as to which of the various opportunities for using those resources should be pursued. If we opt to produce product A we shall be unable to turn out product B. The cost of the opportunity we pursue is the lost opportunity we reject. The opportunity cost is defined in *Official Terminology* as 'the value of a benefit sacrificed in favour of an alternative course of action'. When cash is used to finance a particular form of activity or to purchase materials or capital goods, it may well be possible to invest in something else instead, which would produce a greater return. For example, large sums may be used to purchase materials which are held in stock for a long time. The money tied up in stocks, or at least some of it, could probably have been used to finance some more profitable form of activity. The money tied up is therefore an opportunity cost, and the income which is lost is based on the average time that materials are held before use, and the use of a rate of interest which is considered appropriate at the time.

Opportunity costs are in effect connected with policy decisions; for example, whether to make or buy a particular product (see Unit 8.10), or whether to use other designs, or manufacture using different methods. It is necessary to make comparisons and to use estimates or budgets related to the project or items involved. One can use the *incremental cost method* which limits the items of cost to those that change, because there is no point in including costs on each estimate which are the same. This incremental cost method is often called *differential costing*.

Differential costing is a technique which uses marginal costs in the preparation of *ad hoc* information in which only the differences in cost and income between alternative courses of action are taken into consideration. There may be problems and constraints which limit the production of a particular product, and investigations may be carried out to consider alternative courses of making or buying. Whereas marginal costing refers to the routine system which ascertains marginal costs, where only variable costs are charged to cost units and fixed costs are written off in full against the contribution for that period, differential costing uses the information provided by marginal costs to consider alternative courses of action.

In profit planning, it may be necessary to consider the effect of price changes or to calculate the volume required to attain a certain increase in profits. It should be remembered that fixed costs and profits are interrelated as they represent contribution, and as sales and contribution are in direct proportion to each other, the C/S ratio can be used to estimate the sales required to attain a particular profit.

For example, with present sales of 10 000 units at £10 each, fixed costs of £16 000, a C/S ratio of 36 per cent and profits of £20 000, what volume and sales value will be needed to increase profits by 45 per cent?

$$45\% \text{ of } £20\,000 = £9\,000 \text{ (Total profit } £29\,000)$$

$$\text{Sales required} = \frac{\text{Fixed cost} + \text{Profit}}{\text{C/S ratio}}$$

$$= \frac{£16\,000 + £29\,000}{36\%}$$

$$= \frac{£45\,000}{36} \times 100 = \underline{\underline{£125\,000}} \text{ (12 500 units)}$$

This is an increase of 2 500 units at £10 each, which is equal to extra sales amounting to £25 000. As fixed costs have already been covered in the current turnover the extra could have been calculated as follows:

$$\frac{\text{Extra profit}}{\text{C/S ratio}} = \frac{£9\,000}{36} \times 100 = \underline{\underline{£25\,000}} \text{ (2 500 units)}$$

With reference to make or buy, the comparison should be between the outside supplier's price and the marginal cost of one's own manufacture up to the same stage. If other factors are favourable it will be profitable to manufacture when the marginal cost is lower than the purchase price. If two or more methods of manufacture are possible the marginal cost of each method should be ascertained. The most advantageous and profitable method should take into account the method yielding the greatest contribution per unit of limiting factor of output. Remember that the word 'contribution' means the contribution made by the sale of a unit of product to the coverage of fixed costs and to profit (once the break-even point has been reached).

When the bought-out price is less than the marginal cost, it will be profitable to buy from an outside supplier, but care has to be taken especially where a number of different products are manufactured. A statement can be prepared showing the marginal cost of the products. The total costs and further figures can be shown, giving such details as the selling price, contribution per unit, profit per unit, contribution per man hour, profit per man hour, contribution per machine hour or profit per machine hour.

Pricing decisions

In certain industries where there is a large amount of unused capacity, such as in undertakings carrying out jobbing work, it is often necessary to accept orders with a low contribution in order to provide work. In extreme circumstances any reasonable amount over marginal cost will provide contribution towards the fixed costs, enabling the firm to break even and possibly show an acceptable profit. Unused capacity represents the loss of potential contribution, and as long as future business will not be harmed by the acceptance of lower prices, it is often beneficial to reduce the normal price. Trade can expand by a variation of selling prices, and the most profitable relationship between costs, prices and volume of business should be ascertained.

Proposals to reduce prices in order to increase sales should always be carefully investigated. This is because of the additional volume required to compensate for the decline in prices. A reduction in price reduces the C/S ratio, and shortens the margin of safety, because the break-even point is reached at a much greater volume of sales.

For example, if the unit price of £10 is reduced by 10 per cent to £9, the example given on p. 202 would appear as:

	£	
Sales 10 000 units @ £9	90 000	
Less Marginal cost	64 000	
Contribution	26 000	(C/S ratio 28.89%)
Less Fixed cost	16 000	
Profit	£10 000	

In order to maintain profits, extra volume is required.

$$\text{Sales required} = \frac{\text{Fixed cost} + \text{Profit}}{\text{C/S ratio}}$$

$$= \frac{£16\,000 + £20\,000}{28.89\%}$$

$$= \underline{\underline{£124\,611}} \quad \text{(13 846 units @ £9 each)}$$

3 846 extra units will have to be sold just to hold the profit at £20 000. In connection with pricing, remember that a decrease in fixed or variable costs will improve the margin of safety as the break-even point will be reached at a smaller volume of sales.

8.9 Limiting factor

Unless a plan or forecast is capable of fulfilment, it is a waste of time trying to calculate turnover and profits and to project them on a break-even chart. A *limiting factor* is the factor in the activities of an undertaking which, at a particular time, or over a period, limits the volume of output. The limiting factor is sometimes called the *key factor* or the *principal budget factor*. Marginal costing has been examined generally on the basis that only one product is manufactured, but a company may make a number of products with different rates of contribution and different production problems.

Sales are frequently a limiting factor because of lack of demand and other causes. Other limiting factors are a shortage of skilled labour or materials, a shortage of space or of suitable plant and equipment, or a lack of capital to provide the necessary facilities. In such circumstances, the area of constraint should be examined together with the contribution so that it can be seen which products are yielding the greatest individual contribution, and what steps can be taken to improve the situation. For example, floor space may be a limit to expansion and therefore it is advisable to examine departments or products and to compare the contribution provided, and to rank these products in order of profitability. Consider Example 8.2.

EXAMPLE 8.2

Product	Area (m^2)	Contribution provided £	Contribution per m^2 £	Ranking
A	5 000	22 000	4.40	1
B	4 800	10 800	2.25	3
C	10 200	26 520	2.60	2
	20 000	£59 320		

On the assumption that 2 000 square metres of floor space used for producing product B could be adapted to make product A without any changes in fixed costs or selling prices, and if the turnover of A increases by 40 per cent, the results would be as follows:

Product	Area (m^2)	Contribution provided £
A	7 000	30 800
B	2 800	6 300
C	10 200	26 520
	20 000	63 620
Less Present contribution		59 320
Increased contribution		£ 4 300

This is a simplification of the practical problems because there may be other factors determining the turnover, such as sales of product B having to be maintained in order to retain the customers who are purchasing our other products and, if B is not available, may go elsewhere for A and C. Limiting conditions must be used in the best possible way, and when deciding what product or combination of products to manufacture, each item must be examined to determine the contribution per unit of limiting factor.

An analysis to show the contribution per unit of limiting factor should precede the forecast of a sales and production budget as it may be possible to change the normal sales mix in order to improve profitability. The analysis below indicates that product X has the best contribution to sales at 38½ per cent and the highest contribution per £ of materials, whereas product Z has the best contribution per £ of wages. Decisions will be made after consideration of limiting factors and other conditions which may arise in a trading period.

Analysis of cost of production and sales								*Contribution per £ of*		
Product	Materials (£'000)	Wages (£'000)	Variable overhead (£'000)	Marginal cost (£'000)	Contribution (£'000)	Sales (£'000)		Sales £	Material £	Wages £
X	85	35	40	160	100	260		0.385	1.176	2.857
Y	160	90	90	340	180	520		0.346	1.125	2.000
Z	95	30	80	205	95	300		0.317	1.000	3.167
	£340	£155	£210	£705	£375	£1 080				

8.10 Make or buy decisions

If there is a shortage of capacity the remedy is to expand or to purchase certain items from an outside source. The amount of capital expenditure and the likely cost savings must be carefully considered. Purchasing may be advisable where suppliers have specialised equipment and can supply at reduced prices, but the effect of fixed costs on internally made products must be taken into account. The cost comparison should be between the supplier's price and the marginal cost of producing the goods on the premises. This is because it is assumed that the fixed costs have already been incurred and that the other costs are the variable costs. If there is a limiting factor, products which earn the highest rate of contribution per unit of limiting factor should be retained.

When facilities are available for production to be carried out at an economic price, it is advantageous to make the product oneself. Complete control is established over the quality of the materials used, the manufacturing process and delivery of the final product. If a product manufacturing process or design is unique, it may also be essential to make the item in order to maintain secrecy.

When a product is manufactured under licence, there may be a condition that all work is carried out by the licensee, and the item has to be made and not bought. The disadvantages of buying often mean that drawings, specifications, patterns, jigs, tools and dies have to be supplied, as well as advice on the manufacturing process. There is also the problem of late deliveries and the suspension of assembly when parts for the main product have not arrived. If items such as castings are supplied, and some are unsatisfactory and need to be replaced, there may be a considerable delay in completing products.

Sub-contractors may accept work and give satisfactory service when their business is slack, but may provide poor service when their own trade returns to normal.

If it is discovered that certain parts can be purchased at or near the making price, it is advantageous to buy them only when the production facilities made available can earn more than they did under the other process.

Cost of bought-out items and cost of production

Article	A	B	C
	£	£	£
Purchase price	18.00	35.00	45.00
Production:			
Man hours	4	5	5
Machine hours	1	2	4
Cost:	£	£	£
Marginal cost	20	25	30
Fixed cost	4	8	10
Total cost	£24.00	£33.00	£40.00
Excess of purchase price over marginal cost:			
Per article	(2.00)	10.00	15.00
Per man hour	(0.50)	2.00	3.00
Per machine hour	(2.00)	5.00	3.75

With article A, the purchase price is less than the marginal cost, so it is profitable to buy outside. Article A also shows the lowest rate of contribution per man hour, and if manpower is the limiting factor, again this article could be purchased outside. If manpower is so short that further outside purchases must be made, then article B should be purchased outside. When machine power is the limiting factor, A is again the first choice for outside purchase, since it yields the lowest rate of contribution per machine, and C is the second choice at a contribution of £3.75.

To give a further example, the one shown below refers to a manufacturing company producing four different components. Consideration is being given to purchasing one or more of these components from outside suppliers.

	Units	Hours per week	Material	Labour	Variable overheads	Fixed overheads	Selling price
			£	£	£	£	£
Part A	65	300	850	800	400	550	3 250
Part B	200	1 050	220	2 750	750	1 080	6 400
Part C	40	150	300	500	200	300	1 560
Part D	80	100	250	350	150	250	1 400

Purchase prices: A £2 300; B £2 600; C £1 000; D £650; as offered by possible suppliers.

Costings if products are made by the company:

Product	*A*	*B*	*C*	*D*	
Units	65	200	40	80	
Hours	300	1 050	150	100	
					Total
	£	£	£	£	£
Material	850	220	300	250	1 620
Labour	800	2 750	500	350	4 400
Variable overhead	400	750	200	150	1 500
Marginal cost	2 050	3 720	1 000	750	7 520
Fixed cost	550	1 080	300	250	2 180
Total cost	2 600	4 800	1 300	1 000	9 700
Selling price	3 250	6 400	1 560	1 400	12 610
Profit	650	1 600	260	400	2 910
Purchase prices on offer	2 300	2 600	1 000	650	6 550
Less Marginal cost	2 050	3 720	1 000	750	7 520
	250	(1 120)	Nil	(100)	(970)
	£	£	£	£	
Profit per unit	10	8	6.50	5	
Profit per man hour	£2.17	£1.52	£1.73	£4.00	
	£	£	£	£	
Contribution	1 200	2 680	560	650	
Contribution per unit	£18.46	£13.40	£14.00	£8.13	
Contribution per man hour	£4.00	£2.55	£3.73	£6.50	

The company is producing four different components in conditions of full capacity and only product A has a marginal cost below the bought-out price. Of the others product B provides the largest amount of contribution towards fixed overheads and profit and the lowest contribution per man hour, whereas product D has the highest contribution per man hour.

There may be limiting factors or other problems and the company must decide to purchase in the most effective way and increase production of the product or products showing the best return. It will be necessary to direct the sales effort to those particular products.

8.11 Exercises

1. George Williams is a manufacturer. He prepares a budget on a monthly basis, which provides the following information:

   - Budgeted profit is £6 000;

- Fixed costs are expected to be £10 000 per month;
- Selling price has been set at £10 per unit;
- Variable costs are £8 per unit;
- The business has an output capacity of 10 000 units per month, but at the above selling price can expect to produce and sell 8 000 units per month.

George has asked you to help him to consider the possibility of changes which could occur within his business environment to affect his budget.

(a) (i) Using the budget information George has supplied, produce a break-even chart.

(ii) Advise George of the advantages and disadvantages of presenting data in this form.

(b) Consider each of the following assumptions in isolation. For each assumption (i, ii, iii and iv) calculate the effect on *both* the break-even point *and* the budgeted profit.

(i) **Increase in output and sales.** Suppose that due to reduction in competition, George estimates he could produce and sell 9 000 instead of 8 000 units.

(ii) **Reduction in selling price.** Due to a reduction in the selling prices of competitors, George needs to reduce his own selling price to £9.60 in order to maintain production and sales of 8 000 units per month.

(iii) **An increase in variable cost per unit.** As a result of a new union agreement on wage rates, variable costs per unit of output will increase to £8.50.

(iv) **Reduction in fixed costs.** Due to economies in administration the fixed costs will be reduced by £2 000 to £8 000.

2. *(a)* Explain what is meant in accountancy when reference is made to the break-even point.

(b) State the information which can be obtained from a break-even chart.

3. Gadgets (Camside) Ltd produce a quarterly budget for their patent can-opener as follows:

		Per unit		Total
Sales (65 000 units)	£	£		£
		5.00		325 000
Cost of sales (production)				
Variable	1.50		£97 500	
Fixed	2.00		£130 000	
		3.50		227 500
		1.50		97 500
Selling and administration (fixed cost)		0.25		16 250
Profit		1.25		£81 250

Sales, stocks and production for the first two quarters are as follows:

> Sales are 59 000 units in the first quarter and 62 000 units in the second quarter; production amounted to 69 000 units in the first quarter and 59 000 units in the second quarter. There was no opening stock at the beginning of quarter one but the closing stock in quarter one was 10 000 units, and at the end of the second quarter the stock was 7 000 units.

You are required to produce a Trading and Profit and Loss Account in tabular form for the first and second quarters of the year using the method known as marginal costing.

4. The production records of a department which manufactures a single product are given below for the three months October, November and December 19..:

	October	November	December
	£	£	£
Prime cost	67 500	78 750	101 250
Overhead	62 500	66 250	73 750
Total	130 000	145 000	175 000
Production (units)	9 000	10 500	13 500

(a) Examine the above figures in connection with their behaviour and use them to obtain any information that may be useful in the control of costs.

(b) Prepare a simple cost statement to show the costs in a month when production is recorded at 12 000 units.

(c) Show by the use of diagrams the behaviour of costs as represented above.

5. A business manufactures a product with variable cost of £8, which is sold for £12. There are fixed costs which amount to £35 000 per annum, and sales which vary between 8 000 and 11 000 units. Consideration is being given to a new production process which will increase fixed costs to £60 000 but which will enable an improved product to be marketed, at possible sales of 15 000 units. The variable costs are expected to remain at the same value as those in the original process. In order to compare the costs and profit of the original process, A, and the new process, B, three levels of sales are to be taken:

	A	B
	Units	Units
Level (i)	8 000	13 000
Level (ii)	9 000	14 000
Level (iii)	11 000	15 000

(a) Prepare a statement of sales, costs and profits for each process (this should be shown in columnar form).

(b) From the information in *(a)*, construct two charts of sales, costs and profits.

(c) Recommend to management a course of action which they should take in view of the information gathered from *(a)* and *(b)*.

6. A business has fixed costs which amount to £18 000 and variable expenses which are 20 per cent of sales value. The cost of sales which represents the sale of 60 000 articles is a variable cost and the gross profit is 60 per cent. You are required to calculate the break-even point and to draw up a break-even chart after selecting a suitable sales revenue.

7. What do you understand by the term *limiting factor*? Explain the ways in which this condition can affect the profitability of a business.

8. A partnership was formed on 1 January by A and B, with A contributing £60 000 and B £42 000. They also secured a loan on that date for £30 000 at 15 per cent per annum. The partners expect a return on their capitals of $33\frac{1}{3}$ per cent in order to remunerate them for their services to the business and to cover a reasonable rate of interest on their capital. Premises have been taken over at an annual rent of £15 000, rates are £1 250 half-yearly, and insurance costs £500 annually.

Equipment was purchased on 1 January for £50 000 and this is to carry depreciation at the rate of 15 per cent. Variable costs other than materials are 20 per cent of sales value. 80 000 units are to be sold at prices which are fixed by multiplying material cost by 250 per cent.

Calculate *(a)* the fixed cost, *(b)* the total return required by the partners, *(c)* the contribution/sales ratio and contribution, *(d)* total sales and sales at break-even point and *(e)* total cost; also *(f)* draw up a break-even chart.

9. A manufacturing company operating in a single region contemplates expanding its activities by stages to cover the whole country. Market research and extensive cost investigation indicate that the following figures will be applicable to the first stage of expansion:

Additional sales annually	70 000 units at £10 each
Additional buildings required	£600 000
Additional equipment	£900 000

Depreciation of buildings (5 per cent per annum) and of equipment (10 per cent per annum) is charged using the straight-line method.

Fixed overhead, other than depreciation, is estimated to increase by £80 000. Sales and costs before expansion are as follows:

Annual sales	90 000 units at £10 each
Fixed overhead, annually	£200 000
Materials annually	£200 000
Wages and variable overhead, annually	£400 000

The proposed scale of operations is expected to yield some minor economies in material purchases for all of the output, so that the proposed sales total will be reached if a further £110 000 annually is spent on materials. Similarly, other economies will result in a less than proportional increase in the wages and variable overhead, upon which annual outlay will be increased by £90 000.

(a) Prepare a statement setting out the present and proposed costs and indicating (i) unit sales, (ii) total sales value, (iii) marginal cost, (iv) contribution, (v) profit, (vi) contribution/sales ratio and (vii) sales at break-even point.

(b) Draw up a break-even chart to show the results as planned for the first stage of expansion.

10. *(a)* XY Limited is operating at a normal level of activity of 80 per cent which represents an output of 5 600 units. The statement shown below gives basic details of cost and sales at three operating levels of activity. In view of the depressed market in which the company may have to operate in the near future, the production director believes that it may be necessary to operate at 60 per cent level of activity.

As management accountant of XY Limited, you are required to prepare a forecast statement to show the marginal costs and contribution at the proposed level of activity of 60 per cent.

	Level of activity		
	70%	80%	90%
	£	£	£
Direct materials	73 500	84 000	94 500
Direct wages	44 100	50 400	56 700
Overhead	45 400	49 600	53 800
Sales	196 000	224 000	252 000

(b) Explain the meaning of contribution and discuss its relevance in a marginal costing system.

(CIMA)

11. *(a)* 'Fixed costs are really variable: the more you produce the less they become.' Explain the above statement and state whether or not you agree with it.

(b) You are required to sketch a separate graph for each of the items listed below in order to indicate the behaviour of the expense. Graph paper need not be used but your axes must be labelled.

(i) Supervisory labour;
(ii) depreciation of plant on a machine hour basis;
(iii) planned preventive maintenance plus unexpected maintenance;
(iv) monthly pay of a salesman who receives a salary of £3 000 per annum plus a commission of 1 per cent paid on his previous month's sales when they exceed £20 000; assume that his previous month's sales totalled £30 000.

(CIMA)

12. Using the information given below, prepare profit statements for the months of March and April using *(a)* marginal costing and *(b)* absorption costing.

Per unit:

	£
Sales price	50
Direct materials cost	18
Direct wages	4
Variable production overhead	3

Per month

	£
Fixed production overhead	99 000
Fixed selling expenses	14 000
Fixed administration expenses	26 000

Variable selling expenses were 10 per cent of sales value.
Normal capacity was 11 000 units per month.

	March units	April units
Sales	10 000	12 000
Production	12 000	10 000

(CIMA)

13. *(a)* From the data given below you are required to present on graph paper a contribution/sales graph to show the expected company performance based on the budget for one year.

	£(000s)
Sales	600
Marginal cost	350
Fixed cost	150

Determine the break-even point and the margin of safety.

(b) Discuss briefly the limitations of a contribution/sales graph.

(CIMA)

14. A company manufactures four products which overall show a contribution/sales ratio of approximately 50 per cent. A, C and D make a contribution towards the fixed costs and profit but product B shows a negative contribution.

You are required to draw up a contribution/sales graph to show the cumulative effect of sales and contribution from the following information:

	Sales	Contribution/sales ratio
	£	%
A	120 000	38
B	30 000	(10)
C	70 000	42
D	180 000	70

Fixed costs amount to £100 000.

UNIT 9

Variance accounting (standard costing)

9.1 Introduction

A mass of cost data arises as a result of business transactions and manufacturing processes. This information is historical and either represents actual cost or records past performance. If this information is collected periodically, the cost of performance in the current period can be compared with similar details recorded previously, but if there is no previous record, the cost accountant has to accept what is received without question. When comparisons are made and variations are disclosed, there is no real evidence of inefficient performance or of the payment of uneconomic prices because no standard of measurement is available to check the cost or the performance. For example, costs may be distorted by changes in the volume of production, and variations in buying or selling prices may hide the fact that productivity has improved or that inefficiency has occurred. No information is available to prove that the best use is being made of materials and labour or of plant and equipment, because no planning or investigation has been made to establish standards or to install procedures to measure the efficiency of the business. Variance accounting, also known as standard costing, is a method of overcoming these difficulties by setting standards for a business. The CIMA handbook *Official Terminology* has this definition of standard costing: 'It is a control technique which compares standard costs and revenues with actual results to obtain variances which are used to stimulate improved performance.'

An analysis is made of the causes of the variations so that, where necessary, corrective action can be taken to improve the situation. This is to maintain efficiency by executive action and is called *management by exceptions*. Management is not concerned with the mass of data which is equivalent to standard cost or standard performance, but only with the exceptional variations from standard which occur during a production period.

A full system of standard costing involves a considerable amount of preparatory work because of the need to establish standards for all the elements of cost.

A good traditional definition of standard cost is:

> standard cost is a predetermined calculation of how much costs should be under specified working conditions. It is built up from an assessment of the value of cost elements and correlates technical specifications and the quantification of materials, labour and other costs to the prices

> and/or wage rates expected to apply during the period in which the standard cost is intended to be used. Its main purposes are to provide bases for control through variance accounting, for the valuation of stock and work in progress and, in some cases, for fixing selling prices.

Standards are not set by guesswork but are determined by people with the necessary technical knowledge to assess scientifically what the cost or the performance should be under certain conditions.

9.2 Standard costing v. budgetary control

The same basic ideas apply to standard costing and to budgetary control for they are both predetermined and used as measuring sticks within a business. The term *variance accounting* is now used to describe the unified technique of budgetary control and standard costing, both of which compare planned performance with actual performance in the analysis of variances, but, for convenience, they are shown as separate units in this book. The fundamental idea is predetermination of costs, followed during the operating period by a comparison of actual cost with the value of the allowance set, and the reporting of deviations from the set target. Whereas budgetary control fixes objectives for all aspects of income, expense and other functions of a business, standard costing is concerned with the detailed production operations and the products of a business. The setting of standards gives close attention to the study of work, the human factor, methods of production and the efficiency of operations, while budgetary control sets limits on spending, and is generally less concerned with detailed analysis but more concerned with controlling the expenditure of cost centres.

9.3 Standard conditions: normal, attainable, ideal

The introduction of standard costing requires a decision on the type of standards to set. Are they to be fixed on the basis of *normal conditions* or of *expected, attainable conditions*, or should the aim be to set standards based on best performance which can only be attained under *ideal conditions*?

Production under normal conditions is not usually acceptable because output is based on normal capacity and average sales, probably with little attention being given to the efficiency of labour, machines or the economic use of materials. Standards are fixed instead on the assumption that certain conditions and circumstances will prevail and that operations will be related to normal capacity or a particular volume of output. Therefore standards may be worked out on expected actual costs and are based on the volume of production and efficiency which the manufacturer hopes to achieve, and on the prices which s/he expects to pay for materials and services. The standards allow for waste and a degree of inefficiency, which is unavoidable in most circumstances. A high level of efficiency is expected but the standards are realistic and are capable of attainment. Ideal standards are only attainable in perfect conditions, and as these seldom, if ever, occur, they are not a reasonable or realistic proposition. Such conditions would result in a stream of unfavourable variances which would discourage effort, and have a disincentive effect on the employees.

The best basis for standards is therefore expected, attainable conditions. The various standards are described below:

(i) Basic standard This is a standard established and set for use over a long period. From it a *current standard* can be developed.

(ii) Current standard This is related to current conditions and established for use over a short period of time.

(iii) Attainable standard This refers to a standard which can be attained if a standard unit of work is carried out efficiently, with a machine properly operated and material properly used. It is set by allowing for normal shrinkage, waste and machine downtime. Attainable standards tend to have a motivational effect on employees, and the standards are useful when budgeting and during inventory valuation.

(iv) Ideal standard This is only attainable under the most favourable conditions, with no allowance for normal losses, wastage or machine downtime. Those who use this particular standard believe that the resulting unfavourable variances will encourage management to improve all phases of operations.

The best basis for standards is expected or attainable conditions, as explained above.

9.4 The establishment of standard costs

Installing a system of standard costing may be a long and costly business, but once installed, the records are there for continuous use to check the efficiency of operations. The biggest problem probably concerns the revision of standards. When standards no longer apply because of changes in price, manufacturing methods or product specifications, they must be revised. The cost of revising standards may be excessive and requires a great deal of clerical effort. A period has to be chosen within which the current standards will apply, and this is normally one year. If a system is to be operated for several years without revision, then basic standards can be established, using index numbers which change according to the movement in prices. This is not entirely satisfactory because over a period of years the index number is often not a true reflection of the current value.

(a) Studying the product and the processes

Before standards are set for materials, labour and expense, it is essential to carry out a careful examination of the products and manufacturing processes. Fixing standards in a large company requires the services of many people, particularly technical and accounting staff. In general, records have to be made of the type and quality of material to be stocked and used in the product, the sequence of operations in the manufacture, and the equipment and machinery to be used. In order to be effective, everything connected with the organisation needs to be scientifically studied so that the standards set are fair, reasonable and correct and, when the operating results are measured, show how efficient or inefficient the departments and employees are within each period of control.

(b) What is a standard?

It is 'a predetermined measurable quantity set in defined conditions' (CIMA, *Official Terminology*). 'Actual performance can be compared with the standard, usually for an element of work, operation or activity. While standards may be based on unquestioned and immutable natural law or facts, they are finally set by human judgement and consequently are subject to the same fallibility which attends all human activity. Thus a standard for 100 per cent machine output can be fixed by its geared input/output speeds, but the realisable output standard is one of judgement.'

(c) Standard hours or standard minutes

Standard hours or standard minutes are the units used to measure the quantity of work achievable at standard performance in an hour or a minute. The standard hour is a hypothetical hour which measures the amount of work which should be performed in that time at standard performance by an experienced worker. In current practice, 60 or 1 standard units are produced in one hour when unrestricted work is carried out at standard performance. A standard unit of work is expressed in terms of standard minutes or standard hours.

(d) Standard time

This is the total time in which a task should be completed at standard performance, that is, basic time, plus contingency allowance, plus relaxation allowance.

(e) Physical and value standards

Standards are planned and determined in advance and consist of:

(i) **Physical standards.** These relate to relative quantities and the physical relationships between input and output units.

(ii) **Value standards.** These are factors concerned with values of cost, revenue or profit per physical unit.

(iii) **Standard performance – labour.** This is 'the rate of output which qualified workers can achieve, as an average over the working day or shift, without over-exertion provided they adhere to the specified method and are motivated to apply themselves to their work' (CIMA, *Official Terminology*). This is represented by 100 on the BS scale (BS 3138).

9.5 Material standards (direct material)

Materials are controlled on the basis of *price and usage* after allowing for expected shrinkage, waste, scrap and other losses. The technical expert decides on the best and most economical material to use for each purpose and, after allowing for normal losses, specifies the exact size, quantity or weight required for each item included in the product to be manufactured. Such a review of materials is valuable as it often discloses a large range of different sizes and types of material, many of which could probably be eliminated after a study of them all. A reduction in variety can lead to economies in purchasing, material handling and storage, and a reduction in the amount of capital invested in stocks.

Standard prices

The buyer or purchasing officer prepares lists of materials and indicates the prices to be included in the standard cost for the period ahead. These prices will be based on current or forecast market prices, allowing for anticipated increases, or they may be based on the price paid in recent months together with any expected increases. In some cases it may be necessary to obtain quotations from possible suppliers. Standards will be set for purchased components as well as for raw materials.

9.6 Labour standards (direct labour)

Direct labour costs are controlled according to the *rates paid* and the *efficiency* of the operator, measured by the time taken and the standard time allowed for each job. In order to control labour costs efficiently, the planning department or similar authority has to establish standards by:

(a) listing the operations necessary to make the product;
(b) specifying the department or production centre where the work is to be carried out;
(c) indicating the tools or equipment needed or the machine which is to be used;
(d) stating the grade of labour or grade of employees for each operation;
(e) setting the standard operation times in standard direct labour hours or expressing it in money where piece-work prices are in use.

Standards are used to reveal variances in respect of:

(*a*) the efficiency when the actual time differs from the standard time allowed;
(*b*) the efficiency when there is a change in methods due to the use of different tools or to changes in operations;
(*c*) the non-utilisation of labour when cash is paid for periods of sickness, absenteeism, etc.;
(*d*) payment for idle time when there are production delays;
(e) the cost of correcting defective work;
(f) productive hours when the mix of pay grades is not as planned.

Standard product costs

As costs have to be assembled for standard products, a standard cost form or card is prepared for each item to be produced. This shows the details mentioned above and, by using standard costing rates for wages and overheads, the operations can be priced and the complete cost can be shown. A standard wages rate has to be established for each grade of labour, and is the trade union rate for each grade, or the average rate paid where union rates do not apply. Account must be taken of any wage plans or special incentive schemes which are in use.

9.7 Overhead standards (fixed and variable)

Overheads are controlled by the budgeted allowances for each cost centre and the actual expenditure, according to efficiency and the volume or capacity available. Management has to make decisions on the volume of production in each of the producing cost centres and the work to be carried out by the service cost centres. The decisions will probably be based on the normal capacity to manufacture. This figure is arrived at by taking maximum capacity and deducting from it an amount to cover the usual losses caused by, for example, holidays, material shortages, breakdowns and absenteeism.

The procedure for arriving at the overhead rate for each producing cost centre is similar but more precise than the method used in historical costing. When fixing standards for materials, labour and overheads, advice is sought from experienced people, and work study techniques such as *time study* and *method study* will probably be used. For expenditure control purposes, a firm's indirect labour, purchased services and materials should be related to measurable units of activity.

9.8 Variance analysis

Variances are analysed into constituent parts as shown in Fig. 9.1 (p. 220) and the actual performance is compared with the planned performance. The main variances are given below in detail.

(a) Total profit variance

This is the difference between budgeted and actual profit, which arises from the normal activities of the business. It is in respect of the sale of manufactured goods or services before taking account of extraneous transactions such as those of a purely financial nature. The formula is:

(Budgeted sales units × Standard profit per unit) – (Actual profit)

Note that where the volume of output is different from the budgeted output in the original budget we would adjust the budget with a flexed allowance before doing the calculation. (See Unit 9.13 for flexed allowances.)

(b) Profit variance due to sales

This consists of variances arising from selling prices, sales volume and the mix of sales. The total of these variances is the difference between the budgeted profit and the profit margin between the actual sales figure and the standard cost of those sales. The formula in each case for the individual sales is given later in this unit.

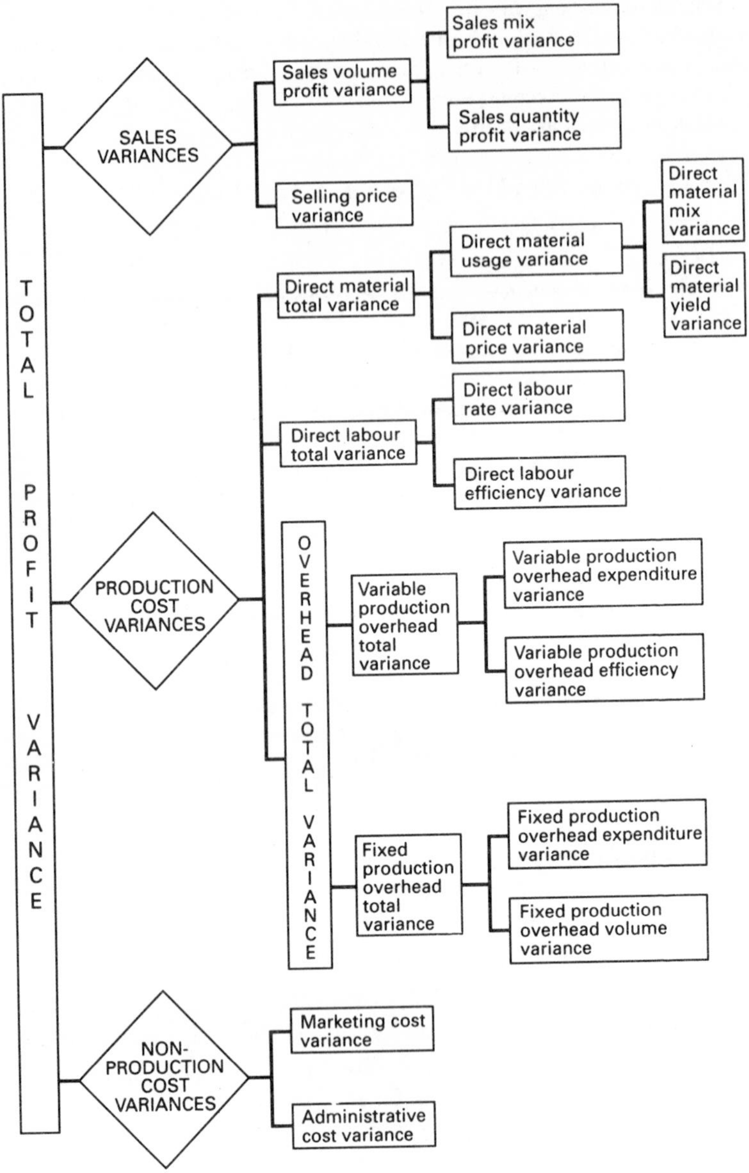

Fig. 9.1 Chart of variances (absorption costing principles)
(Reproduced by courtesy of CIMA – slightly adapted from Official Terminology)

(c) Profit variance due to costs

As shown in Fig. 9.1, total profit variance has three chief sources: the variances due to sales (described above) and the variances due to changes in costs, which may be subdivided into production costs and non-production costs. However carefully we have tried to set standard costs of production, prices of raw materials, labour and overheads are bound to vary and give rise to cost variances. As Fig. 9.1 shows, numerous variances arise on the production side, all of which require explanation. Similarly on the non-production side, in marketing and administration, the actual costs may prove to be different from the costs we used to draw up our budgets.

A first list of cost variances is:

(i) production cost variances, which consist of a number of variances grouped into three groups, direct materials, direct labour and overhead costs. These have special sections of this unit allotted to them;
(ii) marketing cost variance;
(iii) administration cost variance.

(i) Production cost variance This is the difference between the standard production cost of the actual production volume and the actual production cost over the specified period. The formula is:

(Actual number of units produced × Standard production cost per unit)

− (Actual total cost of materials, wages and production overhead)

(ii) Marketing cost variance This refers to the difference between the budgeted costs of marketing (including selling and distribution costs) and the actual marketing costs incurred in a specific period, and the calculation is:

Budgeted marketing costs − Actual marketing costs

(iii) Administrative cost variance This concerns the difference between the budgeted cost of administration for a specified period and the actual expenditure during the specified period. The formula is:

Budgeted administration costs − Actual administration costs

We must now look in greater detail at these various variances. In order to do so we have devised an example to provide some figures for use in the calculations. These are given on p. 222.

9.9 Total profit variance

The total profit variance is the difference between the budgeted profit and the actual profit achieved. The calculation is:

Variance = (Budgeted profit) − (Actual profit)
= £90 000 − £127 215
= £37 215 (F)

Supporting information for the examples and calculations:

	Budget	Flexed budget	Actual
Sales			
Value	£600 000	£650 000	£682 500
Quantity	6 000	6 500	6 500
Unit price	£ 100	£ 100	£ 105
Direct materials			
Value	£42 000	£45 500	£46 035
Quantity	6 000	6 500	6 600
Price	£7.00	£7.00	£6.975
Direct labour			
Value	£144 000	£156 000	£161 250
Hours	36 000	39 000	43 000
Rate	£4.00	£4.00	£3.75
Production overhead			
Variable	£90 000	£97 500	£103 000
Fixed	£108 000	£108 000	£115 000
Rate per hour			
Variable	£2.50	£2.50	
Fixed	£3.00	£3.00	
Production cost of sales			
Value	£384 000	£407 000	£425 285
Marketing cost	£54 000	£54 000	£55 000
Administration cost	£72 000	£72 000	£75 000
Operating profit	£90 000	£117 000	£127 215

Note: Although the flexed budget shows the same fixed overhead as the original budget (because it is fixed) there will actually be a further £9 000 absorbed (3 000 hours at £3 per hour).

Details of production	*Materials*
Actual price paid	£6.975 per unit
Standard price set	£7.000 per unit
Materials requisitioned	6 600 units
Articles produced	6 500 units

Note to 9.9 (p. 221):

(i) When an actual cost is lower than standard cost the difference is a *favourable variance* and is shown as (F); for example, £1 000 (F).

(ii) When an actual cost exceeds the standard cost the difference is an *adverse variance* and is shown as (A); for example, £2 500 (A).

(iii) Similarly, where an actual profit exceeds a budgeted profit it is shown as a favourable variance - for example, £37 215(F) above - while an actual profit below the budgeted profit would be shown as an adverse variance (A).

9.10 Total sales variance

This is that part of the total profit variance which can be attributed to changes in the sales figure (the turnover figure) achieved. It is found by taking the difference between the budgeted manufacturing profit and the profit margin between the actual sales figure and the standard cost of those sales. The budgeted manufacturing profit referred to is the profit before marketing and administrative costs have been deducted. The calculation is:

Variance = Budgeted manufacturing profit − (Actual sales − Standard production cost of actual sales)
= £216 000 − (£682 500 − £416 000)
= £216 000 − £266 500
= £50 500 (F)

Note: The standard production cost of actual sales is found as follows:

Cost per unit = £7 (materials) + £24 labour (6 × £4) + £33 overhead (6 × £5.50)
= £64

∴ Standard production cost of actual sales = 6 500 × £64 = £416 000

This total sales variance is made up of two elements, the *selling price variance* and the *sales volume profit variance*.

(a) Selling price variance

This is the difference between the actual sales figure and the sum that would have been received had those sales been achieved at the standard selling price per unit. The calculation is:

(Actual sales units × Standard selling price) − (Actual sales)
= (6 500 × £100) − (£682 500)
= £650 000 − £682 500
= £32 500 (F)

(b) Sales volume profit variance

This is an element of variance in the profit of the business which arises from the sales department either over-achieving or under-achieving on the sales expected in the period. The formula for this variance is:

(Budgeted sales units × Standard profit per unit) – (Actual sales units × Standard profit per unit)

As illustrated in Fig. 9.1, the sales volume profit variance may be caused in two ways. First the mix of products sold may have been different from the expected mix when the standard was drawn up. This gives rise to a *sales mix profit variance*. The other element is the sales quantity, which may have varied from the expected quantity. This gives rise to a *sales quantity profit variance*. These are both explained below.

The calculation for the sales volume profit variance is:

(Budgeted sales units × Standard profit per unit) – (Actual sales units × Standard profit per unit)
= (6 000 × £36) – (6 500 × £36)
= £216 000 – £234 000
= £18 000 (F)

We will now consider the sales mix profit variance and the sales volume profit variance.

(i) Sales mix profit variance This is an element of variance in the profit of the business which arises from the differences in the achieved sales of the various products made. Since the profit on the products varies and the budget has been based on a weighted average profit, variations in the actual sales achieved are bound to throw up a variance, since the weighting of the actual sales will be different from the weighting used in the budget. The formula for the sales mix profit variance is:

(Total actual sales units × Budgeted weighted average standard profit per unit) – (Actual sales units × Individual standard profit per unit)

This variance does not enter into the example used in this unit.

(ii) Sales quantity profit variance Since the mix does not enter into our exercise, the whole of the sales volume profit variance must have been caused by the change in quantity. The calculation is:

(Budget sales units × Standard profit-to-sales ratio) – (Total actual sales units × Budgeted weighted average standard profit)
= (6 000 × £36) – (6 500 × £36)
= £216 000 – £234 000
= £18 000 (F)

The sales variances can now be reconciled:

Selling price variance	32 500 (F)
Sales volume profit variance	18 000 (F)
Total sales variance	£50 500 (F)

9.11 Production cost variance

The formula for this variance is:

Variance = (Actual units produced × Standard production cost per unit) − (Actual total cost of materials, wages and production overhead)

In our example we have:

$$\begin{aligned} \text{Variance} &= (6\,500 \times £64) - (£46\,035 + £161\,250 + £218\,000) \\ &= £416\,000 - £425\,285 \\ &= £9\,285 \text{ (A)} \end{aligned}$$

This variance must be the result of changes somewhere in the costs involved in production - either a materials variance or an overhead variance - or some combination of these variances.

9.12 Material variances

As shown in Fig. 9.1, the material variances form a group of interlinked variances. Detailed explanations of these are given below.

(a) The direct material total variance

The direct material total variance is the difference between the budgeted direct material costs and the actual direct material costs. It is made up of two elements, the direct material usage variance and the direct material price variance. It is obvious that if the actual costs of the material used vary from the budget this must be due either to changes in the quantity of material used or to changes in the prices of the material. What is not quite so obvious is that, as far as usage is concerned, the change in usage may result from a different mix of materials, or from variations in the yield achieved. For example, the use of a brass rod to make small fittings for kitchen cabinets may result in 12 parts being produced instead of the expected 15, because of a flaw in the rod at one point.

The *Official Terminology* booklet simply defines the direct material total variance as:

(Direct material usage variance) + (Direct material price variance)

More usefully, perhaps, we can say it is the difference between the actual cost of the material used and the standard cost of material for the production achieved. When direct material total variance is calculated at the time of issue to production, it is:

(Standard quantity of material specified for actual production × Standard price) − (Actual cost of material used)

Variance = (Standard quantity × Standard price) − (Actual quantity × Actual price)
= (6 500 × £7.000) − (6 600 × £6.975)
= £45 500 − £46 035
= £535 (A)

The (A) stands for an adverse variance since actual cost exceeded standard cost.

The total variance as far as direct materials are concerned could be made up of two parts, i.e.:

(Direct material usage variance) + (Direct material price variance)

(b) Direct material usage variance

This is the difference between the cost at the standard price of the standard quantity of material used for the production achieved and the cost of the actual quantity of material used at the standard price.

Variance = (Standard quantity × Standard price) − (Actual quantity × Standard price)
= (6 500 × £7) − (6 600 × £7)
= £45 500 − £46 200
= £700 (A)

Note: The material used by the operator exceeds the amount required to produce the goods as represented by the standard quantity. The usage variance indicates whether more or less material has been used than is needed to produce the standard quantity. Although the variance is expressed in money, it is related not to price but to the quantity of material actually used and the quantity which should have been used.

A variance may be caused during production or by spoilage in handling. It may also be caused by losses after issue from the stores as a result of pilferage or slack methods of control. If there is no apparent reason for a variance, an explanation will be required from the production controllers.

The direct material usage variance is the sum of the direct material mix variance and the direct material yield variance.

(c) Direct material price variance

This is the difference between the amount that should have been paid for the quantity purchased and the amount that was actually paid for that quantity. The *Official Terminology* booklet shows the formula for this variance as:

Variance = (Actual material purchased × Standard price) − (Actual cost of material purchased)

The second part of this formula must be the actual quantity purchased × actual price. We therefore have:

Variance = (Actual quantity purchased × Standard price) − (Actual quantity purchased × Actual price)

Where this is calculated not at the time of the purchase of the goods but at the time of their issue to production, the formula is:

(Actual material used × Standard price) − Actual cost of material used

In the present example we have:

$$\begin{aligned} \text{Variance} &= (6\,600 \times £7.000) - (6\,600 \times £6.975) \\ &= £46\,200 - £46\,035 \\ &= £165\ (F) \end{aligned}$$

This is a favourable variance – we actually purchased the materials more economically than is standard.

Note: The direct material price variance must be related to the material requisitioned or purchased, because the profit or loss caused by the variance in the price is in respect of the material actually supplied and used by the operator. A price variance may be a result of changes in market prices, a change of suppliers, purchasing at special prices or purchasing supplies of the wrong grade or quality. Invoices are examined as they are received and major variances are reported, so that management can take any necessary action. The purchasing officer is asked to explain when prices deviate from the standard.

The direct material price variance and the direct material usage variance can now be reconciled with the direct material total variance:

	£
Direct material price variance	165 (F)
Direct material usage variance	700 (A)
Direct material total variance	£535 (A)

When some variances are favourable and some adverse, it is necessary to state the net result. This means that the smaller variance is set against the larger one to show the net effect.

One further point about the material price variance is that it will come to our attention at the time the materials arrive with the advice note, to be followed shortly by the invoice. The goods received note is made out and the price is recorded. Where there is a variance and the materials are immediately issued to production there is no problem, as the variance can be immediately drawn to the attention of the cost accountant. Where there is a price variance but the goods are not immediately issued to production the question arises as to when to deal with the price variance. As losses should be taken into account at the earliest opportunity it is considered prudent to deal with the adverse variance at the time when the invoice is received, and to be logical it follows that favourable variances should be dealt with at the same time.

When materials are taken into stock at the actual price but no attention is paid to the variance from budgeted price, there is a chance that when they are issued to production the variance may be overlooked.

(d) Direct material mix variance

This refers to a process which uses several different materials. If these are combined in a standard proportion, a variance can be calculated in order to show the effect on cost of variances from the standard proportion. Any variance of the mix of materials used is best regarded as a sub-set of the usage variance. If the latter method is used the definition is as follows: *The direct material mix variance is the difference between the total quantity in the standard proportion, priced at the standard price, and the actual quantity in the actual mix priced at the standard price.* This does not apply to the example we have been considering.

The formula may be stated as:

Variance = (Total material input in a standard mix × Standard prices) − (Actual material input × Standard prices)

(e) Direct material yield variance

For a variety of reasons the quantities produced are often different from those planned. An example arises in chemical plants where a given input should produce a given output over a period, but the actual output may differ. This may have no connection with operator or machine performance.

The formula given in the *Official Terminology* booklet is:

Variance = (Standard quantity of materials specified for actual production × Standard prices) − (Actual total material input in standard proportions × Standard prices)

We may define the yield variance as the difference between the standard yield of the actual material input and the actual yield, both valued at the standard material cost of the product.

This variance does not apply to the example we have been considering.

9.13 Direct labour variances

(a) Direct labour total variance

The direct labour total variance is the difference between the standard and the actual cost of labour. This variance could have been caused by changes in the wages paid, or by changes due to over-achieving or under-achieving the standard output. We must therefore discover the *direct labour rate variance* and the *direct labour efficiency variance*, because these variances have caused the direct labour total variance.

The formula for this total variance is:

Variance = (Standard hours of actual production × Standard direct labour rate) − (Actual direct labour hours × Actual rate per hour)
= (39 000 × £4) − (43 000 × £3.75)
= £156 000 − £161 250
= £5 250 (A)

Although the rate paid was lower than the standard rate set, there were 4 000 extra hours taken and this resulted in an adverse variance.

Special note: When dealing with variances it is sensible to ensure that they are not caused by clerical errors when the standard was set and calculated, or when the comparison was made between standard and actual.

We can now calculate the two sub-variances which caused the total variance.

(i) Direct labour rate variance This variance is similar to material price variance and may be the result of changes in wage rates because of awards, or a change in wage plans such as the introduction of piece-work, or because the wrong grade of labour has been used (such as an apprentice instead of a skilled worker, or a highly skilled worker performing low-grade work). When a different grade of worker is used, a note to this effect will probably be made on the job card; otherwise the supervisor will be contacted for an explanation.

The formula for the direct labour rate variance is the difference between wages payable under the standard rate and those payable under the actual labour rate per hour for the total hours worked. For our example, the calculation is:

Variance = (Actual hours worked × Standard direct labour rate) − (Actual hours worked × Actual hourly rate)
= (43 000 × £4) − (43 000 × £3.75)
= £172 000 − £161 250
= £10 750 (F)

The lower rate paid when compared with the standard produces a favourable variance of £10 750.

This can be abbreviated to:

Variance = (Standard rate per hour − Actual rate per hour) × Actual hours
= (£4 − £3.75) × 43 000
= £0.25 × 43 000
= £10 750 (F)

(ii) Direct labour efficiency variance This variance relates to the gain or loss made by achieving or failing to achieve the standard output per hour. It is as well to remember that the wages cost is now at standard cost because any rate variance has been removed. Therefore, these are time variances priced at the standard rate and are found by comparing the actual time with the standard time recorded on job cards. The excess time taken may be a result of incorrect instructions given to the employee, poor supervision, using materials of the wrong quality or using tools, machinery or equipment which may be faulty or of the wrong type. Poor efficiency may also be caused by using workers who are insufficiently trained, or who are working in substandard conditions. Sometimes, organisational problems cause a hold-up in the supply of materials, tools and so on.

When employees are idle because of delays in material supplies and break-downs of machinery, the idle time should be charged to an *Idle Time Account* so that the management is aware of the problems that exist. When calculating labour variances, the standard cost is not actual hours at the standard rate but standard hours for the production achieved at the standard rate. The direct labour rate variance is calculated using the rate of wages actually paid and the rate which should have been paid (standard rate) for the grade of worker selected to perform the work as specified when the standards were set.

When there is a difference between the actual hours and the standard hours for the production achieved (Units produced × Standard hours per unit), it indicates that the work has been carried out in a shorter or longer period of time than the standard hours allowed. The standard rate is used because the application of the rate variance has reduced the actual rate paid to the standard rate. The profit or loss shown by the direct labour efficiency variance is the result of efficient or inefficient working, always provided that the rate is fairly set.

Returning to our example, and the direct labour efficiency variance, we know that this is the difference between the wages payable at the standard rate for the standard hours for the actual production achieved and those payable for the hours actually worked, valued at the standard labour rate. The calculation is:

Variance = (Standard hours of actual production × Standard direct labour rate) − (Actual hours worked × Standard direct labour rate)
= (39 000 × £4) − (43 000 × £4)
= £156 000 − £172 000
= £16 000 (A)

This can be abbreviated to:

Variance = (Standard hours produced − Actual hours worked) × Standard rate per hour
= (39 000 − 43 000) × £4
= 4 000 × £4
= £16 000 (A)

The direct labour variances can now be reconciled:

	£
Direct labour rate variance	10 750 (F)
Direct labour efficiency variance	16 000 (A)
Direct labour total variance	£ 5 250 (A)

(b) Flexed allowances

These provide the link between the original budget for the manufacture and sale of 6 000 units and the standard applicable to the manufacture and sale of 6 500 units. The allowances are as follows:

	Quantity	*Standard*	*Value*
		£	£
Sales	+ 500 units	100.00	50 000
Materials	+ 500 units	7.00	3 500
Direct labour	+ 3 000 hours	4.00	12 000
Variable overhead	+ 3 000 hours	2.50	7 500
Fixed overhead	+ 3 000 hours	3.00	9 000

Note: The flexed budget increases (or decreases) the original budget using the same standard prices and allowances as the original budget.

9.14 Overheads and overhead variances

(a) Fixed and variable overheads

Indirect costs which vary in direct ratio to production are *variable overheads*. *Fixed overheads* represent the fixed costs of the organisation and the fixed overhead cost per unit is set so that the total quantity represents the budget or the constant cost. If the budget quantity is not reached, or if it is exceeded, a variance arises, because of the under-absorption or over-absorption that occurs.

The budget for the period will show separately the fixed and variable overheads and the budgeted or standard hours of production. The information will provide the details to calculate the *fixed overhead absorption rate* and the *variable overhead absorption rate* by dividing the cost in each case by the budgeted standard hours of production.

The use of *flexible budgets* is advisable as allowances should be set in accordance with the activity achieved. If there is a change in the number of working days a *calendar variance* can be calculated. It is part of the volume variance and is equivalent to the standard hours lost or gained.

(b) Controllable variances and uncontrollable variances

Variances are favourable or adverse and can be separated into those which are controllable and those which are uncontrollable. A controllable variance is one which is the primary responsibility of a specified person, whereas an uncontrollable variance is one for which no individual can be held responsible, as, for example, a national wage award, or an increase in the cost of rent. An individual can, however, be answerable for the efficiency of a group of workers under his or her control or for material usage.

The terminology, methods of analysis and ledger entries about overhead variances vary considerably from business to business, and the published material on this subject tackles the problem in a variety of ways. It is essential to understand the basic terms, explained below, before proceeding with the analysis.

(c) Budget

This is a financial and quantitative forecasted statement, based on estimated cost and an anticipated volume of activity expressed in units, direct labour hours, machine hours, etc. A standard cost is established for hours and units.

(d) Volume

The volume of production, whether budgeted or actual, is represented by the quantity of units produced or the number of standard hours of labour or machine time used in the production of those units. The cost of this volume is obtained by multiplying the volume by the predetermined (standard) cost. It should be noted that there is a budgeted (planned) volume and an actual volume. When expressed in hours, there are the standard hours planned and the standard hours produced.

(e) Production actually achieved

This is the actual volume of production and represents the standard hours in the units produced. For example, the actual hours may be 43 000 and the number of standard hours per unit may be 6. If 6 500 units are produced, the production actually achieved is equivalent to 39 000 hours. This means there is an adverse variance of 4 000 hours at the standard rate per hour.

(f) Budget cost allowance

Costs are ascertained during a costing period of, say, four weeks and this is the control period during which comparisons are made between budgeted and actual results. The *budget cost allowance* is the amount allowed to budget centres during this control period. A proportion of the annual budget is allowed for fixed cost, based on the benefits expected during the period and not on any actual payment made at that date. The allowance for variable cost is in direct proportion to the volume of production.

(g) Overhead variance

This is referred to as a cost variance or total variance and is the difference between the actual cost of overheads and the standard cost absorbed in the production achieved. It is defined and analysed as fixed production overhead expenditure variance and variable production overhead expenditure variance, in the section on analysing overhead variances below. Referring to the CIMA terminology, the variances consist of:

(i) Fixed production overhead total variance, subdivided into:
  (i_1) Fixed production overhead expenditure variance, and
  (i_2) Fixed production overhead volume variance
(ii) Variable production overhead total variance, subdivided into:
  (ii_1) Variable production overhead expenditure variance, and
  (ii_2) Variable production overhead efficiency variance

(i) Fixed production overhead total variance = [Standard absorbed cost] *Less* [Actual fixed production overhead]

(i_1) Fixed production overhead expenditure variance = [Budgeted fixed production overhead] *Less* [Actual fixed production overhead]

(i_2) Fixed production overhead volume variance = [Standard absorbed cost] *Less* [Budgeted fixed production overhead]

Fig. 9.2 Fixed production overhead variances

It is possible to run the two total variances shown as (i) and (ii) above into one, as shown in Fig. 9.1. This is the overhead total variance.

These variances are described below and illustrated in two charts (see Figs 9.2 and 9.3, above and p. 234).

In order to make the definitions easier to understand we will define them and explain them with reference to Example 9.8.

EXAMPLE 9.8 (Overhead analysis)

Budget		*Actual*	
Fixed overheads	£108 000	Fixed overheads	£115 000
Variable overheads	£90 000	Variable overheads	£103 000
Standard hours	36 000	Standard hours	43 000
Units of production	6 000	Units of production	6 500

Standard hours per unit

$$= \frac{\text{Hours}}{\text{Units}}$$

$$= \frac{36\,000}{6\,000}$$

$$= \underline{\underline{6}}$$

Standard hours achieved by production

= Units produced × Standard hours per unit

$= 6\,500 \times 6$

$= \underline{\underline{39\,000}}$

Absorption rate per hour

Fixed overhead

$$= \frac{\text{Budgeted fixed overhead}}{\text{Budgeted standard hours}}$$

Standard variable overhead absorbed in the production achieved

= Standard hours achieved × Variable overhead absorption rate

Variance				
(ii) Variable production overhead total variance	=	Standard variable production overhead cost of actual production	*Less*	Actual cost
(ii_1) Variable production overhead expenditure variance	=	Actual hours worked × Standard variable overhead rate	*Less*	Actual cost
(ii_2) Variable production overhead efficiency variance	=	Standard variable production overhead cost of actual production	*Less*	Actual hours worked × Standard variable overhead rate

Fig. 9.3 Variable production overhead variances

$$= \frac{£108\,000}{36\,000}$$

= £3.00 per hour

Variable overhead

$$= \frac{\text{Budgeted variable overhead}}{\text{Budgeted standard hours}}$$

$$= \frac{£90\,000}{36\,000}$$

= £2.50 per hour

= 39 000 hours × £2.50

= £97 500

Variable overhead cost of actual hours, at variable overhead absorption rate

= Hours worked × Variable overhead absorption rate

= 43 000 × £2.50

= £107 500

Notes:

(i) It is necessary to calculate the budgeted standard hours per unit and the budgeted (standard) absorption rates for fixed and variable overheads, which are 6 hours per unit and £3.00 and £2.50 per hour respectively.

(ii) For the actual results it is necessary to calculate the standard hours achieved by production and the variable overhead absorbed by this production, which are 39 000 hours and £97 500 respectively.

(iii) The next calculation is to obtain the budgeted variable overhead cost for the actual hours worked, which is £107 500.

This information shows that variable overheads cost £103 000, but for the hours worked they should have cost £107 500 and the value absorbed in the production achieved is only £97 500. There is also a variance between the budgeted fixed overhead cost and the actual fixed overhead cost.

(i) Fixed production overhead variances

Fixed production overhead total variance This is the difference between the standard fixed overhead cost specified for the actual production achieved (i.e. the standard absorbed cost) and the actual fixed production overhead incurred.

The formula is:

Standard absorbed cost − Actual fixed production overhead
= (39 000 hours × £3) − £115 000
= £117 000 − £115 000
= £2 000 (F)

This total variance is really made up of two elements:

(i_1) Fixed production overhead expenditure variance This is the difference between budgeted and actual fixed production overhead expenditure.

The formula is:

Budgeted fixed production overhead − Actual fixed production overhead
= £108 000 − £115 000
= £7 000 (A)

(i_2) Fixed production overhead volume variance This is the difference between the standard absorbed cost for the actual production achieved and the budgeted fixed production overhead. The formula is:

Standard absorbed cost − Budgeted fixed production overhead
= (39 000 hours × £3) − (£108 000)
= £117 000 − £108 000
= £9 000 (F)

The fixed production overhead variances can now be reconciled:

	£
Volume variance	9 000 (F)
Expenditure variance	7 000 (A)
Total fixed variance	£2 000 (F)

(ii) Variable overhead variances

Variable production overhead total variance This is the difference between the standard variable production overhead cost specified for the production achieved, and the actual variable overhead incurred.

The formula is:

Standard variable production overhead cost of actual production − Actual variable overhead
= (39 000 hours × £2.50) − (£103 000)
= £97 500 − £103 000
= £5 500 (A)

This is again made up of two elements:

(ii_1) Variable production overhead expenditure variance This is the difference between the overhead absorbed by charging for the actual hours worked at the standard variable rate, and the actual cost of the variable overheads.

The formula is:

(Actual hours × Standard variable overhead rate) – (Actual variable production overhead)
= (43 000 hours × £2.50) – (£103 000)
= £107 500 – £103 000
= £4 500 (F)

(ii_2) Variable production overhead efficiency variance This is the difference between the standard variable production overhead cost of the production achieved and the standard overhead cost of the actual hours taken.

The formula is:

(Standard variable production overhead for production achieved) – (Actual hours taken × Standard variable overhead rate)
= (39 000 × £2.50) – (43 000 × £2.50)
= £97 500 – £107 500
= £10 000 (A)

The variable overhead variances can now be reconciled:

	£
Expenditure variance	4 500 (F)
Efficiency variance	10 000 (A)
Total variable overhead variance	£ 5 500 (A)

We can now put the two overheads (variable and fixed) together to find the overhead total variance.

The calculation for this is:

Variance = Standard overhead cost (both fixed and variable) for the production achieved – Actual overhead (both fixed and variable)
= (39 000 × £5.50) – (£115 000 + £103 000)
= £214 500 – £218 000
= £3 500 (A)

Check:

		£
Fixed production overhead total variance	=	2 000 (F)
Variable production overhead total variance	=	5 500 (A)
Net effect		£3 500 (A)

(h) Summary of production cost variance

Note:

(A) means costs were more than budgeted, i.e. an adverse variance.
(F) means costs were less than expected, i.e. a favourable variance.

Unit 9.11 Production cost variance			£9 285 (A)
Direct material usage variance	£700 (A)		
Direct material price variance	£165 (F)		
Direct material total variance			£535 (A)
Direct labour rate variance	£10 750 (F)		
Direct labour efficiency variance	£16 000 (A)		
Direct labour total variance			£5 250 (A)
Variable production overhead expenditure variance	£4 500 (F)		
Variable production overhead efficiency variance	£10 000 (A)		
Variable production overhead total variance		£5 500 (A)	
Fixed production overhead expenditure variance	£7 000 (A)		
Fixed production overhead volume variance	£9 000 (F)		
Fixed production overhead total variance		£2 000 (F)	
Overhead total variance			£3 500 (A)
Production cost variance			£9 285 (A)

9.15 The non-production cost variances

(a) The marketing variance

This is the difference between the budgeted marketing cost and the actual marketing cost. In our example it is very simple:

Variance = Budgeted marketing cost − Actual marketing cost
= £54 000 − £55 000
= £1 000 (A)

(b) The administrative cost variance

This is the difference between the budgeted administrative cost and the actual administrative cost. Once again, in our example it is very simple:

Variance = Budgeted administration cost − Actual administration cost
= £72 000 − £75 000
= £3 000 (A)

(c) Summary of variances

We can now summarise the variances as follows:

Unit 9.9	Total profit variance	£37 215 (F)

The three elements of variance illustrated in Fig. 9.1 are:

(i) Unit 9.10	Total sales variance	£50 500 (F)
(ii) Unit 9.11	Production cost variance	£9 285 (A)
(iii) Unit 9.15	Non-production cost variances:	
	Marketing variance	£1 000 (A)
	Administrative variance	£3 000 (A)
		£37 215 (F)

(d) Reporting to management on variances: operating statements

An operating statement is defined in the CIMA's *Official Terminology* as 'a regular report for management of actual costs and revenues, as appropriate'. The phrase 'as appropriate' means 'to suit the needs of the particular business, or section of a business concerned'. An operating statement usually compares actual costs with budgeted costs and shows the variances. These are set against the operating results (the profit) to show how the actual profit differed from the budgeted profit. The variances explain how the differences in operating results arose.

The operating statement shown below is about an organisation which uses absorption costing. A similar statement can be drawn up for an organisation which uses marginal costing. Such an operating statement is shown in Unit 9.16.

Operating statement (standard absorption costing) for quarterly period ending 30 September 19..

		£	£
Budgeted operating profit			90 000
Variance analysis			
Marketing director			
Selling price		32 500	
Sales volume profit		18 000	
Marketing cost		(1 000)	
Total sales and maketing variance			49 500
Production director			
Direct material usage variance	(700)		
Direct material price variance	165		
Direct material total variance		(535)	
Direct labour efficiency variance	(16 000)		
Direct labour rate variance	10 750		
Direct labour total variance		(5 250)	
Variable overhead efficiency variance	(10 000)		
Variable overhead expenditure variance	4 500		
Variable overhead total variance		(5 500)	
Fixed overhead volume variance	9 000		
Fixed overhead expenditure variance	(7 000)		
Fixed overhead total variance		2 000	
Total production cost variance			(9 285)
Finance director			
Fixed administrative cost variance			(3 000)
Actual operating profit			£127 215

9.16 Variances with marginal costing

The segregation of fixed and variable costs is the fundamental feature of marginal costing and therefore when showing marginal costing principles in the form of a diagram it is necessary to set apart the fixed cost variances from the variable cost variances, as shown in Fig. 9.4 (p. 240).

The chart takes account of the fact that marginal costing is concerned with the behaviour of costs by distinguishing between fixed and variable costs. Therefore the diagram omits production cost variance (see Fig. 9.1) and shows variable cost variances, with a separate section indicating the fixed

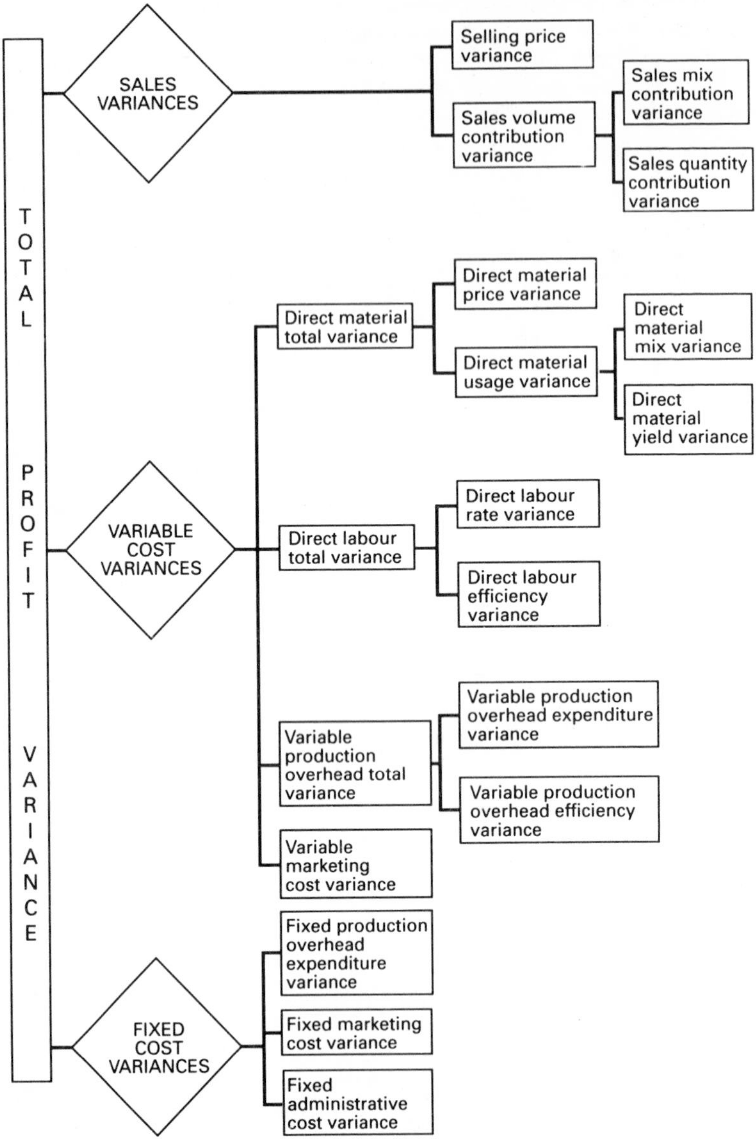

Fig. 9.4 Chart of variances (marginal costing principles)
(*Reproduced by courtesy of CIMA*)

cost variances. This is necessary because of the need to show the contribution which the product or production is making towards the fixed costs.

When comparing this chart (Fig. 9.4) with the chart shown earlier (Fig. 9.1) it will be seen that the fixed overhead volume variance is eliminated. This is because in marginal costing the absorption of fixed overhead costs (which are affected by the volume) is not a major consideration. It is contribution which is important. It will also be seen that under the fixed cost variances there are additions for fixed marketing cost variance and fixed administrative cost variance. Also at the top of the chart the sales mix profit variance and the sales quantity profit variance of Fig. 9.1 are replaced by the sales mix contribution variance and the sales quantity contribution variance. When illustrating marginal costing principles it is necessary to deal with the contribution which is made towards paying for the fixed costs and, when these are covered, towards profits.

In a marginal costing operating statement actual costs are shown, not absorbed costs. Therefore the operating statement begins with a flexed budget which revises the fixed budget to take account of the changes in output. We can now draw up an operating statement showing marginal costs. Remember that such an operating statement is a report to management showing the success (or otherwise) of the operations viewed from a marginal costing point of view, where jobs and orders are accepted on the basis of whether they will cover variable costs only - and, in addition, make some useful contribution to fixed costs and (when fixed costs have been covered) to profits.

The sales volume contribution variance is calculated as follows. It is the difference between budgeted and actual sales units multiplied by the standard contribution per unit. Contribution is sales value less variable cost of sales, and each unit contributes towards the fixed costs and the profit.

(Budgeted sales units × Standard contribution per unit) − (Actual sales units × Standard contribution per unit)
= (6 000 units × £54) − (6 500 units × £54)
= 500 units × £54
= 27 000 (F) *(see pp. 242–3 for operating statement)*

9.17 Reports

Variance analysis should be followed by the intelligent use of reports, so that investigations can be made to find out why the performance has failed to reach the level planned. The object of standard costing is to plan operations systematically in advance, in order to improve processes, methods and procedure, and to secure low costs as well as keeping spoilage, waste and loss to a minimum. It provides a check on the efficiency of supervision and of direct and indirect labour and shows to what extent plant capacity is being utilised. The reporting system should allow for a feedback of information so as to generate corrective action and to enable revisions to be made where necessary.

Operating statement with flexed budget (marginal costs) for quarterly period ending 30 September 19..

	Standard per unit	Fixed budget	Flexed budget	Actual	Budget variances
No. units made and sold	1	6 000	6 500	6 500	
	£	£	£	£	£
Sales	100	600 000	650 000	682 500	32 500
Direct material	7	42 000	45 500	46 035	(535)
Direct labour £4 per hr	24	144 000	156 000	161 250	(5 250)
Variable production overhead £2.50 per hr	15	90 000	97 500	103 000	(5 500)
Total variable costs	46	276 000	299 000	310 285	
Contribution	54	324 000	351 000	372 215	
Fixed production overhead £3 per hour	18	108 000	108 000	115 000	(7 000)
Factory profit	36	216 000	243 000	257 215	
Fixed marketing cost		54 000	54 000	55 000	(1 000)
Fixed administrative cost		72 000	72 000	75 000	(3 000)
		126 000	126 000	130 000	
Operating profit		90 000	117 000	127 215	10 215

£27 000 Sales volume contribution variance

£10 215 Price, usage and expenditure variances

Fixed budget profit − Actual profit = £37 215
Total profit variance

9.18 Other variances

There are many variances in use, some of which are peculiar to particular industries. We give a few examples:

(a) Calendar variance

This variance applies to overheads and is a result of the difference between the *number of working days* in the budget period and the number of working

Operating statement (standard marginal costing) for quarterly period ending 30 September 19..

	Contribution/ sales ratio	Contribution	Fixed costs	Profit
	%	£	£	£
Budget	54.00	324 000	234 000	90 000
Actual	54.54	372 215	245 000	127 215
Variance	0.54	48 215	11 000	37 215
Variance analysis				
Marketing director:				
Sales volume contribution		27 000		27 000
Selling price		32 500		32 500
Fixed marketing cost			(1 000)	(1 000)
Sub-total, marketing		59 500	(1 000)	58 500
Production director:				
Direct material usage		(700)		(700)
Direct material price		165		165
Direct labour efficiency		(16 000)		(16 000)
Direct labour rate		10 750		10 750
Variable overhead efficiency		(10 000)		(10 000)
Variable overhead expenditure		4 500		4 500
Fixed overhead expenditure			(7 000)	(7 000)
Sub-total, production		(11 285)	(7 000)	(18 285)
Finance director:				
Fixed administrative cost			(3 000)	(3 000)
Total variances		48 215	(11 000)	37 215

Note: In the marginal costing operating statement actual costs are shown, not absorbed costs.

---

days in the period to which the budget applies. For example, fixed overhead costs would be under-recovered if, for some special reason, a working day was suddenly declared a public holiday.

(b) Revisions variance

This variance is the difference between a current standard cost and a revised standard cost, brought about by a change in costs or prices during a budget period. There may be a change in wage rates because of a national award, a permanent increase in certain expenses, or extra fixed payments to certain employees, for example. It is frequently of an uncontrolled type and the adjustment of standard costs should be held up until the next review of standards. The costs should be segregated by charging to a Revisions Variance Account.

(c) Seasonal variance

This relates to a volume variance, and is the difference between standards based on average output and output which is budgeted to allow for seasonal fluctuations.

(d) Quality cost variance

This is the difference (arising from failure to conform to quality specification) between the amount included in standard costs and the actual cost or loss incurred in scrapping, rectifying, or selling at sub-standard prices.

The quality cost variance formula is:

Budgeted quality cost − Actual quality cost

In greater detail this is:

(Number of units produced × Standard allowance per unit) − (Number of units rejected or returned × Cost per unit) + Rectification cost − Disposal value

(e) Exchange variances

Exchange variances arise when the exchange rates used in buying goods from overseas countries or selling goods to overseas countries fluctuate to change the effective sterling costs, or the sterling proceeds. If we consider purchases from abroad we may have budgeted for a standard price of $2 250 for a machine, based on an exchange rate of £1 = $1.50, a sterling cost of £1 500. The actual price proves to be $2 106, which at a rate of exchange of £1 = $1.50 would have meant a sterling cost of £1 404. This would have been a favourable variance in the price of the machine of £96 (i.e. £1 500 − £1 404).

Unfortunately, however, the rate of exchange has now changed to £1 = $1.25. In other words the £1 has weakened and we get only $1.25 instead of $1.50 for every £. The cost is now:

$$\frac{2\,106}{1.25} = \underline{\underline{£1\,684.80}}$$

If we call this £1 685 our price has changed from £1 500 (according to our budget) to £1 685, an adverse variance of £185. Since the exchange rate has turned a favourable variance of £96 into an adverse variance of £185 the full impact of the exchange rate variance is £96 + £185 = £281. This is the difference between the sterling cost had the rate not varied (£1 404) and the sterling cost at the new rate £1 685; i.e.:

£1 685 − £1 404 = £281

Of course had the £ strengthened so that it became worth more than $1.50 we should have had to give fewer pounds for the dollars we require, and the purchasing price variance on exchange would have been favourable.

(f) Sales turnover variance
The *Official Terminology* handbook refers to this variance, which it specifically states is not part of the chart of interrelated variances shown in Fig. 9.4.

The formula is:

Sales turnover variance = (Budgeted sales units × Standard selling price) − (Actual sales units × Standard selling price)

9.19 Measures of performance in production (production ratios)

It is helpful when appraising production to have measures of performance from which current performance can be judged. Such measures of performance are usually in ratio form because ratios bring out relative performance in the efficiency achieved, the level of activity and the usage of capacity. We therefore calculate control ratios concerning production, when quantities of goods produced or services provided are expressed in either standard direct labour hours or standard machine hours.

The CIMA publication *Official Terminology* defines ratios concerning production as follows:

(i) Production volume ratio This ratio is calculated as:

$$\text{Production volume ratio} = \frac{\text{Standard hours produced}}{\text{Budgeted capacity}} \times 100$$

'Standard hours produced' means the number of standard hours equivalent to the production achieved (whether completed units or work-in-progress). 'Budgeted capacity' is explained below.

(ii) Capacity ratio This measures the performance achieved in the use of capacity. The ratio is calculated by the formula:

$$\text{Capacity ratio} = \frac{\text{Actual hours worked}}{\text{Budgeted capacity}} \times 100$$

The more commonly used capacity levels are:

- full capacity – output, expressed in standard hours, that could be achieved if sales order, supplies and workforce were available for all installed workplaces (100 per cent);
- practical capacity – full capacity less an allowance for known unavoidable volume losses (say 95 per cent);
- budgeted capacity – standard hours planned for the period, taking into

account budgeted sales, supplies, workforce, availability and efficiency expected (say 90 per cent of full capacity) at 90 per cent efficiency = 81 per cent).

(iii) Idle capacity ratio This measures the unutilised capacity as a percentage of the practical capacity to show to what extent capacity that could have been used was lying idle. The formula is:

$$\text{Idle capacity ratio} = \frac{\text{Practical capacity} - \text{Budgeted capacity}}{\text{Practical capacity}} \times 100$$

$$= \frac{(\text{say } 95\% - 81\%)}{95\%} \times 100 = \frac{1\,400}{95} = 14.7\%$$

(iv) Efficiency ratio This ratio measures the efficiency of the workforce in terms of the production achieved (measured in standard hours of work). It is calculated by the formula:

$$\text{Efficiency ratio} = \frac{\text{Standard hours produced}}{\text{Actual direct labour hours}} \times 100$$

Considering these ratios in a practical example we have:

EXAMPLE 9.1

Standard time	4 hours per unit
Budget	192 units (768 standard hours)
Actual production	197 units (788 standard hours in 800 actual hours worked)

Production volume ratio

$$= \frac{\text{Standard hours produced}}{\text{Budgeted capacity}} \times 100$$

$$= \frac{788}{768} \times 100 = \underline{\underline{102.6\%}}$$

Capacity ratio

$$= \frac{\text{Actual hours worked}}{\text{Budgeted capacity}} \times 100$$

$$= \frac{800}{768} \times 100 = \underline{\underline{104.2\%}}$$

Efficiency ratio

$$= \frac{\text{Standard hours produced}}{\text{Actual direct labour hours}} \times 100$$

$$= \frac{788}{800} \times 100 = \underline{\underline{98.5\%}}$$

Note: In this example there can be no idle capacity, for the capacity is being used to 104.2 per cent.

A comparison of budgeted and actual production shows that five extra units were produced and this accounts for the increase of 2.6 per cent in the volume of production. However, this volume was achieved in 800 hours, compared with 768 hours budgeted for the usage of capacity, and this accounts for the increase of 4.2 per cent shown by the capacity ratio. As the increase in the use of capacity was greater than the increase in the volume of production, this indicates that the efficiency was below 100 per cent.

These ratios are related to each other, and the efficiency ratio can be calculated or proved by using the production volume ratio and the capacity ratio as follows:

$$\text{Efficiency ratio} = \frac{\text{Production volume ratio}}{\text{Capacity ratio}} \times 100$$

$$= \frac{102.6}{104.2} \times 100 = \underline{\underline{98.5\%}}$$

At the standard rate of production, 200 units should be produced in 800 hours.

$$\text{Efficiency ratio} = \frac{\text{Actual production}}{\text{Production at standard rate}} \times 100$$

$$= \frac{197}{200} \times 100 = \underline{\underline{98.5\%}}$$

The efficiency ratio is also referred to as the *rate of efficiency* or simply as the *efficiency*.

9.20 Exercises

1. What are the main differences between *historical costing* and *standard costing*?

2. Explain the meaning of the following terms used in a standard costing system:
   (a) direct labour efficiency variance;
   (b) fixed production overhead expenditure variance;
   (c) revisions variance;
   (d) calendar variance.

3. You are in the process of making arrangements for the installation of a standard costing system, and management are particularly interested in the types of standard and the standard conditions that will apply to the new costing system. Explain the following terms: *(a)* standard conditions, *(b)* current standard and *(c)* basic standard.

4. Explain briefly how material and labour standards are established and

indicate the main variances which would occur if these standards were used in a manufacturing business.

5. A manufacturing company produces a component which is made up of four identical pieces of material. Standard costing has recently been installed and you are required to calculate (*a*) the direct material variances and (*b*) the direct labour variances. Calculate the variances from the information given below.

   Components produced during the period = 8 500
   Standard direct material (4 units per component) = £1.50 per unit
   Material issued = 34 500 units at £1.60 per unit
   Standard hours of direct labour per component = $2\frac{1}{2}$ hours
   Standard direct labour rate = £4 per hour
   Actual hours worked = 22 600 at £4.10 per hour

6. A manufacturing company has a system of financial and production control which uses budgetary control and standard costing to isolate the variances which occur during each period of operations.

   Product Z is produced in departments F and M and in a certain month 750 units were produced. Information extracted from the budget for the year is as follows:

	Overhead expenditure £	Standard hours of production on product Z	Standard hours allowed per unit of product Z
Department F	140 000	56 000	7
Department M	312 000	96 000	12
	£452 000	152 000	19

   Actual overhead expenditure incurred during the month:

Department F	£13 005
Department M	£29 405

   You are required to calculate the costs and variances for the month and to present these clearly in the statement you prepare, showing:
   (*a*) the standard overhead cost per unit of Z;
   (*b*) the standard overhead cost for the month for each department;
   (*c*) the overhead variance for the month for each department.

7. A manufacturing company has the following budgeted costs for one month which are based on a normal capacity level of 40 000 hours. A departmental overhead absorption rate of £4.40 per hour has been calculated, as follows:

Overhead item	Fixed	Variable per hour
	£'000	£
Management and supervision	30	—
Shift premium	—	0.10
National insurance and pension costs	6	0.22
Inspection	20	0.25
Consumable supplies	6	0.18
Power for machinery	—	0.20
Lighting and heating	4	—
Rates	9	—
Repairs and maintenance	8	0.15
Materials handling	10	0.30
Depreciation of machinery	15	—
Production administration	12	—
	120	
Overhead rate per hour: Variable		1.40
Fixed		3.00
		£4.40

During the month of April, the company actually worked 36 000 hours, producing 36 000 standard hours of production and incurring the following overhead costs:

	£'000
Management and supervision	30.0
Shift premium	4.0
National insurance and pension costs	15.0
Inspection	28.0
Consumable supplies	12.7
Power for machinery	7.8
Lighting and heating	4.2
Rates	9.0
Repairs and maintenance	15.1
Materials handling	21.4
Depeciation of machinery	15.0
Production administration	11.5
Idle time	1.6

Prepare a statement showing for April the flexible budget for the month, the actual costs and the variance for each overhead item.

(CIMA)

8. You are required to calculate the variances in respect of the following:

(a) Materials: standard price £8.30 per unit; actual price £8.56 per unit; material requisitioned 1 000 units; production achieved 1 020.

(b) Labour: standard rate £3.60 per hour; rate paid £3.90 per hour; standard time allowed per article 8 minutes; hours worked 170.

9. From the following information, calculate the variances for *(a)* materials, and *(b)* labour:

800 units of material were requisitioned and 780 articles were produced. The standard price of the material was £4.20 per unit and the price paid as shown on the stores record card was £4.00 per unit. The standard rate of wages was £3.80 per hour and the rate paid was £3.70 per hour for 195 hours. The standard time for the production of each article was 16 minutes.

10. A company has budgeted to produce 2 750 articles in 22 000 hours, with fixed overheads of £88 000 and variable overheads of £55 000. In the event, production during the period of the budget amounted to 2 700 articles in 21 500 working hours, with fixed overheads costing £90 000 and variable overheads £58 000.

Calculate the following variances and prepare a summary:

(a) overhead total variance;
(b) fixed overhead total variance;
(c) variable overhead total variance;
(d) fixed production overhead expenditure variance;
(e) fixed production overhead volume variance;
(f) variable production overhead expenditure variance;
(g) variable production overhead efficiency variance.

11. Budgetary control and standard costing is used in a manufacturing company and the budget and production records for the most recent period showed the following:

Budget	£	*Actual*	£
Fixed overheads	126 000	Fixed overheads	130 000
Variable overheads	88 200	Variable overheads	99 000
Standard hours	25 200	Hours worked	26 000
Units of production	8 400	Units produced	8 200

Calculate the variances for overheads, and show them in the form of a summary.

12. *(a)* Explain briefly:

(i) how standards are compiled for material and labour costs for a product;
(ii) the nature of material and labour variances, and the purpose of investigating them.

(b) Calculate the material and labour variances from the data set out below and present your answers in the form of a statement for presentation to management.

	Standard
Weight to produce one unit	12 kilograms
Price per kilogram	£18
Hours to produce one unit	10
Wage rate, per hour	£4

Actual production and costs for week ended 12 November 19..:

Units produced	240
Materials used	2 640 kilograms
Material cost	£52 800
Hours worked	2 520
Wages paid	£11 088

(CIMA, adapted)

13. The cost department of a manufacturing company recorded the following information for 19 May..:

Number of units produced	180
Overhead costs (fixed £12 000)	£19 400
Hours worked	4 050
Number of working days	20

The company's budget and standard costing system provided the following details:

Standard hours per unit	20
Standard overhead rate per hour	£6.25
Standard fixed overhead rate per hour	£4.00
Budgeted hours per month	4 000
Budgeted working days per month	20

You are required to calculate:

(a) the overhead total variance;
(b) the fixed overhead total variance;
(c) the variable overhead total variance;
(d) the fixed overhead expenditure variance;
(e) the fixed overhead volume variance;
(f) the variable overhead expenditure variance;
(g) the variable overhead efficiency variance.

14. The budgeted and actual results of a catering company are as shown on p. 252:

Budget:		*Actual:*	
Sales:			
	£		£
1 240 meals at £3.60 per meal	4 464	1 260 meals at £3.60 per meal	4 536
Less Cost of sales	2 232	*Less* Cost of sales	2 154
Gross profit	2 232	Gross profit	2 382

There were two ingredients, A and B, and the actual quantity used amounted to 300 kg for A and 150 kg for B at a price of £3.58 and £7.20 per kg respectively. The standard material allowed per meal was 250 g for A and 125 g for B, and the standard price set amounted to £3.48 per kg and £7.44 per kg respectively.

(a) Calculate (i) the sales volume profit variance, (ii) the ingredient price variances and (iii) the ingredient usage variances.

(b) Prepare a summary to show the variances and reconcile these with actual profit.

(c) Briefly comment on the significance of the variances disclosed.

UNIT 10

Budgetary control

10.1 Planning and forecasting

The success of an enterprise is dependent on the objectives, policies and practices of those who direct it. The managers have to state their policy and determine the end results they want and, in so doing, must plan the activities necessary to achieve their objectives.

The old patterns of management, where intuition was used as a guide in directing an organisation, have changed and been replaced by the establishment of control points which clarify responsibilities and accountability.

Management is concerned with three factors of control:

(i) The control of money The management of money is carried out by using ratio analyses to investigate current assets and current liabilities, inventory and sales, fixed assets and net worth and similar items, and the net return on invested capital. This area is part of financial accountancy, rather than management accountancy.

(ii) The direction of operations The management of operations is to do with day-to-day activities concerning sales, rate of stock turnover, operating expenses, gross margins, and so on, and the net profit on sales.

(iii) The management of people This relates to customers and employees.

Budgetary control is a carefully worked out financial plan based on forecasts and the best possible estimates that can be made at the date when the budgets are prepared. Those concerned with forecasting and planning future action must consult and communicate with many people in order to obtain vital information which is needed in the preparation of budgets. The purpose of the plan is to ensure that the business is operated as a unified whole rather than as a group of separate departments. Co-operation is essential if the plan is to be a success, and by assigning responsibilities to people in charge of a particular function of the business, a budget regulates spending.

There is a distinction between a forecast and a plan: the forecast is a prediction of what is likely to happen under certain conditions and is concerned with probabilities, whereas a plan is an objective which takes account of policy. The budget provides a means of control.

A budget is defined by the CIMA as:

> a plan expressed in money. It is prepared and approved prior to the

> budget period and may show income, expenditure and the capital to be employed. It may be drawn up showing incremental effects on former budgeted or actual figures, or it may be compiled by zero-based budgeting. (*Official Terminology*)

Budgetary control is defined by the CIMA as:

> a technique for the establishment of budgets relating the responsibilities of executives to the requirements of a policy, and the continuous comparison of actual with budgeted results, either to secure by individual action the objective of that policy or to provide a basis for its revision.

The complex business of preparing budgets requires various officials to produce the figures within their field of responsibility by definite deadline dates. A *budget manual* will assist in allocating responsibilities.

Budget manual

This contains a set of instructions governing the responsibilities of persons, and the procedures, forms and records relating to the plan and objectives of a system of budgetary control. It is a guide which describes the functions of those involved in the preparation and control of budgets. It will indicate the duties and responsibilities of the budget committee (see Unit 10.2) and other officials, and will state the dates for the submission of estimates and reports and the procedure for the approval and revision of budgets. It will provide information on the preparation of the sales budget and the steps which will follow in establishing materials, labour and expense budgets and any other budgets such as plant and equipment.

10.2 Budget committee

The volume of work and the problems associated with the preparation of budgets invariably require the constitution of a *budget committee*. The chair is usually the chief executive and the secretary, who carries out the routine work, is normally the *budget officer*. Much preliminary work has to be done and this is started at an early stage in order to prepare the final figures well before the new period begins. The budget committee consists of the senior executives of the business, whose function is to consider past performance by an analysis of income and expenditure, and to take account of present trends and likely changes in the future. They will make their plans in accordance with the policy of the board of directors, and as interpreted by the managing director or general manager.

The budget officer confers with each person who is responsible for sectional budgets, and provisional figures will be agreed; but notice has to be taken of the *principal budget factor*, which is the factor that restricts the operations and progress of the business. It may be sales or a shortage of cash, materials, labour or other factors, and decisions will have to be made by the committee before the sectional budgets can be finalised, as this factor controls all the other budgets. The principal factor is the main restriction on operations but there may be other limiting factors similar to those mentioned above which also have to be taken into account (see Unit 8.9). Despite these limiting factors it is generally agreed that if persons who are in charge of particular functions prepare their own budgets by planning and forecasting, then they are more likely to be in states of mind which will encourage them to attempt to achieve the targets set.

10.3 The budget period

This is determined by the nature of the business and the types of budget which are to be prepared. The natural period of time is one year, but industries connected with fashion or seasonal trades may need a shorter period. Others may need a longer period, and capital expenditure budgets may be set for three to five years. However, frequent revision is usually essential, because of changes in prices and policies.

For purposes of control, some budgets are broken down into shorter periods, such as the cash budget, which is normally set on a monthly basis, and the budget for a supervisor, which is probably on a weekly basis.

10.4 Functional budgets

Budgetary control is a technique which is used in the management and direction of operations and is applied by the use of *functional budgets* for each activity in the business. Budgets differ slightly between one industry or organisation and another, but the objective is the same. In order that control can be exercised when the period of operations begins, budgets are prepared which can be compared with the operating statements for each manufacturing or trading period. This comparison will disclose variances which, after examination and investigation, will generally reveal the cause of the difference between the actual cost and the allowance set. Before operations start, the budgets are summarised, and the details provide information which is used to prepare the *master budget*. This budget is a forecasted Profit and Loss Account and all these budgets are completed by preparing a forecasted Balance Sheet.

Functional budgets include the following:

sales budget;
production budget;
manufacturing budget (direct materials, direct wages, factory overhead);
administration, selling and distribution cost budgets;
purchases budget;
cash budget;
plant utilisation budget;
capital expenditure budget;
research and development budget.

10.5 The sales budget

The preparation of this budget begins with a *sales forecast*, which is a difficult task because of fluctuations in sales which take place over the year. It is on this budget that many of the other budgets are based. The work of forecasting usually starts with an examination of the sales analysis for the current year as far as it is available. In the work of developing the forecast, the following details may be required:

(i) unit sales by product lines;
(ii) sales expected in each area or country;
(iii) sales for each month;
(iv) sales to customers or through agents at non-standard prices.

Policy conditions, such as a decision to increase production facilities by shift-working or to expand plant capacity, are taken into account. There may be changes in prices, and a forecast will have to be made of business conditions in general, including changes in population or in the income available to consumers. The initial forecast will be in quantities or units which will later be evaluated by using standard or budget prices or, where applicable, non-standard prices.

10.6 The production budget

The production budget is based on the sales budget, and this relationship requires a co-ordination of sales and production policy so that sales targets can be aligned with the production capacity of the factory, after allowing for the available stocks and for supplies that can be obtained outside the factory. A production programme has to be drawn up which will indicate in terms of output the hours of work required to meet the requirements of the sales department. The budget is a statement of the units of product to be made and the hours of work expected from each department and cost centre. The objects are to manufacture the products so that they are available on the dates specified by the customer or the sales department and, at the same time, to maintain a reasonably low level of stocks in order to avoid excessive obsolescence.

10.7 The manufacturing or production cost budget

This budget sets out the allowed expenditure for the output indicated in the production budget. As this is a cost of production budget, it is closely linked with the cash budget and the master budget. There are subsidiary budgets for direct materials, direct wages and overhead expenses, and the production budget referred to above could, if desired, be included under the heading of this section.

(a) Direct material cost

Standard costing greatly facilitates the preparation of a materials budget, but when standard cost records are not available the details have to be obtained from previous costs or estimates, which have to be adjusted so that they are relevant to the period when manufacture takes place.

(b) Direct labour cost

A similar procedure applies to estimating the cost of wages. The hours shown in the production budget are used with the wage rates which are likely to apply during the period of production.

(c) Overhead expenses

This budget has to be assembled from a large amount of detailed information from past records, and updated to allow for changes in future costs and budgeted activity. It is compiled on the basis of departmental overhead expense budgets and cost centre budgets. These are laid out to conform with the expense classification records so that the budgeted costs are available for use in the manufacturing period when actual costs are compared with budgeted figures. Budgetary control is not only concerned with costs but should also, as a means of control, be concerned with quantities. As far as possible, the costs should be set alongside units of material and hours of labour. Controllable and uncontrollable costs are also important factors and costs can be analysed as fixed, variable and semi-variable. This is necessary when budgeted costs are fixed on the basis of allowances set out in a *flexible budget*, which is one where costs are separated into fixed, semi-fixed and variable, and where the budgeted costs are set for various levels of activity. In this way, the spending allowance for each item of overhead is adjusted to the volume of production and the allowance changes in relation to the level of activity attained. A flexible budget is shown in Table 10.1 (p. 258).

10.8 The selling and distribution cost budget

This deals with the costs of selling and distributing the goods or services of the business. It covers expenditure incurred in promoting sales, retaining custom, packing for transport, storage of finished goods, advertising and publicity and similar costs.

10.9 The purchasing budget

This budget includes all materials used in the business such as direct and indirect materials required for production, selling and administration, capital expenditure, and those used in research and development. Allowance is made for outstanding orders and closing stocks, and for any changes in the levels of stocks of raw materials, finished goods or bought-out items.

The budget provides information to enable the purchasing department to arrange for goods to be supplied when prices are at the most economic level, or to take advantage of special prices. As this budget involves a large outwards flow of cash, it is related to the cash budget, and the plans made will give

Table 10.1 Flexible budget – works maintenance department

Activity	0%		95%	100%	105%	110%
		Variable	Hours			
	Fixed	cost				
Expense	cost	per hour	23 750	25 000	26 250	27 500
	£	£	£	£	£	£
Materials	–	3.00	71 250	75 000	78 750	82 500
Labour	9 000	4.50	115 875	121 500	127 125	132 750
Salaries	18 000	–	18 000	18 000	18 000	18 000
Tools and equipment	2 400	1.50	38 025	39 000	41 775	43 650
Fuel	–	0.90	21 375	22 500	23 625	24 750
Depreciation	3 000	–	3 000	3 000	3 000	3 000
	£32 400		£267 525	£279 900	£292 275	£304 650
Rate per hour			£11.264	£11.196	£11.134	£11.078

Notes:

(i) The budget is in steps of 5 per cent with a range between 95 per cent and 110 per cent. Certain items of expense are fixed, while others include a fixed charge and a variable charge. Where the cost includes both types of expense, the difference in cost between each column is a result of the change in activity or volume of output. For example, the change in hours for 5 per cent activity is 1 250 hours, and in the case of labour 1 250 hours at £4.50 is £5 625, which is the difference between each column and the next. At 100 per cent activity the cost is £9 000 fixed cost plus 25 000 hours at £4.50 per hour, which gives £121 500. At 95 per cent activity, the cost includes £9 000 fixed costs plus 23 750 hours at £4.50 per hour, which totals £115 875.

(ii) Normal capacity is represented by 100 per cent and 25 000 hours. At this level the overhead rate per direct labour hour is £11.196, which includes:

$$\frac{\text{Fixed costs}}{\text{Hours worked}} = \frac{£32\,400}{25\,000} = £\ 1.296$$

$$\frac{\text{Variable costs}}{\text{Hours worked}} = \frac{£279\,900 - £32\,400}{25\,000} = £\ 9.900$$

$$£11.196$$

indications of the cash requirements, and, in some cases, may have to be adjusted to the availability of cash as shown in the cash budget.

10.10 The cash budget

A cash budget is a summary of the expected cash receipts and payments during the period of the budget. This budget is usually drawn up on a monthly basis and begins with the balance at the beginning of the year. After taking account of receipts and disbursements during the month, it shows the balance which is then carried forward.

Cash receipts include:

Payments by debtors, cash sales, dividends received, sales of assets (capital), loans received, and issues of shares and debentures.

Payments include:

Wages and salaries, payments to creditors, rent and rates, taxes, capital expenditure, dividends payable, commission payable and repayments of debentures.

The cash budget is an important one as it indicates whether cash is available to meet demands and whether additional finance will be required. It also shows any surplus cash which could be invested outside the business.

Note that the cash budget is drawn up on a receipts and payments basis, whereas the other budgets are concerned with income and expenditure and are related to activity. An example of a cash budget is given below.

EXAMPLE 10.1

A company prepares budgets on a monthly basis for the quarter ending 31 March 19 . 1. In order to produce the necessary budgets, the following forecasts have been made for the five months from November 19 . 0 to March 19 . 1.

	Purchases	Sales	Overheads	Depreciation	Wages
	£	£	£	£	£
November	77 000	157 500	14 000	1 050	42 000
December	50 400	87 500	11 200	1 050	28 700
January	42 000	100 100	10 500	1 050	29 400
February	52 500	105 000	11 500	1 050	37 800
March	58 100	126 000	12 600	1 050	38 500

Further information may be applicable to a cash budget:

(a) All purchases are on credit; suppliers will be paid two months after the date of the transaction.

(b) 20 per cent of sales are on credit. Debts are paid in the month after the transaction takes place. The balance of the forecast is in respect of cash sales.

(c) Overheads include charges for the following:

(i) Electricity – November £800; December £810; January £630; February £735; March £840. Quarterly accounts are received for this expense.

(ii) The electricity bill for the quarter ending 31 December 19 .0, which is estimated to amount to £2 150, will be paid in January 19 . 1.

(iii) The rent is £8 400 per annum and is paid quarterly in advance on 1 January, 1 April, 1 July and 1 October.

(iv) Annual rates are paid in advance on 1 April and 1 October. The rates for 19 .0/19 .1 amount to £12 600; £6 300 has been paid in April and £6 300 in October.

(v) All other overheads are paid in cash as they occur.

(d) Wages are paid in cash as they become due for payment.

(e) Capital expenditure is in respect of office equipment to be received by the company in February 19 . 1. The cost is £7 000 and the account will be settled in March 19 . 1.

(f) The bank balance at 1 January 19 . 1 is expected to be £10 500. The cash budget is prepared and presented as shown in Fig. 10.1.

10.11 The plant utilisation budget

This budget is concerned with the facilities available to carry out the production programme. It shows the machine load of individual machines or groups of machines in different departments or cost centres.

This budget discloses which machines or departments are overloaded and steps can then be taken to:

(a) work overtime or increase the overtime hours;
(b) begin shiftworking or increase the number of shifts;
(c) place work with sub-contractors;
(d) transfer work to other departments;
(e) place work with other factories within the group;
(f) extend the plant.

If it is not possible to arrange for the desired volume of production, an amendment would have to be made to the sales and associated budgets. This could lead to spare capacity in other sections and efforts would then be needed to find ways of filling the gap.

10.12 The capital expenditure budget

This refers to the purchase or manufacture of fixed assets for replacements, extensions as a result of expansion or overloading, and new techniques requiring modern machinery or equipment. The items included in this budget apply to the production, administration and selling functions of the business.

It is a long-term budget, usually set for three to five years, and requires frequent revision because of changes in costs of land, buildings, machinery and equipment. With a long-term budget, there is often a change of outlook: new proposals are made, or a revision may be needed because of economic conditions.

This budget gives an indication of the cash requirements, and if financial

---

Notes to Fig. 10.1:

(i) For the purpose of preparing budgets, the forecasts include *depreciation* which is a non-cash item and must not be included in a cash budget.

(ii) Overhead expenditure includes costs which are incurred on a credit basis and these must be deducted. The items must be included in the cash budget only when they are actually paid.

Cash budget for quarter ending 31 March 19 . 1

	January	February	March
	£	£	£
Balance brought forward	10 500	(10 690)	(3 885)
Receipts			
Sales	97 580	104 020	121 800
	£108 080	£ 93 330	£117 915
Payments			
Purchases	77 000	50 400	42 000
Electricity	2 150	—	—
Rent	2 100	—	—
Rates	—	—	—
Other overheads	8 120	9 015	10 010
Wages	29 400	37 800	38 500
Capital expenditure	—	—	7 000
	£118 770	£ 97 215	£ 97 510
Balance carried forward:	(10 690)	(3 885)	£20 405

Workings

	Sales January	Sales February	Sales March	Purchases
	£	£	£	
	100 100	105 000	126 000	November £77 000
Less 20% credit sales	20 020	21 000	25 200	(paid January)
Cash sales	80 080	84 000	100 800	December £50 400
Add Credit sales from				(paid February)
previous month	17 500	20 020	21 000	January £42 000
	£ 97 580	£104 020	£121 800	(paid March)

Overheads

		£		£		£
	January	10 500	February	11 500	March	12 600
Less Electricity	630		735		840	
Rent	700		700		700	
Rates	1 050		1 050		1 050	
		2 380		2 485		2 590
		£ 8 120		£ 9 015		£ 10 010

Fig. 10.1 Example of a cash budget

resources are not available within the company, arrangements have to be made to borrow the cash so that the project can be carried out. It is always important to consider the effect of capital expenditure on the other budgets, in connection with the reduction or increase in costs or selling prices.

10.13 Other budgets

There are many different types of budget which may be used in planning operations.

(a) Research and development budget

This expenditure is concerned with the improvement of existing products, and the development of new ones or of new methods of production. It may involve the design of special machines or equipment, the testing of raw materials or pure research. Research and development expenditure may represent an essential part of a company's costs but it is an element which has to be carefuly controlled. The usual procedure is for directors to sanction or appropriate an amount that they consider reasonable, which is either based on costs of a previous period or on the basis of requests made by the head of research. S/he will submit a programme of work to be carried out in the budget period, supported by estimated costs.

(b) Personnel budget

This budget provides details of the labour force required to carry out the work planned in the various budgets, and shows the direct and indirect workers in number, grades and wages. It is a manpower planning exercise which defines the labour force for the budget period and tends to stabilise the ratio of direct to indirect workers.

(c) Administrative expense budget

Salaries are the most important item in this budget and most of the expenses can be estimated on the basis of previous costs with an adjustment for salary awards and likely increases in the budget period.

(d) Forecast, control and appropriation budgets

These terms apply to the way in which budgeted expense allowances are determined. The forecast budget provides a basis for planning and is sometimes called a *fixed budget*, as opposed to a *flexible budget*, because the amounts are not adjusted for volume. The control budget is a flexible budget which determines the amount on a volume basis. The appropriation budget establishes a limit on spending, such as for advertising or research.

10.14 General procedure

Budgetary control is a system which places responsibility where it belongs, and accounts for the term *responsibility budgets*. Co-operation among all those concerned with the operation of budgetary control is essential and details of the system should be explained to each of those involved.

Control is exercised by assigning responsibility and measuring results and then reporting the deviations from budget to those in charge of operations and expenditure. The budget officer analyses the variances and decides on the significance of the results. S/he should concentrate on those matters requiring attention in order to ascertain which variances are the result of internal operations and the actions of employees, and which variances are caused externally, and are probably uncontrollable. When preparing the reports, the budgeted figures and the actual costs should be set side by side and only the relevant facts should be reported, but adequate explanations should be given. Variations may be as a result of price changes (*price variances*) or gains or losses caused by volume (*volume variances*) or changed conditions (*revisions variances*). Other variations may be due to the use of methods different from those planned (*methods variances*) or to many other causes. *Controllable variances* are those for which a particular individual is responsible and which indicate success or failure in controlling the expenditure. This applies to items such as the usage of material and the employment and supervision of labour, which results in different degrees of efficiency.

After allowing for comments from those receiving the reports, decisions should be made to take corrective action where this is possible and advisable, to make further investigations, to change the methods or to revise the budget.

10.15 An exercise in setting budgets

This exercise and the budgets which follow have, of necessity, been simplified and abbreviated. The budgets are quarterly rather than monthly. A draft Balance Sheet has been prepared for the current year as certain details are required in the preparation of budgets, and this Balance Sheet will be needed when the master budget is prepared (see Fig. 10.2, pp. 264–5).

The sales manager received reports from the area representatives of expected sales of machines in their regions, and from this compiled Tables 10.2 and 10.3 (pp. 266 and 267).

From the detailed information received from the areas, the sales manager prepared a sales forecast which was agreed with the chief executive, and eventually this forecast was the basis of the sales budget. The forecast and budget are shown in Tables 10.4 and 10.5 (pp. 268 and 269).

Using the sales forecast as a basis the budget committee considered the production forecast for the year, and it was decided to use the production facilities to manufacture a slightly larger quantity of machines than that shown in the sales budget. It was suggested that the surplus machines should be treated as stock at the year-end and shown as such in the master budget, but the sales department was to try to sell these machines as they became available. A statement of the stocks and planned production is as follows:

(continued on p. 266)

Balance Sheet as at 31 December 19 . 0

Assets employed	Cost £	Less Depreciation £	Value £
Fixed assets			
Land and buildings	1 177 500	9 000	1 168 500
Machinery and plant	300 000	53 400	246 600
Motor vehicles	75 000	33 000	42 000
Office furniture	15 000	6 000	9 000
	1 567 500	101 400	1 466 100
Quoted investments (market value £142 500)			142 425
Current assets			
Stock: General stores	715 686		
Finished goods (machines)	82 200		
		797 886	
Debtors		241 500	
Cash at bank and in hand		235 884	
		1 275 270	
Less Current liabilities			
Creditors	303 000		
Wages due	13 500		
Preference dividend proposed	52 500		
Proposed ordinary dividend	75 000		
Corporation tax	266 775		
		710 775	
Net current assets			564 495
			£2 173 020

Financed by

			£	£
Preference shareholders' interest in the company			Authorised	
750 000 7% Preference shares of £1 each fully paid			750 000	750 000
		Authorised £		
750 000 Ordinary shares of £1 each fully paid		750 000	750 000	
Reserves				
Revenue reserves:	£			
Staff pension fund		148 500		
General reserve		219 000		
Profit and Loss Account	11 250			
Less Preliminary expenses	5 730			
		5 520		
			373 020	
Ordinary shareholders' equity				1 123 020
Long-term liability				
6% debentures				300 000
				£2 173 020

Note: Stock of finished machines consists of:

Product X 2 @ £7 800 =	£15 600
Product Y 4 @ £7 200 =	£28 800
Product Z 6 @ £6 300 =	£37 800
	£82 200

Fig. 10.2 Draft Balance Sheet

Table 10.2 Estimated quarterly sales for year ending 31 December 19 . 1

Machine type	X	Y	Z	*Totals*
Quarter ending				
31 March	35	56	42	133
30 June	28	50	29	107
30 September	19	39	24	82
31 December	30	50	34	114
Totals	112	195	129	436
Selling price	£10 800	£9 600	£8 640	
Total sales	£1 209 600	£1 872 000	£1 114 560	£4 196 160

Product	X	Y	Z
Budgeted sales	112	195	129
Less Estimated opening stock	2	4	6
Production required to meet the sales forecast	110	191	123
Add Closing stock	7	11	16
Planned production	117	202	139

The works manager and production controller estimated the quarterly production as shown in Table 10.6 (p. 270).

Information is now available which indicates what is to be produced and the quantities, in terms of machines, to be produced in each quarter.

This information will enable the production budget to be produced in two ways:

(a) *Production volume* in terms of hours to be worked in each department;
(b) *Production cost* by using subsidiary budgets for the elements of cost.

The production records (Table 10.7, p. 270) showed the direct labour hours required to manufacture the machines.

On the basis of these hours of direct labour, the production budget (volume) for the year was prepared for each quarter, showing the number of machines to be produced and the hours of work for each type of machine in each of the departments (see Table 10.8, p. 271).

The purchasing officer made a general statement to the committee on the expected movement in prices during the budget period and was requested to prepare and present to the budget officer a schedule of material prices for direct and indirect materials, so that the budget for direct materials and the budget for factory overhead could be drawn up (Tables 10.9 and 10.11, pp. 272 and 274). The personnel manager stated that the rates of wages payable during the period of the budget were estimated to be: *(continued on p. 268)*

Table 10.3 Estimated area sales for year ending 31 December 19 . 1

Machine type Selling price	X £10 800		Y £9 600		Z £8 640		*Totals*	
	Units sold	£	Units sold	£	Units sold	£	Units sold	£
Area A	35	378 000	125	1 200 000	70	604 800	230	2 182 800
Area B	17	183 600	27	259 200	20	172 800	64	615 600
Area C	27	291 600	18	172 800	15	129 600	60	594 000
Area D	33	356 400	25	240 000	24	207 360	82	803 760
Totals	112	£1 209 600	195	£1 872 000	129	£1 114 560	436	£4 196 160

Table 10.4 Sales forecast of machines for period ending 31 December 19 . 1

	Current year 19.0	Quarter ending 31 Mar.	30 June	30 Sept.	31 Dec.	*Totals*
Area A						
Product X	30	10	9	7	9	35
Product Y	120	35	32	28	30	125
Product Z	60	20	18	15	17	70
	210	65	59	50	56	230
Area B						
Product X	15	5	4	3	5	17
Product Y	30	8	7	5	7	27
Product Z	15	6	5	4	5	20
	60	19	16	12	17	64
Area C						
Product X	25	8	7	5	7	27
Product Y	16	5	5	4	4	18
Product Z	12	6	3	2	4	15
	53	19	15	11	15	60
Area D						
Product X	35	12	8	4	9	33
Product Y	28	8	6	2	9	25
Product Z	20	10	3	3	8	24
	83	30	17	9	26	82
Totals	406	133	107	82	114	436

Department 1	£3.00 per hour
Department 2	£4.50 per hour
Department 3	£6.00 per hour

The direct wages budget was drawn up by the budget officer by using the information shown in the production budget for the direct labour hours and the rates of wages already given. This budget is shown in Table 10.10 (p. 273).

On the basis of the production forecast the committee considered the effect of this output and other matters on the cost of factory overheads. The works manager was asked to consult with departmental heads in order to establish the extent of work to be carried out in respect of maintenance and services during the budget period.

Table 10.5 Sales budget for period ending 31 December 19 . 1

	Current year 19 . 0	Standard price	Quarter ending 31 Mar.	30 June	30 Sept.	31 Dec.	*Totals*
	£	£	£	£	£	£	£
Area A							
Product X	306 000	10 800	108 000	97 200	75 600	97 200	378 000
Product Y	1 087 200	9 600	336 000	307 200	268 800	288 000	1 200 000
Product Z	489 600	8 640	172 800	155 520	129 600	146 880	604 800
	1 882 800	–	616 800	559 920	474 000	532 080	2 182 800
Area B							
Product X	153 000	10 800	54 000	43 200	32 400	54 000	183 600
Product Y	271 800	9 600	76 800	67 200	48 000	67 200	259 200
Product Z	122 400	8 640	51 840	43 200	34 560	43 200	172 800
	547 200	–	182 640	153 600	114 960	164 400	615 600
Area C							
Product X	255 000	10 800	86 400	75 600	54 000	75 600	291 600
Product Y	144 960	9 600	48 000	48 000	38 400	38 400	172 800
Product Z	97 920	8 640	51 840	25 920	17 280	34 560	129 600
	497 880	–	186 240	149 520	109 680	148 560	594 000
Area D							
Product X	357 000	10 800	129 600	86 400	43 200	97 200	356 400
Product Y	253 680	9 600	76 800	57 600	19 200	86 400	240 000
Product Z	163 200	8 640	86 400	25 920	25 920	69 120	207 360
	773 880	–	292 800	169 920	88 320	252 720	803 760
Totals	£3 701 760	–	£1 278 480	£1 032 960	£786 960	£1 097 760	£4 196 160

Note: The current year sales were achieved based on prices of £10 200; £9 060 and £8 160.

Table 10.6 Estimated quarterly production

Product	X	Y	Z	*Totals*
Quarter ending				
31 March	37	59	45	141
30 June	29	51	31	111
30 September	20	40	26	86
31 December	31	52	37	120
Planned production	117	202	139	458

Table 10.7 Direct labour hours per machine

Product	X	Y	Z
Department			
1	226	180	170
2	216	200	176
3	130	120	103
Totals	572	500	449

This information was submitted to the budget officer to enable her to prepare a draft budget for presentation to the committee. After revision this appears as shown in Table 10.11 (p. 274).

The costs recorded in the factory overhead budget and those in the direct wages budget provide the details which are required in order to calculate the absorption rates for preparation of the factory overhead (absorbed) section of the production cost budget (Table 10.12, p. 275).

Absorption rates: percentage on direct wages

$$\text{The formula is } \frac{\text{Budgeted overhead}}{\text{Budgeted direct wages}} \times 100$$

Department 1

$$\frac{£259\,296}{£259\,296} \times 100 = \underline{\underline{100\%}}$$

Department 2

$$\frac{£304\,209}{£405\,612} \times 100 = \underline{\underline{75\%}}$$

Department 3

$$\frac{£161\,301}{£322\,602} \times 100 = \underline{\underline{50\%}}$$

Table 10.8 Production budget for period ending 31 December 19 . 1

	Direct labour hours Quarter ending 31 Mar.		30 June		30 Sept.		31 Dec.		*Totals*	
	Units	Hours	Units	Hours	Units	Hours	Units	Hours	Units	Hours
Department 1										
Product X	37	8 362	29	6 554	20	4 520	31	7 006	117	26 442
Product Y	59	10 620	51	9 180	40	7 200	52	9 360	202	36 360
Product Z	45	7 650	31	5 270	26	4 420	37	6 290	139	23 630
	141	26 632	111	21 004	86	16 140	120	22 656	458	86 432
Department 2										
Product X	37	7 992	29	6 264	20	4 320	31	6 696	117	25 272
Product Y	59	11 800	51	10 200	40	8 000	52	10 400	202	40 400
Product Z	45	7 920	31	5 456	26	4 576	37	6 512	139	24 464
	141	27 712	111	21 920	86	16 896	120	23 608	458	90 136
Department 3										
Product X	37	4 810	29	3 770	20	2 600	31	4 030	117	15 210
Product Y	59	7 080	51	6 120	40	4 800	52	6 240	202	24 240
Product Z	45	4 635	31	3 193	26	2 678	37	3 811	139	14 317
	141	16 525	111	13 083	86	10 078	120	14 081	458	53 767
Totals	141	70 869	111	56 007	86	43 114	120	60 345	458	230 335

Table 10.9 Production cost budget for period ending 31 December 19 . 1

Materials	Cost per machine	*Direct materials* Quarter ending 31 Mar.	30 June	30 Sept.	31 Dec.	*Totals*
Group A						
	£	£	£	£	£	£
Product X	1 230	45 510	35 670	24 600	38 130	143 910
Product Y	1 140	67 260	58 140	45 600	59 280	230 280
Product Z	1 050	47 250	32 550	27 300	38 850	145 950
	3 420	160 020	126 360	97 500	136 260	520 140
Group B						
	£	£	£	£	£	£
Product X	1 560	57 720	45 240	31 200	48 360	182 520
Product Y	1 380	81 420	70 380	55 200	71 760	278 760
Product Z	1 302	58 590	40 362	33 852	48 174	180 978
	4 242	197 730	155 982	120 252	168 294	642 258
Group C						
	£	£	£	£	£	£
Product X	834	30 858	24 186	16 680	25 854	97 578
Product Y	657	38 763	33 507	26 280	34 164	132 714
Product Z	483	21 735	14 973	12 558	17 871	67 137
	1 974	91 356	72 666	55 518	77 889	297 429
Totals		£449 106	£355 008	£273 270	£382 443	£1 459 827

The budget officer consulted the sales manager and other officials and prepared the administration overhead budget and the selling and distribution overhead budget. This was placed before the budget committee and approved (see Table 10.13, p. 275).

The cost of administration (see Table 10.13) and the total direct wages from the production budget (see Table 10.10) provided the details for calculating the absorption rate for administration costs, and the total cost of selling and distribution (see Table 10.14, p. 276) together with the total unit sales from the sales budget (see Table 10.4) provided the details for calculating the absorption rate for the selling and distribution expenses.

Absorption rate: percentage on direct wages

$$\text{The formula is: } \frac{\text{Budgeted administration overhead}}{\text{Direct wages}} \times 100$$

$$= \frac{£296\ 253}{£987\ 510} \times 100 = \underline{\underline{30\%}}$$

(continued on p. 276)

Table 10.10 Production cost budget for period ending 31 December 19 . 1

	Rate per hour	31 March		30 June		30 September		31 December		Totals	
		Direct wages — Quarter ending									
Department 1											
	£	Hours	£	Hours	£	Hours	£	Hours	£	Hours	£
Product X	3.00	8 362	25 086	6 554	19 662	4 520	13 560	7 006	21 018	26 442	79 326
Product Y	3.00	10 620	31 860	9 180	27 540	7 200	21 600	9 360	28 080	36 360	109 080
Product Z	3.00	7 650	22 950	5 270	15 810	4 420	13 260	6 290	18 870	23 630	70 890
		26 632	79 896	21 004	63 012	16 140	48 420	22 656	67 968	86 432	259 296
Department 2											
		Hours	£	Hours	£	Hours	£	Hours	£	Hours	£
Product X	4.50	7 992	35 964	6 264	28 188	4 320	19 440	6 696	30 132	25 272	113 724
Product Y	4.50	11 800	53 100	10 200	45 900	8 000	36 000	10 400	46 800	40 400	181 800
Product Z	4.50	7 920	35 640	5 456	24 552	4 576	20 592	6 512	29 304	24 464	110 088
		27 712	124 704	21 920	98 640	16 896	76 032	23 608	106 236	90 136	405 612
Department 3											
	£	Hours	£	Hours	£	Hours	£	Hours	£	Hours	£
Product X	6.00	4 810	28 860	3 770	22 620	2 600	15 600	4 030	24 180	15 210	91 260
Product Y	6.00	7 080	42 480	6 120	36 720	4 800	28 800	6 240	37 440	24 240	145 440
Product Z	6.00	4 635	27 810	3 193	19 158	2 678	16 068	3 811	22 866	14 317	85 902
		16 525	99 150	13 083	78 498	10 078	60 468	14 081	84 486	53 767	322 602
Totals		70 869	£303 750	56 007	£240 150	43 114	184 920	60 345	£258 690	230 335	£987 510

Table 10.11 Factory overhead budget for period ending 31 December 19 . 1

	Quarter ending				
	31 Mar.	30 June	30 Sept.	31 Dec.	*Totals*
	£	£	£	£	£
	Department 1				
Indirect material	8 415	6 000	3 900	6 603	24 918
Fuel and lighting	6 642	3 300	3 000	4 500	17 442
Repairs to machines	4 530	4 200	4 110	4 275	17 115
Indirect wages	35 886	30 024	22 575	31 383	119 868
Factory expenses	21 087	17 994	14 358	18 096	71 535
Depreciation					
Land and buildings	750	750	750	750	3 000
Machinery and plant	1 353	1 353	1 356	1 356	5 418
	78 663	63 621	50 049	66 963	259 296
	Department 2				
Indirect material	9 219	6 900	5 700	7 050	28 869
Fuel and lighting	6 924	3 840	3 585	6 000	20 349
Repairs to machines	5 955	4 884	3 909	5 220	19 968
Indirect wages	44 352	33 165	24 312	39 063	140 892
Factory expenses	26 586	20 604	15 624	21 339	84 153
Depreciation					
Land and buildings	900	900	900	900	3 600
Machinery and plant	1 594	1 594	1 595	1 595	6 378
	95 530	71 887	55 625	81 167	304 209
	Department 3				
Indirect material	4 830	3 600	3 087	3 918	15435
Fuel and lighting	3 600	2 010	1 869	3 180	10 659
Repairs to machines	3 147	2 475	2 289	2 550	10 461
Indirect wages	22 389	20 778	12 711	18 822	74 700
Factory expenses	13 500	10 530	8 706	11 946	44 682
Depreciation					
Land and buildings	600	600	600	600	2 400
Machinery and plant	741	741	741	741	2 964
	48 807	40 734	30 003	41 757	161 301
Totals	£223 000	£176 242	£135 677	£189 887	£724 806

Table 10.12 Production cost budget for period ending 31 December 19 . 1

	% on direct wages	*Factory overhead (absorbed)* 31 Mar.	30 June	30 Sept.	31 Dec.	*Totals*
Department 1		£	£	£	£	£
Product X	100	25 086	19 662	13 560	21 018	79 326
Product Y	100	31 860	27 540	21 600	28 080	109 080
Product Z	100	22 950	15 810	13 260	18 870	70 890
		79 896	63 012	48 420	67 968	259 296
Department 2						
Product X	75	26 973	21 141	14 580	22 599	85 293
Product Y	75	39 825	34 425	27 000	35 100	136 350
Product Z	75	26 730	18 414	15 444	21 978	82 566
		93 528	73 980	57 024	79 677	304 209
Department 3						
Product X	50	14 430	11 310	7 800	12 090	45 630
Product Y	50	21 240	18 360	14 400	18 720	72 720
Product Z	50	13 905	9 579	8 034	11 433	42 951
		49 575	39 249	30 234	42 243	161 301
Totals		£222 999	£176 241	£135 678	£189 888	£724 806

Table 10.13 Administration overhead budget for period ending 31 December 19 . 1

	Quarter ending 31 Mar.	30 June	30 Sept.	31 Dec.	*Totals*
	£	£	£	£	£
Office expenses	39 273	42 804	31 158	43 845	157 080
Salaries	24 480	24 480	25 794	25 794	100 548
Directors' fees	–	7 500	–	7 500	15 000
Audit fees	4 875	–	–	–	4 875
Debenture interest	–	9 000	–	9 000	18 000
Depreciation (furniture)	187	187	188	188	750
Totals	£68 815	£83 971	£57 140	£86 327	£296 253

Table 10.14 Selling and distribution overhead budget for period ending 31 December 19 . 1

	Quarter ending				
	31 Mar.	30 June	30 Sept.	31 Dec.	*Totals*
	£	£	£	£	£
Travellers' salaries	30 000	30 000	36 000	38 835	134 835
Advertising	6 000	7 500	7 500	9 375	30 375
Motor expenses	18 000	18 000	22 800	22 590	81 390
Depreciation (motor vehicles)	3 750	3 750	3 750	3 750	15 000
Totals	£57 750	£59 250	£70 050	£74 550	£261 600

Absorption rate: standard rate per machine

$$\text{The formula is: } \frac{\text{Budgeted selling overhead}}{\text{Budgeted sales (units)}}$$

$$= \frac{£261\ 600}{436} = £600$$

At this stage the information is available for preparation of the budgeted machine costs (see Fig. 10.3) by using selling prices from the sales budget (Table 10.5), direct materials (Table 10.9) and direct wages (Tables 10.7 and

Notes to Fig. 10.3: extra profits

(i) The profit of £629 424 is the standard profit on the basis of standard cost in the current year.

(ii) As the standard costs have increased, an extra profit is made on the opening stock which is valued on a lower standard cost.

(iii) The opening stock (see Fig. 10.2) of £82 200 includes direct materials, direct wages, factory overhead and administration overhead.

(iv) The corresponding costs in the current year are

		£
X	2 × £8 850 =	17 160
Y	4 × £7 560 =	30 240
Z	6 × £6 744 =	40 464
		87 864

This gives an extra profit of (£87 864 − £82 200) = £5 664

As the calculation of £629 424 is based on machines which provided only the current standard profit, the standard profit for the coming year in the budget must be increased because some machines will make a higher profit. These were made more cheaply in a previous period.

						Product			
			X			Y			Z
Materials			£			£			£
Group A			1 230			1 140			1 050
Group B			1 560			1 380			1 302
Group C			834			657			483
			3 624			3 177			2 835
Direct labour									
	Hours	£		Hours	£		Hours	£	
Department 1	226	678		180	540		170	510	
Department 2	216	972		200	900		176	792	
Department 3	130	780		120	720		103	618	
	572		2 430	500		2 160	449		1 920
Factory overhead									
	%	£			£			£	
Department 1	100	678			540			510	
Department 2	75	729			675			594	
Department 3	50	390			360			309	
			1 797			1 575			1 413
Administration overhead (30%)			729			648			576
			8 580			7 560			6 744
Selling expenses			600			600			600
Total cost			9 180			8 160			7 344
Profit (15% on invoice value)			1 620			1 440			1 296
Invoice value			£10 800			£9 600			£8 640

Note: 15% on invoice value = $\frac{15}{85}$ of total cost.

	£
Product X 112 machines at a profit of £1 620 each =	181 440
Product Y 195 machines at a profit of £1 440 each =	280 800
Product Z 129 machines at a profit of £1 296 each =	167 184
	629 424
Add Extra profit on previous year's stock (*see notes on facing page*)	
X 2 at £780 = £2 340	
Y 4 at £360 = £1 440	
Z 6 at £444 = £2 664	
	5 664
	£635 088

Fig. 10.3 Budgeted machine costs

10.10) from the production cost budget, and the absorption rates from the overhead budgets. This will disclose the budgeted profit per machine and a calculation can be made to find the budgeted profit for the year.

Budgeted profit

The purchasing officer together with the materials controller prepared the purchases budget for direct and indirect materials by taking the opening stocks and using information provided by the production budget (direct materials) and the factory overhead budget. These figures will be needed when the cash budget is drawn up, although the payment of accounts will depend on the terms of credit and the policy of the company in respect of when payment should be made. These budgets are shown in Figs 10.4 and 10.5 (pp. 279–80).

The cash budget (Fig. 10.5) has been prepared starting with the balance as shown in the Balance Sheet and using the figures shown in the operating budgets. The receipts from debtors will depend on the sales and the time-lag between the date of dispatch and the date of collection. The amount shown for each period is based on past experience, by taking into account the average collection period. For convenience, the forecast of cash payments for many items is based on the assumption that payment is made in the period when the expenditure is incurred.

At this stage, the operating budgets have been prepared and approved by the budget committee which must give the final approval. A product summary budget (see Fig. 10.6, p. 281) is prepared followed by the master budget and the Balance Sheet.

The master budget can now be prepared using figures shown in the budgets or summary budget and information extracted from the Balance Sheet for the year ending 31 December 19 . 0.

The master budget (Figs 10.7 (a) and (b), pp. 284–5) takes the form of a Budgeted Profit and Loss Account and a budgeted Balance Sheet. There are several sources of figures for the master budget; those for the Profit and Loss Account (column 1) are derived from the sources shown in column 2 (p. 282).

10.16 Variance reporting

Variance reports are an essential part of a system of budgetary control. They are prepared for the period of activity, usually weekly or monthly, which is appropriate and suitable to the work performed or the expenditure which has to be incurred. There is a large number of these reports and they are sent to top management, supervisors and so on. Examples are shown in Tables 10.15 and 10.16 (pp. 286 and 287).

10.17 Zero-based budgets

This is a technique in budgeting which was introduced in 1960 by an American electronics company. It is a procedure for considering *relative values* and re-examining expenditure which, after review, has to be justified. This technique is claimed to improve cost control and to allocate resources more

Purchases budget for period ending 31 December 19 . 1

Direct materials

Materials	Stock 1 Jan.	Usage	Balance	Purchases	Stock at end of quarter
Quarter ending					
31 March	£	£	£	£	£
Group A	260 100	160 020	100 080	120 000	220 080
Group B	311 586	197 730	113 856	135 000	248 856
Group C	114 000	91 356	52 644	75 000	127 644
	715 686	449 106	266 580	330 000	596 580
	Stock 1 Apr.	Usage	Balance	Purchases	Stock at end of quarter
Quarter ending					
30 June	£	£	£	£	£
Group A	220 080	126 360	93 720	150 000	243 720
Group B	248 856	155 982	92 874	210 000	302 874
Group C	127 644	72 666	54 978	90 000	144 978
	596 580	355 008	241 572	450 000	691 572
	Stock 1 July	Usage	Balance	Purchases	Stock at end of quarter
Quarter ending					
30 September	£	£	£	£	£
Group A	243 720	97 500	146 220	96 000	242 220
Group B	302 874	120 252	182 622	120 000	302 622
Group C	144 978	55 518	89 460	54 000	143 460
	691 572	273 270	418 302	270 000	688 302
	Stock 1 Oct.	Usage	Balance	Purchases	Stock at end of quarter
Quarter ending					
31 December	£	£	£	£	£
Group A	242 220	136 260	105 960	159 540	265 500
Group B	302 622	168 294	134 328	231 897	366 225
Group C	143 460	77 889	65 571	87 612	153 183
	688 302	382 443	305 859	479 049	784 908
Totals		£1 459 827		£1 529 049	

(continued overleaf)

Purchases budget for period ending 31 December 19 . 1

	Indirect materials				
	31 Mar.	30 June	30 Sept.	31 Dec.	*Totals*
	£	£	£	£	£
Department 1	8 415	6 000	3 900	6 603	24 918
Department 2	9 219	6 900	5 700	7 050	28 869
Department 3	4 830	3 600	3 087	3 918	15 435
	£22 464	£16 500	£12 687	£17 571	£69 222

Fig. 10.4 The purchases budget

Cash budget for period ending 31 December 19 . 1

	Quarter ending				
	31 Mar.	30 June	30 Sept.	31 Dec.	*Totals*
	£	£	£	£	£
Balance brought forward	235 884	(196 992)	(152 052)	(94 758)	235 884 (March)
Receipts					
Debtors	1 093 386	1 116 000	867 000	1 170 231	4 246 617
	1 329 270	919 008	714 948	1 075 473	4 482 501
Payments					
Creditors: direct and indirect materials	510 000	540 000	375 000	335 094	1 760 094
Wages: direct and indirect	407 388	321 939	254 004	337 944	1 321 275
Dividends: Preference	52 500				52 500
Ordinary	75 000				75 000
Taxation	266 775				266 775
Fuel and light	17 166	9150	8 454	13 680	48 450
Repairs to machines	13 632	11 559	10 308	12 045	47 544
Factory expenses	61 173	49 128	38 688	51 381	200 370
Office expenses	39 273	42 804	31 158	43 845	157 080
Directors' fees		7 500		7 500	15 000
Audit fees	4 875				4 875
Debenture interest		9 000		9 000	18 000
Advertising	6 000	7 500	7 500	9 375	30 375
Motor expenses	18 000	18 000	22 800	22 590	81 390
Salaries	54 480	54 480	61 794	64 629	235 383
	£1 526 262	£1 071 060	£809 706	£907 083	£4 314 111
Balance carried forward (= deficit)	(196 992)	(152 052)	(94 758)	168 390	168 390

Fig. 10.5 The cash budget

Product summary budget for period ending 31 December 19 . 1

Product	X	Y	Z	*Totals*
	£	£	£	£
Opening stock (finished machines)	15 600	28 800	37 800	82 200
Direct materials	424 008	641 754	394 065	1 459 827
Direct wages	284 310	436 320	266 880	987 510
Factory overhead	210 249	318 150	196 407	724 806
Administration overhead	85 293	130 896	80 064	296 253
	1 019 460	1 555 920	975 216	3 550 596
Less Closing stock (machines)	60 060	83 160	107 904	251 124
	959 400	1 472 760	867 312	3 299 472
Selling expenses	67 200	117 000	77 400	261 600
	£1 026 600	1 589 760	944 712	3 561 072
Profit	183 000	282 240	169 848	635 088
Sales revenue	£1 209 600	£1 872 000	£1 114 560	£4 196 160

Calculations

Opening stock (finished machines)

	£
Product X 2 @ £7 800	15 600
Product Y 4 @ £7 200	28 800
Product Z 6 @ £6 300	37 800
	£82 200

Closing stock (finished machines)

	£
Product X 7 @ £8 580	60 060
Product Y 11 @ £7 560	83 160
Product Z 16 @ £6 744	107 904
	£251 124

Fig. 10.6 Product summary budget

Profit and Loss Account

Column 1	*Column 2*
Opening stock	Purchases budget or Balance Sheet 19.0
Purchases	Purchases budget
Closing stock	Purchases budget
Direct material used	Derived from opening stock, purchases and closing stock; production cost budget or summary budget
Direct wages	Production cost budget or summary budget
Factory overhead	Factory overhead budget
Opening stock (finished machines)	Balance Sheet 19.0
Closing stock (finished machines)	Derived from opening stock, production budget and sales forecast. Valued by using budgeted machine costs
Administration overhead	Administration overhead budget
Selling expenses	Selling expenses budget
Corporation tax	Estimated at £300 000
Appropriations	Proposed 20% ordinary dividend and other items as shown

The Balance Sheet is prepared in the usual way by using the information in the previous Balance Sheet and adjusting the figures from the details shown in the budgets and the Profit and Loss Account.

Workings

Debtors

	£
Balance 19.0	241 500
Sales 19.1	4 196 160
	4 437 660
Cash receipts (from cash budget)	4 246 617
Balance 19.1	£ 191 043

(continued on p. 283)

effectively. The usual procedure in budgeting is to start with the previous year's budgets and to adjust these on the basis of *comparative* costs by making allowance for changes in policy, costs and estimated future conditions. Zero-based budgeting, however, is carried out every three to five years. It splits budgets into activity levels and gives consideration to whether the required results can be obtained with a lower level of activity, or more cheaply. It is an exercise which questions every activity, establishes priorities and seeks alternative ways of providing services.

Creditors

	£	£
Balance 19.0		303 000
Purchases 19.1		
Direct materials	1 529 049	
Indirect materials	69 222	
		1 598 271
		1 901 271
Payments (cash budget)		1 760 094
Balance 19.1		£ 141 177

Wages

	£	£
Balance 19.0		13 500
Direct wages	987 510	
Indirect wages		
(Factory overhead budget)	335 460	
		1 322 970
		1 336 470
Payments (cash budget)		1 321 275
Balance 19.1		£ 15 195

10.18 Continuous budgeting

Rapidly changing price levels make annual budgeting difficult because when comparisons are made between actual costs and budgeted allowances, the results are unreliable indicators of true performance. Many companies now use a system which looks at current costs and conditions at the end of each quarter and adjusts the remaining budget values so that a more accurate assessment can be made. Every month or quarter new forecasts are made to give some indication of budget values over the next twelve months.

10.19 Advantages and disadvantages of budgetary control

Budgetary control is a management function which is essential if control is to be established over the different sections of the business. It uses planning and forecasting in order to achieve the objects of the business and seeks to maintain effective performance by co-ordinating the various departments. In this respect budgeting uses consultative management and group participation, so that the activities of these departments can be synchronised. Its final objective is to secure control by measuring what has been accomplished, and by taking appropriate action where required.

Budgeted Profit and Loss Account for year ending 31 December 19 . 1

	£	£		%
Sales		4 196 160		100
Production costs				
Direct materials		1 529 049		
Direct labour		987 510		
Factory overhead		724 806		
Add Opening stock	715 686			
Less Closing stock	784 908			
		(69 222)		
		3 172 143		
Finished machines				
Add Opening stock	82 200			
Less Closing stock	251 124			
		(168 924)		
Cost of sales (deduct from sales above)		3 003 219		71.6
Gross profit		1 192 941		28.4
Less				
Administration costs	296 253		7.1	
Selling expenses	261 600		6.2	
		557 853		13.3
Profit before taxation		635 088		15.1
Less Corporation tax		300 000		7.1
Profit after taxation		335 088		8.0
Balance brought forward		11 250		
Profit available for distribution		346 338		
Appropriation of profits				
Preliminary expenses	5 730			
Transfer to general reserve	75 000			
Transfer to staff pension fund	9 000			
7% Preference dividend	52 500			
Proposed ordinary dividend of 20%	150 000			
		292 230		
Balance (carried forward)		£ 54 108		

Fig. 10.7 (a) The master budget: Budgeted Profit and Loss Account

Budgeted Balance Sheet as at 31 December 19 . 1

Assets employed	*Cost*	*Depreciation*	*Value*
Fixed assets	£	£	£
Land and buildings	1 177 500	18 000	1 159 500
Machinery and plant	300 000	68 160	231 840
Motor vehicles	75 000	48 000	27 000
Office furniture	15 000	6 750	8 250
	£1 567 500	£140 910	£1 426 590
Quoted investments (market value £143 250)			142 425
Current assets			
Stock: General stores	784 908		
Finished machines	251 124		
		1 036 032	
Debtors		191 043	
Cash at bank and in hand		168 390	
		1 395 465	
Less Current liabilities			
Creditors	141 177		
Wages due	15 195		
Proposed preference dividend	52 500		
Proposed ordinary dividend 20%	150 000		
Corporation tax	300 000		
		658 872	
Net current assets			736 593
			£2 305 608
Financed by			
			£
Preference shareholders' interest in the company		*Authorised*	
750 000 7% Preference shares of £1 fully paid		750 000	750 000
Ordinary shareholders' interest in the company	*Authorised*		
	£		
750 000 Ordinary shares of £1 fully paid	750 000	750 000	
Reserves			
Staff pension fund	157 500		
General reserve	294 000		
Profit and Loss Account	54 108		
		505 608	
Ordinary shareholders' equity			1 255 608
Long-term liability			
6% debentures			300 000
			£2 305 608

Fig. 10.7 (b) The master budget: Budgeted Balance Sheet

Table 10.15 Factory overhead cost report for quarter ending 31 March 19..

	Actual cost £	Budgeted cost £	Variance Favourable £	Variance Adverse £
Indirect material	2 900	2 805		95
Fuel and lighting	2 250	2 214		36
Repairs to machines	1 398	1 510	112	
Indirect wages	12 000	11 962		38
Factory expenses	6 999	7 029	30	
Depreciation	701	701		
	£26 248	£26 221	£142	£169

Remarks: (if any).

The advantages of budgetary control are as follows:

(a) it compels management to make clear-cut statements concerning its policy and objectives;
(b) it plans and makes forecasts so that the costs of materials, wages and expenses are set at the most economical levels;
(c) it is a consultative procedure which demands co-operation in the preparation of budgets and the operations which follow, so that the results fixed by the budget can be attained;
(d) it establishes areas of responsibility and sets targets so that the people carrying the responsibility are aware of what must be achieved if the organisation's objectives are to be realised;
(e) by controlling the spending of money, which is regulated in accordance with a well-defined plan, it attempts to avoid a loss of resources;
(f) the organisation is encouraged to examine its products, markets and methods in order that the maximum use can be made of the plant, equipment and assets of the business;
(g) management receives a warning when operations are not proceeding in accordance with the plan. This follows a comparison of budget with actual results when substantial deviations are investigated and reported.

The only disadvantage of budgetary control is that it is time-consuming and requires a high degree of accuracy in its forecasting. However, the great advances in microprocessor technology now allow much of this routine work to be carried out by computer.

10.20 Exercises

1. You work for a firm of business consultants called Thurrock Business Consultancy. The consultancy is approached by different organisations to investigate and analyse problems they face. Your role within the consul-

Table 10.16 Area sales report for quarter ending 31 March 19..

	Actual		Budget		Variance	
	Machines	Value	Machines	Value	Machines	Value
		£		£		£
Area A						
Product X	9	32 400	10	36 000	1 (A)	3 600 (A)
Product Y	33	106 000	35	112 000	2 (A)	6 000 (A)
Product Z	21	60 480	20	57 600	1 (F)	2 880 (F)
	63	198 880	65	205 600	2 (A)	6 720 (A)
Area B						
Product X	5	18 000	5	18 000	–	–
Product Y	9	28 000	8	25 600	1 (F)	2 400 (F)
Product Z	6	17 000	6	17 280	–	280 (A)
	20	63 000	19	60 880	1 (F)	2 120 (F)
Area C						
Product X	8	28 800	8	28 800	–	–
Product Y	5	16 000	5	16 000	–	–
Product Z	8	23 040	6	17 280	2 (F)	5 760 (F)
	21	67 840	19	62 080	2 (F)	5 760 (F)
Area D						
Product X	12	43 200	12	43 200	–	–
Product Y	5	16 000	8	25 600	3 (A)	9 600 (A)
Product Z	10	28 800	10	28 800	–	–
	27	88 000	30	97 600	3 (A)	9 600 (A)
Summary						
Product X	34	122 400	35	126 000	1 (A)	3 600 (A)
Product Y	52	166 000	56	179 200	4 (A)	13 200 (A)
Product Z	45	129 320	42	120 960	3 (F)	8 360 (F)
Totals	131	£417 720	133	£426 160	2 (A)	£8 440 (A)

tancy is to deal with local firms that need advice of a purely financial nature.

You have been instructed to visit a local manufacturer, who has telephoned the consultancy requesting advice concerning his plans to expand his business. Having spent an afternoon with the client, Mr J. Frazer, you have ascertained the following:

(i) The firm manufactures component parts for use in the electronics industry.

(ii) Profits have been increasing steadily since the firm began three years ago.

(iii) Mr Frazer works full time in the firm, employs two members of staff full-time in the factory and one part-time in the office.
(iv) Mr Frazer has plans to produce a new component, which has been requested by his biggest customer.
(v) A new machine will be purchased, specifically to produce the new component, at a cost of £50 000.
(vi) Mr Frazer can raise additional capital from private funds of £20 000, and has approached his bank manager to request a loan to raise the balance.
(vii) The bank manager has requested a cash flow forecast and forecast profit calculation for the first six months, presuming the new component is manufactured.
(viii) Mr Frazer can produce all relevant figures concerning his expected sales of both components and his estimated expenses.
(ix) He does not have the time or expertise to satisfy his bank manager.

You agree to prepare, by May 19 . 1:

(a) a forecast cash budget for the six months July to December 19 . 1;
(b) a forecast profit calculation for the six months to December 19 . 1.

Mr Frazer agrees to provide you with the relevant figures by the end of March 19 . 1. These arrive in the form of a letter, Fig. 10.8, which will enable you to proceed.

2. You have been appointed as the first management accountant to an old-established manufacturing business of medium size which has recently expanded rapidly beyond the capacity of its existing accounting system. It has been agreed by the board of directors that your priority task will be to prepare and introduce a system of budgetary control.

You are required to set out clearly:

(a) the problems you are likely to face in carrying out this task;
(b) the requirements which will have to be satisfied before the proposed budgeting system can operate successfully at the planning stage.

(CIMA)

3. Product Z was manufactured by X Limited at a budgeted selling price of £41.00. The budget for the current year shows the following information:

Four-week period: Budgeted production and sales: 10 000 units

Selling price, costs and profit per unit

		£
Direct costs:	Materials	13.00
	Wages	6.50
		19.50
Overhead:	Variable	1.30
	Fixed	11.70
Total		32.50
Profit		8.50
Selling price		41.00

Thurrock Business Consultancy
Love Lane
Aveley
South Ockendon
Essex

22 March 19.1

Dear Consultant,

I enclose relevant figures as requested by you.

1) I will receive a bank loan of £30,000 on 1 July 19.1.

2) Sales (all credit):
July and August £12,600
September, October and November £15,500
December £19,300
I allow my customers two months' credit.

3) Purchase of raw materials, paid for one month after delivery:
July, August, September and October £6,800
November and December £7,600.

4) Wages and salaries £2,500 per month.

5) Rent £28,000 per annum, paid quarterly in March, June, September and December.

6) Light and heat £200 per month.

7) Office expenses £500 per month.

8) Loan interest at 18 per cent per annum, paid monthly.

9) Business rates £8,000 per annum, paid quarterly in March, June, September and October.

10) Consultancy fee £700 paid in July.

11) Advertising £200 per month.

12) Machinery will be paid for by cheque on 1 July, £50,000.

13) My bank balance on 1 July 19.1 will be £25,000.

14) I take £400 per month for my own expenses.

15) Stock at 31 December will be valued at £3,000.

Yours sincerely

J. Frazer

Fig. 10.8

During a certain four-week period 6 200 units were produced and the actual profit was £1 792. There was an increase in wage rates of 10 per cent and material prices increased by 3 per cent, but material usage and labour efficiency were the same as budgeted.

You are required to *(a)* prepare a statement to show the four-weekly budget with the actual costs and *(b)* state the reasons for the difference between the budgeted profit and the actual profit.

4. A manufacturing company has recorded the following overhead costs and hours worked for the year ended 31 December 19..:

		Hours worked	Overhead
			£
Production departments:	A	185 000	290 000
	B	200 000	275 000
Service departments:	X		104 000
	Y		125 000
	Z		144 000

The service department costs in the budget are apportioned as follows:

		Apportioned to production departments:	
		A	B
Department:	X	$\frac{3}{4}$	$\frac{1}{4}$
	Y	$\frac{3}{5}$	$\frac{2}{5}$
	Z	$\frac{2}{3}$	$\frac{1}{3}$

The budgeted overheads are as follows:

		Absorption rate per hour	Overhead
		£	£
Production departments:	A	3.00	280 000
	B	2.00	250 000
Service departments:	X		96 000
	Y		150 000
	Z		168 000

Draw up a tabulated statement to show for each production department:
(a) budgeted overhead;
(b) actual overhead;
(c) absorbed overhead;
(d) under- or over-absorbed overhead.

5. A department's normal workload has been fixed at 4 500 hours per month. From the following information, you are required to draw up flexible budgets for 3 000 hours, 4 000 hours and 5 000 hours and also a fixed budget for normal workload, and to calculate the departmental hourly overhead rate.

Supervision	£2 000 up to 3 000 hours £240 extra for steps of 500 hours above 3 000 hours A further £120 for steps of 500 hours above 5 000 hours
Indirect wages	£160 for every 250 hours
Consumable materials	£200 for every 200 hours
Rent and rates	£1 480
Heat and light	£360 from 1 500 hours to 2 000 hours inclusive £400 above 2 000 hours and up to 4 000 hours £500 above 4 000 hours
Power	£220 per 250 hours up to 4 750 hours £200 per 250 hours above 4 750 hours
Cleaning	£240 up to 4 000 hours £300 above 4 000 hours
Repairs	£600 up to 2 000 hours A further £100 for steps of 500 hours up to 4 500 hours An additional amount of £160 above 4 500 hours
Depreciation	£3 000 up to 4 000 hours £3 800 above 4 000 hours and up to 6 000 hours

6. The cash budget for the last quarter of 19.. has to be prepared and the details can be extracted from the forecasts made for the last five months of the year, and from the information given below:

	Sales	*Purchases*	*Overheads*	*Depreciation*	*Wages*
	£	£	£	£	£
August	42 000	24 000	4 200	360	13 000
September	26 000	25 000	3 200	360	9 000
October	28 000	14 000	3 600	360	9 600
November	32 000	16 000	3 400	360	12 000
December	38 000	18 000	3 800	360	12 000

Additional information:

(a) All purchases are on a credit basis and the suppliers will in normal circumstances receive payment two months after the date of the transaction.

(b) Twenty-five per cent of sales are on credit (the balance being cash sales); the debtors are expected to settle their accounts in the month after that in which the transaction takes place.

(c) Wages are paid in cash as they become due.

(d) The bank balance on 1 October 19.. is estimated to be £3 600.

(e) Overheads other than depreciation include:
   (i) gas and electricity charges: August £140, September £150, October £160, November £200 and December £220. The accounts for gas and electricity (quarter ending 30 September) will be paid in October 19.., and they are estimated to be £430;
   (ii) rates: these are paid half-yearly in April and October and the rates for the year beginning 1 April 19.. amount to £3 840;
   (iii) certain other items which are all cash transactions.

Prepare the cash budget for the quarter showing the months of October, November and December 19...

7. A sales budget was prepared using standard prices and standard volumes for five standard products. After the budget had been prepared there was an increase in prices and a request was made for a report which would show the extent of changes in price or volume in respect of the products sold. Calculate the sales variances for the month of June 19.. for that purpose. The budgeted and actual sales for June 19.. are as follows:

Sales budget and actual sales for June 19..

Product	*Budgeted sales price*	*Budgeted volume*	*Actual volume*	*Actual invoice value*
	£			£
A	100	1 200	1 800	198 000
B	25	400	300	9 000
C	80	960	1 020	86 700
D	50	240	120	7 200
E	30	850	1 100	36 300

8. Your company has invited a firm of industrial consultants to examine the organisation and to recommend the introduction of new techniques to improve the business and overcome many of the problems which seem to arise. They have made a preliminary survey and have suggested the installation of a system of budgetary control, which in the first instance will need the formation of a budget committee. You have been asked to prepare a report to the managing director describing the functions of such a committee.

9. The ultimate objective of budget preparation is the 'master budget'. In order to develop this summary budget the elements of cost and other items have to be forecast and planned and functional budgets prepared. Explain what you understand by *functional budgets*, by describing those which support the forecast Trading Account, Profit and Loss Account and Balance Sheet.

10. A company manufactures two machines, A and B, using two classes of raw material, X and Y. The company is preparing its budgets for the coming year, and as a first step the Balance Sheet for the current year has been drawn up by using estimates for the remaining weeks of the year.

Balance Sheet as at 31 December 19 . 8

Assets employed:	Cost	Depreciation	Net
Fixed assets	£	£	£
Freehold premises	150 000		150 000
Plant and machinery	90 000	30 000	60 000
Motor vehicles	20 000	10 000	10 000
Office furniture	8 000	2 500	5 500
	268 000	42 500	225 500
Investments (market value £10 150)			10 000
Current assets			
Stock		41 280	
Debtors		15 000	
Cash at bank and in hand		9 220	
		65 500	
Less Current liabilities			
Creditors	32 000		
Wages due	2 000		
		34 000	
Working capital			31 500
			£267 000
Financed by:			
		Authorised	Issued
Ordinary shareholders' interest in the company		£	£
125 000 Ordinary shares of £1 each, fully paid		125 000	125 000
Reserves			
General reserve		35 000	
Profit and Loss Account		7 000	
			42 000
Ordinary shareholders' equity			167 000
Preference shareholders' interest in the company		Authorised	
100 000 8% preference shares of £1 fully paid		100 000	100 000
			£267 000

You are required to draw up the following:

(a) sales budget;

(b) production budget;

(c) production cost budget:

(i) direct materials,

(ii) direct wages,

(iii) factory overhead (absorbed);
(d) factory overhead cost budget;
(e) administration overhead budget;
(f) selling expenses budget;
(g) cash budget;
(h) forecast product costs;
(i) master budget.

The Profit and Loss Account and Balance Sheet are to be drawn up as at 31 December 19 . 9, but the other budgets for the year ending 31 December 19 . 9 are to be drawn up on a quarterly basis. The area sales forecast is shown below:

Area sales forecast (machines)

	Quarter ending 31 Mar.	30 June	30 Sept.	31 Dec.	*Totals*
Area P					
Product: A	10	12	9	14	45
B	8	6	6	10	30
	18	18	15	24	75
Area Q					
Product: A	5	4	3	6	18
B	7	6	4	5	22
	12	10	7	11	40
Area R					
Product: A	8	4	6	7	25
B	5	6	2	2	15
	13	10	8	9	40

The sales budget is to be drawn up on the assumption that the selling prices of product A and product B are £1 690 and £2 030 respectively. The profit margin is 20 per cent on selling price (25 per cent on cost). The following information has been extracted from the company records:

Material content per machine:

	Material group X	Y
	£	£
Product: A	150	87
B	200	61

Direct labour costs per machine:

	Product			
	A		B	
	Hours	£	Hours	£
Department 1 (rate per hour £1.50)	100	150	120	180
Department 2 (rate per hour £2.00)	80	160	106	212

Factory overheads are charged as a percentage on direct labour cost, and the absorption rates can be calculated when the factory, administration and selling cost budgets have been completed for the overhead expenditure. Administration overheads are applied as a percentage on direct labour cost and selling expenses are chargeable at a rate per machine, on the basis of the costs shown in the selling costs budget.

It is to be assumed that the company carries no finished stock or work-in-progress at the end of each quarter and that machines are produced in the same quantities and during the same period as shown in the sales forecast. Purchases of materials amounted to £47 293, which included £41 383 for direct materials and £5 910 as a direct charge to factory overheads. A payment of £50 000 was made in the June quarter for the purchase of freehold buildings.

The factory overhead costs for the year have been estimated as follows:

	Department 1	Department 2
	£	£
Indirect material	3 546	2 364
Fuel and lighting	1 322	882
Repairs to machines	1 380	920
Indirect wages	14 633	9 756
Factory expenses	11 429	3 571
Depreciation: machinery and plant	5 580	3 720
	37 890	21 213

The factory overhead costs are allocated to each quarter on a percentage basis:

Quarter ending:	
	%
31 March	30
30 June	25
30 September	20
31 December	25
	100

Administration costs have been estimated at £53 544 for the year, and consist of:

Office expenses: £7 872 (31 March), £6 560 (30 June), £5 248 (30 September), £6 560 (31 December)
Salaries: £4 074 per quarter
Depreciation: £127 per quarter
Directors' fees: £2 500 (30 June) and £2 500 (31 December)
Training levy: £5 500 (31 March)

Both directors' fees and the training levy are to be apportioned to the administration budget on a quarterly basis.

Selling expenses are estimated at:

	31 Mar.	30 June	30 Sept.	31 Dec.
	£	£	£	£
Travellers' salaries	3 143	3 143	3 144	3 144
Advertising	780	650	520	650
Motor expenses	2 048	1 707	1 365	1 706
Depreciation:				
motor vehicles	312	312	313	313

All accounts for overhead expenses are to be settled as they occur. Other receipts and payments are as follows:

Receipts from debtors for sales: £84 502 (31 March), £70 418 (30 June), £56 335 (30 September), £70 419 (31 December)
Payments to creditors for direct and indirect materials: £15 388 (31 March), £12 823 (30 June), £10 259 (30 September), £12 823 (31 December)
Payments of direct and indirect wages: £23 230 (31 March), £19 358 (30 June), £15 487 (30 September), £19358 (31 December)

The market value of the investments is estimated to be £10 550 on 31 December 19.9.

From the profit available for distribution, a provision is to be made for the preference dividend, and a dividend of 8 per cent on the ordinary shares is proposed. A transfer of £5 000 is to be made to the General Reserve Account. Corporation tax of £28 000 is to be taken into account.

UNIT 11

Integrated and non-integrated accounts

11.1 Alternative solutions to financial and management accounting

Two methods may be used to record cost and financial information. The accounts may be *integrated* using one set of accounts, or they may be *interlocked*, with the cost accounts being distinct from the financial accounts and kept in agreement by the use of control accounts. The CIMA booklet *Official Terminology* describes these methods as follows:

> *Integrated accounts*
> A set of accounting records which provides financial and cost accounts using a common input of data for all accounting purposes.
> *Interlocking accounts* (non-integrated accounts)
> A system in which the cost accounts are distinct from the financial accounts, the two sets of accounts being kept continuously in agreement by the use of Control Accounts; or made readily reconcilable by other means.

This is a difficult area in cost and management accounting where the student must develop his or her accountancy knowledge to cover the entire field (from the start of production to the final determination of profit). It is best to start with interlocking accounts, where the cost accounts are distinct but are interlocked with the financial accounts by a series of Control Accounts. We will then consider integrated accounts.

Since a whole series of Control Accounts has to be considered, students are liable to get confused. Some clarification has been attempted in Fig. 11.1, to which it is hoped students will refer as they read through the text.

11.2 Non-integrated accounts (interlocking accounts)

When it is considered more convenient to have a separate set of cost accounts distinct from the financial accounts, the recording of expenditure in respect of the production function and the related activities of administration, marketing, research and development is made in a *Cost Ledger*. The Cost Ledger is the principal ledger in a costing system using double-entry book-keeping, which is linked with the financial accounts by *interlocking accounts*. We are familiar with the book-keeping system used to record the financial accounts and a similar system can be adopted in the Cost Ledger to record costing information using double-entry book-keeping. This is *cost book-keeping* and the financial accounts and the cost accounts can be kept in agreement by using *Control Accounts.*

In order to avoid overloading the Cost Ledger with detailed accounts, there are subsidiary ledgers. Each ledger contains a group of accounts of a similar nature relating to the various aspects of costing such as stores, wages or overheads. The financial information shown in a subsidiary ledger is recorded in summary form in a Control Account in the Cost Ledger. The Cost Ledger has a separate Control Account for each type of expenditure. As there are no cash or personal accounts in the Cost Ledger the entries for sales, purchases, wages, salaries and overheads are single-sided entries and the double entry is achieved by charging these amounts to the credit side of a *Financial Ledger Control Account*. Similarly any returns, allowances or other reductions in cost credited to the various Cost Accounts in the subsidiary ledgers, and carried from them to the Control Accounts in the Cost Ledger, will have a double entry achieved by debiting the appropriate amounts in the Financial Ledger Control Account. You may follow this better if you now look at the illustration Fig. 11.1, parts 1–3 (pp. 300–1).

We shall see later that the integrated system provides both financial and management accounting information in one ledger (the Financial Ledger) and this avoids what may be considered unnecessary duplication of accounting records.

When the system is non-integrated as in Fig. 11.1, the two sets of accounts are connected or linked by the use of interlocking accounts. Although there is no direct double entry between the two ledgers there is a link when a Memorandum Cost Ledger Control Account is opened in the financial ledger. (A Memorandum Account is one which is provided as a reminder only, and is not part of the double-entry system.) The entries in this Cost Ledger Control Account (in the Financial Ledger) are identical to those which appear in the Financial Ledger Control Account (sometimes called the Cost Ledger Contra Account) in the Cost Ledger, but they are entered on the opposite side. It follows that the Memorandum Account, which is in the Financial Ledger, actually represents on a single page (or computerised record if a computerised system is being used) the entirety of the entries in the Cost Ledger.

Before considering the interlocking of the Cost Ledger and the Financial Ledger we must first consider parts 1, 2 and 3 of Fig. 11.1 in greater detail.

11.3 The analysis of costs

(a) The basic documents

In order to operate a cost system which has Cost Control Accounts in its Cost Ledger, it is necessary to maintain subsidiary books (books of original entry) for costs of a similar nature such as stores materials, wages and overheads. Costs are recorded on basic documents or vouchers and include material requisitions, job cards, goods received notes and any voucher which supports an entry in the cost accounts. Each element of cost will be dealt with separately and sorting is necessary in order to group the items for each cost centre, and also to arrange the items in a logical sequence for posting to the subsidiary ledgers. Materials, wages and expenses are analysed and entered in journals, or listed on analysis sheets.

For example, there will be wages analysis sheets on which direct and indirect wages are listed. The wages shown on each job card or time sheet are posted to account or order numbers which are listed in numerical order for each of the subsidiary ledgers involved. There are sub-totals for each account or order number and there is also the total value to be posted to each subsidiary ledger. The sub-totals are accumulated and at the end of the posting run the total amount should be equal to the total wages paid.

(b) The subsidiary ledgers

All these accumulated cost records have now to be posted to the subsidiary ledgers. There may be as many of these subsidiary ledgers as are necessary to cover the broad areas of activity in the enterprise. What we are effectively doing is collecting together all the detailed costs involved and obtaining sub-totals which will eventually give us a final total for the subsidiary book concerned. The total amount posted in each subsidiary ledger is the amount which is posted to the appropriate Control Account in the Cost Ledger. It is also posted to the Financial Ledger Control Account to preserve the principle of double entry.

(c) Control Accounts

The term 'Control Account' may be used in two ways. First, it can be a total account inserted in a ledger (or section of accounts) to make it self-balancing. A run of debits and credits is posted to the individual ledger accounts, and the total of both, or the net value, is posted to the Control Account. The balance of the account should thus always equal the total of the balances on the individual accounts in the subsidiary ledger. In an exactly similar way, the total account can appear as an account in the main ledger, or in our case the Cost Ledger, where it reproduces on a single page all the information in a subsidiary book. Thus the single entry 'Purchases' would show a total figure for all the purchases debited to every account in the subsidiary ledger, and a single entry 'Returns' would show a total figure for all the returns credited to every account in the subsidiary ledger. When all these total figures are set against one another on the Control Account they exactly represent the whole of the subsidiary ledger on one page. This ensures that *the balance of the Control Account equals the total of the balances on the individual accounts in the subsidiary ledger*.

The principal control accounts are as follows:

(i) Stores Ledger Control Account;
(ii) Wages and Salaries Control Account;
(iii) Production Overheads Control Account;

The Cost Accounting System

1.

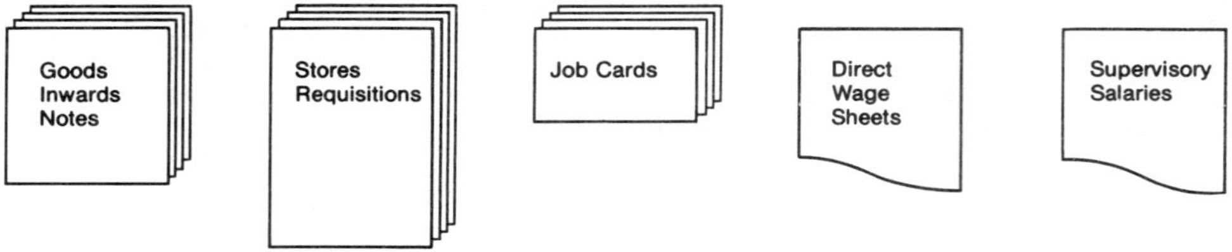
Goods
Inwards
Notes
Stores
Requisitions
Job Cards
Direct
Wage
Sheets
Supervisory
Salaries

Documents, vouchers, job cards and other sources of cost information are analysed, batched up and prepared for posting to a set of subsidiary ledgers. Of course these could be in computerised form, but for the present we will think of them in traditional form.

2.

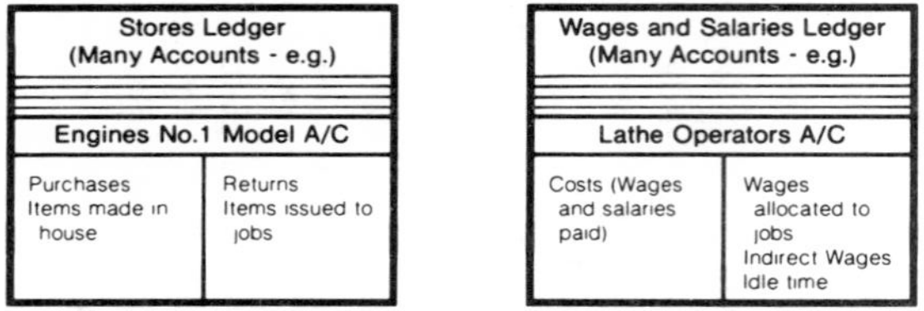
Stores Ledger
(Many Accounts - e.g.)
Engines No.1 Model A/C
Purchases
Items made in
house
Returns
Items issued to
jobs
Wages and Salaries Ledger
(Many Accounts - e.g.)
Lathe Operators A/C
Costs (Wages
and salaries
paid)
Wages
allocated to
jobs
Indirect Wages
Idle time

and so on for all other cost areas e.g. Production Overhead Ledger, Administration Overhead Ledger, etc. The double entry for all these entries is in the

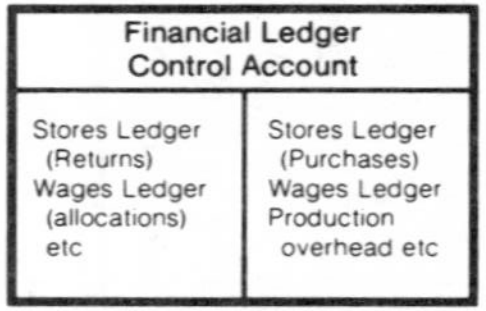
Financial Ledger
Control Account
Stores Ledger
(Returns)
Wages Ledger
(allocations)
etc
Stores Ledger
(Purchases)
Wages Ledger
Production
overhead etc

However many subsidiary ledgers there are, with numerous accounts in each recording particular headings of costs, the entries will be mainly debits (expenses of the business) set against some credit entries (returns, allowances, allocations to jobs, etc). Note that as there are no personal accounts for suppliers and no Cash or Bank Accounts in the Cost Ledger the semblance of double-entry is preserved by opening up a Financial Ledger Contra A/C (sometimes called the Cost Ledger Control Account). It is usually the last page in the Cost Ledger and contains all the double entries for all the entries made in all the subsidiary ledgers. It therefore exactly balances the Cost Ledger - with all the items on the opposite side (hence its name of Contra A/C).

3. The Cost Ledger consists mainly of a series of Control Accounts - each of which contains in summary form on a single page the entire contents of a subsidiary ledger.

The Cost Ledger (Many Control Accounts - e.g.)	
Stores Ledger Control A/C	
Purchases (total) Work in progress (total of in-house manufactures for jobs)	Work in progress (Allocations to jobs - total) Production overhead (materials) (total) Returns (total)

The Control Accounts in the Cost Ledger are:
(a) Stores Ledger Control Account
(b) Wages and Salaries Control Account
(c) Production Overheads Control Account
(d) Administration Overheads Control Account
(e) Selling and Distribution Control Account
(f) Work-in-Progress Control Account
(g) Finished Goods Control Account
and finally the
(h) Financial Ledger Control Account

4. The link with the Financial Ledger

Memorandum Cost Ledger Control Account (in the Financial Ledger)	
Stores Ledger (Purchases) Wages Ledger Production Overhead etc	Stores Ledger (Returns) Wages Ledger (Direct wages allocated to jobs) etc etc

This Memorandum Account in the Financial Ledger puts the whole Cost Ledger into the Financial Ledger on a single page. It is purely a Memorandum Account and not part of the double entry, but it is a mirror image of the Financial Ledger Control Account. The term 'mirror image' implies that the Memorandum Account will be exactly the same as the Financial Ledger Control Account except that everything will be recorded on the opposite side.

5. The reconciliation in the Financial Ledger

Memorandum Reconciliation Account (in the Financial Ledger)	
Profit in Financial Books Selling Expenses Distribution Expenses Variances in stocks and all other losses not in Cost Accounts	Profit in Costing Books Interest Received Dividends Received Variances in stocks and all other profits not in Cost Accounts
Note: totals will balance	Note: totals will balance

The Financial Accountant will have the net profit on his/her Accounts. The costing profit will be different. The two will be reconciled in a Reconciliation Account, (or a Reconciliation Statement).

Fig. 11.1 Cost accounting with interlocking (non-integrated) accounts

(iv) Administration Overheads Control Account;
(v) Selling and Distribution Control Account;
(vi) Work-in-progress Control Account;
(vii) Finished Goods Control Account;
(viii) Financial Ledger Control Account.

We must now consider each of these in turn. We show (i) and (viii) in detail as accounts. The others are similar, and the various entries are described in the text.

(i) Stores Ledger Control Account This account controls the activities involved in the receipt and issue of materials, in respect of purchases and material requisitions, and any adjustments which are necessary when stock-taking takes place or when discrepancies are discovered.

Stores Ledger Control A/c

Dr.			Cr.		
		£		£	£
Balance	b/d	x	Material requisitions:		
Purchases *less* returns:			(a) Work-in-progress		
(Financial Ledger Control A/c)		x	Control A/c	x	
Components and spare parts:			(b) Production Overheads		
(Work-in-progress Control A/c)		x	Control A/c	x	
Materials returned and scrap			(c) Administration Overheads		
left over (Work-in-progress			Control A/c	x	
Control A/c)		x	(d) Selling and Distribution		
			Control A/c	x	
					x
			Stock discrepancies:		
			(Costing Profit and Loss A/c)		x
			Balance (inventory) c/d		x
		£xxx			£xxx
Balance	b/d	x			

Notes:

(i) The amount shown for purchases represents the total value of all the items taken into stock as received from suppliers and as indicated on the goods received notes. It also takes account of goods returned as shown on the credit notes received.

(ii) Stock items such as components and spare parts, manufactured internally, are taken into stock and their value is credited to work-in-progress.

(iii) Materials issued in excess of requirements, unsuitable materials and scrap materials are taken into stock and credited to work-in-progress.

(iv) Material requisitions are analysed and their values are credited to the above account. The respective amounts are debited to work-in-progress, and to the overhead accounts and selling and distribution.

(v) Avoidable losses (stock discrepancies) are credited and charged to the

Costing Profit and Loss Account as a debit.

(vi) The balance brought down represents the total inventory in the stores at the end of the period under review.

(ii) Wages and Salaries Control Account The cost of employees' remuneration is analysed in order to divide this into direct wages cost and indirect wages cost. Direct wages represent the employees' skills and efforts when applied directly to a product or saleable service. Indirect wages consist of wages costs other than direct wages and include production overhead, general administration costs and costs in respect of selling, distribution, research, etc. If there are separate Control Accounts for wages and salaries, Wages Control Account is credited with the amounts transferred to work-in-progress and production overheads, and Salaries Control Account is credited with administration and selling and distribution costs. The total wages cost is shown on a wages analysis sheet, which is a detailed record of the separate amounts relating to individual cost units or cost centres for a particular period.

(iii) Production Overheads Control Account This account is debited with the amounts transferred from the Wages and Stores Accounts and the indirect expenses as detailed on an Expenses Analysis Sheet. The account is credited with the amount transferred to work-in-progress and any under-recovery of overheads, which is debited to the Overhead Adjustment Account.

(iv) Administration Overhead Control Account Costs debited to this account include amounts transferred from stores for materials used and from wage and salaries account for indirect costs relating to administration. There are also debits for expenses detailed on an Expenses Analysis Sheet. The account is credited with amounts charged to finished goods and for any under-recovery of administration costs, which is debited to the Overhead Adjustment Account.

(v) Selling and Distribution Control Account Debits are in respect of salaries, and for any materials from stores and other expenses detailed in the Expenses Analysis Sheet. Credits are for the cost of sales and any under-recovery which may occur.

(vi) Work-in-Progress Control Account The subsidiary ledger for the detailed accounts for work-in-progress shows entries which are recorded in the Control Account as debits for the opening balance at the beginning of the period, and for the amounts credited to the Control Accounts for stores, wages and production overheads. There are also debits for direct or special purchases for production orders as requisitioned. The Work-in-progress Control Account is credited with the value of goods and tools returned to stores. It is also credited with the value of items debited to the Finished Goods Account and with the value of work-in-progress carried forward as a balance at the end of the period.

(vii) Finished Goods Control Account This account controls the Finished Goods Stock Ledger and has debits for the opening balance and the amounts transferred from work-in-progress and administration overhead. There is a credit for the amount debited to the Cost of Sales Account and also for the value of the finished goods in stock at the end of the period.

(viii) The Financial Ledger Control Account This is an essential part of the double-entry costing system as it makes the Cost Ledger self-balancing and allows a Trial Balance to be drawn up. The transactions in this account include all or most of the following items.

Financial Ledger Control Account

Dr.		£			£	£ Cr.
Costing Profit and Loss A/c (sales)		x	Balance	b/d		x
Capital Expenditure		x	Purchases:			
			(a) Stores Ledger Control		x	
Balance	c/d	x	(b) Work-in-progress Ledger Control		x	
			(c) Overhead Control:			
			Production		x	
			Administration		x	
			Selling and Distributioin		x	
			(d) Capital Expenditure		x	
						x
			Wages and Salaries Control			x
			Expenses:			
			(a) Production Overhead Control		x	
			(b) Administration Overhead Control		x	
			(c) Selling and Distribution Overhead Control		x	
						x
			Costing Profit and Loss A/c (profit)			x
		£x				£x
			Balance	b/d		x

Notes:

(i) The balances at the start and end of the financial period represent and are equal to the total value of the balances on the accounts in the Cost Ledger, e.g. Stores + Work-in-progress + Finished Goods.

(ii) In order to provide the figures which eventually finish up on this account the vouchers, original documents, posting slips and any other documents which support entries in the cost accounts are sorted and analysed. Costs must be arranged and classified so that the components of the selling price are in logical sequence. They can then be posted in an orderly manner to the accounts in the subsidiary ledgers. This will enable totals to be obtained under the different headings for posting to the control accounts.

(iii) An analysis is made of purchases (goods received notes) in order to ensure that the items are arranged correctly for posting to the subsidiary ledgers, and to obtain in each case the total value of purchases charged to stores, work-in-progress, overheads and capital expenditure. These figures are then debited to the accounts in the subsidiary ledgers and credited to the Financial Ledger Control Account. Purchases which are not stock items are special purchases for charging direct to work-in-progress orders, overheads or capital expenditure. These are identified by the production order numbers or expense codes shown on the goods received notes.

(iv) A profit is assumed and this is a debit in the Costing Profit and Loss Account. As this is likely to differ from the profit shown in the Financial Ledger there is a need for a statement to list the variations. The object of the reconciliation statement is to prove that the profit in each ledger is correct, but that certain items are included or excluded because they are peculiar to a particular situation or because of the requirements of an accounting standard. Goodwill is an example under SSAP 22. It must be valued on a fair value basis, its value can fluctuate considerably over short periods and the standard expresses a preference for an immediate write off against reserves.

(v) The account described above is sometimes referred to as a General Ledger Adjustment Account. It thus has three different names, which reflect its three functions:

- *Cost Ledger Contra Account*. This reflects its function of providing a double entry for all the entries made in the subsidiary ledgers.
- *Financial Ledger Control Account*. This reflects its function as a double entry for all the entries recorded in total in the Control Accounts of the Cost Ledger, making that ledger self-balancing.
- *General Ledger Adjustment Account*. This reflects its function as a link with the General Ledger in the financial accounting system, where it provides a double entry for the Memorandum Cost Ledger Control (or Adjustment) Account.

11.4 Other accounts in the Cost Ledger

(a) Overhead Adjustment Account

Overheads are included in the cost of specific products or saleable services and are applied to these items by means of absorption rates which are based on estimates. Therefore at the end of the period the amount absorbed may exceed the amount of overhead incurred, or there may be an under-absorption. The debits in this account represent an under-absorption of production, administration or selling and distribution overhead, and credits indicate that overheads are over-absorbed. The balance of this account is transferred to the Costing Profit and Loss Account.

(b) Cost of Sales Account

This account is debited with the amount transferred from the Finished Goods

Control Account and with the selling and distribution overhead, and the account is closed by a transfer to the Costing Profit and Loss Account.

(c) Costing Profit and Loss Account
There are debits for the cost of sales and probably for under-absorbed overheads from the Overhead Adjustment Account. Sales as shown in the Financial Ledger Control Account are credited, and there may be a credit entry for over-absorbed overheads if the Overhead Adjustment Account indicates that this is the situation at the end of the period. The balance of the account which shows the profit or loss is transferred to the Financial Ledger Control Account.

11.5 The link with the Financial Ledger

Returning to Fig. 11.1 for a moment we now see that the Final Account in the Cost Ledger is the Financial Ledger Control Account. This account serves the following purposes:

(a) It is used as a double-entry account to provide the entries made in all the subsidiary ledgers with a double entry that balances them.
(b) It makes the Cost Ledger a self-balancing ledger, thus giving us confidence that all double entries have been performed.
(c) If a Memorandum Cost Ledger Control Account is now set up in the Financial Ledger as a mirror image of the Financial Ledger Control Account in the Cost Ledger, it will effectively put the whole of the Cost Ledger into the Financial Ledger on a single page. The Cost Ledger and the Financial Ledger have thus been interlocked, even if they are not integrated.

The reader should now study Fig. 11.2 (pp. 308–9) which gives some idea of how a set of non-integrated accounts leads to the Costing Profit and Loss Account.

11.6 Statements prepared in order to prove and reconcile the accounts

(a) Trial Balance
To prove the accuracy of the postings a Trial Balance is extracted. There are normally debit balances for stores, work-in-progress and finished goods, and the total value of these is equal to the credit balance in the Financial Ledger Control Account.

(b) Reconciliation statement
This is a memorandum statement which is prepared at the end of each accounting period. The object is to reconcile the profit shown in the Cost Ledger with that shown in the Financial Ledger. The profit in the Financial Ledger is established after allowing for some expenses and costs which are

not directly related to the manufacturing activities, and for appropriations of profit which are not the concern of the cost accountant. There may be a profit variation, because items similar to the following may appear in the Financial Ledger or the Cost Ledger:

(i) Financial Ledger Dividends and interest received or paid; profit or loss on sale of investments and fixed assets; cash discounts; rent receivable; penalties and damages payable; legal charges; charitable donations which are not related to the main business activities or to the welfare of employees; bad debts; expenses written off, such as those connected with the formation or financing of the business; transfers to reserves or provisions in respect of sinking funds and taxation; depreciation, when the rates or methods differ from those used in the cost accounts.

(ii) Cost Ledger Variations in the valuation of stocks and work-in-progress when a different method is used such as LIFO or average price.

It is appropriate to refer to SSAP 2, 'Disclosure of Accounting Policies', and specifically to the 'Cost' concept, which states that the assets of the business should be recorded normally at the price paid for them, except where a diminution in value has occurred, in which case the prudence concept requires that the lower value be incorporated.

(c) Repairs and capital expenditure

Repairs are carried out in order to ensure that the value and operating condition of fixed assets are maintained. The cost is classified as revenue expenditure and is charged to repair or service orders and to the overhead account of the department which receives the benefit of those repairs. Capital expenditure consists of the original or additional expenditure on fixed assets which are purchased or manufactured by the firm's employees. If the capital expenditure is carried out by the work's employees a job order is issued to collect the actual expenditure, and on completion the cost is transferred to an asset account in the Financial Ledger. In the Cost Ledger the Capital Expenditure Account is debited with the amount transferred from the Work-in-progress Account. At the end of the accounting period the asset is capitalised and a transfer is made from the Capital Expenditure Account to the debit of the Financial Ledger Control Account. When work of this type is undertaken a decision has to be made in respect of the amount of overheads which is to be included in the cost. It may be decided that it would be unfair to charge capital orders with the same rate of overheads as are charged to the ordinary production orders.

11.7 Cost Ledger exercise

The XY Engineering Company keeps a Cost Ledger, and at 1 January 19.. the balances were as follows:

(continued on p. 310)

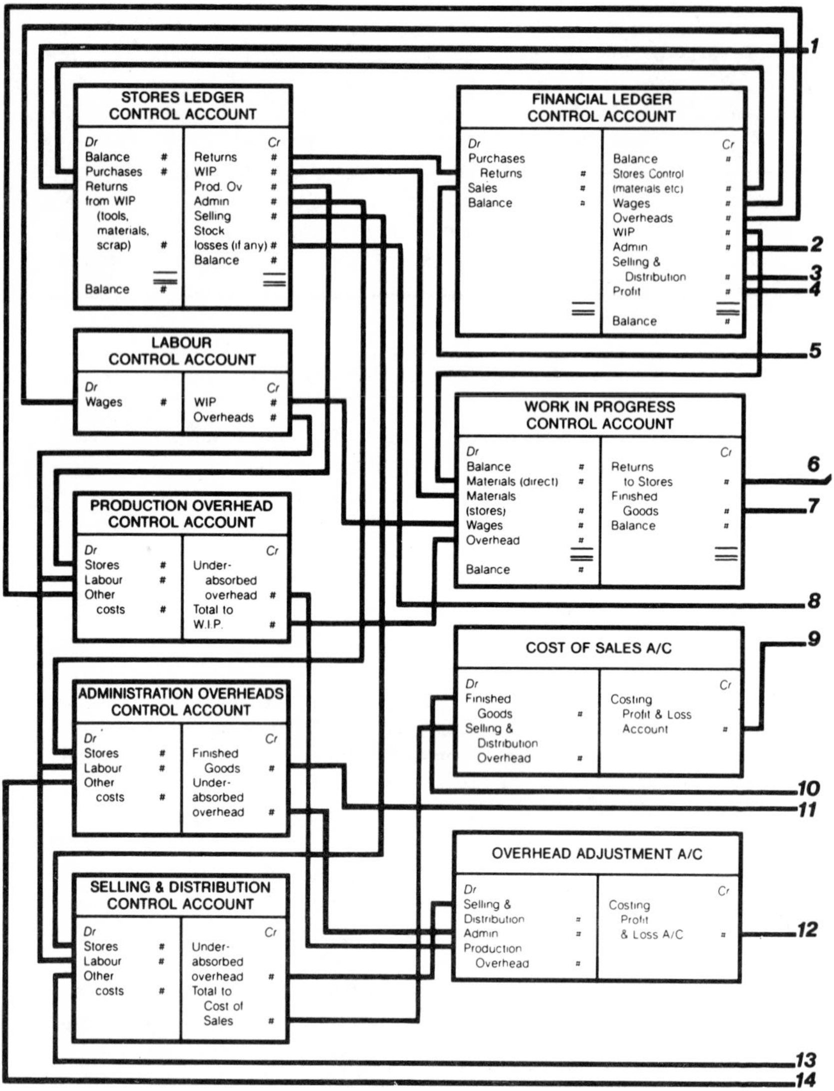
STORES LEDGER CONTROL ACCOUNT
Dr Balance # Purchases # Returns from WIP (tools, materials, scrap) # Balance #
Cr Returns # WIP # Prod. Ov # Admin # Selling # Stock losses (if any) # Balance #
FINANCIAL LEDGER CONTROL ACCOUNT
Dr Purchases Returns # Sales # Balance #
Cr Balance # Stores Control (materials etc) # Wages # Overheads # WIP # Admin # Selling & Distribution # Profit # Balance #
LABOUR CONTROL ACCOUNT
Dr Wages #
Cr WIP # Overheads #
WORK IN PROGRESS CONTROL ACCOUNT
Dr Balance # Materials (direct) # Materials (stores) # Wages # Overhead # Balance #
Cr Returns to Stores # Finished Goods # Balance #
PRODUCTION OVERHEAD CONTROL ACCOUNT
Dr Stores # Labour # Other costs #
Cr Under-absorbed overhead # Total to W.I.P. #
COST OF SALES A/C
Dr Finished Goods # Selling & Distribution Overhead #
Cr Costing Profit & Loss Account #
ADMINISTRATION OVERHEADS CONTROL ACCOUNT
Dr Stores # Labour # Other costs #
Cr Finished Goods # Under-absorbed overhead #
OVERHEAD ADJUSTMENT A/C
Dr Selling & Distribution # Admin # Production Overhead #
Cr Costing Profit & Loss A/C #
SELLING & DISTRIBUTION CONTROL ACCOUNT
Dr Stores # Labour # Other costs #
Cr Under-absorbed overhead # Total to Cost of Sales #
1
2
3
4
5
6
7
8
9
10
11
12
13
14

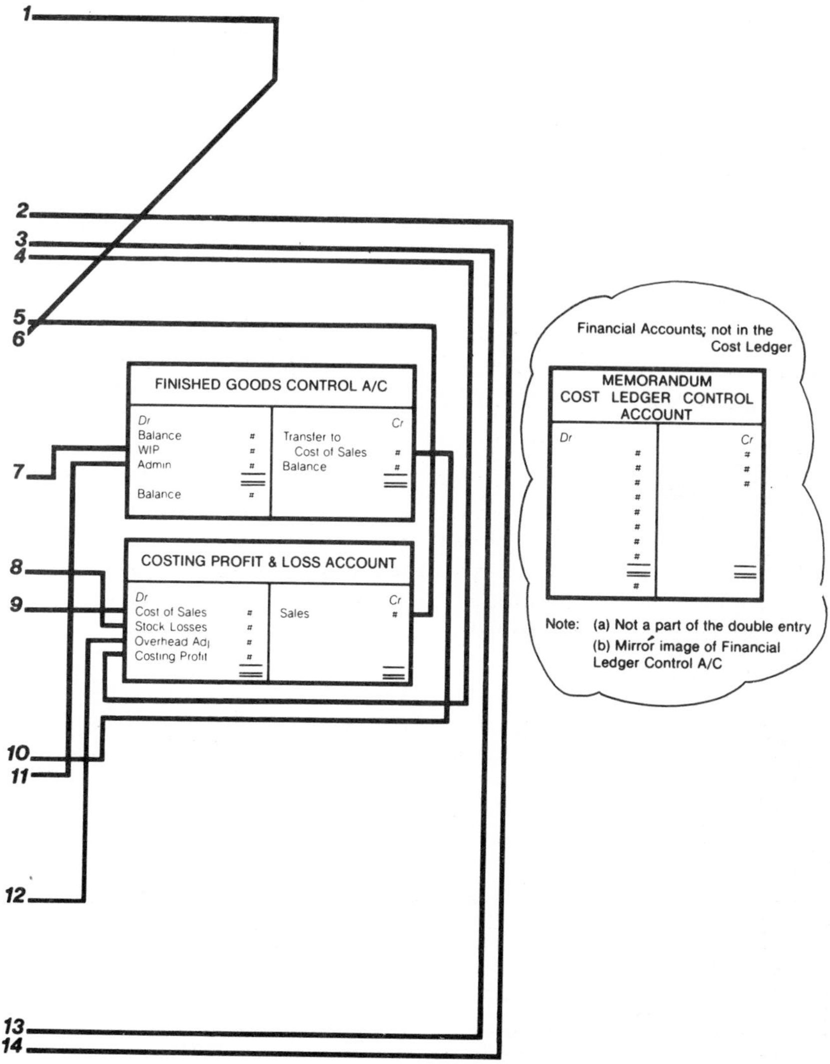

Fig. 11.2 Non-integrated cost accounts

	£	£
Financial Ledger Control A/c		311 245
Stores Ledger Control A/c	109 456	
Work-in-progress Control A/c	78 206	
Finished Goods Stock Ledger Control A/c	123 583	
	£311 245	£311 245

Transactions during the year to 31 December 19.. were as follows:

	£	£
Purchases		
Stores stock (£256 304 *less* Returns £653)	255 651	
Production orders (work-in-progress: direct materials)	34 672	
Production expenses (overheads: indirect materials)	17 028	
Sales department (selling costs)	1 576	
		308 927
Material requisitions (stores issues)		
Work-in-progress (direct materials)	264 147	
Production expenses (overheads: indirect materials)	9 265	
Administrative departments (overhead expenses)	143	
Sales department (overheads: selling costs)	768	
Suppliers (materials returned to suppliers)	653	
		274 976
Wages analysis		
Production orders (work-in-progress: direct wages)	207 826	
Production expenses (overheads: indirect wages)	48 472	
		256 298
Salaries analysis		
Production costs (overheads: indirect costs)	14 034	
Administration costs (overheads: indirect costs)	62 753	
Selling costs (overheads: indirect costs)	25 985	
		102 772
Expenses analysis (Financial Ledger)		
Production overhead	3 209	
Administration overhead	2 063	
Selling and distribution overhead	4 728	
		10 000
Capital Expenditure (ex work-in-progress)		3 291
Sales (ex Financial Ledger)		894 000
Parts manufactured for stores stock		50 000
Materials returned to stores stock from work-in-progress		1 250

	£	£
Production overheads absorbed by work-in-progress		91 808
Administration overheads charged to finished goods		65 063
Selling and distribution overheads charged to sales		32 928
Value of finished goods transferred to stock from production orders		597 543
Valuation of stores stock as carried out after stock-taking at 31 December 19..		142 034
Cost of finished goods sold (transfer to Cost of Sales A/c)		755 169

Enter the above items in the Cost Ledger, and then:

(a) Balance the overhead accounts and transfer the under- or over-absorption to the Overhead Adjustment Account.

(b) Transfer the balance of the Overhead Adjustment Account to the Costing Profit and Loss Account.

(c) Capitalise the capital expenditure and transfer the value to the Financial Ledger Control Account.

(d) Balance the following accounts and carry down the amounts as opening balances for the new period of account:

(i) Financial Ledger Control Account (after transferring profit or loss from the Costing Profit and Loss Account);
(ii) Stores Ledger Control Account (the balance is stock valuation at the end of the period);
(iii) Work-in-progress Ledger Control Account;
(iv) Finished Goods Stock Ledger Control Account.

(e) Reconcile the balance in the Financial Ledger Control Account with the total value of the balances in the other accounts in the Cost Ledger, by drawing up a Trial Balance.

Notes:

The procedures for tackling such an exercise are as follows:

(i) Open the accounts which have opening balances, as shown at the start of the exercise on 1 January 19.. These are the Financial Ledger Control A/c, the Stores Ledger Control A/c, the Work-in-progress Control A/c and the Finished Goods Stock Ledger Control A/c.

(ii) Do the double entry for all the transactions taking place during the year. Note that each outside expense will go in its appropriate Control Account and the double entry for it will be in the Financial Ledger Control A/c, which is the special Contra Account we have opened to make an effective double-entry system. If you cannot understand why we need this, consider purchases of stores. 'Stores stock (£256 304 *less* £653)' is the first item. This is clearly goods coming into stores (and the returns going out). We debit the goods in the Stores Ledger Control A/c, but we cannot credit the supplier. The Supplier's Account is in the financial accounting system, not the cost accounting system. So we credit the Financial Ledger Control A/c, an account we have opened just to receive all these double entries. Similarly the credit notes are going to mean a credit of £653 in the Stores Ledger Control A/c, and a debit in the Financial Ledger Control A/c, because we cannot debit the supplier who is receiving back the goods as we have not got a supplier's account in the Cost Ledger - it is in the Financial Ledger.

(iii) Where an entry is not from an outside source - for example, when we requisition materials from stores to send to work-in-progress - the entries will not affect the Financial Ledger Control A/c, but will involve a move from one cost account to another cost account. Carry on with all these entries until you get to the end of the year and the start of the adjustments (designated *(a)*, *(b)*, etc.).

(iv) Now carry out each of the adjustments in turn and complete the work by drawing up a Trial Balance.

Financial Ledger Control A/c

	£		£	£
Capital Expenditure A/c	3 291	Balance b/d		311 245
Costing Profit and Loss A/c (sales)	894 000	*Purchases*		
Balance c/d	197 629	Stores Ledger Control A/c	256 304	
		Less Returns	653	
			255 651	
		Production Overhead Control A/c	17 028	
		Work-in-progress Ledger Control A/c	34 672	
		Selling and Distribution Overhead Control A/c	1 576	
				308 927
		Wages Ledger Control A/c		256 298
		Salaries Ledger Control A/c		102 772
		Expenses		
		Production Overhead Control A/c	3 209	
		Administration Overhead Control A/c	2 063	
		Selling and Distribution Overhead Control A/c	4 728	
				10 000
		Costing Profit and Loss A/c		105 678
	£1 094 920			£1 094 920
		Balance b/d		197 629

Stores Ledger Control A/c

		£			£
Balance	b/d	109 456	Work-in-progress Ledger Control A/c		264 147
Financial Ledger Control A/c (purchases)		256 304	Production Overhead Control A/c		9 265
Work-in-progress Ledger Control A/c			Administration Overhead Control A/c		143
Manufactured parts		50 000	Selling and Distribution Overhead Control A/c		768
Materials returned		1 250	Financial Ledger Control A/c (purchase returns)		653
			Balance	c/d	142 034
		£417 010			£417 010
Balance	b/d	142 034			

Wages Ledger Control A/c

	£		£
Financial Ledger Control A/c	256 298	Work-in-progress Ledger Control A/c	207 826
		Production Overhead Control A/c	48 472
	£256 298		£256 298

Salaries Ledger Control A/c

	£		£
Financial Ledger Control A/c	102 772	Production Overhead Control A/c	14 034
		Administration Overhead Control A/c	62 753
		Selling and Distribution Overhead Control A/c	25 985
	£102 772		£102 772

Production Overhead Control A/c

	£		£
Financial Ledger Control A/c (purchases)	17 028	Work-in-progress Ledger Control A/c	91 808
Stores Ledger Control A/c	9 265	Overhead Adjustment A/c	200
Wages Ledger Control A/c	48 472		
Salaries Ledger Control A/c	14 034		
Financial Ledger Control A/c (expenses)	3 209		
	£92 008		£92 008

Administration Overhead Control A/c

	£		£
Stores Ledger Control A/c	143	Finished Goods Stock Ledger Control A/c	65 063
Salaries Ledger Control A/c	62 753		
Financial Ledger Control A/c (expenses)	2 063		
Overhead Adjustment A/c	104		
	£65 063		£65 063

Selling and Distribution Overhead Control A/c

	£		£
Financial Ledger Control A/c (purchases)	1 576	Overhead Adjustment A/c	129
Stores Ledger Control A/c	768	Cost of Sales A/c	32 928
Salaries Ledger Control A/c	25 985		
Financial Ledger Control A/c (expenses)	4 728		
	£33 057		£33 057

Work-in-progress Ledger Control A/c

		£			£
Balance	b/d	78 206	Capital Expenditure		3 291
Financial Ledger Control A/c		34 672	Stores Ledger Control A/c		
			Manufactured parts		50 000
Stores Ledger Control A/c		264 147	Material returns		1 250
Wages Ledger Control A/c		207 826	Finished Goods Stock Ledger Control A/c		597 543
			Balance	c/d	24 575
Production Overhead Control A/c		91 808			
		£676 659			£676 659
Balance	b/d	24 575			

Capital Expenditure A/c

	£		£
Work-in-progress Ledger Control A/c	3 291	Financial Ledger Control A/c	3 291

Finished Goods Stock Ledger Control A/c

		£			£
Balance	b/d	123 583	Cost of Sales A/c		755 169
Work-in-progress Ledger Control A/c		597 543	Balance	c/d	31 020
Administration Overhead Control A/c		65 063			
		£786 189			£786 189
Balance	b/d	31 020			

Cost of Sales A/c

	£		£
Finished Goods Stock Ledger Control A/c	755 169	Costing Profit and Loss A/c	788 097
Selling and Distribution Overhead Control A/c	32 928		
	£788 097		£788 097

Overhead Adjustment A/c

	£		£
Production Overhead Control A/c	200	Administration Overhead Control A/c	104
Selling and Distribution Overhead Control A/c	129	Balance to Costing Profit and Loss A/c	225
	£329		£329

Costing Profit and Loss A/c

	£		£
Cost of Sales A/c	788 097	Financial Ledger Control A/c (sales)	894 000
Overhead Adjustment A/c	225		
Financial Ledger Control A/c (profit)	105 678		
	£894 000		£894 000

Trial Balance as at 31 December 19..

	£	£
Financial Ledger Control A/c		197 629
Stores Ledger Control A/c	142 034	
Work-in-progress Ledger Control A/c	24 575	
Finished Goods Stock Ledger Control A/c	31 020	
	£197 629	£197 629

11.8 Reconciliation of cost and financial accounts

The preparation of a reconciliation statement has already been referred to in this unit (see 11.6) and an example is given below (Example 11.1). Generally the items which are responsible for the difference between the profit as shown in the Costing Profit and Loss Account and the profit as shown in the financial books are the result of policy decisions made by the management and abnormal profits or losses, and these are found in the financial accounts, but certain items in the cost accounts may differ due to valuation procedures or the inclusion of items which do not appear in the financial accounts.

Purchases, wages, expenses and sales are normally the same in each ledger because they are derived from the same original documents.

EXAMPLE 11.1

	£
Profit in financial accounts	85 028
Profit in cost accounts	105 678
A comparison of the two sets of accounts shows that the following items appear only in the financial accounts:	
Loss on sale of investments	5 000
Dividends received	3 000
Staff bonus as a reward for extra duties during flooding of offices	5 000
Special commission to sales staff	1 000
Profit on sale of buildings	8 000
Depreciation on machinery and plant in addition to that in the cost accounts	10 000
Provision against possible loss on sale of certain finished goods	2 400
Valuation of stores stock at the close of the year is on a different basis in the financial accounts and is lower by:	1 500
The following items are different in the cost accounts:	
Notional rent (rent charged to manufacturing costs although not actually payable)	6 000
Interest included in contract accounts	750

The accounts are reconciled by drawing up a memorandum statement which is presented either in the form of an account or in vertical form. When the statement is in the form of an account the financial profit may be shown on the left-hand side and the costing profit on the right.

Proceed as follows:

(a) Enter the profit as indicated.

(b) Enter all the items which differ and do not appear in the cost accounts.

(i) Under financial profit enter the items which have *reduced* the financial profit. These are *debits* in the financial accounts, such as loss on investments.

(ii) Under costing profit enter the items which have *increased* the costing profit. These are *credits* in the financial accounts, such as dividend received.

(c) Enter all the items which differ and do not appear in the financial accounts.

(i) Under financial profit enter the items which have *increased* the costing profit. These are *credits* in the cost accounts, such as notional rent, which was included in costs although no rent was payable.

(ii) Under costing profit enter the items which have *reduced* the costing profit. These are *debits*, such as cost of sales, which was of greater value in the cost accounts due to closing stock being valued at a lower level.

The reconciliation statement in the form of an account is as follows:

Memorandum Reconciliation Statement

	£		£
Profit in Financial Ledger	85 028	Profit in Cost Ledger	105 678
Loss on investments	5 000	Dividends received	3 000
Staff bonus	5 000	Profit on sale of buildings	8 000
Special commission to sales staff	1 000		
Depreciation	10 000		
Provision against loss on finished goods	2 400		
Valuation of closing stock	1 500		
Notional rent	6 000		
Interest in contract accounts	750		
	£116 678		£116 678

The reconciliation statement in vertical form is shown below:

Memorandum Reconciliation Statement

	£	£
Costing profit		105 678
Add Amounts credited in Financial Ledger:		
Dividends received	3 000	
Profit on sale of buildings	8 000	
		11 000
		116 678
Less Amounts credited in Cost Ledger:		
Production overhead:		
Notional rent	6 000	
Work-in-progress:		
Interest in contract accounts	750	
		6 750
		109 928

		£	£
Less	Amounts debited in Financial Ledger:		
	Loss on sale of investments	5 000	
	Provision against loss on finished stock	2 400	
			7 400
			102 528
	Production overheads:		
	Depreciation		10 000
			92 528
	Administration overheads:		
	Staff bonus		5 000
			87 528
	Selling and distribution overheads:		
	Special commission to sales staff		1 000
			86 528
	Stock valuation:		
	Lower valuation of closing stock		1 500
Profit as per financial accounts			£85 028

The effect of stock valuation on profits

Because stock may be valued on a different basis in the financial accounts the cost of sales and the profit may be different from those shown in the cost accounts. If a Trading Account shows the same values for opening and closing stock, the value of the purchases is equal to the cost of sales.

EXAMPLE 11.2

(i) Purchases = cost of sales

Stock values		£	£
£	Sales		100 000
10 000	Opening stock	10 000	
	Add Purchases	80 000	
		90 000	
10 000	*Less* Closing stock	10 000	
	Cost of sales		80 000
	Profit		£20 000

It is therefore the purchases figure, adjusted up or down by the change in stock values, which represents the cost of sales, and it is this adjustment which influences the amount of profit or loss shown in the accounts. It should be noted that the value of opening stock has a different effect on cost of sales and profit to that which arises from the value of closing stock. This is because opening stock is an addition to stocks, and closing stock is a deduction. When the value of opening stock is at a higher level there is an increase in cost of sales and a lower profit arises, whereas if closing stock is higher, costs are lower and the profit is at a higher level.

(ii) Opening stock Higher value – lower profit; lower value – higher profit.
(iii) Closing stock Higher value – higher profit; lower value – lower profit.

The following examples show the effect on cost of sales and profit when there are different values for opening and closing stocks.

Financial accounts (with higher opening value of £15 000)

Stock values		£	£	£
	Sales			100 000
£				
15 000	Opening stock	15 000		
	Purchases	80 000		
			95 000	
10 000	*Less* Closing stock		10 000	
+ 5 000	Cost of sales			85 000
– 5 000	Profit			£15 000
—				

Cost accounts (with lower opening value of £8 000)

Stock values		£	£	£
	Sales			100 000
£				
8 000	Opening stock	8 000		
	Purchases	80 000		
			88 000	
10 000	*Less* Closing stock		10 000	
– 2 000				
+ 2 000	Cost of sales			78 000
—	Profit			£22 000

The difference in opening stock is £7 000 (i.e. £15 000 – £8 000) and this corresponds to the difference in profit of £7 000 (i.e. £22 000 – £15 000). The extra profit in the cost accounts is due to the lower value of the opening stock in the cost accounts.

It is necessary to find the difference between the opening stocks and the difference between the closing stocks. The account with higher opening stock has a lower income and the account with the higher closing stock has a higher income.

11.9 An integrated system of accounts

As the name implies, an integrated system of accounts is one that deals with all the accounts in a single system. The two chief branches of accounting, the financial accounts and the cost accounts, both use similar inputs of information and there is really no reason why they should be separated apart from the general problem of complexity. When all entries had to be made on paper records there was some sense in keeping the two sets of accounts apart, giving two manageable sets of information which could be interlocked towards the end of the financial year and reconciled if they gave slightly different results.

There is rather less reason for keeping the systems apart when a computerised system can be programmed to deal with all the uses of a particular piece of information, and prepare both the costing records and the financial records from a single set of inputs. Naturally there will be a good deal of work required to analyse the requirements of a company and draw up suitable programs, or possibly to adapt the existing system to one of the available packages on the market. Methods can be used and a system designed with the object of economising in time and effort and with the intention of satisfying the requirements of both the management accountant and the financial accountant. The problems associated with the preparation of a reconciliation statement are avoided and the need for a separate Cost Ledger is eliminated. Systems vary and it is necessary to determine the degree of integration. All the records may be integrated, duplicate entries may be eliminated and the cost accounts can be in a form very similar to separately prepared cost accounts.

In the case of a manufacturing company which produces a number of different products it may be advantageous to break the figures down so that costs and profits and losses can be shown for each type of product. There will be Control Accounts and also a series of accounts for each type of product in respect of materials, labour, overheads, work-in-progress, finished goods and other items. It will require a great deal of analysis of Nominal Ledger entries, and tabulations will provide the costs in summarised form for Journal entries, and for the Control Accounts and other accounts used in the system. It will be necessary to open Suspense Accounts to take account of accrued expenses.

Table 11.1 shows the accounts and entries which may be found in the different systems used. Note that in each case the integrated accounts do in one double entry that which requires two double entries if separate systems are used.

When seeking to understand integrated accounts problems arise, because

Table 11.1 Accounts and entries in different systems

	Financial accounts	*Integrated accounts*	*Cost accounts*
	Materials		
Debit	Purchases A/c	Stores Ledger Control A/c	Stores Ledger Control A/c
Credit	Creditors' A/cs	Creditors' A/c	Financial Ledger Control A/c
	Wages		
Debit	Wages and Salaries A/c	Wages and Salaries Control A/c	Wages and Salaries Control A/c
Credit	Bank A/c	Bank A/c	Financial Ledger Control A/c
	Overheads		
Debit	Various nominal a/cs	Production, Administration and Selling Overhead Control A/cs	Production, Administration and Selling Overhead Control A/cs for Stores, Wages and Salaries
Credit	Various creditors' a/cs	Various creditors' a/cs	Financial Ledger Control A/c
	Work-in-progress		
Debit	Finished Stock A/c	Finished Stock A/c	Work-in-progress Control A/c
Credit	Manufacturing A/c	Stores, Wages and Overhead A/cs	Stores, Wages, and Overhead Control A/c
	Finished Stock		
Debit	Finished Goods Stock A/c	Finished Goods Stock A/c	Finished Goods Control A/c
Credit	Manufacturing A/c	Work-in-progress A/c	Work-in-progress Control A/c
	Expenses		
Debit	Various nominal a/cs	Control A/cs for Production, Administration, Selling and Work-in-progress	Control A/cs for Production, Administration, Selling and Work-in-progress
Credit	Expense Creditors' A/cs	Expense Creditors' A/cs	Financial Ledger Control A/c

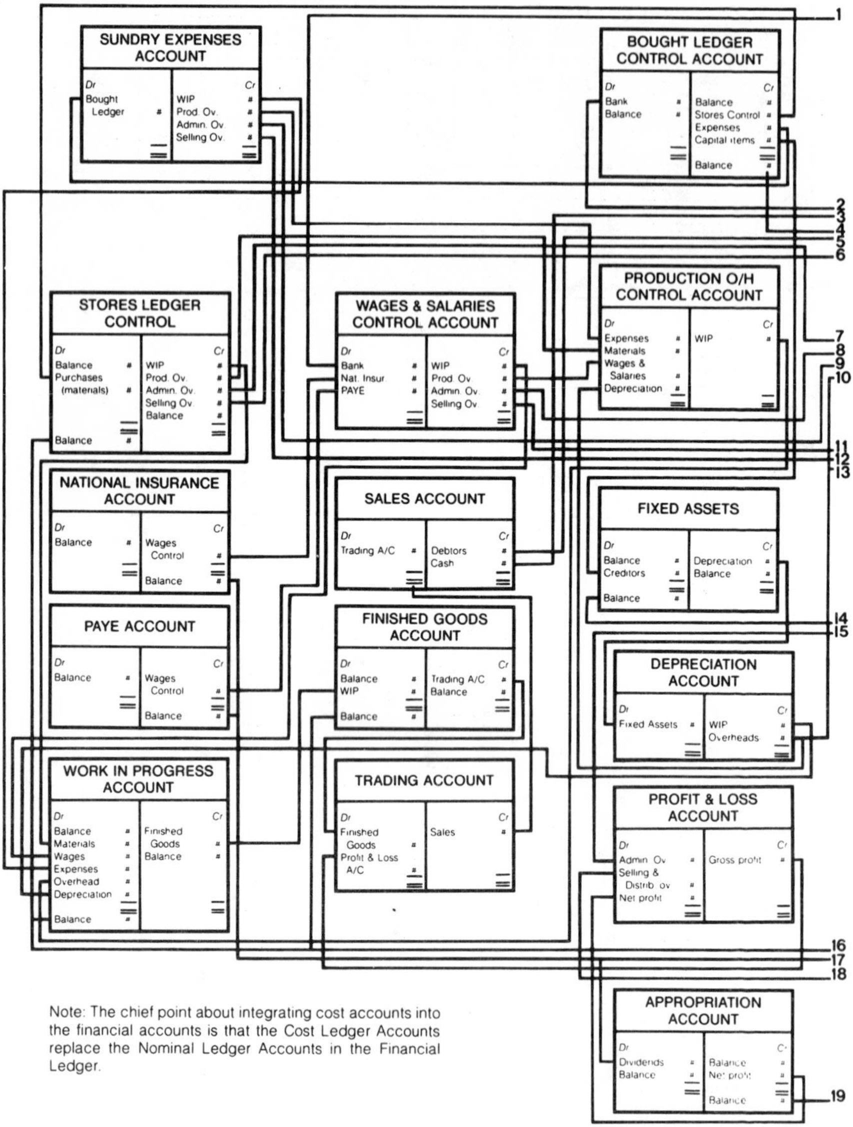

Note: The chief point about integrating cost accounts into the financial accounts is that the Cost Ledger Accounts replace the Nominal Ledger Accounts in the Financial Ledger.

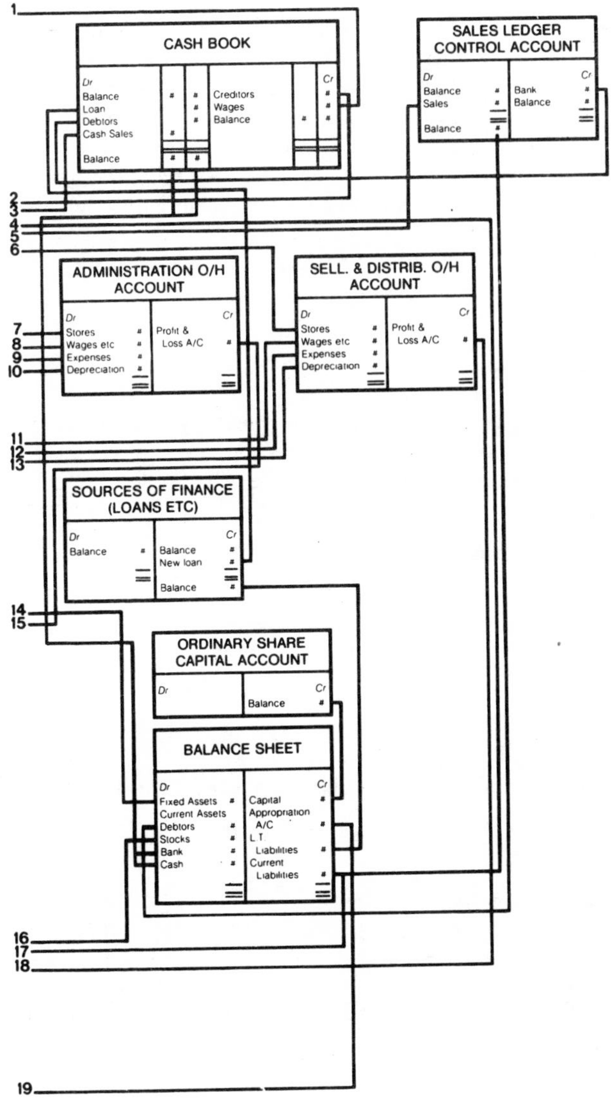

Fig. 11.3 An integrated set of accounts

the whole exercise is lengthy and involved and requires numerous accounts in T form, with many double entries to be achieved through a complex network of accounts. It is therefore usual in practice to use a computerised spreadsheet approach in which figures at the start of the year (the opening Balance Sheet) are given in vertical style on the right-hand side of the presentation. A columnar ledger approach permits the various figures for the year to be posted in the various columns, modifying the opening Balance Sheet figures and eventually arriving at the Balance Sheet at the end of the year on the left-hand side.

Fig. 11.3 (pp. 324–5) gives some idea of how the cost accounts can be integrated with the financial accounts.

11.10 Exercises

1. *(a)* Discuss the way in which double-entry book-keeping is used to record and present cost information.
   (b) Explain the meaning and purpose of the following:
      (i) integrated accounts;
      (ii) interlocking accounts;
      (iii) Control Accounts.

2. When a cost department keeps its own set of accounts there may be a difference between the profit shown in the Cost Ledger and the profit in the Financial Ledger.
   (a) What kind of statement is prepared to show the difference which may occur?
   (b) What items are likely to be responsible for this state of affairs?

3. The balances in a Cost Ledger on 1 January 19 . 7 were as follows:

	£
Stores	49 000
Finished goods	35 000
Work-in-progress	70 000

During the year the following transactions were recorded:

	£
Sales	1 600 000
Employees' remuneration	
Direct wages	800 000
Indirect wages	250 000
Expenses ex General Ledger:	
Works	60 000
Administration	110 000
Selling	50 000

	£
Purchases for stores	260 000
Purchases for production orders	23 000
Stores issued	
Production orders	240 000
Works expenses	27 000
Works overheads absorbed	275 000
Administration costs recovered	110 000

Sixty per cent of indirect wages are to be charged to works expenses and 40 per cent to administration expenses. At the end of the year the stocks were valued as follows:

	£
Stores	42 000
Finished goods	56 000
Work-in-progress	98 000

You are required to enter the balances and transactions in a Cost Ledger and to prepare a Trial Balance as at 31 December 19 . 7.

4. You are required to enter the following items in accounts in a Cost Ledger. You should also prepare a Trial Balance and close the accounts at 31 December 19 . 8.

The opening balances at 1 January 19 . 8 were as follows:

	£
Financial Ledger Control A/c	640 648
Stores Ledger Control A/c	224 209
Work-in-progress Control A/c	197 375
Finished Goods Stock Ledger A/c	219 064

The transactions during the year were as follows:

Purchases	
Stores stock	371 926
Production orders	46 591
Production overheads	32 484
Administration costs	1 342
Selling costs	2 917
Materials issued	
Work-in-progress	392 246
Production overheads	15 498
Administration overheads	397
Selling and distribution overheads	1 024

	£
Wages	
Work-in-progress	348 976
Production overheads	59 463
Salaries	
Production overheads	21 862
Administration overheads	87 654
Selling and distribution overheads	39 863
Expenses (ex Financial Ledger)	
Production overheads	4 209
Administration overheads	3 876
Selling and distribution overheads	5 843
Capital expenditure transferred from Work-in-progress Ledger	12 793
Parts manufactured for stores stock (ex work-in-progress)	72 785
Materials returned to stores from work-in-progress orders	2 106
Sales	993 494
Production overheads absorbed by work-in-progress	133 841
Administration overheads absorbed by finished goods	92 971
Selling and distribution overheads absorbed by sales	49 343
Value of finished goods transferred from work-in-progress	806 790
Stocktaking: abnormal loss transferable to Stock Discrepancy Account	234
Cost of finished goods sold	820 771
Stock valuation at end of year	261 627

5. *(a)* What is the object of opening the following accounts in a cost ledger?

(i) Work-in-progress Account
(ii) Finished Goods Stock Ledger Account
(iii) Overhead Adjustment Account
(iv) Cost of Sales Account

(b) Indicate what steps you would take to check the accounts and so ensure that the costing profit is correct when it differs from the profit shown in the Financial Ledger.

6. A company operates a system of cost accounting which uses separate cost ledgers to record the costs and activities of its manufacturing and administrative departments. At the end of the year there is a difference of £6 106 between the profit in the financial accounts and that shown in the Costing Profit and Loss Account. Using the following information, draw up reconciliation statements in horizontal and vertical form.

	£
Financial profit	122 982
Items which do not appear in the cost accounts	
Loss on sale of obsolete computer	7 000
Golden handshake to member of staff	25 000
Dividend received	3 000
Profit on sale of machinery	7 294
Items which appear only in the cost accounts	
Extra depreciation on machinery	5 000

Stock valuation

	Opening stock	Closing stock
	£	£
Financial Ledger	93 964	107 542
Cost Ledger	99 252	112 230

7. *(a)* A company operates a financial accounting system and a cost accounting system with its own set of ledgers. Extracts from the final accounts for the year are shown below. You are required to prepare a reconciliation statement.

The final financial accounts included the following:

	£
Debenture interest	2 000
Interest received	1 000
Discount allowed	8 000
Discount received	3 000
Net profit	57 000

Stock valuations

	Opening stock	Closing stock
	£	£
Raw materials	152 000	198 000
Work-in-progress	66 000	72 000
Finished goods	84 000	87 000

The final cost accounts included the following:

	£
Interest on capital	30 000
Notional rent	20 000
Administration overhead over-absorbed	10 000
Production overhead under-absorbed	15 000
Selling and distribution overhead over-absorbed	14 000
Net profit	1 000

Stock valuations

	Opening stock	Closing stock
	£	£
Raw materials	164 000	187 000
Work-in-progress	61 000	68 000
Finished goods	90 000	94 000

(b) Explain the meaning of (i) interest on capital, and (ii) notional rent. Discuss briefly the reason why the cost accountant may choose to introduce these items into the cost accounts.

8. The chief accountant of a manufacturing company is responsible for the correct presentation of the financial accounts. The cost accounts, which are interlocked with the financial accounts, show a profit for the year of £249 005, but the financial accounts (which appear below) show only £211 275. It is therefore necessary to examine both sets of final accounts and prepare a statement listing the items which make up the difference in profit. You are required to prepare this statement from the information given below.

Manufacturing Account

	£	£		£
Opening stock			Works cost of	
Raw materials		8 550	production transferred	
Purchases		247 050	to Finished Stock A/c	501 300
		255 600		
Less Closing stock		8 100		
		247 500		
Direct wages	159 750			
Works overhead	96 300			
		256 050		
		503 550		

	£	£		£
Work-in-progress				
Opening stock	37 800			
Closing stock	40 050	2 250		
		£501 300		£501 300

Depreciation amounting to £26 428 is included in the works overhead.

Finished Stock Account

	£		£
Opening stock	52 200	Cost of sales to Trading Account	498 150
Goods transferred from Manufacturing A/c	501 300	Closing stock	55 350
	£553 500		£553 500

Trading Account

	£		£
Cost of sales from Finished Stock A/c	498 150	Sales	830 250
Gross profit to Profit and Loss A/c	332 100		
	£830 250		£830 250

Profit and Loss Account

	£		£
Administration expenses	70 200	Gross profit	332 100
Selling expenses	45 819	Discount received	8 127
Discount allowed	6 799	Dividend received	1 516
Debenture interest	4 625		
Loss by fire	3 025		
Net profit	211 275		
	£341 743		£341 743

The following items appeared in the cost accounts:
interest on capital £18 500; notional rent £12 750; depreciation (included in works overheads) £27 657.

Valuation of:	Raw materials	Work-in-progress	Finished stock
	£	£	£
Opening stock	8 860	37 260	51 282
Closing stock	8 325	39 285	57 645

9. What are the advantages and disadvantages of accounts which are integrated and those which are reconciled?

10. A company operates an integrated accounting system and the following information is given:

	£'000	£'000
Capital		500
Reserves		100
Creditors		75
Freehold buildings at cost	250	
Plant and machinery at cost	150	
Provision for depreciation of plant and machinery		50
Expense creditors		10
Debtors	100	
Stock of		
Raw materials	110	
Work-in-progress	20	
Finished goods	30	
Bank	75	
	£735	£735

	£
Wages and salaries paid	212
Deductions from wages and salaries	25
Cheques from debtors	1 175
Paid creditors	448
Paid expense creditors	365
Sales on credit	1 250
Administration	
Salaries	50
Expenses incurred	130
Overhead absorbed in finished goods	190
Selling and distribution	
Salaries	40
Expenses incurred	60
Absorbed in cost of sales	105

	£
Carriage inwards	22
Finished goods sold	1 000
Production at standard cost	800
Cash discount allowed	18
Cash discount received from trade creditors	12
Production overhead absorbed	212
Provision for depreciation of plant and machinery	25
Production	
Wages	125
Salaries	30
Expenses	160
Materials	
Purchased on credit	495
Returned to suppliers	20
Issued to production	425
Variances	
Direct material:	
Usage (favourable)	10
Price (adverse)	18
Direct labour efficiency (favourable)	15
Direct wages rate (favourable)	8
Production overhead:	
Expenditure (adverse)	12
Efficiency (favourable)	20
Bad debts written off	13

All 'price' variances (i.e. direct material, direct wages rate, production overhead expenditure) are recorded in the relevant expenditure accounts; 'quantity' variances (i.e. direct material usage, direct labour efficiency, production overhead efficiency) are recorded in the Work-in-progress Account.

You are required to: (*a*) enter the transactions in the appropriate ledger accounts and (*b*) prepare a Trial Balance for the year.

UNIT 12

The computerisation of management accounting

12.1 Introduction to computerisation

The essential raw data of management accounting are the various cost figures collected and collated by the cost system in use. Computerisation of cost accountancy procedures is highly desirable, for costing procedures are in many respects routine matters of collecting and recording cost data and these lend themselves to computerisation, being relatively easy to collect, record and store. They then have to pass through a number of processes, some more appropriate for one type of business and others more appropriate for other types of activity. Thus we may have to allocate the costs to a particular job, contract or product, or we may have to absorb the costs into on-costs on various products, projects or cost centres. These are again relatively routine activities which lend themselves to data processing, which enables the correct proportion of costs to be fed through to the various destinations where costs are being assembled. Finally a whole range of number-crunching activities, such as budgetary control, variance analysis, score-keeping activities and report writing, can be devised to assist management decision-making at various levels. Such reports can be prepared at electronic speeds, with some of them becoming routine print-outs to alert management to problems that are about to arise – the need to pay accounts, or order stock, or chase the progress of particular orders, or book warehouse or shipping space. Others may be required for periodic reviews of production, sales, budget utilisation, profitability, etc.

Many readers will no doubt be familiar with many aspects of computerisation, but for those whose background is less well developed a short introduction is given in the rest of this unit, before we look at some specifically costing applications.

12.2 The early history of computers

The father of modern computing is generally agreed to be the Englishman Charles Babbage, who drew up the concept of an analytical engine in 1833. He conceived the engine as having an *input device* to feed numbers into the machine, a *store* to hold them while they were in it, a *program* of instructions to manipulate them in various ways, a *control unit* to keep the sequence of operations correct, a *mill* to do the actual calculations and *output devices* to put the answers arrived at out to the end-user. He envisaged punched cards and printed outputs as possible methods of making the results available.

Most of the words given in italics above are in common use today, but over a hundred years were to pass before the full implementation of Babbage's ideas. In the meantime a mechanical 'engine' of sorts, the Hollerith Tabulator, had been produced in America to analyse election results, using punched cards and magnetic forces to attract iron rods through the holes to make and break an electrical circuit.

The first generation of real computers was produced in the years leading up to 1950. An essential element in the idea of a computer is that current must be able to flow, or not flow, according to the information which is being processed, because the whole system works using binary arithmetic, which has only two numbers, namely 1 and 0 (see Unit 12.3). One number can be indicated when current is flowing, and the other when current is not able to flow. The original semi-conductor designed to control the flow was the thermonic valve, used in first generation computers. As these required to heat up before current could flow at all, and since thousands of them were needed, computers required special premises, with air conditioning and other devices.

Within twenty years the development was:

(a) first generation computers with thermionic valves;
(b) second generation computers with transistors – very small semi-conducting devices the size of a peanut and more efficient than the thermionic valve;
(c) third generation computers with the semi-conductor activity performed by a silicon chip – a natural product which possessed the semi-conductor property;
(d) fourth generation computers with VLSI technology (very large scale integration). Integration is a procedure for putting more than one circuit on a silicon chip, and by 1971 the first complete computer on a silicon chip – a microprocessor – had been developed. Fourth generation computers have many silicon chips, each with a microprocessor on it.

As yet there is no fifth generation of computers, though research into robotics (machines which are almost human in their ability to think) may eventually prove to be so distinctive as to merit the name. What we do have at present is a massive expansion of power (more and more capacity packed into the same space) and a huge extension of the use of computers into every field of business activity. The change to user-friendly software, so that everyone can use the computer and the subject is no longer one of mystique for specialist staff, is also an important development. Networking, the interlinking of computers to form a network of data-processing and information facilities accessible on a multi-user basis, is another important feature.

Today the variety of computers is enormous, with lap-top computers that can be used on a journey and are as powerful as the original computers which needed their own air-conditioned premises. The three main classifications are:

(i) Mainframe computers These are large, sophisticated computers with enormous capacities, able to handle the work of a major government department or public company. Often those who possess such computers act as bureaux for other firms that need data processing, and (for a fee) the mainframe owner will sub-contract to do the work for hundreds of other firms.

(ii) Mini-computers These are smaller than mainframes, but able to do all the data processing required by most medium-sized firms. Costing between £15 000 and £50 000, these machines are relatively small, robust, easily housed and able to do an enormous amount of work.

Even the biggest organisation may find it more flexible and convenient to use two or three mini-computers controlling various sections of its work, rather than a single mainframe.

(iii) Microcomputers These small, relatively inexpensive computers are able to handle all the work required by many small firms, and are also available as personal computers (PCs) for individual clubs, societies and people.

The essential point of computers is that they can carry out their simple functions – reading input data, reading a program of instructions, carrying out the calculations required and putting out the answers in readable form – at simply fantastic speeds, so that the results appear to be instantaneous. In fact they are carried out in logical sequence just like any human calculation; but at a speed of about 700 million calculations a second. Even a complicated calculation, with several hundred different processes, does not take long at such speeds.

12.3 Hardware and software

(a) Hardware

This is the machinery required to make up a computer layout, commonly known as a *configuration*. The central item is the computer itself, called the *CPU*, the central processing unit. It consists of a number of components housed in the same machine body: an *arithmetic and logic unit*, a *control unit* and a *main memory* (or *immediate access store*).

All other items of hardware may be viewed as grouped around the CPU and are therefore given the name *peripheral units*. Typical peripheral units would be a *keyboard* (or *console communicator*) with alphabetical and numerical keyboards through which the computer may be accessed; a variety of other input devices such as *floppy discs* or *hard discs*; a *VDU* (visual display unit) or *monitor* with a screen where the computer can display information; *backing store devices* of various sorts where programs and results can be stored until required either for processing (when they are fed into main memory in the CPU for immediate access) or for output to a suitable output device such as a *printer*, a VDU, a *microfilm device*, etc.

(i) Binary numbers When we use a computer we have to represent all the letters of the alphabet and all the numbers we wish to use in a special form or system called the binary system. The term 'binary' means the system has only two numbers, 1 and 0. The numbers 1 and 0 can be easily represented in electronic circuits and on magnetic media by the presence or absence of flowing current.

We can represent all the numbers in the decimal system and all the characters in the alphabet, using only 1 and 0, by their place value. Just as the number 365 represents 3 hundreds, 6 tens and 5 units in the decimal system, any number can be represented by a place value using 2 instead of 10 as the required figure for moving to a higher position in the system. Thus:

0 = 0	
1 = 1	
2 = 10	(one two and nothing else)
3 = 11	(one two and one more)
4 = 100	(one 2^2 and nothing else)
5 = 101	(one 2^2 and one more)
6 = 110	(one 2^2, one 2 and nothing else)
7 = 111	(one 2^2, one 2 and one more)
8 = 1000	(one 2^3 and nothing else)

Instead of hundreds, tens and units we have 2^3, 2^2, 2^1 and 2^0 (units). (Those who remember their algebra will remember that anything to the power nothing = 1 (a unit).)

Clearly some numbers in binary form are going to be very long but as the computer works so fast – several hundred million processes in a second – even the largest number can be readily distinguished in a fraction of a second. What an input device does is turn the information supplied in words and figures into binary data which the machine can 'read'. The data are said to be in machine-readable form. The machine obeys the program it has been fed with in order to process the data in binary form. It then delivers the revised data to an output device capable of turning it back into ordinary alphabetical, numerical or graphical form and printing it out, or making it available in some other way, such as on a screen or a film. We will now consider the devices (illustrated in Fig. 12.1 on pp. 344–5) in a little more detail.

(ii) Input devices There are many types of input device. As shown in Fig. 12.1, they include punched cards, paper tape, keyboards, magnetic tape, magnetic discs, floppy discs, bar codes, punched tags and various methods of reading paper records, including MICR (magnetic ink character recognition), OMR (optical mark recognition) and OCR (optical character recognition). The VDU can have its display modified or built up by the keyboard, and this revised display can then be re-passed to the computer in its modified form. As Fig. 12.1 shows, there is a section of storage in any computerised system called the *backing store*, where data of every sort can be put out of the computer and into store in machine-readable form, only to be called on when required and input again. The great advantage of this is that there is no need for such data to be in a form comprehensible to the end-user. So long as the computer can recall them and 'read' them when it is required, there is no need to change them back to readable form.

Punched cards and paper tape The earliest types of computer input were punched cards and paper tape inputs, which may still be met with in companies using large mainframe computers. The punching operation is relatively slow, and so is the reading of the cards with light beams by bands of photo-electric cells - about 1500 cards per minute with 80 characters per card, or 1000 characters per second with paper tape. The passage of light through the card or tape conveys data to the photo-electric cell which passes them to the computer in machine-readable form.

Keyboards The keyboard is the chief way of putting data into the computer today although there are various ways that this can take place. For example, we might call a particular account out of the computer's memory on to a VDU screen and update it with a purchases invoice, a credit note or a cheque sent in payment. Where we have a whole collection of documents to enter we would *batch them up* and key them in to a fast peripheral, such as a magnetic tape or a floppy disc, ready for feeding into the computer at some slack period when other work will not be disturbed. Keyboards may therefore be used by key operators for routine work or as a console communicator to access the computer itself directly and give instructions, interrogate the computer on some point or view existing data stored somewhere in the computer. In this direct role, where the keyboard is accompanied by a VDU, the computer is most helpful if it is what is known as *user-friendly*. This means that the screen either tells the operator what the computer is doing - for example, 'One moment - I am loading the Contract no. 1 cost file' - or it anticipates the operator's needs - for example, 'Please enter crane charge now' - or it prevents a disaster - for example, 'You are asking me to delete the crane charge from the cost of the contract. Is this right? Y/N.' If the operator touches the Y key the computer may then ask, 'Are you sure? Y/N'. If the operator touches the Y key again the computer will delete the crane charge and say 'Crane charge deleted. Next entry please!'

Where we have keyboards integral with a VDU they are often called *terminals*. These may act as console communicators, or they may be remote from the computer but able to access it over *dedicated* telephone lines (i.e. lines entirely given over to that purpose). Where a number of terminals are able to access a central computer we have a *network*. A *LAN* (local area network) is a series of terminals connected to one another within an office or factory. The terminals are not only able to contact one another but can use shared facilities such as printers or microfilm or microfiche outlets. Larger networks can not only link up with international branches of multinational firms but can access outside databases such as DIANE (Direct Information Access Network for Europe). The many 'automatic teller' cash-dispensing machines are a typical network.

Magnetic tape, magnetic discs and floppy discs These are all fast input peripherals on which whole programs and collections of data can be held to be fed into the computer either as original inputs or as backing store devices. While all three are fast, the disc system is faster than magnetic tape, since a tape can only be read in sequence as the tape is run, whereas a particular piece of information can be located on a disc more quickly. Tapes can be read at speeds of about 180 000 characters per second.

Hard discs are packs of between one and twelve metal discs, up to a foot or more in diameter, and coated with iron oxide tracks similar to the grooves on a gramophone record. They are read off (or written to) by a read–write head mounted on an arm which operates over the grooves to find the correct place. A floppy disc is a single plastic disc coated with iron oxide and protected by a plastic or cardboard cover. A read–write head operates in a slot to locate the correct area of the disc and read off the data or write to the disc with new data. Not all discs can be both read and written to. Thus a *ROM* disc is a Read Only Memory disc – one which is purchased or hired by a subscriber to obtain information on some topic, such as medical problems. The patient could not write back to the disc and change anything, for s/he would not have the necessary knowledge.

Many small business accounting systems work off a single floppy disc which has all the programs required. Details of the costs incurred are fed into the computer after loading a particular program (for example, the Wages program) and are then recorded on a second disc which accumulates all the year's entries as the months pass. Wise cost accountants take a duplicate copy of such a disc at the end of the day and store it in a separate place, since it would be a disaster if the data disc were stolen or inadvertently used for some other purpose. If one has a duplicate the most you can 'lose' is the data inserted today, which are fairly easy to re-key into the system.

Other input devices There are a number of specialist input devices which are available and can be adapted to particular industries if required. For example, *magnetic ink character recognition* (MICR) is widely used in banking on cheques, credit transfers, etc., and can equally be used on invoices and similar documents. Some of the features are pre-printed on the document, such as the account number. Others have to be encoded before the document is read – for example, the value of the invoice, the VAT content, etc.

The clothing industry makes considerable use of *punched tags*, which are removed by the assistant when the garment is sold and provide stock records and other useful data. *Bar codes* are becoming enormously important in the retail trade, where they not only provide the price to be charged on a screen and a line of print on the customer's bill but update stock records and lead to print-outs to re-order stock when the minimum stock level is reached. *Magnetic strips* are widely used on credit cards, cheque cards and EFTPOS cards (electronic funds transfer at point of sale). Some of these are of course not costing applications, but we are considering the general range of input devices.

Optical mark recognition (OMR) systems are used in statistical work, and in examinations, where the ticking of a box can be distinguished by the computer. For example, if there are five boxes and one of them has a tick in it the reduced intensity of the light reflected from that square can be sensed and recorded as the student's answer, which will then be marked as right or wrong. Situations where the student has changed his or her mind and marked two boxes will be rejected by the computer, and these will have to be marked manually by staff at the end of the run.

Optical character recognition (OCR) is similar to MICR, but the computer can detect the typeface being used. Some sophisticated computers can distinguish between a whole range of printing styles and call up from their memories any typeface, so that the typeface read can be converted to a different one if required.

(iii) Output devices When results are finally put out to an end-user from the computer they must be converted back from machine-readable form to ordinary numbers or language, or perhaps into graphical or pictorial form. The chief output device is the printer, of which there are five main types. Other output devices are the visual display unit, COM equipment, graph plotters and audio-response devices. A word about each of these is desirable.

VDU outputs The VDU output is a non-permanent display on the end of a cathode ray tube which gives a 'data-view' facility to all who are interested in the data concerned. Since it may usually be accessed by the keyboard it is susceptible to updating and the amended result may then be re-input, so that a VDU display is often both an input device and an output device. However, if it comes from a ROM source (see above, 'input devices') it cannot be 'written to' or amended. If a hard copy is required of the screen display it can be obtained by attaching a printer.

Print-out Print-out may come from a wide variety of printers. Print-outs may be called for on request, many menus having a line for requesting a print-out, or a user-friendly computer may ask 'Would you like a print-out? Y/N'. Print-outs may also be generated by the computer itself when it detects a problem, as when stock levels fall to the re-order level and the computer generates an order form, or it detects an unacceptable input and prints a rejection slip, perhaps saying what the fault is – for example, 'Unauthorised exceeding of budget', etc.

Printers include the line-printer, the work-horse of the print-out system, which typically produces 4 000 lines (of 132 characters) per minute. It uses continuous stationery which folds to give a neat pack that can be stored in special folders, which often hang in a frame where they can be easily consulted. A typical printout might consist of monthly sales figures, showing the numbers of items of each product sold, the sort of outlet, the prices achieved, etc.

There are also matrix printers, ink-jet printers, thermal printers and laser printers. These are described in Unit 12.8 (see pp. 355–67).

COM outputs COM stands for 'computer output to microfilm' or 'computer output to microfiche'. The computer output appears in page form as a micro-image, printed sequentially on a film or a 150 mm × 100 mm rectangle of film (the microfiche). A 30-metre roll of film holds 2 000 pages of records; a 150 mm × 100 mm microfiche holds either 98 pages or 270 pages. Naturally these images must be read in a viewer which expands them up to ordinary size. They are chiefly used for archiving long-term records, but also for such documents as export documents where the computer has the ability to produce many different documents from the same bank of data - for example, the invoice, bill of lading, bank documentary collection form, insurance cover note, etc., are all very similar.

Graph plotters These devices produce charts, maps, diagrams, etc. from computerised output to give a clear presentation of facts and figures for management purposes.

Audio-response devices An audio-response device is one which can give an intelligent message from a bank of computer stored sounds. The result sounds a little mechanical but is a great saver of time. For example, if you dial directory inquiries an operator will ask you the name of the person you wish to call, and where s/he lives, but once the operator has found the number on the databank a computer, with a stored computer voice, will give you the number.

(b) Software

The programs prepared to instruct the computer how to carry out a particular set of activities are known by the general name *software*. Any costing activity has a number of sections of work and each requires its own program and files. The general procedure is to have a main menu, or list of activities, which can be selected by touching a particular key. When one of these is selected it will probably lead to the display of a futher sub-menu. For example, an original menu might read:

1. Purchases
2. Expenses
3. Stocks
4. Sales
5. Audit trail
6. VAT Records
7. Close down

Please select menu option.

The user who specifies 1 might then be presented with a second menu:

Purchases Activities

1. Capital items
2. Raw materials
3. Components
4. Other manufacturing requirements
5. Consumable items
6. Hirings
7. Special contracts
8. Return to main menu

The selection of 2 would result in the loading of a program to deal with purchase of raw materials and the display of information calling for an entry to be made. For example:

Code of raw materials purchased . . .

The processing of the data is carried out in the central processor unit (CPU) where the existing file, the program which tells the computer what to do to the data and the updating material which has recently been input are all called into main memory, at enormous speeds. The whole collection of data (the database) consists of a large number of files each with its particular code and sub-sections which are also coded. The program tells the computer to find the right place in the file and update the records at a particular point. It could be a change of supplier, or a change of a supplier's address or telephone number. It could be a changed price for a component, or a change of re-order level or re-order quantity. It could be an additional product for which a component can now be used, requiring a minor change of the component's specification or an increase in stocks to be held.

Once dealt with, the revised data are returned to the main memory and 'queued' to be put out to a suitable output device in due course. This may be to a backing store device in machine-readable form for re-use at a later date, or to a printer, VDU or other output device in ordinary language or pictorial (chart) form. The program will also be returned to store until once again required for some activity affecting the purchase of raw materials.

Fig. 12.1 (pp. 344–5) shows a wide-ranging computer configuration for costing data, with an element of licence in that most of the various input devices and output devices have been shown to indicate the versatility of the facilities being offered. No single costing operation would make use of all these facilities, of course, but somewhere there will no doubt be a costing system that takes advantage of their availability. For those new to computerised activities the opportunity to ponder upon the place of each in the configuration may be helpful, and even those familiar with a costing computerised system at their own place of employment may find items with which they are not familiar.

12.4 Computerisation of the cost accounts system

In most modern companies of any size and complexity most functions will be computerised. These could include the accounting, stock control, purchasing, payroll and factory processing functions. The computers and methods (i.e. systems) used vary enormously in complexity, sophistication, scope and functionality. They all effect the same result as the historical manual function but usually much faster, with greater control and providing a great deal more information. There is no one definite computerised cost accounting system, but one can describe typical methods that may be used in such a system.

In all cases data have to be fed into the computer, programs are run to process those data and information (results) have to be put out to the human user. Such a set of activities is no different from what happens in a manual system. In a manual system a person, or persons, collates source information from source documents (such as job sheets or stores requisitions), checks for accuracy, performs calculations, records the results (e.g. on ledger sheets) and analyses the data to provide information (i.e. reports). The same functions occur in a computer system. We must now consider each element in the computerisation of cost accounts.

(a) Input

A typical means of input to the computer is the terminal. Terminals will be strategically placed throughout the company for keying data from source documents. Terminals consist of a keyboard and monitor screen and will be linked to the main computer over a telecommunications line (if the main computer is in a different city from the terminal user, for example) or over a local area network (LAN) where, for example, the terminals are scattered around the various cost centres in a large plant or factory.

Each source document, (say a stores requisition) will contain data forming a *record*, typically contract number, stock item, code description, quantity, date/time, etc. A blank record will be depicted on the terminal screen and the information will be keyed in by the key operator accordingly. The screen record may be user-friendly, each item of the data being called for in correct sequence to build up a full screen record. When a full screen of data has been keyed it will be transmitted to the main computer, where it will be validated by a purpose-built program. If the entry is invalid for some reason, the key operator at the terminal will receive a message via the screen that the record is unacceptable, indicating the field or fields (i.e. items of data within the record) that are invalid. Once the record is valid it will be written to a master file (updated). This may take place immediately if the system is *on-line*, i.e. with immediate access to the computer. Alternatively the record may be held on a temporary file until some off-peak time. The temporary file accumulates similar records until the computer becomes available, when it updates the master file. This is known as a *batch update*.

As stated, on-line terminals are just one typical means of input. Whatever the method used, however, the function of getting source data on to a computer file in as accurate a form as possible remains common throughout.

(b) Master files

In a manual system, master files may consist of contract account ledger sheets, customer name and address cards, supplier ledger sheets, etc. In a computer system the content of a master file is no different; only the medium on which it is held and the method by which it is updated are different.

Computer files may be stored on magnetic disc or tape. Magnetic disc is by far the most common medium, because it is faster and provides more flexible access methods. Magnetic tape is more common as a back-up or transit medium for mini- and mainframe computers.

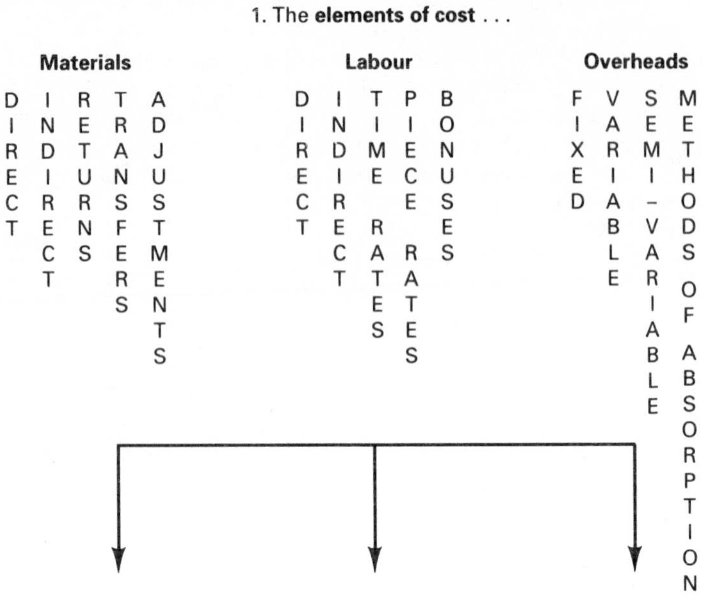

2. . . . are detected as they arrive on invoices, credit notes, clock cards or similar internal documents. They are encoded with suitable coding marks to identify their place in the system and are input to the computer by an appropriate input device.

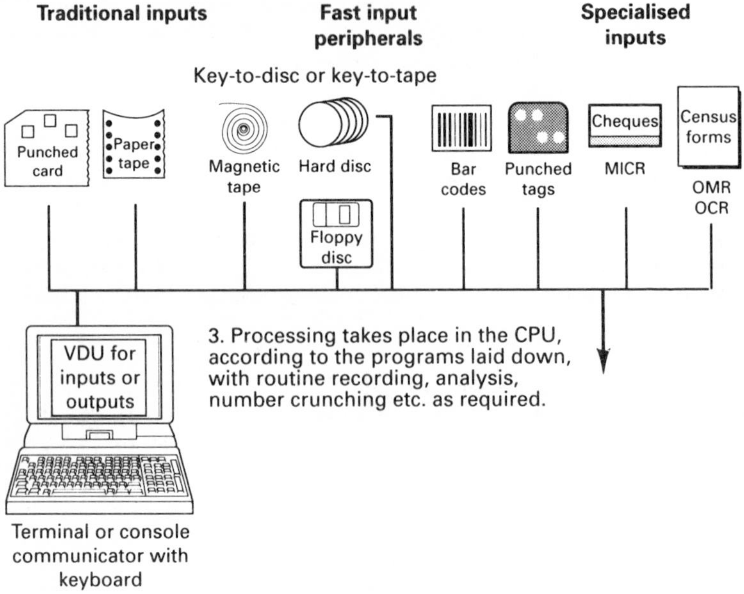

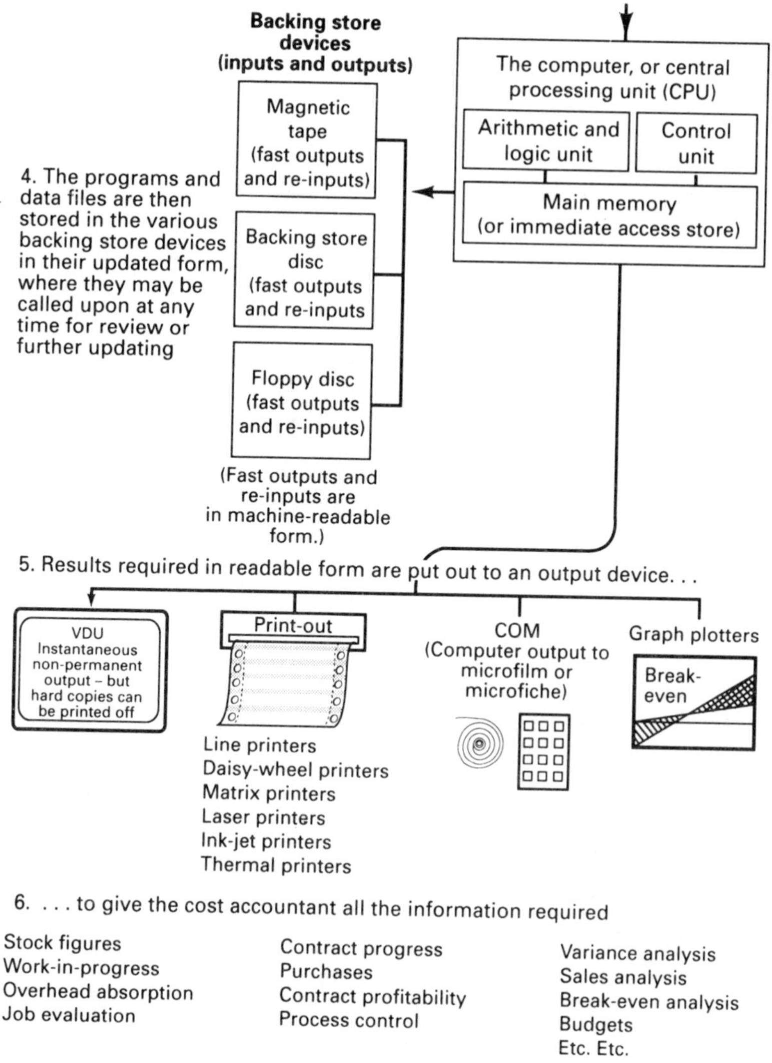

Fig. 12.1 A general computer configuration for costing activities

Again, the method of updating master files on disc varies from one system to another. One method is direct updating, whereby a record is read in from the file, updated and written back to the *same* file - or, if it is a new input record, it is added to the file. The other method is serial updating. In this method the master file will be in a specific sequence (e.g. by contract number) and the input records will be sorted to the same sequence. The user thus has a brought-forward master file which is read record by record, matched with each input record, updated and written to a *new* carried forward file record by record. Whatever the method, the underlying fact is that files consist of data in logical groupings called records - exactly the same as manual records.

(c) Data processing

Data processing is effected by programs which 'process' the data in that they can read and write data, perform calculations, change data, add to data, delete data and present them in report formats. It is the programs that perform what we may consider as the 'thinking' rather than the mechanical processes within a computer. It is the programs that read and validate stores requisitions from the terminal and then match and apply them to the associated contract record on the master file. In a contract accounting system there will be many programs performing the various functions. On a large system there may be several *suites* of programs which perform the major functions of input, update and output. A comprehensive accounting system would rarely consist of less than twenty programs, and often many more.

(d) Output

Excluding the carried forward master files, which are themselves a form of output, output will be in the form of reports. The normal output medium is paper (i.e. printed reports) but smaller, urgent reports can be output to the terminal screen if required. Normally these reports to screens would be in response to an inquiry via the screen, such as specific customer name and address, a specific contract cost to date, latest stock item cost, etc. Programs produce the reports and each type of report calls for its own program. Thus if a report had to be generated whenever a contract went over budget, it would require a special program to generate such a report.

Reports may be of many types. Examples are statutory documentation such as audit lists and ledger print-outs; formal documents such as purchase orders or customer invoices; management information such as 'actuals' versus 'budgets', turnover by supplier, turnover by customer. If the information is somewhere in the computer files or can be derived from data on the files then a program or programs can be written to present that information in a report in any way that is desired. Fig. 12.2 gives some impression of a typical layout.

We shall now consider one or two specialised applications of computers to particular situations.

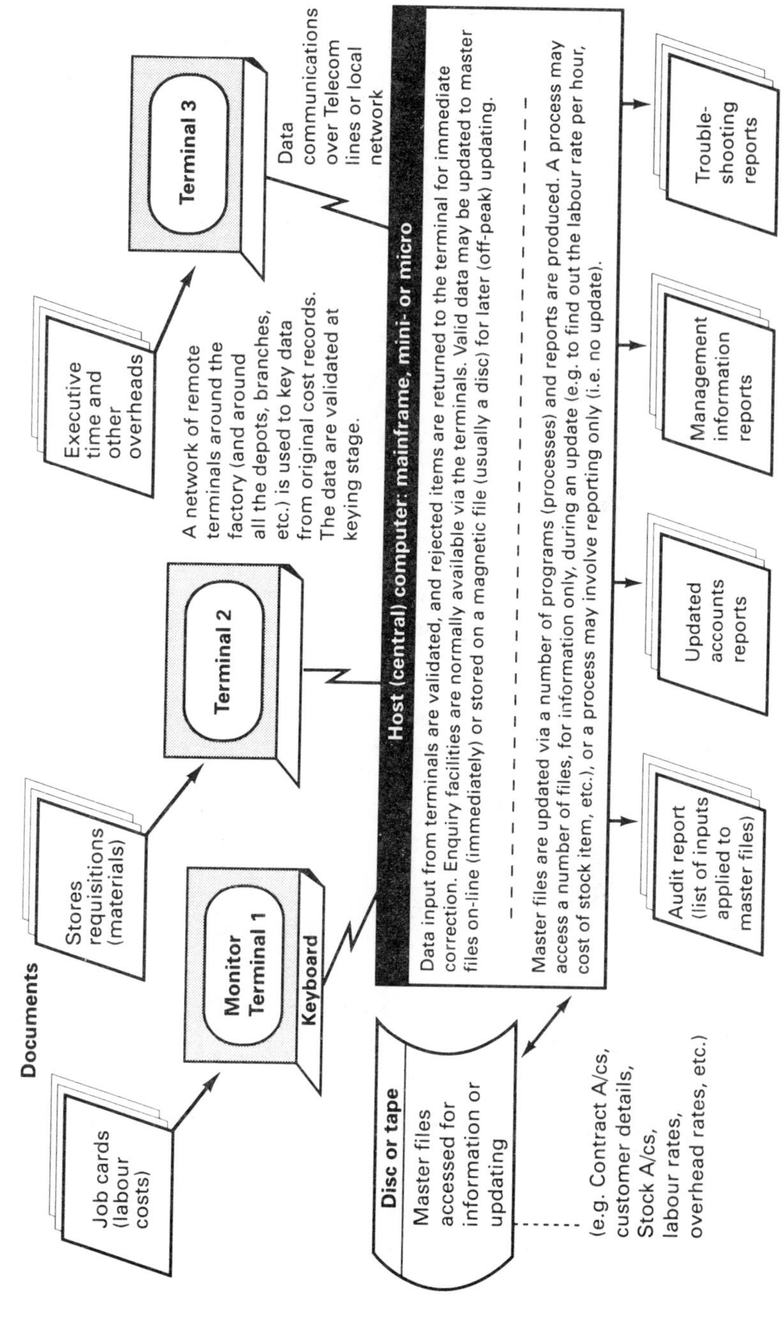
Documents
Job cards (labour costs)
Stores requisitions (materials)
Executive time and other overheads
Monitor Terminal 1
Keyboard
Terminal 2
Terminal 3
A network of remote terminals around the factory (and around all the depots, branches, etc.) is used to key data from original cost records. The data are validated at keying stage.
Data communications over Telecom lines or local network
Host (central) computer: mainframe, mini- or micro
Data input from terminals are validated, and rejected items are returned to the terminal for immediate correction. Enquiry facilities are normally available via the terminals. Valid data may be updated to master files on-line (immediately) or stored on a magnetic file (usually a disc) for later (off-peak) updating.
Master files are updated via a number of programs (processes) and reports are produced. A process may access a number of files, for information only, during an update (e.g. to find out the labour rate per hour, cost of stock item, etc.), or a process may involve reporting only (i.e. no update).
Disc or tape
Master files accessed for information or updating
(e.g. Contract A/cs, customer details, Stock A/cs, labour rates, overhead rates, etc.)
Audit report (list of inputs applied to master files)
Updated accounts reports
Management information reports
Trouble-shooting reports

Fig. 12.2 Computerised cost accounting

12.5 Systems analysis and design

Although many organisations today introduce computerisation using some sort of software package available on the market, and perhaps call in consultancy services to decide what packages are appropriate for them, it is helpful to have some background in systems analysis to know what the various packages are trying to do and evaluate their suitability. Systems analysis starts with an in-depth study of existing activities to discover exactly what is done, why it is done, who does what, etc. The systems analyst might begin by calling for a brief account from heads of departments of all the work of their departments: the activities performed, the part played by the department in the firm's affairs, outputs in terms of product produced or services rendered, the reports that result and to whom they are made, etc.

This will be followed by drawing up a schedule of systems and sub-systems covering all the activities of all departments, with a view to more detailed study of each sub-system. This will involve detailed questioning of those actually doing the work, so that the full facts can be established and the whole sub-system can be appraised. The main activities will probably include the following:

(a) Identification of a sub-system and its position within the whole network of operations.
(b) Fact-finding by close examination of the sub-system. How does it work? What does it do? Who does what? A diagram of the sub-system should be built up.
(c) Analysis of the sub-system. Do we need it at all? If it is necessary, how is it performed at present? Could it be done in a better way? What are the systems alternatives for this activity?
(d) Included in the analysis of sub-systems will be most of the following:

   (i) collection and codification of all the data relating to each product;
   (ii) collection and codification of data relating to classes of materials used, supplier sources, current prices, etc.;
   (iii) collection and codification of machines used, or machines which might be used, and development of a maintenance system (including staff training required, etc.);
   (iv) standardisation of tools in use and envisaged, and associated problems of tool room system, staff training, etc.;
   (v) development of a stores system, requisition procedures, authorisation procedures for ordering and receiving stores, etc.

(e) Assessment of whether a suitable package is available on the market or must be designed in-house.
(f) Development of a system proposal.
(g) Design of the system, including routeing, machine loading, time-keeping, etc.
(h) Testing and evaluation of the design.
(i) System construction, and training programmes prior to implementation,

including supervision procedures, control of work-in-progress, methods whereby the system alerts management to failures or impaired quality, variances from budget, etc.

(j) Implementation alongside manual system for a trial period.

(k) Feedback and follow-up as the system comes into use.

(a) Cost system changeover

The cost accounting system will usually follow the implementation of a wide variety of computerised systems and sub-systems in a factory, and a detailed scrutiny of the existing cost system, the nature of costs incurred, the cost records kept and the cost statements prepared, the allocation and absorption of overheads, etc. The end result is a set of prepared working papers, prepared forms, manuals of operation and procedural instructions, all of which should be ready before the system is introduced. These working papers should have been the subject of staff training activities, dummy run trials, etc., before the set date for implementation.

Usually the software for the system must have been chosen or designed before the hardware can be chosen, and only when both are in position can the preparatory work for implementation of the new system begin. The basic files for the system must be set up and filled with data. For example, we may need customer files and supplier files, complete with all the data needed. Once a customer file has been set up, for example, it must be kept up to date, so that the file is current when the new system comes into use. The period leading up to the implementation of the new system may be used as a good opportunity to get staff used to entering 'live' data and to test out various user-friendly techniques built into the system. At the set date the old system is cut off, all records and data are transferred to the new system, supervisors and managers stand by to deal with problems, and the new system takes over.

The run-in period calls for considerable supervision by the systems analyst. Changes will almost certainly need to be made to solve snags not envisaged earlier and such developments as changed names and addresses, changes in overhead rates, changes in material prices, labour rates, etc., will occur as a continuing process over the years ahead.

(b) Accounting packages

In the early days of computerisation it was necessary to develop dedicated software, i.e. software tailor-made to meet the needs of the particular firm or company and achieve the same results as the manual system being replaced. Such systems programming is expensive, and wasteful in many cases, because the double-entry system is a universal system and a package designed for one firm may very well do for other firms. As a result firms that had spent a fortune on programming began to sell their software systems to others needing similar programs. A vast array of packages is now available, many of them relatively cheap. A consultant will advise about the various packages available, but it is always advisable to have a good list of questions to ask about any particular package, because of course a non-dedicated package is probably going to be less satisfactory than one tailor-made to your own system, and you have to be sure that it fits fairly closely with your requirements.

12.6 Computerised control of project management

We saw in Unit 10 that budgetary control is a complex and time-consuming activity which in its manual form calls for much detailed work and complex analysis of variances of various sorts. The computer can assist enormously in these complex activities because a suitable program can accept data into the system and apply them throughout the system wherever they should be used. It is impossible to discuss such a system abstractly, and the following account of the Institute of Hydrology System TRAMS is reproduced by kind permission of the Institute of Hydrology (IH). Although originally designed as a dedicated program to meet IH requirements, it is available for sale to institutions with similar needs. Those who are interested in purchasing the package should apply to the Director of the Institute of Hydrology (Professor Brian Wilkinson), Wallingford, Oxon. OX10 8BB.

The IH Time and Resources Allocation Management System, TRAMS, is designed to assist in allocating staff to projects, monitoring the progress achieved month by month, with special reference to the use of financial and staff resources, and reporting each month to line managers on the progress achieved.

The system recognises the NERC (Natural Environment Research Council)'s eight-character numbering system for projects, and is capable of handling up to 400 projects or sub-projects, and up to 500 members of staff. It can recognise all the MSA (Management Systems America) cost centres, all the MSA programme areas, all the five funding classes and the NERC CR (commissioned research) pricing bands, as well as 31 different customer classifications. It can accommodate a wide range of staff charge rates (so that the work performed by staff on any particular project can be charged at an appropriate rate to the project). This ensures that each project bears the true costs incurred for labour. Similarly machine time (for example, computer time) can be charged at an appropriate rate to each project. Cash costs can also be fed into the system, as can any special project-specific charges.

TRAMS is centred on the current year, holding planning information and the operational history of every project month by month. Future commitments for the next four years can be stored and the storage of contract summaries for the previous five years is in the planning stage. TRAMS deals with time as per cent, months, days and hours. The standard year comprises 216 working days (12 months of 18 working days). Each day consists of 7.4 hours. It accepts the flexitime operations used in IH, calculates work in excess of standard hours (overtime) and is geared to charging customers on the basis of a daily charge (i.e. one day every 7.4 hours of work).

As is usual with computer systems TRAMS is menu-driven. When the program is loaded the main menu appears and offers seven choices. Six of these are optional programs and the seventh offers the user the next menu. This menu offers seven reporting options or the next menu. This final menu offers five more reporting options and a return to the previous menu.

TRAMS exists primarily to provide output to senior IH management, to plan staff deployment to new commissioned research (CR) and to reformat the Institute's planned programmes of research upon the award of new contracts. It provides monthly reports to project leaders for budgetary control and monitoring of CR project performance relative to the original contract. It reports to the accounts department to assist in customer billing. The system is operated by a single system administrator who co-ordinates IH project information flow not only internally but also to the directorate and NERC.

The information available from TRAMS is as follows.

(a) Project information

TRAMS holds the following information relating to each IH project:

(a) project numbers and titles;
(b) project leader and sub-project leader;
(c) start and end dates;
(d) funding source, customer(s) and charge band;
(e) details of non-recurrent costs allocated and spent:

  (i) NCS (NERC Computing Service) computing;
  (ii) chemical analysis;
  (iii) capital expenditure;
  (iv) equipment rental;
  (v) equipment manufacture;

(f) details of recurrent costs allocated and spent:

  (i) T&S (travel and subsistence) UK;
  (ii) T&S overseas;
  (iii) printing and stationery;
  (iv) general equipment;
  (v) scientific equipment;
  (vi) non-pool transport;
  (vii) non-NCS computing;
  (viii) packing/freight/insurance;
  (ix) consultants/contractors data;
  (x) overtime;
  (xi) other;

(g) staff by grade to show their allocation – days, costs as cash/FEC (full economic cost);

(h) staff by grade to show actual costs - cash and FEC;
(i) total allocation, staff costs and actual as cash and FEC;
(j) total project costs as cash and FEC.

Updating of information is done on a monthly basis and at any point in the current year details of project allocations and costs (cash and FEC) to date can be obtained. Information is also held for the next four years as this becomes available from project fact sheets.

(b) Staff information
Monthly distribution of staff time to projects (in hours, days or as a percentage; and in cost terms - cash/FEC) can be obtained, and comparisons made between original time allocations and actual time worked. The balance of any unused allocation can be shown, and time worked on unallocated projects highlighted: overtime can be listed separately showing hours worked for any/all staff for any month or year-to-date. A simple list of percentage allocations to projects for any staff member is available.

(c) Manpower resources
Summaries grouped by:

CR projects
SB (science budget) projects
Mixed funding projects
Dummy projects

can be obtained for the following categories:

Institute
Programme area
Cost centre
Grade
Staff member.

These are overviews of time/costs for the current or next year showing allocations and actuals for a specified month and/or year-to-date.

From the management accountant's viewpoint it is clear that such a system operating in a field where high-level (and consequently expensive) staff are busy on a wide variety of complex projects carried out all over the world must give much better control to the directorate than would be possible otherwise. The reports generated give clear and objective reviews of the state of each project to the team leader and the directorate, drawing attention to approaching deadlines, expenditures going over budget, the need to bill customers for services rendered so far, and many other matters.

12.7 Accounting and stock control systems for retailers

While accounting is a requirement for all businesses, the needs of accounting systems differ according to various factors. In the smallest retail business, a control over the Bank Account and the total level of bills outstanding may well be sufficient. In a large retail store, full stock control with integrated accounting may be required to control the most important asset of a retail business – its stock. Retail businesses are rarely successful if the right goods are not on the shelves at the right time at the right price. There are a number of different methods of controlling stocks for retailers.

(a) Unit stock control

This method of stock control requires every item of stock to have a unique identity, which usually means the item has a stock number. When the item is sold, the stock code and price are recorded and the stock file is told of the sale. This may be done manually or by connecting the Stock File on a computer to the cash register on the counter. The cash register may have a bar code reader or scanner attached.

The Stock File has a record for each item held in stock and various pieces of information are held to assist in the control of the stock. These may include:

(i) code number (often called an SKU – stock keeping unit);
(ii) supplier;
(iii) description;
(iv) unit of stock (e.g. each, litre, 100);
(v) quantity in stock;
(vi) re-order level;
(vii) minimum stock;
(viii) maximum stock;
(ix) re-order quantity;
(x) selling price;
(xi) cost price;
(xii) VAT rate;
(xiii) statistics – sales this week/period/year, sales last week/period/year.

The purpose of the Stock File is to ensure that:

(a) The stock is properly controlled.
(b) The optimum quantities are available on the shelves.
(c) Stock is always available in the right shop at the right time.
(d) Managements optimise profit and minimise stock values.

(b) Colour and size stock control

Additional information is held on the Stock File for retailers who sell items which are available in a range either of colours or of sizes or both. If the business deals in high-quality leatherwear for instance, the proprietor will want to know which styles, colours and sizes are the best sellers. S/he may have a number of shops and will therefore want to know, if requested by a customer for a particular garment, whether that size and colour is available at another branch. This will save ordering an item which is already available elsewhere. Furthermore, the trader can see from the stock records where one shop has too many of one colour and size while another shop may be short or have no stock at all.

(c) Financial stock control

A further method of stock control for the retailer is to use financial stock control. This is suitable particularly for department stores, furniture and carpet stores and some types of fashion retailer. The principal difference relates to the fact that the goods being sold may not be repeatable. In other words, they may be an exclusive fashion line for which the shop cannot obtain replacement supplies when it has sold out during the season. In addition, the goods may only be in fashion for a few months during, say, the spring season. To create a stock record for each would be time consuming and many of the benefits of unit stock control would not apply.

The principle of financial stock control is based on the control of stocks, margins and profit by department or merchandise category within the shop. A stock record is held for each stock category or department, which contains information relating to:

(i) purchases at cost price;
(ii) purchases at planned selling prices;
(iii) sales;
(iv) mark-downs;
(v) adjustments.

The method of operation is as follows:

(a) At the start of the year the values of opening stocks by department or mechandise level are recorded. This is usually done quite easily at year-end or half year-end from the stock check sheets.
(b) During the year goods purchased for resale are entered into the Purchase Ledger at both cost and expected selling values. This is done at department or category level.
(c) Sales by department or category are recorded and these values are entered into the stock record.
(d) It is also necessary to record the values of mark-downs. A mark-down is the difference between what you originally decided to sell an item for and the price you now plan to sell it for.
(e) A statement of the stock movements is produced for a sales period and for the year-to-date and a report is produced.

The purpose of the procedure is to calculate the realised margin (profit) for that period and the year-to-date for each of the departments or categories in the store. The margin percentage by department shows management at a glance how each category of merchandise is performing. It shows anticipated selling margins and is a constant guide to the adequacy of initial mark-ups. The margin obtained on sales with information on mark-downs quickly highlights those departments which are not performing to target and may therefore need more attention and control. The value of profit earned by each department and by the shop as a whole on both a period and year-to-date basis quickly shows if the return being achieved is enough to cover the known overheads of either the department or the business as a whole. The easy calculation of current stock in hand values by department makes it easy to do a quick departmental physical stock valuation to determine what, if any, stock has been lost through shrinkage or pilferage. (A computerised version of financial stock control is available for various sizes of business from Micro Retailer Systems Ltd, 84 Mill St, Macclesfield, Cheshire SK11 6NR, tel. 0625 615375.)

12.8 Glossary of computer terms

All items in *italics* within an entry refer to other entries in the glossary.

Address The location of an item in the computer's *memory*.

Algorithm A set of logical rules for solving a problem in a finite number of moves.

Arithmetic and logic unit That part of the *central processor unit* which carries out specific instructions assigned to it by the *control unit*. The instructions tend to be arithmetical in nature (e.g. 'Add one number to another' or 'Subtract one number from another number').

Array A series of storage locations in a computer arranged in a continuous pattern, like pigeon-holes in a hotel lobby for correspondence for guests. These storage locations can be accessed using index values.

Backing storage A storage device to hold *programs* and *data 'off-line'* from the computer when they are not required by the *central processor unit*. For example, after entering a batch of purchases invoices affecting a number of contract accounts, the updated contract accounts would be put out to backing store until required again. Backing storage is always in machine-readable form. The usual backing storage devices are *magnetic tape* and *magnetic disc*, but many small businesses use *floppy discs*, which can hold a complete set of programs and a year's data.

Bar codes A specialised *input device* which can be read with a light pencil or wand, or by passing the strip over a light-sensitive window. The computer then searches its *memory* to name the item, record its price and adjust stock records. Computerised stock records increase the rate of stock turnover, since re-ordering only takes place when existing stocks reach an agreed low point, and only the optimum order is placed – often on a just-in-time basis.

BASIC A simple computer language – the Beginners All-purpose Symbolic Instruction Code.

Batch A collection of documents or other computer work collected together and coded prior to running in sequence. Where a computer gives *real-time* access to users from remote *terminals*, it is usual for batches to be run in the background – interrupted by real-time users seeking access – so that a highly efficient use of computer time is achieved.

Batch total The total of a *batch* used to check that all amounts to be entered have been accepted.

Binary code This is the representation given by the *binary system* to any numeric or alphabetical character, using only the digits 1 and 0. Each character is represented by a different combination of ones and zeros to give it a unique code. An *input device* gets information into the computer by translating the information into its binary coded form, which the machine can recognise, accept and process.

Binary number The representation of a character in numerical form using the *binary system*.

Binary system A number system based on two, where each place value is not ten (as in the decimal system) but two (i.e. when we get more than one unit we move into the next place). Thus the numbers 0–7 in binary code are respectively 0, 1, 10, 11, 100, 101, 110 and 111. Any number or letter, punctuation mark, etc., can be allocated a *binary code*.

Bit An abbreviation for binary digit. Each position (i.e. each place value) in a *binary number* is called a bit. Thus the decimal number 7, which in binary is 111, has three bits: 1 unit; 1 two (the second place in the binary system is a two, not a ten) and 1 four (the third place in a binary system is 2^2 (four) not 10^2 (one hundred) as in the decimal system). So 111 is a 4, a 2 and a 1, which is 7.

Blank A space; a character where nothing is printed. As in printing, in a computer *memory* the space takes just as much room as any other character.

Buffer A storage device where information arriving too fast from another device can be diverted until the slower device can absorb it.

Bug An error in *coding* which causes a *program* to fail, or perform incorrectly.

Bus A *data* highway; a number of transmission lines along which data are moved.

Byte A byte is 8 *bits*, and may be used to hold two small numbers (because any number up to 15 only needs four bits – for example, decimal 15 is 1111 in the *binary system*) or one alphabetic or special character.

Casette A storage medium for *microcomputers* and personal computers, with narrow tape only 0.15″ wide. *Data* are written along the length of the tape, not across it, so the speed of reading and writing is slow.

Central processor unit The CPU, the central unit of a computer, consisting of three elements: *(a) control unit*, *(b) arithmetic and logic unit* and *(c) main storage* (sometimes called 'main *memory*' or 'immediate access memory'). The function of the CPU is to process *data* according to a *program* of instructions.

Chips Small portions of a wafer of silicon on which photograph-like images have been printed and developed to give integrated circuits of great complexity; virtually a computer on a chip.

COBOL Common Business-Orientated Language: a programming language (see *Program*) which is designed to be used to solve business-based problems.

Coding A system of symbols which enables costs and similar items to be allocated a place within the costing system so that entry, processing, allocation or absorption, retrieval, etc. can be easily managed.

COM Computer *output* to microfilm or microfiche: specialised outputs used for archiving vital records – 2 000 pages on a 30-metre roll of film; 98 or 270 pages on a 150 mm × 100 mm microfiche. The main uses are in insurance companies, banks, libraries and public record offices. They are not widely used in costing activities.

Compiler A *program* which translates statements made in a high-level language into *machine code*, so that the machine can actually execute the program.

Console A typewriter *keyboard* used by a computer operator to interrupt the computer and feed in further instructions. It will have a *VDU* attached to assist the process of inputting instructions, and to receive responses from the computer.

Control unit That part of the *central processor unit* which accesses the *program* instructions held in *main storage* one at a time, and in the correct sequence. It interprets the coded instructions and assigns one of the other elements in the CPU to carry out the instruction, whatever it may be. Control units operate at a great speed, measured in *mips*. Common speeds are 5–12 mips.

Core Another term for *memory*; where *data* can be stored for immediate access.

CPU The *central processor unit*.

Cursor A blinking light which draws the operator's attention to the point on the screen where entries will appear if keyed in. It may be moved by pressing appropriate keys and in other ways.

Daisy-wheel printer A *printer* which works from a daisy-wheel – a circle of metal or plastic with the characters embossed on 'petals' sticking out from the edge of the circle. The wheel rotates to bring the correct character to the ribbon, where a hammer strikes it to print the character through the ribbon. This can be done at about 90 characters per second (cps). This type of printer is mainly used in word-processing (see *Word-processor*) because of the high-quality output.

Data Any items of information in machine-readable form – the basic material that computers process.

Data administrator The person in charge of a database who may alone authorise changes in the *data* since the integrity of the data for one type of user might be adversely affected if another user, with different needs, was allowed to make changes which did not reflect the needs of all.

Data checking See *Data validation*.

Data processing The automatic performance of operations on *data*. A *program* of instructions to the computer instructs it what operations to perform; for example, 'Compare Q with 200; if Q is less than 200 print out an urgent re-order memo to stock controller for the EOQ (economic order quantity)'.

Data transfer The action of transferring *data* from one unit to another within the computer (for example, from storage into main *memory*). Other movements include the input of data to computer from an *input device* or from the computer to an *output device*.

Data transmission The communication of *data* from one location to another. It may be local (within the computer, or between the computer and a *peripheral input device* or *output device*), or it may be from one remote *terminal* to another over dedicated telephone lines (usually direct-connect lines at present but eventually over a full network of fibre-optic lines or by satellite).

Data validation A system for checking *data* to ensure they are within a permitted range of values – for example, a percentage must be within the range 0–100. Works numbers for personnel may lie within certain limits. If we insert an account number the computer may be able to check that such an account does exist. Data outside the limits will be rejected and a *print-out* of rejections will be produced.

Degrees of integration The number of transistor circuits on a silicon *chip*, e.g. SSI – small-scale integration; MSI – medium-scale integration; VSLI – very large-scale integration.

Digital device A device where the *data* are represented by numerical quantities. For example, the wave of an ordinary telephone message is sampled 8 000 times a second to measure the amplitude of the wave and these measurements are turned into a *binary code* of numerical data. The original wave is reconstituted at destination by a device called a *modem*.

Direct access Any system of storage which enables a particular body of *data* to be located and consulted irrespective of where it is in the system.

Disc drive A device which can read from and write to a disc, so that *data* or *programs* can be read from the disc into the computer's main *memory*, where the programs can be used to carry out operations on the data, adding new data or deleting data no longer required.

Dump The transfer of the contents of a *memory* or a *file* to another device, such as a *printer*.

EFTPOS Electronic funds transfer at point of sale: a system which permits a bank customer to pay for goods by means of a bank card. The computer is accessed by the banker's card to check that funds are available in a customer's account and, if they are, it sanctions payment. The customer is debited (s/he has received back some of the funds on deposit) and the store credited with the amount paid.

File A store of information on a particular topic which can be read into the computer at any time to accept *input*, answer queries, show the state of the system and keep a log of events as an audit trail.

Floppy disc A single disc of plastic coated with magnetic oxide, and protected by a thin card envelope. They may be 8″, 5¼″ or 3½″ in diameter with a capacity of up to 2 *megabytes*. The *read–write head* of the *disc drive* operates in a slot in the protective envelope to access the *data* or *programs* on the disc.

Flowchart A stage in the development of a *program*. It is a graphical representation of the steps involved in a procedure or program.

FORTRAN FORmula TRANslator: a high-level programming language designed to deal with mathematical computations.

Generation A term used to describe the development of computers. First generation computers used valves; second generation used transistors; third generation used integrated circuits; fourth generation use VSLI (very large-scale integration: see *Degrees of integration*).

Gigo Garbage in, garbage out: a computing maxim which reminds us that no computer can produce good *output* from bad *input*. Any results cannot be better than the input supplied, since they are based upon it.

Graph plotters Devices which produce graphs, maps, charts, etc. They consist of a pen, or several pens, driven by a computer *program*. There are two types, drum plotters and flat-bed plotters.

Hard copy A permanent record on paper of *output data* or of a *program*. Often taken from what appears on a *VDU* screen, by attaching a *printer*.

Hard disc A method of storing *programs* and *data*. Unlike a *floppy disc*, which can be stored in a filing box or cabinet and only read into a computer from a *disc drive* as required, a hard disc is a more permanent piece of *hardware*, with very large capacity, able to operate at high speeds and permanently *on-line* to the computer.

Hardware The durable mechanical, electrical and electronic components of a computer configuration; for example, the *central processor unit*, *terminal*, *printer*, *disc drive*, etc.

Immediate access memory The main *memory* in the *central processor unit*, where *data* and *programs* are held while awaiting processing. The first stage of any processing operation is to load the program required and the *file* of data into the immediate access memory.

Ink-jet printers A non-impact *printer* which sprays characters onto the paper at about 150 characters per second. Since these printers are silent they are often used in hospitals, offices, etc.

Input *Data* from an external source fed into a computer from an *input device* for processing.

Input device A means of passing information into a computer. The information is passed in machine-readable form and may be *data* or instructions about how data is to be processed - the *program*. The chief input devices today are terminal *keyboards*, *magnetic tape*, *magnetic disc* and *floppy disc*, *bar codes*, *magnetic ink character recognition* (MICR), *optical mark recognition* (OMR), *optical character recognition* (OCR), tags and *magnetic strips*. The original input devices were *punched cards* and *paper tape*.

Integrated circuit A very small electronic circuit on a *chip* of semi-conducting material such as silicon.

Joystick An attachment that allows an operator to move the field of view on a screen, and draw a line or a curve, or store a position.

K An abbreviation for 1 000 (actually 1 024) and used to denote the number of transistors on a silicon *chip memory*. Thus 1k = 1 024 *bits* per chip, and we have 4k, 16k, 64k and 256k bit chips available.

Keyboard A communicating device used to *input data* and commands to the computer. In many ways it is similar to a typewriter keyboard.

Key-to-disc system A system whereby large volumes of *data* can be keyed by *VDU* operators directly to a disc *file*. When all the data have been keyed, the data on the disc can be input into the computer.

Laser printer Top-quality *printer*, printing a page at a time and up to 200 pages a minute, i.e. 26 000 characters a second. As the machines are very expensive and the *output* is of the highest quality, the main users are companies with *mainframe computers*.

Light pen Also called a sensing wand: a photosensitive detector housed in a case which can be held in the hand, and connected to the *VDU* controls by a cable. The computer can detect the position of the pen on the screen and display the details on record of the particular item pointed at, e.g. customer's address if a list of names is displayed.

Line printer A fast *printer* for the commercial field printing a line at a time at speeds of 4 000 lines per minute, on continuous stationery. Normal line width is 132 characters.

Listing The printed *output* from a computer.

Loop The repeated execution of a *program* instruction. It is a fault in the program and can only be stopped by aborting the program.

Machine code The basic code on which a machine actually operates, a low-level numeric format. Early *programs* were written in this format. Today they are written in higher-level languages, but these languages have to be converted to the machine code applicable to the computer before the programs can be operated.

Magnetic disc A pack of discs (or platters) coated with magnetic oxide on which *data* can be recorded in 800 tracks per disc, with about 20 recording surfaces in each pack. Access is by a *read–write head*, which can access about 2 500 *megabytes* on a fixed disc unit, or about 200 megabytes on an exchangeable disc drive. It takes about 50 milliseconds (thousandths of a second) to locate data on the disc, which can then be read at 2 megabytes per second.

Magnetic ink character recognition A system for reading documents such as cheques, paying-in slips, etc., at speeds of 2 500 documents per minute. The vital details are printed on the cheque with magnetic ink in special type-faces. The magnetic ink character reader can detect the electric field created by each magnetic pattern as the characters pass under the read-head. Some of the information is pre-printed, but other information (for example, the amount to be paid on the cheque, written in by the customer) has to be encoded before the documents are fed into the reader.

Magnetic strips A specialist *input device* used by some major retailers to record *POS data* for stock taking and customer billing. They act rather similarly to *bar codes*.

Magnetic tape A tape coated with ferrous oxide, chiefly used as a *backing storage* medium but also as an *input* (and *output*) *device*. It is usually ½″ wide and 2 400 feet long. Characters are recorded across the width of the tape and are read in sequence along the tape. Tape can hold either 1 600 characters per inch or 6250 bpi (*bytes* per inch). A full tape at 1 600 bpi holds 46 million bytes (46 *megabytes*). The tape is read, or written to, at speeds of 112.5″ per second (about 180 000 bytes per second).

Mainframe computers Very large computers; direct descendants of the original valve computers, with great power and many functions, but expensive to build, *program* and operate. They typically have at least 100 K *bytes* of primary (main) storage.

Main storage The short-term storage medium, part of the *central processor unit*, in which *programs* and *data* are stored temporarily while they are being processed. This also includes data that have been processed and are waiting to be put out to a particular *output device*.

Management information system A system which is designed to supply managers with all the *data* they need to plan, organise, staff, direct, control and report on all the operations required of any major company or institution.

Matrix printer A *printer* that prints by building up characters from sets of dots made by firing needles at a carbon paper which makes a dot on the print paper below it.

Megabyte A million *bytes*. Used as a measure of capacity for any storage medium.

Memory That part of a computer capable of storing *programs* and *data* for manipulation (see also *Main storage*).

Menu A list of alternative procedures from which a user may select one particular activity. This will result in the loading of the required *program* for viewing, updating, interrogation, etc.

MICR See *Magnetic ink character recognition*.

Microcomputers Small computers, available at very low cost, flexible in application and adequate for most small businesses and for home use. Low-cost secondary storage is provided by *floppy discs*.

Microfiche See *COM*.

Microfilm See *COM*.

Microprocessor A complex set of integrated circuits on a silicon *chip*, which is therefore virtually a computer on a chip of silicon. Introduced in 1971 by the Intel Corporation, of California's 'Silicon Valley'.

Mini-computers Medium-size computers – competitors for *mainframe computers* at a medium size and functionality.

Mips Millions of instructions per second: the speed at which the *central processor unit* operates. Most *mainframe computers* work at speeds between 5 mips and 12 mips.

Modem Modulator-demodulator: a device which codes or decodes computer *data* from digital to wave form and vice versa so that they can be transmitted accurately over telephone cables.

Mouse A device which can direct the *cursor* very rapidly to any point on the screen of a *VDU* so that entries can be made quickly and easily. In many applications (for example, filling complex forms) the box pinpointed can be enlarged to permit completion (for example, of the address of the consignee) before being reduced down to screen size again while other boxes are completed. The final document will be printed full size.

Nanosecond One thousand-millionth of a second

Network An interconnected pattern of communications which permits access to computers with large databases from anywhere in the network on a many-to-many basis. One such system is DIANE (Direct Information Access Network for Europe). British Telecom is developing System X as a network which will handle all communications in digital form. The minimum size of a network is two computers interlinked.

Number crunching The calculation of useful ratios and other complex *data* using the ability of the computer to calculate at enormous speeds.

OCR See *Optical character recognition*.

Off-line A term used to describe any device, such as a *backing storage* disc, which is not *on-line* to the *central processor unit* but is in reserve until required.

OMR See *Optical mark recognition*.

On-line Describes equipment which is connected to and controlled by the computer. Such equipment is available for immediate use and can access the computer, interrogate it and receive responses immediately. (See also *Real-time*.)

Operating system A collection of *software* which controls the basic computer operations.

Optical character recognition Similar to *optical mark recognition*, but the computer can recognise alphabetical and numerical characters printed in one of the special type styles. The light reflected by a character creates a special pattern on the detector which is unique to the character concerned.

Optical mark recognition A specialised *input device*, used on pre-printed questionnaires and other documents. The respondent fills in a box, or joins a pair of dots to show his or her choice of answer. The documents are fed into a hopper, where light beams are shone on to each document and reflected back to a detector. The selected answer reflects back less light and can be detected. 10 000 copies per hour, with a failure rate of 1 per cent, can be processed. Unreadable forms are rejected into a special stacker and must be checked manually.

Output Computer results or information ready for transfer to an *output device*.

Output devices Devices which will pass on the processed results of the computer's calculations to the computer user, or to a storage device for further use when required. Until sufficient *data* have accumulated, results from the *central processor unit* are held temporarily in main *memory*. The chief output devices are *VDUs*, *printers* of various types, *graph plotters* and *COM*.

Paper tape A method of inputting *data* and outputting data, by punching characters across paper tape with a pattern of holes. Ten characters per inch can be punched on the tape. They are read by a paper-tape reader at about 1 000 characters per second. The punching is a much slower operation because the punch is mechanically operated.

Parity channel A channel on *paper tape* which enables the computer to validate each character, to detect any failure in the punching method.

Peripheral device The collective name for any device which is not part of the *central processor unit* itself, but is in the surrounding area to *input data*, or *output* data, or store it in some permanent way until required.

POS Point-of-sale: a POS device can read *bar codes*, credit cards, etc., and call up *data* from the *memory* to give customer activity in each trading area, the price of the goods, etc. (See also *EFTPOS*.)

Printer An *output device* that produces the results on paper; the most common form of computer output especially in the commercial field, where bank statements, wage slips, invoices, etc., are the end products after processing. The common types of printer are *line printers*, *matrix printers*, *daisy-wheel printers*, *laser printers* and *ink-jet printers*.

Print-out The listing from a computer.

Processor The part of the computer actually performing the computing.

Program A set of instructions in correct order which tells the computer how to carry out the task it is being asked to perform.

Programmer A person who designs, writes, tests and updates *programs*.

Punched card An early *input device*, still in use, which is punched with 80 columns, with 12 punchable rows in each column. A character is punched so as to give a unique pattern in a column, and there can therefore be 80 characters per card. They are read by photo-electric cells at speeds of 1 500 cards per minute, but punching the cards is a slower process. Their use is declining because of their slow speeds and bulky nature when stored.

Punched tags *POS* tags used in clothing stores to identify garments, sizes and prices. The codes are punched into the tag in two places. One half is torn off and these tags are sent at the end of the day to the central computer where they give a daily update of sales from all stores, and the stock position. They are a way of capturing POS *data*.

RAM Random access memory: the components of a *memory* that can be accessed at any point and both read from and written to. A computer advertised as 64k (see *K*) has 64 × 1024 *bytes* of random access memory. (See also *ROM* and *Random access*.)

Random access The ability to access a *file* and find a record independently of all the other records in the file.

Read The process of transferring information from an *input device* or a *backing storage* device into the *central processor unit*.

Read–write head The essential element of a *disc drive* which can find and read any *program* or item of *data* stored on a disc, and take it into main *memory* for processing. When the processing is complete the program, or revised data, will be returned to disc storage (that is, it will be written back on to the disc by the read–write head).

Real-time Any *on-line* system which can feed *data* directly into a computer and use the resulting *output* to control a system (such as a railway network, oil refinery or airport landing operation).

ROM Read only memory: the components of a *memory* which can be read from but not written to. It is used among other things for holding the operating system and utility *programs* of a computer. ROM discs are also used as databases for all sorts of areas, such as medical information, educational courses, etc. (See also *RAM*.)

Semi-conductor Any device which restricts electron flow to one direction only – for example, a valve, transistor or silicon *chip*.

Silicon chips See *Chips*.

Software The operating system and application *programs* which organise the computer's resources and make the whole set of separate elements operate together to function as a computer.

Systems analysis The process of examining documents and systems of work to detect what has to be done, what is the best method of doing it, and how can it be computerised. It leads eventually to a *program* of procedures which the computer will follow.

Terminal A device made up of a *keyboard* and a *VDU* which has become the standard means of communicating with a computer. *Input* is achieved via the keyboard, and *output* appears on the VDU screen (or in some earlier terminals it was typed out on a typewriter to give a hard copy). What appears on the screen can be produced as a hard copy if a *printer* is attached. Used more generally the term can mean any device at the end of a transmission of *data*, such as a VDU, teleprinter, cash receipting machine, badge or credit card reader, *modem* or *mini-computer*.

Time sharing The interleaved use of the computer by two or more end-users so that each appears to have the computer's entire attention. Made possible by the fantastic speed of the computer.

Thermal printer A non-impact *printer*, which makes characters appear on a special heat-sensitive paper by means of heated wires in the print head. They are silent and therefore useful in hospitals, but their speeds are slow (100 characters a second).

Transistor A *semi-conductor* device, smaller than the original device (the thermionic *valve*). It restricts electron flow to one direction. Transistors are more efficient than valves, since they do not require heat to stimulate electron flow, and replaced valves in computers about 1960.

Validating The process of proving the correctness of a piece of *data*.

Valve The thermionic valve was the original *semi-conductor* device, which restricts the flow of electrons to one direction. In America it is called a vacuum tube. It can act as an amplifier of electrical signals and as an on/off switch. Valves were used in the earliest computers, but are bulky and use a lot of energy.

VDU A visual display unit, or monitor, usually part of a *terminal* and giving instantaneous displays of *output* from the computer. Hard copies may be taken if a *printer* is attached. The VDU also acts as an *input device* either *on-line* (for example, having direct access to the *central processor unit* as in air-line bookings) or *off-line* (for example, the *key-to-disc system*.)

Visual display unit See *VDU*.

Volatility The capacity of a component to lose its *data* if switched off or if there is a power failure. Loss of data must always be guarded against by having back-up records, and by having sound layouts which are clear so that wrong plugs will not be pulled out, wrong switches turned off, etc.

Winchester discs *Hard discs* for *microcomputers*, either single platter or multi-platter (see *Magnetic disc*), and either integral parts of the computer or 'stand-alone' versions as separate units. More expensive than *floppy discs*, they have faster performance and larger storage capacities (5–40 *megabytes*).

Word-processor A computerised system for producing all types of written correspondence, reports, etc., with enormous advantages over the ordinary typewriter, and usually available as packages today. The text that results appears on a screen for instant checking, is stored in the computer *memory* for recall (to update drafts, for example) and can be printed out at high speeds with many of the features of printed text.

12.9 Exercises

1. Explain the following terms:

- *(a)* microprocessor
- *(b)* user-friendly
- *(c)* computer configuration
- *(d)* hardware
- *(e)* software
- *(f)* terminal

2. As far as input devices are concerned, what is meant by each of the following terms?

- *(a)* machine-readable data
- *(b)* floppy disc
- *(c)* bar code
- *(d)* MICR
- *(e)* punched tag
- *(f)* OMR

3. From your knowledge of job costing draw up a schedule of matters which the systems analyst would need to be familiar with to design software programs which would meet the accountant's needs in this field.

4. 'All our supervisors are trained to input costing data from the terminal in their workshop cost centre. The facility is available during working hours, though it is not on-line, and all records are updated overnight so that they are up to date at the start of every new working day.'

Explain the system outlined above.

5. What are the advantages to the management accountant of a fully computerised cost accounting system? Refer in your answer, *inter alia*, to cost estimation, production scheduling, budgeting and variance reporting and analysis.

6. *(a)* List the functional budgets which enter into a master budget.
   (b) What problems are likely to be encountered in attempting to computerise the budgeting process?

UNIT 13

Other aspects of management accounting

13.1 Presentation of reports and information to management

One of the most important aspects of management is to avoid as far as possible the loss or waste of resources. The efficiency of an organisation depends to a large extent on the supply of information which presents the facts in such a way that the effectiveness of the business can be increased and managerial action can lead to improvement and to a reduction of costs. Quick remedial action is necessary and this requires the provision of information and reports which are designed and adapted to the needs of executives.

There are various divisions and levels of management, and effective communication will only be satisfactory when the subject matter meets the need of the individual concerned. There is a pyramid of control, and at the top level it is usually possible to avoid getting into too much detail and reports may be presented less frequently.

(a) Levels of management

These include:

(a) the board of directors under its chairperson, with the managing director as the chief executive. Other directors may have executive responsibilities, while others will be non-executive, part-time directors;
(b) divisional managers;
(c) departmental managers engaged in general management;
(d) shop superintendents, foremen, forewomen and charge hands.

The directors formulate policy and the managing director is responsible for carrying this into effect. The divisional and departmental managers assist the managing director by planning and carrying out the programme laid down. The foremen or forewomen and charge hands will allocate tasks, issue instructions and generally supervise the activities.

(b) The presentation of reports

There is no standardised practice in the method of presentation of reports because the subject matter, amount of detail and operating conditions will vary depending on the type of industry, the size of the company and the requirements of executives. Every report must clearly show:

(a) The subject matter, which must be identified by a title.
(b) The date on which it is presented and the period to which it relates.
(c) The name of the department concerned with the report.
(d) The nature of the report, written in simple form using language which will be understood by the person(s) for whom the report is intended.
(e) The information, which in appropriate cases should be in comparative form, indicating what has actually happened set against what the performance should have been (for example, to what extent planned programmes have been achieved). Some helpful hints are:
    (i) Columns should be headed with details which are clear and concise.
    (ii) Information should be arranged in a way which facilitates reading and enables a quick grasp of the facts.
    (iii) The object is to present operating and cost information so as to reveal actual working conditions. This will help in attaining, as near as possible, maximum efficiency and will assist in determining policies.
    (iv) Reports should contain significant facts and indicate operating results and costs. They should be presented promptly to those responsible for the division, department or unit they control.
    (v) Analysis takes place in order to control costs, to revise methods and change policies when this is necessary. It helps in the process of eliminating unfavourable conditions and in the improvement of procedures.

(c) Types of report

There are *routine reports* and *special reports*. Routine reports cover all the main activities of the organisation. Special reports deal with aspects of the business which require investigation and with occasions when information is needed for special purposes. These include such items as make-or-buy decisions, market research, the effect of closing down a department, etc. Routine reports are presented monthly, weekly, daily or at other regular intervals suited to the needs of the recipients.

Routine reports include the following:

(a) those which are general in content and are of interest to top and general management;
(b) production reports in which production management and certain other executives are particularly interested;
(c) sales reports of primary interest to sales management, but which may also be used by other members of top management;
(d) reports which deal with distribution activities;
(e) matters concerning administration; administration reports which deal with internal matters including the actual and budgeted cost of administering the various departments and the variation in cost, if any;
(f) financial and cost reports that include reports for several levels of management – examples are: cash flow statements; costing profit and loss statements in detailed or summarised form; budgets; actual cost reports

and variances from budget for many functions of the business; Profit and Loss Accounts; Balance Sheets, etc.

(d) Conclusions

Those who direct the affairs of the organisation are concerned with objectives, policies and practices. Information should furnish them with the essential facts which will enable them to take action to increase effectiveness and reduce costs. Such action can lead to an increase in productivity and job satisfaction for all those engaged in the enterprise.

Although the presentation of information to management is important, there should be a constant watch on reports because conditions change and the information provided may be redundant. From time to time it may be useful to ask the recipients of particular reports if they consider that the report serves a useful purpose, whether it can be improved and whether it should be discontinued.

In the next few years information technology and just-in-time techniques will be changing the kind of information presented and the way it is presented. In many situations it should be possible at the touch of a button to obtain the information necessary for making decisions on courses of action.

Figs 13.1–13.4 (pp. 372–4) show a range of types of report.

13.2 Performance evaluation

Performance evaluation is not fully discussed in this introductory text, but it seems appropriate to refer to it briefly since it is a topic of growing importance. Management accounting is concerned with the efficiency of an organisation, and with large-scale businesses the efficiency of the whole is clearly dependent on the efficiency of the various parts. Manufacturing processes are continually changing and competitors may leapfrog ahead if they are able to adopt new technologies. The whole character of business activities is changing too, with support functions requiring an increasing proportion of operating costs.

Performance appraisal followed by effective communication has never been more important, and information must be clear and effective if the business is to survive in today's highly competitive conditions. While close control of costs and rapid feedback when problems arise, or variances from budget are detected, have become to some extent second nature in manufacturing, this is not quite so true of support areas. There is a need to look at all areas of a business, with regular reviews of the activities of each functional area and a detailed evaluation of its performance.

The stages in such a performance evaluation may be as follows:

(a) Defining boundaries

First, define the boundaries of the functional area under consideration. It may be a subsidiary company, or a manufacturing or service department. It may be a support area with links to other functional areas which it has to service and support.

Copies to:
Managing Director
Executive Directors
Secretary

COST ACCOUNTS REPORT – September 19.5

	Invoicing	Profit (or Loss)	Profit (or Loss) as percentage of invoicing	
			Month	To date
	£	£	%	%
Product A				
Product B				
Product C				
Product D				

Results to date with comparable results for 19.4

	19.5 Invoicing	19.5 Profit (or Loss)	19.4 Invoicing	19.4 Profit (or Loss)
	£	£	£	£
Product A				
Product B				
Product C				
Product D				

Remarks:

Product A Fourteen machines invoiced at £ show a loss of £ after allowing for £ Discount and Sales Expenses.

Product D Eight machines invoiced at £ show a loss of £ after allowing for £ Commission and £ Discount and Sales Expenses.

Fig. 13.1 Monthly sales return and profitability statement

FORECAST OF PRODUCTION Month: ________			
Product	Budget centre Foundry	Budget centre Machine shop	Budget centre Assembly
A B C D			

Fig. 13.2 A production forecast

MACHINE UTILISATION REPORT Week ending: ________									
Machine no.	Description	Hours worked	Idle hours	A	B	C	D	E	F

Idle time caused by:

A Shortage of labour	D Machine breakdown
B Shortage of raw material	E Shortage of work
C Shortage of machine tools	F Other causes

Fig. 13.3 Machine utilisation report

SELLING EXPENSES

Month: May 19.9

Copies to: Managing Director
Sales Managers
Secretary
File

	Home				Export				Totals			
	Month		Cumulative		Month		Cumulative		Month		Cumulative	
	Actual	Budget	Actual	Budget	Actual	Budget	Actual	Budget	Actual	Budget	Actual	Budget
Sales	£	£	£	£	£	£	£	£	£	£	£	£
Expenses:												
Head office salaries												
Head office expenses												
Travellers' salaries												
Travellers' commission												
Travellers' expenses:												
Car expenses												
Other travelling												
Hotels												
Entertaining												
Other costs												
Total												
Total % of sales												

Fig. 13.4 Selling expenses report

(b) Listing broad objectives

Second, list the formal objectives of the functional area - the broad achievements it must realise during the course of its activities. These will then establish a framework for comparison purposes which can be used to evaluate the performance of the functional area as a whole - and by implication the degree of success of its top executives.

(c) Listing detailed objectives

Third, continue this definition of objectives down through the function's organisation to list the objectives of each sub-area, and to list the activities which will be necessary to achieve the objectives. This may mean detailed activity surveys of what each sub-area actually does; who is responsible for each activity; what reports are generated; etc. Such reports are often called *returns*, because official forms have to be returned to superiors who feed the information through to top levels. The analysis may involve the preparation of work-flow charts, the completion of questionnaires, interviews, etc.

(d) Devising control measures

The aim in the course of these investigatory activities is to devise a number of control measures or ratios which can be calculated on a regular basis - for management information rather than rigid control. In many of these areas we are dealing with human beings, not inanimate objects. For example, a retailer might find it helpful to know sales per foot of display counter and an administration officer may be keen to know the number of letters typed per typist, but too rigid a control of the latter may be unwise. One government department with a huge turnover in the typing pool found that the chief cause of complaint was a supervisor who checked up every hour how close each typist was to achieving his or her 'norm' of letters completed. Staff were totally resentful of this approach, for it often meant that those who took the trouble to answer letters in detail, and perhaps had to phone round for information, were less well regarded than those who sent terse and unhelpful replies.

Wherever possible the result of the investigation should be a computerised system of data capture. If this is too sophisticated, regular returns at appropriate intervals (weekly, four-weekly, monthly or quarterly) should be fed upwards and consolidated to the point where it is worthwhile feeding them in as electronic input to the general management information service (MIS). At this point the actual number crunching (see Unit 12.8) to throw up the control ratios or measures would provide senior management with the figures from which the performance of departments and individuals could be evaluated.

The aim is to collect data promptly and accurately. It should be up to date and confined to significant facts. Many of these should be in the form of comparisons. Recognition should be given to differences thrown up by the data. The causes should be identified, and they should indicate where efforts could be made to effect an improvement in operations and lead to a reduction in costs. Where appropriate the previous results should be shown, such as previous week, previous month, or same month in the previous year.

A performance evaluation system should generate a set of measures appropriate to the business concerned which enable management to monitor performance in each crucial area. The measures may relate to functions, subfunctions or individual staff, and should pinpoint less than acceptable performance and suggest areas where performance might be enhanced. Action to correct adverse trends and improve achievement based on the information made available should be such as to improve the quality of achievement without producing behavioural unrest, high labour turnover or stress in the working situation. Positive measures to improve performance rather than negative criticism are desirable.

An an illustration of the sort of measures that can be devised for a particular industry, the following list of measures designed for inter-branch comparison in the banking field is interesting:

(i) **Routine statistics**
(a) Number of personal current accounts.
(b) Number of business current accounts.
(c) Number of personal deposit accounts.
(d) Number of business deposit accounts.
(e) Number of savings accounts.
(f) Number of budget accounts.
(g) New personal accounts opened per quarter.
(h) New business accounts opened per quarter.
(i) Private loan accounts opened per quarter.
(j) Overdrafts sanctioned per quarter.
(k) Ratio of cheque guarantee cards to the number of personal current accounts.
(l) Ratio of credit cards to the number of personal current accounts.
(m) Ratio of company credit cards to the number of business current accounts.

(ii) **Other statistics**
(a) Total export business handled.
(b) Total import business handled.
(c) Ratio of export transactions to business accounts open.
(d) Foreign commission earned.
(e) Domestic commission earned.
(f) Specialist commission earned (insurance, executorship and similar services).
(g) Ratio of commission to general charges.
(h) Average personal lending per personal current account.
(i) Average business lending per business current account.
(j) Number of counter transactions per counter position.
(k) Average value of a counter transaction.
(l) Average cash balance.
(m) Cash handled as a percentage of average cash balance.
(n) Normal man-hours and overtime man-hours.

(o) Overtime as a percentage of normal man-hours.
(p) Commission earned per man-hour paid.

Clearly there are any number of such ratios which could in fact be calculated and would throw light on particular areas. For example, many branch premises occupy prime town centre sites with generous space allowances for customer service. While the banks have not yet descended to the level of superstores interested in how much sales are achieved per foot of counter space, they must begin to ask themselves whether there is too much space for the money being handled. In 1980 personal accounts were estimated to be costing about £750 million, of which only about £100 million could be recouped in charges. The balance had to be made up by 'lending on' the balances in the personal accounts at interest.

With the interest rates prevailing in 1980 this was not an uneconomic operation, but if interest rates fell to, say, half the 1980 levels the whole range of personal services offered would become uneconomic. (Courtesy of *Money and Banking Made Simple*)

Those of us who have bank accounts will be only too aware how right the author of this extract was - not that interest rates in the 1990s have been smaller than those in the 1980s, but the margins of income to be loaned on have fallen (for example, with the advent of interest-bearing current accounts). Many of the services previously offered as 'free' by the banks are now the subject of direct charges, and some of them (for example, going into the red without prior approval) incur computerised knee-jerk penalties of - say - £10. In these cases, the computer senses the unauthorised overdraft and immediately charges the fixed penalty. Routine statistics can certainly help management understand what is happening, but allied with a computer program can secure instant recompense for losses suffered or expenses incurred.

13.3 Investment appraisal and capital budget decisions

There are various factors that influence capital expenditure decisions. A business has to replace assets as they wear out and become obsolete. It is also necessary for management to create circumstances and adopt policies which will maintain and improve the efficiency and performance of the organisation. These may be concerned with improving the quality of the product, increasing the volume of output and decreasing the cost of production. There is also the question of expansion by extending the facilities of the existing business, by opening a new branch or by taking over another business. A modernisation programme or similar project should lead to a saving in costs, but whatever is proposed the costs should be measured against the expected extra profits.

Long-term investment in capital projects is subject to varying degrees of risk, and there are often alternative courses of action, when money is available for investment.

Capital expenditure consists of an outflow of cash and as operations proceed this is normally followed by cash inflows of various amounts. The cash receipts or cash inflows may take place at different times and each of the projects under consideration may have a different life-cycle. Cash is required to cover the cost of production and to provide a profit, but when these projects are examined, the *cash inflow* which is used in the investment appraisal consists of the *estimated profit (net of tax when this is paid) plus the depreciation.* An assessment should therefore be made of the profitability of investments by comparing the cash flows with the value of the proposed investments, and this involves calculations of future *increases* in cash inflows or *net savings* in cash outflows. The comparability of projects is complicated by the fact that they may have different lives and the inflows of cash may vary in amount and be received at different intervals.

The basic problem when proposed investments are considered concerns the choice of a method which will indicate the return on capital employed or the real benefit or return which is likely to result from a particular course of action or from the alternatives. It is possible to calculate the time it may take to *pay back* the amount invested, to apply a rate of interest which must be earned, and to calculate the estimated rate of return on the capital. We have to forecast the cash inflows as accurately as possible and to assume that over the life of the project they consist of the initial investment plus the return on the capital expenditure.

When projects are compared, the cash flows must be dealt with on a common basis so that the comparisons are valid. The return on the capital expenditure is the *interest*, which is often referred to as the time value of money, and this element in the cash flow is treated as being at *compound interest*. This is interest which is not withdrawn at the end of each year but is added to the investment. If the compound interest is eliminated by deducting this from the cash flow, the amount which is left is the *present value* of the cash flow. This present value has to be compared wtih the cost of the investment, and if common methods and similar rates of interest are applied to the cash flow from various projects, valid comparisons can be made.

(a) Methods of appraisal

In the selection of the most profitable project a procedure is followed whereby certain methods are used to provide information which will enable the projects to be ranked and which will disclose the project with the shortest pay-back period or the one which shows the highest rate of return. Four methods are used and these consist of:

(a) the pay-back period;
(b) average rate of return as a percentage of the investment;
(c) average rate of return as a percentage of the average investment;
(d) discounted cash flow.

These methods will be examined and applied to a particular problem concerning proposals which have been made to invest in Project A or Project B. Investigations which have been carried out by a planning department have established that an investment in either of the two projects is likely to cost £160 000, and the cash flows are estimated as follows:

Year	*Project A*	*Project B*
	£	£
1	16 000	52 000
2	52 000	70 000
3	72 000	90 000
4	105 000	52 000
5	70 000	37 000
6	–	18 000

At the end of year five, no further cash flows are expected in respect of Project A and there is no residual value, but Project B provides cash flows for six years and at the end of that period the scrap value of the plant is expected to amount to £10 000. Over the life of the projects the market rate of interest is assumed to be 20 per cent and the directors require a return of at least 7 per cent above the market rate.

(i) Pay-back period This method of appraisal merely calculates the period of time it takes to recover the expenditure when proposals are made for capital projects. It does not measure the profitability as a percentage or rate of return, but observes the estimated cash flow in the early years in order to estimate how long it will take to obtain the cash to pay for the capital cost of the project. The cash flows are therefore accumulated period by period until the total cash flow equals the cost of the investment.

	Project A			*Project B*		
Year	*Cash flow*	*Total cash flow*	*Amount outstanding*	*Cash flow*	*Total cash flow*	*Amount outstanding*
	£	£	£	£	£	£
0	–	–	160 000	–	–	160 000
1	16 000	16 000	144 000	52 000	52 000	108 000
2	52 000	68 000	92 000	70 000	122 000	38 000
3	72 000	140 000	20 000	90 000	212 000	–
4	105 000	245 000	–	52 000	264 000	–

The above statement indicates that if Project A is adopted, the accumulated cash flows will recover the cost of the investments during year four, but if Project B is adopted the cost of the investment will be recovered during year three.

Project A The cost is reached when £20 000 is taken from the cash flow of £105 000 received in year four. The pay-back period is therefore 3 years plus a part of year four, represented by £20 000 as a proportion of £105 000.

$$3 + \frac{20\,000}{105\,000} = \underline{\underline{3.2 \text{ years}}}$$

Project B This is also calculated by using the final amount to find the proportion of the cash flow in the year when the pay-back is completed and when £38 000 is taken from the cash flow of £90 000 received in year three.

$$2 + \frac{38\,000}{90\,000} = \underline{\underline{2.4 \text{ years}}}$$

This is simply a method of accumulating the cash flows until the amount which is to be invested is reached. The cash which completes the pay-back is a proportion of the cash flow for that year and this is the point in the year when pay-back is completed.

In order to reach a decision on the proposals, it is necessary to compare the pay-back period of the projects, and on this basis Project B might be chosen as it has the shorter pay-back period (2.4 years). However, to arrive at the best results we have to resolve the problems by examining the facts, and therefore the problems have to be identified and the risks assessed. Appraisal by the pay-back method may be satisfactory when short-life projects are considered, but as some projects have a high degree of risk it is most important to examine the timing of cash flows and the profitability. With projects of high risk it may be preferable to choose the project which has a slightly longer pay-back period if the bulk of the cash is received in the early period of that project and the reverse applies to the other project. It should also be noted that early pay-back makes cash available for reinvestment, although it should not be overlooked that the earnings of the alternative project may be considerable after the pay-back date. Example 13.1 gives an illustration of Projects Y and Z, with Project Z providing most of its income in the early part of its life.

EXAMPLE 13.1

There is an investment of £100 000.

	Project X			*Project Z*		
	Cash flow			*Cash flow*		
Year	*(annual)*	*(accumulated)*	*Recovered*	*(annual)*	*(accumulated)*	*Recovered*
	£	£	%	£	£	%
1	10 000	10 000	10	60 000	60 000	60
2	30 000	40 000	40	30 000	90 000	90
3	70 000	110 000	110	10 000	100 000	100
4	40 000	150 000	—	10 000	110 000	—
Pay-back period =	2.86 years				3 years	

Project Z, with a slightly longer pay-back period, repays 90 per cent of the capital cost within two years compared with only 40 per cent recovered by Project Y. Taking the use of this money into account we might regard Project Z as the better investment.

(ii) Average annual rate of return as a percentage of the investment To find the rate of return the depreciation or cost of the investment is deducted from the cash flow. The net cash flow is then divided by a figure which represents the life of the project. This provides the *average annual return*, which is then related to the capital invested in order to find the annual earnings as a percentage of the sum invested.

Using the figures for Projects A and B again we have:

	Project A	*Project B*	
	£	£	
Total cash flow	315 000	319 000	
Less Depreciation or cost of investment	160 000	150 000	(£160 000 *less* £10 000 scrap)
Net return	155 000	169 000	
Life of investment	5 years	6 years	
Average annual return	£31 000	£28 167	

$$\textit{Rate of return} = \frac{\text{Average annual profit}}{\text{Capital invested}} \times 100$$

The calculations are therefore:

Project A	*Project B*
$\frac{£31\,000}{£160\,000} \times 100$	$\frac{£28\,167}{£160\,000} \times 100$
$= 19.4\%$	$= 17.6\%$

This method is an improvement on the pay-back period method as it covers the whole of the period and deals with the net return on an average annual basis. The defect of this method is that interest is calculated as simple interest on an average amount. It does not recognise the fact that when money is invested for a period of time, with variable earnings being received at intervals, then compound interest considerations have to be included in the sums involved.

(iii) Average rate of return as a percentage of the average investment This method records double the rate of interest shown by the previous method. It assumes that only half the original capital is invested for the whole period, on the basis that if capital is returned at regular intervals and at a standard rate throughout the period, then only half of the original investment is really invested during the life of the project. In the project being analysed, the rate of return under this method is 38.8 per cent for Project A and 35.2 per cent for Project B.

(iv) Discounted cash flow (DCF) This method reduces the amount received by discounting the cash flows. The previous methods either ignore the earnings after the pay-back period or fail to take account of the timing of the cash flows. Timing is important if money is invested at compound interest. The combined amount of original investment and interest earns interest in the following year, thereby increasing the amount of interest earned in that year, and this process continues from year to year. The rate of interest remains fixed but the annual amount of interest earned increases due to the effect of compounding. Therefore when money is invested for a stated period of time at a fixed rate of interest, the return of the investment together with the interest on it is in the form of a single payment a number of years from the date when the original investment was made. This single payment covers the return of the original investment and the compound interest. In project analysis the cash flow at each date is equivalent to the single payment, as the cash received includes a portion of the original investment and compound interest. The date of the cash flow is important because the amount of compound interest included in the payment increases year by year, and these earnings of interest affect the discount which has to be deducted to reduce the cash flow to its *present value*.

Present value Discounted cash flow is a technique which reverses the compound interest calculations in order to arrive at the present value of an amount to be received in the future. For example, at 10 per cent interest £1 210 received in two years' time has a present value of £1 000. This is shown below first at compound interest and then using the reverse procedure.

The calculation for compound interest is as follows:

Formula: $C = P\,(1 + r)^n$

where C = cash flow (i.e. the amount received including interest at the end of the period)

P = present value

r = rate of interest as a percentage

n = number of years

$C = £1\,000\,(1 + 0.10)^2 \quad (1.10 \times 1.10) = 1.21$

$C = £1\,000 \times 1.21$

$C = £1\,210 \quad$ (interest £210)

The calculation for present value of £1 210 at 10 per cent interest is as follows:

Formula: $$P = \frac{C}{(1 + r)^n}$$

$$P = \frac{£1\,210}{(1 + 0.10)^2}$$

$$P = \frac{£1\,210}{1.21}$$

$$P = £1\,000$$

The discounting procedure is considerably simplified by the use of tables which indicate the *discount factors* for the present value of £1 at various rates of interest and periods of time. There is an example of these tables in Fig. 13.7 (p. 401).

EXAMPLE 13.2

Rate of interest 10%: 1 year = 0.909: 2 years = 0.826

These factors can be found by dividing £1 by the amount to be received at the end of each period.

$$\text{Present value of £1 at 10\%, receivable in 1 year's time} = \frac{£1}{£1.10} = £0.909$$

$$\text{Present value of £1 at 10\%, receivable in 2 years' time} = \frac{£1}{(£1.10)^2} = £0.826$$

These three-figure factors are approximations but they indicate that if 90.9 pence is invested today at 10 per cent interest, the value at the end of one year is £1, and if 82.6 pence is invested today, the value at the end of two years is £1. If five- or six-figure tables are used the calculations will produce more accurate results. For £1 received in two years' time the six-figure factor at 10 per cent interest is 0.826 446.

To find the amount to invest today at 10 per cent in order to receive £1 210 at the end of two years the calculation is as follows:

$$£1\,210 \times 0.826\,446 = £999.999\,66\ (£1\,000)$$

The whole of the cash flows is valued on this basis, and in the examples it is assumed that cash flows are received at the end of each year.

In order to appraise investment proposals certain details are required, including the estimated cost of the project in the form of the capital employed or the cost of the investment. Also required is the minimum rate of return which will pay for the cost of borrowing or as compensation to the shareholders for investing in the business. The life of the projects should be stated and a forecast should be made of the cash flows for each period throughout the life of each of the projects. The next problem concerns the rate of interest to use when discounting the cash flows.

(b) Interest

The cost of capital is represented by the interest paid to debenture holders or others when money is borrowed. It is also represented by the dividends paid to, or expected by, the shareholders. The establishment of rates for discounting will depend on the type of capital involved and the kind of information desired. A decision can be made as to whether the internal rate of return (see below) is desired or whether a specific rate is to be applied to the cash flows in order to disclose whether there is a balance which is positive or negative. If a specific rate is used for discounting and the present value exceeds the cost of the project the result is positive and may be considered favourable, but if the cost exceeds the present value the result is negative and the proposal will be rejected. There are therefore two methods of discounting, one which uses specific rates to disclose the *net present value* and the other which determines and applies the *internal rate of return.*

(i) Net present value method As stated above this method reduces the cash flows to present value by adopting a particular rate of interest and discount and deducting the capital employed from the total of the present values. This then shows that the cost of the investments has been covered and a particular rate of interest has been earned. If there is a balance it is the net present value, which is the surplus or deficit after allowing for the cost and the earnings at the rate of interest selected. There is a cut-off point where the present values have accumulated to the cost of the project and the rate used is referred to as the cut-off rate.

At this stage consideration can be given to the comparability of the projects and they can be ranked, but apart from financial considerations, due regard must be given to any risks which may be attached to the projects.

Whether money is borrowed or taken from company funds, a rate may be fixed which is the minimum the company is prepared to accept. Projects A and B are now dealt with, using 20 per cent as the borrowing or cut-off rate.

	Project A			*Project B*			
Year	*Cash flow inwards* £	*Present value factor* 20%	*Discounted cash flows* £	*Cash flow inwards* £		*Present value factor* 20%	*Discounted cash flows* £
1	16 000	0.833	13 328	52 000		0.833	43 316
2	52 000	0.694	36 088	70 000		0.694	48 580
3	72 000	0.579	41 688	90 000		0.579	52 110
4	105 000	0.482	50 610	52 000		0.482	25 064
5	70 000	0.402	28 140	37 000		0.402	14 874
6	–	–	–	18 000		0.335	6 030
				+ 10 000	scrap	0.335	3 350
	£315 000		£169 854	£329 000			£193 324
Less Cost of capital at beginning of year 1			£160 000				£160 000
Net present value			£ 9 854				£ 33 324

Project B has a higher net present value and, as the cost of Projects A and B is identical, Project B would be preferred provided there were no other factors to be considered. When the *costs of projects* vary, the results can be compared by the use of a profitability index. This reflects the relationship between the gross present value and the cost of a project.

If it is assumed that Project A costs £140 000, and rounding off the above figures:

	Project A	*Project B*
	£	£
Gross present value	170 000	193 000
Cost of capital	140 000	160 000
Net present value	£ 30 000	£ 33 000
Ranking	2	1
Profitability index		
$\frac{\text{Gross present value}}{\text{Cost of capital}}$	$\frac{170}{140}$	$\frac{193}{160}$
=	1.214	1.206
Ranking	1	2

This information indicates that, after allowing for interest, £1 of investment produces £1.214 for Project A and £1.206 for Project B, and because of the smaller investment in the case of Project A, the ranking is now in its favour. It will be seen that Project B has much larger cash flows in the early years and this is an important consideration, especially where there is a risk factor and early returns enable cash to be reinvested.

(ii) Internal rate of return or yield method Using the present value method of evaluation, a rate of discount can be selected which is the internal rate of return, achieved by each of the projects. This method equates the total of the present values with the cost of the investment and there is therefore no net present value. When the two figures are exactly alike, with no net present value, the rate of discount applied to the cash flows represents the rate of return. It is a method which is carried out by trial and error until the estimated rate of return is found. A rough idea can sometimes be established in respect of the rate of return by looking at the net present value to see by how much the discounted cash flow exceeds or is lower than the cost of the investment. When the difference is fairly small the rate used is close to the internal rate of return.

In the example above, Project A has a net present value of only £9 854 and this indicates that the rate is close to 20 per cent, whereas Project B has £33 324 and is much further away from 20 per cent. It is necessary to approach this problem by trying a rate of discount such as 20 per cent and noting whether the net present value is positive or negative. Project A at 20 per cent showed a positive figure of £9 854 and this indicated that the internal rate of return was higher than 20 per cent.

The effect of discounting is to extract the interest, leaving the discounted cash flow in the form of the principal amount or the capital cost. If the amount is in excess of the capital cost the rate of interest is too low, and a higher rate must be applied to the cash flow. This can be summarised as follows:

(a) Net present value: positive – percentage too low.
(b) Net present value: negative – percentage too high.

(c) Net present value: zero – percentage represents the internal rate of return.

It is not usually possible to find the actual rate of return at the first attempt. If the percentage gives a positive amount, try higher percentages until the amount is negative and fairly close to the capital cost. If the first attempt gives a negative amount the reverse procedure is followed. As the figures are already available at 20 per cent for Project A, we can now try a higher rate, say 25 per cent.

Project A

Year	*Cash flow* £	*Present value factor* 25%	*Discounted cash flow* £
1	16 000	0.800	12 800
2	52 000	0.640	33 280
3	72 000	0.512	36 864
4	105 000	0.410	43 050
5	70 000	0.328	22 960
	£315 000		£148 954
Less Cost of capital			160 000
Net present value			(£11 046)

The change which takes place between the two sets of calculations is the *range* between them. The distance is represented by 5 per cent and £20 900 of discounted cash flow, because 5 per cent is the difference between 25 per cent and 20 per cent, and £20 900 is the addition of the net present values, £9 854 + (£11 046). £20 900 is also the difference between the present value of the cash flows of £169 854 and £148 954. If £20 900 is equivalent to 5 per cent, it will be found that £9 854 is 2.4 per cent, and this is the addition to the lower rate of discount of 20 per cent which provides the internal rate of return of 22.4 per cent. This can be illustrated as shown in Fig. 13.5.

Project A The internal rate of return is as follows:

$$\text{Low rate of interest} + \frac{\text{(Net present value of low rate)}}{\text{(Difference between high and low discounted cash flow)}} \times \text{Range \%}$$

$$= 20 + \frac{£9\,854}{£20\,900} \times 5\%$$

$$= 20 + 2.4\%$$

$$= \underline{\underline{22.4\%}}$$

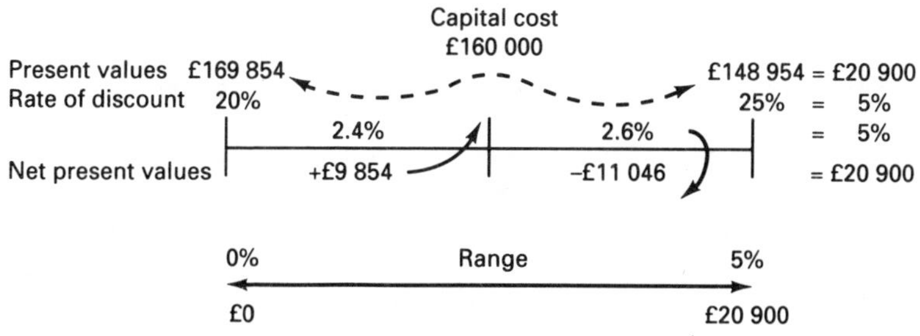

Fig. 13.5 The range between rates of return

Project B The net present value at 20 per cent is £33 324 and discounting is now tried at 25 per cent.

Year	*Cash flow* £	*Present value factor* 25%	*Discounted cash flow* £
1	52 000	0.800	41 600
2	70 000	0.640	44 800
3	90 000	0.512	46 080
4	52 000	0.410	21 320
5	37 000	0.328	12 136
6	28 000	0.262	7 336
	£329 000		£173 272
Less Cost of capital			£160 000
Net present value			£13 272

This shows that 25 per cent is too low a rate to reduce the flows to the cost of the capital, so discounting is now tried at 30 per cent.

Year	*Cash flow* £	*Present value factor* 30%	*Discounted cash flow* £
1	52 000	0.769	39 988
2	70 000	0.592	41 440
3	90 000	0.455	40 950
4	52 000	0.350	18 200
5	37 000	0.269	9 953
6	28 000	0.207	5 796
	£329 000		£156 327
Less Cost of capital			£160 000
Net present value			(£ 3 673)

The calculations shown above indicate that the internal rate of return is somewhere between 25 per cent and 30 per cent, and the small negative amount of £3 673 suggests that it is fairly close to 30 per cent. The range is 5 per cent (30% − 25%), and this is equivalent to £16 945 of discounted cash flow; that is, (£173 272 − £156 327) or (£13 272 + £3 673). Using the method of taking the low rate and calculating a proportion of the range percentage, the internal rate of return is 25 per cent plus a proportion of 5 per cent as represented by the relationship of £13 272 to £16 945. The internal rate of return for Project B is therefore as follows:

$$25\% + \left(\frac{£13\,272}{£16\,945} \times 5\%\right)$$

$$= 25\% + 3.9\%$$
$$= 28.9\%$$

Project B is preferred as it has the highest rate and is 1.9 per cent above the minimum rate set by the directors.

The merits of Projects A and B can now be compared by summarising the results under the various methods of evaluation.

Method	*Project A*	*Project B*
Pay-back	3.2 years	2.4 years
Average annual return on investment	19.4%	17.6%
Average annual return on average investment	38.8%	35.2%
Net present value at 20 per cent	£9 854	£33 324
Internal rate of return	22.4%	28.9%

On the assumption that the risk factor is the same for both projects, it is likely that Project B would be preferred as showing the best results. (The slightly lower average annual return on investment and average investment is due to the low cash flows towards the end of the project.)

(c) The improvement of performance and profitability

In order to improve performance and profitability it is necessary to measure and evaluate the activities of a business, and this procedure will require the use of the most effective techniques. Profitability may be improved in various ways, such as an increase in turnover and a reduction in unit costs, or an improvement in the methods of production, and the development and marketing of new products. Investment decisions should be made after the problems have been analysed and the alternatives considered. A most effective method is the appraisal of projects is the use of discounting techniques. Priorities have to be established in the use of capital as some projects are connected with essential replacements or have to conform with local or national government regulations. Other proposed projects will have to compete for the funds which are, or may be, made available, and the important considerations include the borrowing rate and an internal rate of return (that is, a rate of return on the operations of the company) which will satisfy the providers of capital. The techniques described in this section assist in the selection of projects which are viable propositions.

13.4 Costing in the hotel and catering industries

The hotel and catering industry covers anything from fast food services which are purely retail outlets to large hotels dealing with ordinary guests, travel tour operations and services such as banqueting. In the smaller organisations there may be very little financial control, and costing or pricing may consist of taking the cost of food as being 40 per cent of the selling price of portions or meals. Apart from the sale of food and other services it is often the revenue received from the sale of accommodation which makes the business a commercial success. In the hotel and catering industry at the higher level there is financial planning and control and a better understanding of finance, costs and the effect on profit of decisions made by managers and other controllers in the industry. Budgetary control is an important part of the plans made and so is the use of operating ratios to check the progress of the business. These ratios include the rate of room occupancy, rate of guest occupancy and rate of restaurant occupancy. Average spending power (ASP) is another important ratio because the total turnover of a business depends on two factors, the number of customers and the average amount spent by them. If this is adequate menus can be planned more efficiently. The ASP is calculated by dividing sales by the number of covers. These may be sales of food, beverages or other items. In the small units of this industry food, which tends to be the largest item of cost, is often bought, prepared, sold and paid for all in the cycle of one day. The more efficient organisations prepare operating statements showing budget and actual figures for net sales of rooms, food, liquor and tobacco and for the related costs, including wages and staff costs and the cost of service departments and general expenditure.

Hotels may have limiting factors, such as the accommodation available, which make it impossible to increase sales, and this also applies to seating capacity in restaurants. There may also be a shortage of suitable labour, insufficient capital and consumer demand. Canteen sales is another catering activity which needs to be costed carefully because it is often a service which is heavily subsidised.

(a) Problems when costing meals

The cost of food fluctuates considerably especially when seasonal lines are involved. Food is not the easiest of materials to deal with especially when using quantity control in relation to portions. In order to obtain an adequate return there must be food control, and this requires the application of cost accounting to the peculiar production and selling methods of the catering industry.

Hotels and caterers need to obtain the highest possible return on food sales, but the gross profit must be consistent with the policy of the management as to quality and size of portions. The kitchen is the equivalent of the manufacturing section in other organisations, and it has difficult problems with food control. It is dealing with highly perishable goods and should there be over-production there may be a substantial loss. The object of food control is to search for the commodities which may be adversely affecting operating results. Units in the catering industry vary considerably in size and the kind of goods they produce. A method which has been used successfully is a detailed food sales and costs analysis, but such systems often require a large amount of clerical work.

Another problem with food and portion control is the fact that certain items of food may be handled in the kitchen by several persons. Stores requisitions should indicate the department to which the goods are to be issued, the brand name and the exact quantity, description and size of the units.

During the process of determining the cost per portion, standard recipes must be adhered to. Weight and volume measures should be used and standard pans of known size. Observation should be made at the point of service of the size of portions and the number sold. The standard cost method is an effective system for comparing the particular food cost against the established standards. Purchase specifications and portion standards have to be established and portion costs determined for all food on the menus.

(b) Costing canteen services

Hotels have to provide their guests with many services such as food, drink, accommodation, laundry, etc. The canteen is more concerned with the preparation and service of food. The service has to be fast, and the canteen may well be subsidised, which will add to the problems of the canteen manager. As with hotels there will be daily planning of production and sales. The transactions, though small in amount, have to be carried out with speed and efficiency and there is a high rate of stock turnover. Provided there are adequate cold-store facilities waste can be avoided and buying can be more economical. It is the duty of the manager to estimate the food requirements for each day.

The staff will probably consist of cooks, kitchen porters, kitchen assistants, waitresses and supervisors. Other expenses include consumable stores such as cutlery, crockery, washing-up cloths and cleaning materials. Depending on the costing system and the requirements of management the canteen may have to bear the cost of rent, rates, depreciation, etc. It is fairly common for the canteen manager to be responsible to the personnel manager.

In order to present the appropriate cost information to management the analysis and allocation of expenditure is necessary. This will determine the cost of meals and services and reveal possible sources of economies. A Canteen Cost Statement can be drawn up on a monthly basis showing details of wages and salaries, provisions provided and a list of expenses. The income from sales and any subsidy provided will be deducted to show the net result. The statement will show, in 'budget' and 'actual' columns, the figure for the month and also the cumulative total, as shown in Fig. 13.6.

COST STATEMENT				
Canteen	For the month of			
	Budget		Actual	
	This month	Cumulative total	This month	Cumulative total
Wages and salaries: Supervision Cooks Kitchen assistants Counter service				
Provisions: Meat Poultry Vegetables Fruit Butter Eggs Cheese Milk Coffee, tea, cocoa Bread and cakes Soft drinks Groceries Ice cream Seafood Expenses: Crockery and glassware Table linen Consumable stores Rent Gas Electricity Steam Insurance				
Cost *Less*: Sales income Subsidy				
Surplus/(Deficit)				

Fig. 13.6 A Canteen Cost Statement

13.5 Costing road haulage operations

Motor transport costing is a special case of operation costing which has unique features. First of all it is largely regulated by administrative requirements imposed from above, and enforced by a network of inspectors including those for European Community standards. Second, it is not as susceptible to control as a factory because most of the staff are on the road, and outside the direct control of management. Movements are subject to the exigencies of traffic movements everywhere. One cartoonist showed a map of a day's journey in any direction from Hyde Park Corner which showed Newcastle, Land's End, the Lake District and the Tower of London as a typical day's driving.

From an economic viewpoint vehicles should aim to run at full capacity in both directions, but light or empty running is to some extent unavoidable. The filling of 'empty legs' is a major aim of operators, often at very cheap rates; for example, enough to cover fuel and tyre costs. Vehicles must be properly serviced to comply with legislation as well as to prevent breakdown, and standard mileages and journey times are important. However, the tachometer system makes it difficult to keep to standard times when delays occur because excessive speeds are easily detected if attempts are made to make up for lost time. The fines are heavy, while the loss of an operator's licence is fatal to the business.

Important features are:

(a) The repair and servicing department should use a system of job-costing and comparisons should be made between own-labour and outside-contractor charges.

(b) Efficiency should be monitored as to timing on actual journeys between known collection points and delivery points. Loading and unloading times should also be monitored and delays examined to determine whose fault they are.

(c) Running cost comparisons should be made between different types of vehicle to ensure the fleet is the most appropriate one for the class of business involved. Running costs include fuel, lubricants, tyres, maintenance

Table 13.1 Weekly costing statement for 5-day week ending . . .

Revenue earned (actual)		£ —
Expenses		
Wages (actual)	—	
Running costs (based on actual mileage)	—	
Licences/Insurance (as per budget)	—	
Depreciation (as per budget)	—	
Overhead expenses (as per budget)	—	
Total expenses		—
Profit for week		£ —

and repairs and are usually calculated as a standard cost per mile or kilometer run.

(*d*) Fixed costs are independent of the distance run and include vehicle costs (less the value of the tyres), licence costs, insurance and administration. Standard charges per tonne of the vehicle are calculated.

(*e*) Depreciation of vehicles is chiefly affected by the age of the vehicle, but wear and tear increases with the distance run. It is essential to work out standard rates for depreciation which fully recover replacement costs of the vehicle, bearing in mind that prices rise year by year.

(*f*) Tyre histories should be maintained, and tyres with a short life should be detected. If this extra cost can be related to a particular contract the contract burden should be increased. Tyre histories make it easier to decide a fair charge per mile or kilometer for tyres. Similarly a vehicle maintenance record will help detect improper use of the vehicle, and enable a standard maintenance charge to be calculated for each type of vehicle.

Some typical transport statements are shown in Tables 13.1 and 13.2 (pp. 392 and 394–5).

13.6 Local government finance

The finance of local government is a very complex subject and the authors are grateful for background material supplied by the Chartered Institute of Public Finance and Accountancy.

There are three elements in local government structure for England and Wales: London, the metropolitan areas outside London, and the non-metropolitan areas known as the shire counties. This structure covers county councils, district or borough councils, joint authorities and other directly elected bodies. Their functions include the following:

Strategic planning	Refuse collection	Social services
Highways and traffic	Refuse disposal	Libraries
Housing	Transport	Leisure and recreation
Building regulations	Police	Environmental health
Weights and Measures Act	Fire	
Food and Drugs Act	Education	

Local authorities' functions are laid down in various statutes but they often have discretion on the extent to which they carry them out. The Local Government Act 1988 to some extent restricts their freedom and they now have to seek competitive tenders for some of the functions. A local authority must have a sound financial planning system and one of the most important activities is the preparation of the annual budget.

(a) Budgetary control

Local authorities generally use computerised systems to handle the large amount of data involved. Officers have to monitor the actual trends in spending on a periodic basis, usually monthly. It is physically impossible for chief officers to control all the details of spending but there has to be accountable

Table 13.2 Budget for road haulage operations (January–June 19..)

Details	*Costs and revenue Vehicle no. 1 for period*	*Costs and revenue Vehicle no. 1 per working day*	*Vehicle no. 2 costs, etc.*	*Total fleet*
Vehicle no.	2123 ABC			
Date of purchase	1.1.19..			
Capacity	44 tonnes			
Cost	£32 500			
Less tyres	£ 2 500	*(a)*		
	£30 000			
Running costs per km in pence		*(b)*		
Fuel and oil	8.425			
Tyres	1.325			
Repairs/Maintenance	1.236			
	11.786	pence		

Notes:

(a) Since tyres are regarded as a running expense it is usual to deduct these from the value of any vehicle purchase.

(b) These costs are based on current prices at the time the budget is prepared.

Estimated km	40 000	*(c)*	320	*(c)* This estimate is based on previous experience, and 125 days' operations.
Estimated revenue	£25 000	*(d)*	£200	*(d)* As above.
Deduct				
Estimated costs				
Wages	£10 400		£83.20	*(e)* As above.
Licence/Insurance	£ 840		£6.72	*(f)* Factual at the time the estimate is prepared.
Depreciation	£ 6 000		£48.00	*(g)* Straight-line method.
Overheads	£ 1 215		£9.72	*(h)* Allocated on vehicle tonnage basis.*
Running costs	£ 4 795		£38.36	*(i)* Based on estimates above.
	23 250		186.00	
Profit	1 750		14.00	
	£25 000		£200.00	

*Note on *(h)* above:
Total vehicle tonnage = 880 tonnes

Total overheads = £24 300
This vehicle = 44 tonnes

$\frac{44}{880} \times £24\ 300 = £1\ 215$

management, and this will define the roles of the treasurer, chief officers and named line managers in budgetary control. Financial responsibility is often delegated to those nearest to the provision of services, such as officers in charge of residential homes. Because of the Education Reform Act 1988, local education authorities (LEAs) have had to develop new monitoring arrangements to ensure that locally managed schools are keeping within their spending allocations.

To ensure that spending is in line with the budget provision, inflation has to be monitored because budget figures are set on a fixed (usually November) price base, and this has to be taken into account when actual spending is compared with budget.

(b) Virement

This is the permission given to spend more than originally planned on a particular budget head. There should be an avoidance of an increase in aggregate commitments and the object is merely a switch of resources between budget heads. Spending more under one budget head should be matched by a corresponding reduction on some other head. Generally, permission is not given if it gives rise to a continuing commitment such as salaries.

In the past budgetary information tended to relate solely to financial information. Because local authority managers, officers and elected members should also be concerned with work done (output) so that there is value for money, non-financial data are now presented. This acts as an incentive to improving the management of a local authority. A few examples are given below:

(a) refuse collection (number of premises) output measured on number of premises per collector week, and (tonnes collected) measured on cost per tonne collected;

(b) education (number of pupils on roll, by category, and number of places provided, by category) measured by pupil/teacher ratio and cost per pupil week;

(c) social services (number of places provided in centres or homes) measured by an occupancy ratio, and (number of occupiers and period of occupancy) measured by cost per client week.

(c) Day-to-day funding

The management of the cash flow rests with the treasurer, who must carry out the task at minimum cost. S/he is required to collect funds, monitor arrears and take action to recover outstanding amounts as promptly as possible. Payments to creditors are to be managed within an agreed policy on payment periods and any surplus is to be invested for an appropriate period to earn interest. Should there be a deficit it should be covered by borrowing at minimum cost.

The treasurer forecasts cash flow for a period six or twelve months ahead, taking into account the dates and size of each pay bill, when capital expenditure payments fall due and other spending throughout the year, as well as the amounts and dates when any loans may be due for repayment. S/he will also note the dates when major items of income are expected, such as police grant precept income from the collection fund, and will note the pattern of other income receipts throughout the year. The treasurer will usually be aware of the authority's bank balance at the close of the previous day and will be in a position to estimate closely the payments and income during the day. This will enable him or her to make a decision should it be necessary to borrow or lend on that day.

The external auditor will need to be satisfied that an authority has a sound cash management system which is cost effective and secure. The treasurer has to report should there be unlawful expenditure, unlawful action or unlawful entry in the authority's accounts by the authority, one of its committee or one of its officers. S/he should work closely with the management team, being responsible for borrowing and capital finance, cash flow, arranging insurance and managing the investments. There is a duty to collect the income, pay the bills, keep the financial records generally and attend to their presentation for audit.

(d) Internal audit

The Accounts and Audit Regulations 1983 require every local authority to maintain an adequate and effective internal audit. This is intended to be a service to all levels of management and for the review of activities. The internal audit within the organisation is independent and functions as an assessment of the system. It is concerned with the effectiveness of financial and non-financial controls and with the efficient use of resources. It is a report on the soundness, adequacy and application of administrative controls in each department or service, and of controls on computer systems. It is also concerned with the extent to which assets and interests are accounted for and safeguarded from losses. It examines the measures taken to protect the authority from losses arising from waste, extravagance or poor value for money.

There is also a review, appraisal and report on steps taken to prevent and detect fraud and the suitability and reliability of financial and other management data developed within the organisation.

(e) External audit

The Local Government Finance Act 1982 established a new framework for the audit of local authorities in England and Wales. Under Section 15 of the Act, the auditors have to satisfy themselves that the accounts are prepared in accordance with regulations made under Section 23 and comply with the requirements of all statutory provisions applicable to the accounts. The auditors must also be satisfied that proper practices have been observed in the compilation of the accounts and that the body whose accounts are being audited has made proper arrangements for securing economy, efficiency and effectiveness in its use of resources. There is a Code of Audit Practice which sets out the way in which auditors are to fulfil their functions. When the external auditor makes a report in the public interest the elected member should pay particular attention to it, because it is a public document usually drawing attention to things that have gone wrong.

(f) Public inspection facility before audit

The accounts and documents must be available for public inspection for 15 full working days before the audit.

(g) New powers

One section of the Local Government Act 1988 gave the external auditor a 'stop power' in certain circumstances. S/he can issue a prohibition order to a local authority or one of its officers requiring it (or him or her) not to adopt or continue with a specified course of action.

(h) Housing finance

Housing is one of the most important services. The whole system of housing finance changed on 1 April 1990, but it is too involved a subject to be dealt with here. Those with a particular interest should consult *Housing Finance* (2nd edition), published by the Chartered Institute of Public Finance and Accountancy, Publications Dept, 3 Robert St, London WC2N 6BH (tel. 071 930 3456).

(i) Conclusion about local government finance

Clearly this comprehensive range of responsibilities includes both financial accounting aspects and management accounting aspects. In particular the importance of budgeting in local authority work is paramount, while the close auditing of all activities and the possibility that council members will be surcharged for unauthorised expenditures makes local authority finance a serious matter for all concerned.

13.7 Strategic management accounting

The CIMA's *Official Terminology* handbook defines strategic management accounting as 'the preparation and presentation of information for decision making, laying particular stress on external factors'. Another CIMA definition says, 'It is the provision and analysis of management accounting data relating to a business strategy: particularly the relative levels and trends in real costs and prices, volumes, market share, cash flow and the demands on a firm's total resources.' Strategy is defined as 'a course of action, including the specifications of the resources required, to achieve a specific objective'. Therefore it may be the corporative objective, the clearly stated aim of the organisation which should be obtainable with the resources available and provided the necessary effort is applied. There will be a reference to the company's products, to future products and to the share of the market which is expected in the future. The aim is to improve the return on capital employed.

In order to achieve the objectives many factors have to be considered including the resources available, such as factory space, and what will be needed in the future. Manpower requirements, machinery, equipment and layout are other considerations. New systems may have to be installed and all such matters will require finance if the products are to be successfully marketed. The decision on the course of action involves examining the present situation and the corporate objectives for the future concerning finance, marketing and product development and the internal changes which management will have to deal with if the objectives are to be met. Strengths and weaknesses will have to be identified and steps taken to ensure that there will be sufficient working capital to meet the commitments.

When the agreed strategy has been implemented the plan will have to be checked progressively against what has already been achieved. The plan will have to be monitored and updated and the management accountant must provide accounting information to management so that corrective action can be taken if the plan is not being achieved, or so that the plan can be modified if this shoud be necessary. Feedback can occur at a variety of levels; for example, each strategically important area may be subject to immediate feedback in which it might become apparent that the plan is not being achieved or is running ahead of schedule, with consequent cash flow or other implications. Where the general accounting evidence indicates that the plan was not as well conceived at it might have been, or where economic or political changes have made it unattainable, or revealed that the plan could have been more ambitious still, there is a *revision of plans* feedback. This will lead to a new set of instructions to production or service centres. Finally, at the topmost level there can be a *review of policy*. This will usually be started by a report to the board from the chief planning officer, or the chair of the standing committee or *ad hoc* committee charged with putting the strategy into effect.

13.8 Developments in retailing

Nowhere are the economics of large-scale activity more apparent today than in retailing, where the supermarket or hypermarket on the edge of towns is not only eliminating countless local shops, but making good profits because it can take advantage of the consumer revolution in enjoying pre-prepared meals rather than traditional home-cooked meals. Profitability is excellent in this area, but does depend on long-term strategic planning. Competition is intense and in order to maintain profits with a high fixed-cost structure it has been necessary to increase volumes considerably. Emphasis is placed upon outlet size, geographical location, planned geographical coverage and careful control of operations. Rates of growth have to be considered fully and the actions of competitors taken into account. Quality is very important, and product labelling, environmental aspects, etc. play a new and important role. Price is less important than presentation – one chain regularly asks three times as much for its white cabbage as does the local greengrocer.

Capital expenditure planning is a crucial element in the strategic planning of supermarket chains. With expansion depending upon the building of very expensive, highly computerised stores, depots and warehouses, the generation of profits to finance them requires close attention to all aspects of costing. The budgeting process for each store usually starts about four months before the end of the financial year, using 13 four-week 'months', and considers sales, margins, occupancy costs, personnel costs, etc., and net profit. This is followed by a detailed consideration of cost centre responsibilities before a final draft plan is put up for board approval. The budget is then considered over the first few 'months' of the new year, culminating in a reappraisal of objectives for the rest of the year at the end of the sixth four-week period. Supervision of the second half of the year then follows as the next annual plan is prepared.

13.9 Exercises

1. (*a*) What is a report?
(*b*) What would be the chief features of a report to top management on a major matter of company policy?

2. (*a*) What is performance appraisal?
(*b*) If you are in employment explain what your job is and suggest how you would organise an exercise in performance appraisal on the department in which you work. If you are not in employment suggest how you would arrange an exercise in performance appraisal for the educational department in which you are studying. In either case remember to keep your discussion impersonal and objective (that is, viewed from the point of view of a disinterested outsider, seeking only greater efficiency).

3. The production department of your company has prepared a report to management, complaining about the difficulty of maintaining output with the existing equipment, which is now very old. The report makes two suggestions for improving the present situation, (i) the replacement of the plant with identical equipment and (ii) a complete redesign of all the operations, using automation as the objective.

Discuss the procedure and methods which could be used to appraise the proposed projects, in order that management can be supplied with adequate information before making a decision on this problem.

4. You have recently been appointed to the position of chief accountant to a large engineering company and in the course of your investigations into the systems and reporting procedures you have noted that the company uses the pay-back period method when making investment decisions. Write short explanatory notes on this method and other methods which can be used to provide management with suitable information when investment decisions have to be made.

5. The planning department of a manufacturing company are in the process of investigating the merits of two proposed projects. They have collected information on investment costs and cash flows and this is given below.

Investment cost: Project A £200 000 Project B £250 000

Cash flow:

Year	*Project A* £	*Project B* £
1	90 000	60 000
2	80 000	80 000
3	70 000	100 000
4	60 000	120 000

You are required to calculate: (*a*) the pay-back period; (*b*) the average annual return on investment and (*c*) the average annual return on average investment. Taxation is to be ignored.

6. Using the investment cost and the cash flows in the previous question, you are required to discount these by the net present value method. You are to assume that the investment cost is incurred at the beginning of year 1, and that the cost of capital is 20 per cent. Taxation is to be ignored. A table of present value factors is provided in Fig. 13.7. After completion of the cash flow statement and the establishment of the net present value, you are required to write a short note indicating the significance of the figures provided.

7. You are required to calculate the internal rate of return on a proposed project which has been estimated to cost £235 000. The company's minimum rate of return has been set at 20 per cent. Cash flows have been forecast as follows:

(continued overleaf)

	Present value factors							
	5%	10%	15%	20%	25%	30%	35%	40%
Year								
1	0.952	0.909	0.870	0.833	0.800	0.769	0.741	0.714
2	0.907	0.826	0.756	0.694	0.640	0.592	0.549	0.510
3	0.864	0.751	0.658	0.579	0.512	0.455	0.406	0.364
4	0.823	0.683	0.572	0.482	0.410	0.350	0.301	0.260
5	0.784	0.621	0.497	0.402	0.328	0.269	0.223	0.186
6	0.746	0.564	0.432	0.335	0.262	0.207	0.165	0.133
7	0.711	0.513	0.376	0.279	0.210	0.159	0.122	0.095
8	0.677	0.467	0.327	0.233	0.168	0.123	0.091	0.068
9	0.645	0.424	0.284	0.194	0.134	0.094	0.067	0.048
10	0.614	0.386	0.247	0.162	0.107	0.073	0.050	0.035

Fig. 13.7 A table of present value factors

Year	£	*Year*	£
1	100 000	4	60 000
2	120 000	5	30 000
3	80 000		

A table of present value factors is provided in Fig 13.7 (p. 401).

8. What are the chief problems in costing hotel services?

9. Explain why the canteen manager is more interested in short-term planning than long-term planning. Draw up a list of expenses likely to be incurred in providing canteen services to a busy factory.

10. What is strategic management accounting? What factors need to be considered in a review of strategy?

PART TWO

Answer section

Most of the answer units in this section of the book give the following types of assistance to students:

(i) Where the question can best be answered by reading the text again and making quite sure you understand the points discussed, the 'answer' simply consists of a text reference (e.g. 'See Unit 1').
(ii) For most questions the answer is given in detail, with workings fully displayed and reasonably comprehensive lists of suggested points for essay type questions.
(iii) In a few cases, where the workings are fairly obvious, only an abbreviated answer is supplied.

The best way to use this answer section is as follows:

(i) Try each question absolutely 'cold' with no reference at all to the answer and the style in which it is set out.
(ii) If you get hopelessly stuck turn to the answer section and this time work the whole question through to the end of the answer, making sure you follow all the stages of the work.
(iii) Now leave the question for at least seven days and try it again absolutely 'cold'. This will decide whether you have mastered the technique or not.

UNIT 1

Introduction to management accounting

1.1 Suggested answers to exercises

1. See Unit 1.1.

2. See Unit 1.1 (b).

3. See Unit 1.6.

4. See Units 1.3 and 1.12.

5. Points to make:

(a) Classification enables an analysis to be made of overhead costs, under the nature of the item, the type of service provided and by department, cost centre, process and so forth.
(b) Items need to be arranged in logical sequence, having regard to their nature or the purpose to be fulfilled.
(c) Detailed information is provided for the control of overhead expenses.
(d) Certain overhead costs have to be apportioned and classification facilitates the task of collecting the costs of a particular service.
(e) The provision of detailed costs enables the behaviour of costs to be observed.

6. Points to make:

(a) Appraisal of existing production systems and design of new cost-effective systems.
(b) Design of factory layout, including access for wholesalers taking the finished product.
(c) Plant design and construction, and the evaluation, purchase and installation of machinery.
(d) Design of supervision area in each cost centre.
(e) Design of in-house documentation procedure to control production and internal distribution of work-in-progress.
(f) Systems appraisal for office activities, including financial and cost accounting.
(g) Appraisal, purchase and installation of office machinery, fittings and furniture, including internal and external telephones.
(h) Computer programming and test runs.
(i) Relocation assistance to key staff.
(j) Personnel acquisition costs including preparation of job descriptions, system of promotion and merit awards, interviewing costs, etc.

(k) Training and retraining costs.
(l) Customer relation costs, notification of changes of address, revision of entries in trade journals, etc.
(m) Redundancy payments to staff not being relocated.
(n) Disposal costs and losses on existing plant and machinery found unsuitable for use in new location.
(o) Additional work study costs due to the need to use new methods and fix new standards resulting from the new layout of plant and the installation of new machinery.
(p) The possible need for extra working capital.
(q) Cost of the provision of recreational facilities for staff.

7. See Unit 1.7.

UNIT 2

Recording material costs

2.1 Suggested answers to exercises

1. See Unit 2.2.

2. See Unit 2.3 and Fig. 2.6.

3. See Units 2.3 and 2.4.

4. See Units 2.1 and 2.2.

5. See Unit 2.3 (Fig. 2.5).

6. Points to make, and documents that should be mentioned:

(a) The authorised officer concerned with production control presents the purchasing officer with 'purchase requisitions' for the materials required for batch production. These are ordered by the purchasing department; as they are received they are entered on the stock record card, and issued as required for batch production. The production controller also arranges for the manufacture of parts which are received by the stores department for eventual issue to the production departments for batch production.

(b) Goods received note.

(c) Bin card.

(d) Stores record card.

(e) Materials requisition.

(f) Materials return note.

(g) Material transfer note.

7. *(a)* See Unit 2.3 (Fig. 2.4).

(b) See Unit 2.2 (Fig. 2.2).

(c) See Unit 2.2 (Fig. 2.3).

(d) See Unit 2.2 (Fig. 2.1).

(e) See Unit 2.3 (Fig. 2.5).

UNIT 3

Stores control and the pricing of requisitions

3.1 Suggested answers to exercises

1. *Functions of the stock controller:*

(a) Management of storehouses and stockyards.
(b) Accepting or rejecting materials after inspection and checking.
(c) Responsibility for the recording of receipts and issues of materials on the bin cards (see Unit 3.3 and Fig. 3.2).
(d) Preparation of purchase requisitions in respect of low stocks.
(e) Issuing materials on the authority of material requisitions.
(f) Responsibility for the safe custody and protection of stock so as to avoid loss and deterioration.

Reasons why the stock control function must be efficiently performed:

(a) Production departments need a balanced flow of materials to suit their requirements.
(b) Excessive handling must be avoided as this increases the cost but not the value of the goods.
(c) Efficient handling improves productivity.
(d) Faulty storage leads to deterioration of materials.

2. *(a)* Weighted average:

Receipts:	10 Sept.	180 at £200 each	= £36 000	
Issues:	14 Sept.	135 at £200 each	= £27 000	
Balance:		45 at £200 each	= £ 9 000	
Receipts:	17 Sept.	180 at £240 each	= £43 200	(£9 000 + £43 200 = £52 200)
Balance:		225 at £232 each	= £52 200	(£52 200 divided by 225 = £232)
Issues:	24 Sept.	135 at £232 each	= £31 320	
Balance:		90 at £232 each	= £20 880	

(b) FIFO:

Receipts:	10 Sept.	180 at £200 each	= £36 000
Issues:	14 Sept.	135 at £200 each	= £27 000
Balance:		45 at £200 each	= £ 9 000
Receipts:	17 Sept.	180 at £240 each	= £43 200
Balance:		225	= £52 200
Issues:	24 Sept.	45 at £200 each	= £ 9 000
	24 Sept.	90 at £240 each	= £21 600
Balance:		90 at £240 each	£21 600 [£52 200 less (£9 000 + £21 600)]

(c) LIFO:

Receipts:	10 Sept.	180 at £200 each	= £36 000
Issues:	14 Sept.	135 at £200 each	= £27 000
Balance:		45 at £200 each	= £ 9 000
Receipts:	17 Sept.	180 at £240 each	= £43 200
Balance:		225	= £52 200
Issues:	24 Sept.	135 at £240 each	= £32 400
Balance:		90	= £19 800 [(45 at £240) + (45 at £200)]

3. *(a)* Points to make:

(i) Personnel required to count, weigh etc. and record the stock.
(ii) Provision of pre-printed stock sheets.
(iii) Decision on 'cut-off' points so that there is no duplication of costs and sales. See Unit 3.5 (d).
(iv) Arranging for identification of obsolete stock and scrap.
(v) Written instructions needed for those engaged on stocktaking.

(b) Points to make:

(i) A stricter control of stock helps to reduce the loss due to pilferage and wastage.
(ii) Deterioration and other storage faults are detected earlier and losses may be avoided.
(iii) Records will provide information for determination of maximum and minimum stock and will enable optimum order size to be established.
(iv) Interim accounts can be prepared without special stocktaking.
(v) With continuous stocktaking the perpetual records can be used, and the dislocation of annual stocktaking can be avoided.

4. *(a)*

Finished Goods Stock Ledger Account, part no. B2481

Date	Receipts: Quantity	Price	Value	Issues: Quantity	Price	Value	Stock: Quantity	Price	Value
19..		£	£		£	£		£	£
June 3							400	8.60	3 440
5				160	8.600	1 376	240	8.60	2 064
9	240	9.000	2 160				480	8.80	4 224
12				300	8.800	2 640	180	8.80	1 584
17	400	9.090	3 636				580	9.00	5 220
23				200	9.000	1 800	380	9.00	3 420
28	120	9.625	1 155				500	9.15	4 575
29				360	9.150	3 294	140	9.15	1 281
30				20	9.150	183	120	9.15	1 098

(b) (i) £9 110; (ii) £1 098; (iii) £183.

5. *(a)*

Stores Ledger Account, part no. C2149

Date	Receipts: Quantity	Price	Value	Issues: Quantity	Price	Value	Stock: Quantity	Price	Value
(i) *Weighted average*		£	£		£	£		£	£
July 1							1 100	10.50	11 550
7	4 400	11.80	51 920				5 500	11.54	63 470
16				3 500	11.54	40 390	2 000	11.54	23 080
23	2 000	12.46	24 920				4 000	12.00	48 000
28				2 500	12.00	30 000	1 500	12.00	18 000
(ii) *First in, first out*									
July 1							1 100	10.50	11 550
7	4 400	11.80	51 920				5 500		63 470
16				1 100	10.50	11 550			
				2 400	11.80	28 320			
				3 500		39 870	2 000		23 600
23	2 000	12.46	24 920				4 000		48 520
28				2 000	11.80	23 600			
				500	12.46	6 230			
				2 500		29 830	1 500	12.46	18 690
(iii) *Last in, first out*									
July 1							1 100	10.50	11 550
7	4 400	11.80	51 920				5 500		63 470
16				3 500	11.80	41 300	2 000		22 170
23	2 000	12.46	24 920				4 000		47 090
28				2 000	12.46	24 920			
				500	11.80	5 900			
				2 500		30 820	1 500		16 270

(b) *Weighted average:* this method is very satisfactory as it assumes that the values of identical items are equal. It tends to even out the fluctuations which may occur with other methods. *First in, first out:* this method is based on cost but the prices charged to contracts, jobs, etc. when parts are issued tend to lag behind current conditions. *Last in, first out:* this method keeps the prices charged when parts are issued close to current conditions, but when valuing stock the final stock value will be out of line with current prices.

6. (a) See Fig. 3.10 (p. 412).

(b)

X	£
Write off 30 units at £42.00 each =	1 260
Adjust stock card balance to 270	
Raise Journal entry:	
Debit Stock Loss A/c	1 260
Credit Stores Ledger A/c	1 260

Y	£
Adjust stock card balance to 195	
Raise Journal entry:	
Debit Stores Ledger A/c	75
Credit Stock Loss A/c	75

Z	£
Adjust stock card balance to 730	
Raise Journal entry:	
Debit Stores Ledger A/c	37.50
Credit Stock Loss A/c	37.50

(c) Possible reasons are:

(i) failure to record.
(ii) clerical errors on the stock record card.
(iii) postings to the wrong card or stock account.
(iv) theft and falsification.
(v) over- (or under-) issue
(vi) losses on breaking bulk, or loss (or gain) of weight by evaporation (or absorption of moisture).

Possible remedies are:

(i) spot checks on issue quantities.
(ii) storekeeper recording stock balance on each material requisition for reconciliation with Stores Ledger balance.
(iii) better control over physical security of stores.
(iv) calculating allowances for breaking bulk, evaporation, etc.

7. (a) FIFO: Receipts: £6 000; £1 575; £3 500; £3 300.
Issues: £4 800; £1 200; £1 575; £2 450.
Balance: 400 £6 000; 500 £7 575; 700 £11 075; 380 £6 275; 580 £9 575; 260 £4 350.

Continuous stock check			Date		Sheet no.				
Item	Description	Physical stock	Balance per: stock card	stores ledger	Cost per unit £	Action to be taken	Authorised	Stock card adjusted	Journal entry made
X		270	300	300	42.00				
Y		195	190	190	15.00				
Z		730	680	700	1.25				

Fig. 3.10 A form for checking stock

(b) LIFO: Receipts: £6 000; £1 575; £3 500; £3 300.
Issues: £3 500; £1 575; £300; £3 300; £1 800.
Balance: 400 £6 000; 500 £7 575; 700 £11 075; 380 £5 700; 580 £9 000; 260 £3 900.

8. *(a)* FIFO: Receipts: £186.00; £87.00; £339.00; £108.00; £22.65.
Issues: £148.80; £37.20; £87.00; £33.90.
Balance: 50 £186.00; 70 £273.00; 170 £612.00; 130 £463.20; 150 £571.20; 110 £413.10; 115 £435.75.

(b) LIFO: Receipts: £186.00; £87.00; £339.00; £108.00; £22.65.
Issues: £135.60; £108.00; £67.80.
Balance: 50 £186.00; 70 £273.00; 170 £612.00; 130 £476.40; 150 £584.40; 110 £408.60; 115 £431.25.

(c) AVCO: Receipts: £186.00; £87.00; £339.00; £108.00; £22.65.
Issues: £144.00; £153.60.
Balance: 50 £186.00; 70 £273.00; 170 £612.00; 130 £468.00; 150 £576.00; 110 £422.40; 115 £445.05.

Reconciliation: *(a)* FIFO: 5 at £4.53 = £22.65; 20 at £5.40 = £108.00; 90 at £3.39 = £305.10. *Total* 115 £435.75.
(b) LIFO: 5 at £4.53 = £22.65; 40 at £3.39 = £135.60; 20 at £4.35 = £87.00; 50 at £3.72 = £186.00. *Total* 115 £431.25.

9. See Unit 3.2.

10. *(a)*

Stores ledger

Date	Receipts: Quantity	Price	Value	Issues: Quantity	Price	Value	Balance: Quantity	Price	Value
		£	£		£	£		£	£
FIFO:									
b/f	100	39.000	3 900				100		3 900
May	100	41.000	4 100				200		8 000
June	200	50.000	10 000				400		18 000
July				250 100	39.000				
				100	41.000				
				50	50.000	10 500	150		7 500
Aug.	400	51.875	20 750				550		28 250
Sep.				350 150	50.000				
				200	51.875	17 875	200		10 375
Oct.				100	51.875	5 188	100		5 187
LIFO:									
b/f	100	39.000	3 900				100		3 900
May	100	41.000	4 100				200		8 000
June	200	50.000	10 000				400		18 000

Date	Receipts: Quantity	Price	Value	Issues: Quantity	Price	Value	Balance: Quantity	Price	Value
		£	£		£	£		£	£
July				250 200	50.000				
				50	41.000	12 050	150		5 950
Aug.	400	51.875	20 750				550		26 700
Sep.				350	51.875	18 156	200		8 544
Oct.				100 50	51.875				
				50	41.000	4 644	100		3 900
Weighted average:									
b/f	100	39.000	3 900				100	39.000	3 900
May	100	41.000	4 100				200	40.000	8 000
June	200	50.000	10 000				400	45.000	18 000
July				250	45.000	11 250	150	45.000	6 750
Aug.	400	51.875	20 750				550	50.000	27 500
Sep.				350	50.000	17 500	200	50.000	10 000
Oct.				100	50.000	5 000	100	50.000	5 000

(b)

Trading Accounts

	FIFO	LIFO	Weighted average
Sales	£	£	£
250 at £64	16 000		
350 at £70	24 500		
100 at £74	7 400		
	47 900	47 900	47 900
Cost of goods sold	33 563	34 850	33 750
Gross profit	£14 337	£13 050	£14 150

(c) The best measurement of profit of the three methods is LIFO, because in a situation where there is a gradual increase in prices, the value of the issues is very close to current costs. Each of the three methods used is based on cost, but LIFO is the one which is at current cost or which is only slightly behind replacement cost.

The weighted average methods deals with the fluctuations in cost, but lags further behind current cost and is usually somewhere between FIFO and LIFO.

The figures can be misleading if purchases are made at special or exceptional prices, and in this example it would depend on whether the quantities ordered are to be repeated. If not, the LIFO price is well below replacement cost and the stated gross profit of £13 050 is somewhat misleading because it is too high; the other figures are even higher, and therefore even more misleading.

Should the normal or replacement cost of £58 (£51.875 + £6.125) be used, the profit would be only £10 600 (£13 050 *less* 400 at £6.125) instead of £13 050 as shown when using LIFO. Therefore it may be more prudent to use replacement cost in order to show more realistic figures. If profits are overstated, cash is likely to be withdrawn from the business in the form of dividends, and it will not be available to maintain stocks at their present levels.

11. Cost and handling charges = 40% of £12.50
$$= £5$$

(a)
$$\text{EOQ} = \sqrt{\frac{2\text{CoD}}{\text{Ch}}} = \sqrt{\frac{2 \times £12 \times 3000}{£5}}$$
$$= \sqrt{2 \times 12 \times 600}$$
$$= \sqrt{14\,400}$$
$$= 120 \text{ units}$$

(b)
$$\text{Number of orders per year} = \frac{3000}{120}$$
$$= 25 \text{ orders}$$

12. *(a)* The economic order quantity is a figure calculated after consideration of the cost of placing an order, the capital costs of stock, the cost of storage and the amount of accommodation available. The re-order quantity is set at a figure which is estimated to secure the lowest cost for each item purchased. It takes into account the fact that frequent re-ordering increases costs, and also that infrequency increases costs due to the amount invested in stocks and the resulting holding costs and other expenses. It is therefore necessary to find a balance between holding and re-ordering in order to find the most favourable quantity. This process can be shown graphically: see Fig. 3.1. in the main text.

The economic order quantity (EOQ) can be calculated by the use of a formula:

$$\text{EOQ} = \sqrt{\frac{2\text{CoD}}{\text{Ch}}}$$

where Co = cost of ordering
D = demand per annum for the item
Ch = cost of capital and handling charges (usually expressed as a percentage on cost)

(b)

Orders per annum	1	2	3	4	5	6
Re-order quantity	600	300	200	150	120	100
Average stock (units)	300	150	100	75	60	50
Value of average stock	720	360	240	180	144	120
Stockholding cost	144	72	48	36	28.8	24
Annual cost of re-ordering	6	12	18	24	30	36
Total cost	150	84	66	60	58.8	60

The lowest cost is shown for a re-order quantity of 120 for five orders per annum. Using the formula:

$$EOQ = \sqrt{\frac{2CoD}{Ch}} = \sqrt{\frac{2 \times 6 \times 600}{0.48}}$$

$$= \sqrt{1500} = \underline{\underline{122}}$$

This is almost the same as the answer of 120 found in the table above.

(c) There are three variables involved which, although difficult to establish, are required if a fairly accurate forecast is to be made.

(i) *The rate of consumption or usage.* This can be found by referring to past records or by an estimate based on production and sales expected in the future.

(ii) *Cost of re-ordering.* This is not an easy calculation, due to the variety of work carried out in the purchasing department for different products and for different purposes, but a figure has to be placed on the cost of dealing with orders and the expenses of receiving and inspecting the goods.

(iii) *The storage and holding cost.* This includes the interest on capital invested in stock, together with other charges such as those of deterioration and obsolescence, insurance and certain handling costs.

13. See Unit 3.13.

14. Points to make:

(a) Just-in-time activities are activities which seek to arrange production and distribution so that materials, components and finished goods reach the workshop, depot or customer just before they are wanted.

The advantages of the system are that stocks are not held, thus saving capital tied up in unutilised stocks and warehousing space. Documentation, security staffing, etc. are almost eliminated. Materials arrive on the factory floor just in time to be used, and are turned into finished goods just in time to be collected by customers. Purchases are ordered up daily for next-day delivery if a variation from the standard daily delivery appears necessary. Any hold-up in production stops the whole line; workers turn over to training sessions, tidying up or other useful activities.

(b) (i) Stocks of materials and components are not held. They are delivered as required by suppliers who have been briefed on requirements and who take responsibility for quality.

(ii) Cost records are kept to a minimum and costs for estimating and invoicing are calculated by working backwards from the finished product.

(iii) To work properly everyone must be brought into the system and made responsible for their own quality of work, delivery times, etc.

UNIT 4

Accounting for labour costs

4.1 Suggested answers to exercises

1. Points to make:
   (a) (i) High unit costs due to low output of new employees.
   (ii) Excessive cost of scrap and spoilage.
   (iii) Low output requiring overtime and extra costs in order to meet production targets.
   (iv) Trainees and inefficient workers increase the cost of tools and the wear and tear on machines.
   (v) High training and recruitment costs.
   (b) (i) Improve morale by better training and improved working conditions.
   (ii) Provide financial incentives for increased output and improve promotion prospects.
   (iii) Ensure that welfare facilities are adequate and arrange for social activities.
   (iv) Transmit information by good communications and improve relations by allowing participation in suitable areas of the business.
   (c) See Unit 4.4.

2. **Order no. 2075**
   (a) Cost under Halsey 50–50 scheme:

Time allowed	12 hours 30 minutes
Time taken	9 hours 30 minutes
Time saved	3 hours

Labour cost = (Time taken + 50% of Time saved) × Time rate
$= (9\frac{1}{2}$ hours + 50% of 3 hours) × £4.50
$= (9\frac{1}{2}$ hours + $1\frac{1}{2}$ hours) × £4.50
= 11 hours at £4.50 = £49.50

(b) Cost under Rowan scheme:

$$\text{Bonus as } \textit{percentage} \text{ of time rate} = \frac{\text{Time saved}}{\text{Time allowed}} \text{ per cent}$$

$$= \frac{3}{12\frac{1}{2}} \times 100 \text{ per cent} = 24\%$$

$$\therefore \text{ Bonus} = 24\% \text{ of } £4.50 = £1.08$$

$$\text{Rate per hour for time taken} = £4.50 + £1.08 = £5.58$$

$$\text{Labour cost} = 9\tfrac{1}{2} \text{ hours at } £5.58 = \underline{\underline{£53.01}}$$

$$\text{Bonus as a } \textit{fraction} \text{ of time rate} = \frac{\text{Time saved}}{\text{Time allowed}} \times \text{Time rate}$$

$$= \frac{3}{12\tfrac{1}{2}} \times £4.50$$

$$= \frac{6}{25} \times £4.50$$

$$= \underline{\underline{£1.08}}$$

$$\text{Rate per hour for time taken} = £4.50 + £1.08 = £5.58$$

$$\text{Labour cost} = 9\tfrac{1}{2} \text{ hours at } £5.58 = \underline{\underline{£53.01}}$$

3. *Time allowed*:

Product	Units produced	Time allowed per unit (minutes)	Total time allowed (hours)
X	80	63	84
Y	160	120	320
Z	300	100	500
			904

Hours worked:

Grade of employee	Number of employees	Hours worked per employee	Total hours worked
L	10	15	150
M	4	32	128
N	16	25	400
			678

(a) Percentage of hours saved to hours taken:
Hours allowed (904) *less* Hours worked (678) = Hours saved (226)

$$\text{Percentage} = \frac{\text{Hours saved}}{\text{Hours worked}} \times 100$$

$$= \frac{226}{678} \times 100 = \underline{\underline{33\tfrac{1}{3}\ \%}}$$

(b) *Total bonus payable:*

Grade of employee	Hours worked	Bonus $33\frac{1}{3}$% (hours)	Rate (= Base rate – £1.50) £	Bonus £
L	150	50	2.50	125.00
M	128	$42\frac{2}{3}$	2.10	89.60
N	400	$133\frac{1}{3}$	2.20	293.33
	678	226		£507.93

(c) *Total wages payable:*

Grade of employee	Hours worked	Base rate £	Wages £	Bonus £	Total £
L	150	4.00	600.00	125.00	725.00
M	128	3.60	460.80	89.60	550.40
N	400	3.70	1 480.00	293.33	1 773.33
	678		£2 540.80	£507.93	£3 048.73

4. Time allowed 58 + 280 + 1 000 = 1 338 hours
Hours worked 400 + 192 + 360 = 952 hours
Percentage of hours saved to hours taken = 40.5%

Bonuses payable £324 + £233.28 + £379.08 = £936.36

Total wages payable £1 524 + £1 001.28 + £1 675.08 = £4 200.36

5. Wages cost of bonus paid, gross wages and units produced:

Employee A:

(a) Time allowed 70 hours
Time taken 49 hours
Time saved 21 hours
Bonus = 21 hours at 50% of £4.00 per hour = £42.00

(b) Time taken 49 hours
Overtime premium 3 hours
Gross wages = 52 hours at £4.00 + bonus £42.00
= £208 + bonus £42 = £250

(c) Wages cost per unit of goods passing inspection:

$$= \frac{\text{Gross wages}}{\text{Units passed inspection}} = \frac{£250}{32} = £7.81$$

Employee B:

(a) Time allowed 90 hours
Time taken 46 hours
Time saved 44 hours
Bonus = 44 hours at 50% of £4.00 per hour = £88.00

(b) Time taken 46 hours
Overtime premium 2 hours
Gross wages = 48 hours at £4.00 + bonus £88.00
= £192 + bonus £88 = £280.00

(c) Wages cost per unit of goods passing inspection:

$$= \frac{\text{Gross wages}}{\text{Units passed inspection}} = \frac{£280}{56} = £5.00$$

6. **Balken Manufacturing Company**
Methods include:

(a) attendance time (book, or mechanically or electronically recorded);
(b) activity or job time (operation cards);
(c) time sheets (daily or weekly);
(d) day-work and piece-work cards.

Some of the disadvantages are;
(i) clerical time involved in calculating operation time on individual jobs and reconciling these with attendance time;
(ii) need to reconcile operation time with attendance time.

7.

Journal

19..			£	£
30 Sep.	Wages Expense Account	Dr. L.98	14503	
	Social Security Account			
	(employees' £947; employer's £984)	L.62		1 931
	Income Tax Account (PAYE)	L.87		1 792
	Recreation club			
	(employees' £58; employer's £342)			400
	Wages Payable Account	L.99		10 380
	Being details extracted from Payroll for week ended 30 September 19..			

UNIT 5

Accounting for overhead costs

5.1 Suggested answers to exercises

1. *(a)* See Units 5.3 and 5.5
   (b) See Units 5.3, and 5.4 and 5.5.
   (c) See Units 5.7, 5.8 and 5.9.

2. *(a)* See Units 5.2, 5.3 and 5.4.
   (b) See Unit 5.4.

3. See Units 5.5 and 5.6.

4. See Units 5.4, 5.6, 5.8 and 5.9.

5. Five methods of absorbing factory overheads are shown below, although the question only calls for three of them. Some of the calculations required are also shown below (under the sub-heading 'Workings').
   Note: There is insufficient information to show the machine hour rate.
   Method (i) Percentage of prime cost:

Product	A		B
Production	800		1 500
	£		£
Direct material	3.350		3.700
Direct labour	8.400		7.500
Prime cost	11.750		11.200
Overhead: 350% of 11.750	41.125	350% of 11.200	39.200
	£52.875		£50.400

Method (ii) Percentage of direct material cost:

	£		£
Direct material	3.350		3.700
Direct labour	8.400		7.500
Prime cost	11.750		11.200
Overhead: 1 114% of 3.350	37.319	1 114% of 3.700	41.218
	£49.069		£52.418

Method (iii) Percentage of direct labour cost:

	£		£
Direct material	3.350		3.700
Direct labour	8.400		7.500
Prime cost	11.750		11.200
Overhead: 510% of 8.400	42.840	510% of 7.500	38.250
	£54.590		£49.450

Method (iv) Rate per direct labour hour:

	£		£
Direct material	3.350		3.700
Direct labour	8.400		7.500
Prime cost	11.750		11.200
Overhead: 7 hours × £7	49.000	5 hours × £7	35.000
	£60.750		£46.200

Method (v) Rate per unit of product:

	£		£
Direct material	3.350		3.700
Direct labour	8.400		7.500
Prime cost	11.750		11.200
Overhead: £39.870 per unit	39.870	£39.870 per unit	39.870
	£51.620		£51.070

Workings:

	£	£
Total prime cost =	800 × 11.750 =	9 400
=	1 500 × 11.200 =	16 800
		£26 200

(i) *Prime cost rate* $= \dfrac{\text{Overhead}}{\text{Prime cost}} \times 100 = \dfrac{£91\,700}{£26\,200} \times 100 = 350\%$

(ii) *Direct material rate*

Total direct material cost $= (800 \times £3.350) + (1\,500 \times £3.700)$
$= £2\,680 + £5\,550 = £8\,230$

Percentage $= \dfrac{\text{Overhead}}{\text{Material cost}} \times 100 = \dfrac{£91\,700}{£8\,230} \times 100 = 1\,114\%$

(iii) *Direct labour rate*

Total direct labour cost $= (800 \times £8.400) + (1\,500 \times £7.500)$
$= £6\,720 + £11\,250 = £17\,970$

$$\text{Percentage} = \frac{\text{Overhead}}{\text{Direct labour cost}} \times 100 = \frac{£91\,700}{£17\,970} \times 100 = \underline{\underline{510\%}}$$

(iv) *Direct labour hour rate*
Total direct labour hours = $(800 \times 7) + (1\,500 \times 5)$
= 5 600 + 7 500 = 13 100 hours

$$\text{Rate per hour} = \frac{\text{Overhead}}{\text{Direct labour hours}} = \frac{£91\,700}{13\,100} = \underline{\underline{£7.00}}$$

(v) *Rate per unit*
Total numbers of units = 800 + 1 500 = 2 300

$$\text{Rate per unit} = \frac{\text{Overhead}}{\text{Units produced}} = \frac{£91\,700}{2\,300} = \underline{\underline{£39.87}}$$

6. *(a)* Budgeted overheads for year 19..:

	X	Y	Z
	£	£	£
Production department	200 000	211 900	95 000
Service departments: A	29 000	40 600	46 400
B	28 500	42 750	23 750
	257 500	295 250	165 150

Overhead rates: $\frac{£257\,500}{206\,000}$ $\frac{£295\,250}{147\,625}$ $\frac{£165\,150}{£275\,250} \times 100$

= £1.25 = £2.00 = 60%

(b) Overhead absorbed June 19..:

		£
Department X	18 000 hours at £1.25	22 500
Y	12 000 hours at £2.00	24 000
Z	60% of £22 000	13 200
		59 700
Overhead incurred June 19..:		61 000
Overhead under-absorbed:		£ 1 300

7. *(a)* First we must calculate the variable cost per unit and the fixed overheads. We can then use this information to find the change in activity (the monthly change in units produced) and the changes in direct material and direct labour costs.

	Units produced	Monthly change in units	Direct material costs £	Change in direct material £	Direct labour costs £	Change in direct labour £
October	6 200	–	43 400	–	34 100	–
November	8 600	2 400	60 200	16 800	47 300	13 200
December	5 000	3 600	35 000	25 200	27 500	19 800

Direct materials:

In November 2 400 extra units costs an extra £16 800 = £7 per unit
In December 3 600 fewer units saved £25 200 = £7 per unit

Direct labour:

In November 2 400 extra units cost an extra £13 200 = £5.50 per unit
In December 3 600 fewer units saved £19 800 = £5.50 per unit

If we calculate the change in activity (the monthly change in units) and compare it with the monthly change in overheads, we shall find what relation exists between them:

	Units produced	Monthly change in units	Overhead expenses £	Monthly change in overheads £
October	6 200	–	77 200	–
November	8 600	2 400	91 600	14 400
December	5 000	3 600	70 000	21 600

November: £14 400 ÷ 2 400 = £6 per unit
December: £21 600 ÷ 3 600 = £6 per unit

These calculations show that when output rises (or falls), the overheads rise (or fall) £6 for each unit of production. There is therefore a *variable overhead cost* of £6 per unit.

We can now eliminate the variable overheads from the total overhead costs and this will leave the *fixed overheads.*

Fixed overheads = Overhead expenses *less* Variable overheads
October: Overhead expenses *less* (6 200 units × £6)
= £77 200 − £37 200 = £40 000
November: £91 600 *less* (8 600 × £6)
= £91 600 − £51 600 = £40 000
December: £70 000 *less* (5 000 × £6)
= £70 000 − £30 000 = £40 000

This establishes that fixed overheads per month are £40 000.

We therefore find that the change in activity shows that material costs are £7 per unit, labour costs are £5.50 per unit, variable overhead costs are £6 per unit and fixed overheads are £40 000.

(b)

Cost Statement
September 19. . : 7 500 units

	Units	*Per unit*	*Cost*
		£	£
Direct material	7 500	7.00	52 500
Direct labour	7 500	5.50	41 250
Prime cost			93 750
Variable overhead	7 500	6.00	45 000
Variable cost			138 750
Fixed overhead			40 000
Total factory cost			£178 750

8. *(a)*

Digby Manufacturing Company: Overhead Distribution Statement

	Production departments			*Service departments*		
	Machining	Fitting	Painting and packing	Tool room	General services	Total
	£	£	£	£	£	£
Indirect materials				4 500		4 500
Indirect labour				8 000	11 000	19 000
Other costs	90 050	29 000	18 010	18 000	5 000	160 060
Total	90 050	29 000	18 010	30 500	16 000	183 560
Distribution of service dept costs:						
Tool room	15 250	12 200	3 050	(30 500)		
General services	6 400	4 800	3 200	1 600	(16 000)	
Tool room	800	640	160	(1 600)		
Production overhead	112 500	46 640	24 420	—	—	183 560

(b) *Absorption rates:*

(i) Machining: Direct labour hours:

11 000
9 000
2 500
22 500

$$\text{Rate} = \frac{\text{Overhead}}{\text{Direct hours}} = \frac{£112\,500}{22\,500}$$

$$= £5.00 \text{ per direct labour hour}$$

(ii) Fitting: Percentage on direct wages:

		£
6 600 hours at £2.60 per hour	=	17 160
4 476 hours at £2.50 per hour	=	11 190
Total direct wages	=	28 350

$$\text{Rate} = \frac{\text{Overhead}}{\text{Direct wages}} \times 100 = \frac{£46\,640}{£28\,350} \times 100$$

$$= 164\% \text{ of direct wages}$$

(iii) Painting and packing: Rate per unit of production:

$$= \frac{\text{Overhead}}{\text{Production units}} = \frac{£24\,420}{3\,000} = £8.14 \text{ per unit}$$

9.

	Basis of apportionment	*Departmental overheads* Machine groups 1	2	3	4	5	Total
		£	£	£	£	£	£
Rent and rates	Area	17 280	34 560	8 640	17 280	8 640	86 400
Insurance of buildings	Area	1 440	2 880	720	1 440	720	7 200
Insurance of machinery	Value	900	4 500	1 800	7 200	3 600	18 000
Depreciation of machinery	Value	7 250	36 250	14 500	58 000	29 000	145 000
Power	Kilowatts	2 520	3 780	2 520	6 300	10 080	25 200
Heat and light	Area	2 880	5 760	1 440	2 880	1 440	14 400
General expenses	Working hours	3 600	5 760	2 160	2 880	7 200	21 600
Supervision	Working hours	28 800	46 080	17 280	23 040	57 600	172 800
Maintenance	Direct	12 600	14 400	21 600	30 600	18 000	97 200
Consumable supplies	Direct	5 400	10 800	18 000	21 600	34 200	90 000
		82 670	164 770	88 660	171 220	170 480	677 800
Machine operating hours		25 000	40 000	15 000	20 000	50 000	150 000
Rates per machine hour		£3.31	£4.12	£5.91	£8.56	£3.41	

Workings (units have been reduced to convenient values):

Machine group	Units of area ($100m^2$)	Units of value (£'000)	Units of power (7½ kW)	Units of operating hours (1 000 hours)
1	10	45	2	25
2	20	225	3	40
3	5	90	2	15
4	10	360	5	20
5	5	180	8	50
Total	50	900	20	150

$$\text{Price per unit} = \frac{\text{Total cost}}{\text{Total units}}$$

Basis of apportionment

Area (per 100m²)	Rent and rates:	$\frac{£86\,400}{50} = £1\,728$
	Insurance of buildings	$\frac{£7\,200}{50} = £144$
	Heat and light	$\frac{£14\,400}{50} = £288$
Value (per £1 000)	Insurance of machinery	$\frac{£18\,000}{900} = £20$
	Depreciation	$\frac{£145\,000}{900} = £161.11$
Power (per 7½ kW)		$\frac{£25\,200}{20} = £1\,260$
Working hours (per 1 000 hours)	General expenses	$\frac{£21\,600}{150} = £144$
	Supervision	$\frac{£172\,800}{150} = £1\,152$

10. *(a)* See Unit 5.9.

(b)

Budgeted Overhead Variance Statement

	Department A	Department B	Department C
	£	£	£
Budgeted overhead	38 500	47 000	100 000
Less Overhead incurred	33 000	44 000	54 000
Overhead variance	£5 500	£3 000	£46 000

Workings:

Department A: overhead absorbed of £30 800 is taken as 80% of normal capacity.

Department B: overhead absorbed of £47 000 is taken as 100% of normal capacity.

Department C: overhead absorbed of £50 000 is taken as 50% of normal capacity.

The budgeted overhead can therefore be found as follows:

For Department A,

$$\text{Budgeted overhead} = \frac{£30\,800}{80} \times 100 = £38\,500$$

For Department C,

$$\text{Budgeted overhead} = \frac{£50\,000}{50} \times 100 = £100\,000$$

11. *(a)* Current overhead absorption rate

$$= \frac{\text{Total budgeted production overhead}}{\text{Budgeted total direct wages cost}} \times 100$$

$$= \frac{225\,000}{150\,000} \times 100 = \underline{\underline{150\%}}$$

(b)

Job no. 657

	£
Direct materials	190
Direct wages	170
Prime cost	360
Production overhead = £170 × $\frac{150}{100}$	255
Production cost	615
Gross profit = $\frac{1}{3}$ × £615	205
Selling price	820

(c) (i) Departmental overhead absorption rates would result in more accurate job costs because departmental overhead costs vary considerably, and when related to departmental direct wages show 480 per cent, 30 per cent and 300 per cent compared with the single rate of 150 per cent. The single rate hides the fact that these costs are not identical, and the individual rates indicate that the incidence of overhead cost on departments is far from equal. The application of an average rate results in incorrect costs, with some work being underpriced and other work overpriced. As selling prices are fixed on a cost-plus basis, any defect in the method of costing is reflected in the selling price, and this may result in lost orders and reduced profits. The use of departmental rates will ensure a more accurate distribution and asborption of overhead costs.

(ii) *Department A:*

From the hourly figures provided it appears that this department is machine-based with employees operating more than one machine. Assuming that the machines are more or less identical, a machine hour rate may be more appropriate for this department. It is calculated as follows:

$$\frac{\text{Overhead cost}}{\text{Machine hours}} = \frac{£120\,000}{40\,000} = \underline{\underline{£3 \text{ per machine hour}}}$$

Should the machines vary considerably in size, cost and so on, then further information would be required in order to fix an equitable rate for each group of machines.

Department B:

This department is only partially mechanised, with direct labour predominating, and in this case the direct labour rate is the ideal base as labour operations are the central factor in production.

$$\frac{\text{Overhead cost}}{\text{Direct labour hours}} = \frac{£30\,000}{50\,000} = \underline{\underline{£0.60 \text{ per direct labour hour}}}$$

Department C:

Here the labour operations are again the central factor, and a direct labour rate would seem to be the best.

$$\frac{\text{Overhead cost}}{\text{Direct labour hours}} = \frac{£75\,000}{25\,000} = \underline{\underline{£3.00 \text{ per direct labour hour}}}$$

(d) Overhead absorbed by job no. 657:

				£
Department	A	40 machine hours	at £3.00 =	120
	B	40 direct labour hours	at £0.60 =	24
	C	10 direct labour hours	at £3.00 =	30
Total				174

(e) Overhead over/under-absorption:

	Dept A	Dept B	Dept C	Total
	£	£	£	£
(i) *Using 150 per cent on direct wages cost:*				
Overhead absorbed	45	120	45	210
Actual overheads	130	28	80	238
Over/under-absorption	(85)	92	(35)	(28)
(ii) *Using departmental absorption rates:*				
Overhead absorbed	135	27	90	252
Actual overheads	130	28	80	238
Over/under-absorption	5	(1)	10	14

12. *(a)* See Unit 5.12.

(b) Points to make:

(i) The engineering costs of setting up are much greater with product no. 2.

(ii) Since the costs are allocated on the basis of volume of turnover, product no. 1 will carry most of the burden. The result will be that it is costed too high and product no. 2 is costed too low.

(iii) If the costs are collected into cost pools relating to the cost-driver that is generating the activity, we shall have a more accurate guide to the costs of the two products, and hence their viability.

13. *(a)* Cost-drivers are a concept in activity-based costing, a new approach to management accounting which argues that in any business activity there are certain activities which drive the business forward and in so doing call for costs to be incurred. If these cost-drivers can be identified we can see more clearly what the costs of the activity are and how to control them.

(b) The importance of this idea is that it enables us to see more clearly how costs should be allocated or absorbed within the company. If we load costs on to products in old-fashioned ways - for example, based on machine hours - we may arrive at incorrect costs for products, if in fact the true cost-drivers are not machine shop costs but other quite different things (for example, marketing costs like television advertising). Most of the cost-drivers are likely to be found in the support departments rather than in the production departments.

UNIT 6

Job and contract costing

6.1 Suggested answers to exercises

1. *(a)*

Dear Arthur,

I provide below information in respect of the charging of indirect costs when quotations are prepared. Indirect costs represent the expenditure on labour, materials or services which cannot be economically identified with a specific saleable cost unit. I suggest that these indirect costs should be recovered by the use of a direct labour hour rate. Therefore I have calculated an overhead absorption rate based on direct labour hours expected to be worked during the year.

	Hours
Total hours worked during the year estimated at 48 weeks × 40 =	1 920
Less:	
Total hours of direct labour charged to jobs = 48 weeks × 30 =	1 440
Total hours chargeable as indirect labour = 48 weeks × 10 =	480

Overhead absorption rate (based on a direct labour hour rate)

	£
Sundry overhead expenses (including rent, rates, etc.)	2 760
Indirect labour (480 hours @ £5)	2 400
Estimated indirect costs	£5 160

Direct labour hours expected to be worked during the year:
= 48 weeks × 30 hours = 1 440 hours
Add part-time labour 2 000 hours

Total direct labour hours = 3 440 hours

Absorption rate:

$$= \frac{\text{Indirect costs}}{\text{Direct labour hours}} = \frac{£5\,160}{3\,440} = £1.50 \text{ per hour}$$

In the following year I would suggest that you adopt a form of budgetary control. This should be based on forecasts and the best possible estimates of what the costs are likely to be during that year. Actual costs during the current year can be used and adjusted on the basis of estimated future costs, taking into account known or expected changes in costs. New absorption rates will have to be calculated based on the above information and month-by-month actual costs can be compared with the estimates.

Note: In preparing the estimate I calculated the material costs as £80.50. The direct costs were £10, the labour costs for 29 hours' work came to £145, and overhead absorbed was £43.50. A profit margin of 10 per cent was added to the total, which was then rounded to the nearest £1.

(b)

Arthur Smith
Painter and Decorator
Quotation
Painting and papering lounge

	£
Materials	89
Direct expenses	11
Stripping old paper and hanging new paper	207
	£307

2.

Job no. 30724

		£
Direct materials		36
Direct wages:		
Department A	54 hours at £4.00 per hour	216
Department B	96 hours at £3.50 per hour	336
Overheads:		
Variable		
Department A	54 hours at £8.00 per hour	432
Department B	96 hours at £7.00 per hour	672
Fixed	150 hours at £10.00 per hour	1 500
Total cost		£3 192
Profit $12\frac{1}{2}\%$		399
Selling price		£3 591

Overhead rates were calculated as follows:

Variable

Department A $\frac{£216\,000}{27\,000}$ hours = £8.00 per hour (direct labour)

Department B $\frac{£224\,000}{32\,000}$ hours = £7.00 per hour (direct labour)

Fixed

$\frac{£670\,000}{67\,000}$ hours = £10.00 per hour (direct labour)

3. *(a)*

Cost sheet: 100 components

Unit cost Estimated cost £	Unit cost Actual cost £				£
6.50	6.50	Direct materials (group 2):			650.00
		Direct wages:	Hours	£	
1.54	1.55	Department A	107	155.00	
2.40	2.50	B	130	250.00	
0.92	0.85	C	50	85.00	
0.67	0.72	D	40	72.00	
5.53	5.62				562.00
		Works overhead:	Rate per direct labour hour £	£	
1.60	1.60	Department A	1.50	160.50	
3.42	3.58	B	2.75	357.50	
1.62	1.50	C	3.00	150.00	
1.16	1.24	D	3.10	124.00	
7.80	7.92				792.00
8.30	8.43	Administration overhead:	150% of wages		843.00
28.13	28.47	Total cost			£2 847.00

(b)

Selling price	100%
Profit margin	45% of selling price
Cost price	55% of selling price

$$\text{Selling price} = \frac{\text{Actual cost}}{55\%}$$

$$= \frac{£28.47}{55} \times 100 = \underline{\underline{£51.76}}$$

4. *(a) Present system:*

$$\text{Wages rate per direct labour hour} = \frac{\text{Direct labour}}{\text{Total direct labour hours}}$$

$$= \frac{£11\,250}{2\,400 + 300 + 1\,800}$$

$$= \frac{£11\,250}{4\,500}$$

$$= \underline{\underline{£2.50 \text{ per hour}}}$$

$$\text{Overhead per direct labour hour} = \frac{\text{Overhead expenses}}{\text{Total direct labour hours}}$$

$$= \frac{£18\,000}{4\,500}$$

$$= \underline{\underline{£4.00 \text{ per hour}}}$$

Proposed system:

Wages rate per direct labour hour = £2.50 as under present system

$$\text{Wages rate for setting-up} = \frac{\text{Wages cost}}{\text{Setting-up time}} = \frac{£3\,750}{1\,250} = \underline{\underline{£3.00 \text{ per hour}}}$$

$$\text{Overhead per direct labour hour} = \frac{\text{Overhead expenses } less \text{ Cost of setting up}}{\text{Direct labour hours including setting-up time}}$$

$$= \frac{£14\,250}{5\,750}$$

$$= \underline{\underline{£2.48 \text{ per hour (approx.)}}}$$

Statement of cost

	Job A			Job B			Job C		
	Hours	Rate		Hours	Rate		Hours	Rate	
Present system:		£	£		£	£		£	£
Direct materials			4 540			525			3 185
Direct labour	2 400	2.50	6 000	300	2.50	750	1 800	2.50	4 500
			10 540			1 275			7 685
Overheads	2 400	4.00	9 600	300	4.00	1 200	1 800	4.00	7 200
			£20 140			£2 475			£14 885

Proposed system:									
Direct materials			4 540			525			3 185
Direct labour	2 400	2.50	6 000	300	2.50	750	1 800	2.50	4 500
Direct labour (setting)	375	3.00	1 125	250	3.00	750	625	3.00	1 875
			11 665			2 025			9 560
Overheads	2 775	2.48	6 882	550	2.48	1 364	2 425	2.48	6 014
			£18 547			£3 389			£15 574

(b) The system as proposed provides costs more accurately than can the present one. The setting-up time for the three jobs bears no relationship to the amount of direct labour hours involved in each case. This is obvious when comparing job A with job B; job B has a small number of direct labour hours but requires a large number of hours in setting up the work. The setting-up time is in fact direct labour as it can be identified and charged as a direct cost to the job to which it relates. There is a more accurate assessment of the prime cost in the proposed system and a more correct charge for overhead expenses. Many overhead expenses are incurred on a time basis and by adjusting the direct labour hours on each job and the rate of overhead expenses a more accurate cost is obtained in each case.

5. *(a)* and *(b)* See Fig. 6.17 (p. 438).

6. Total materials £1 030.96; direct expenses £420.00; direct wages £268.34; works overhead £386.93; total manufacturing costs £2 106.24; selling expenses £216.00; total cost £2 322.24; invoice price £2 700; profit £377.76.

7.

Cost statement

Estimated results in respect of the production of 150 000 calculators

	£	£
Sales: 150 000 at £17.00 each		2 550 000
Less Costs:		
Materials (150 000 at £6.11)	916 500	
Direct labour (150 000 at £3.09)	463 500	
Indirect labour	135 000	
Other costs (150 000 at £2.75 + £65 000 fixed cost)	477 500	
		1 992 500
Profit		£557 500

Customer: Mr X.Y. Brown | Order No. PH 279 | Date 1.1.07

Particulars of Order: Extension to 52 London Road, Somewhere. | Quoted Price £3 050

Week ending	Materials:						
	Purchase order or Stores requisition no.	Description	Weight	Direct purchase	Stores requisition	Other charges	Total
				£	£		£
	G1458	Timber			148		
	G1563	Sundries			75		
	C2037	Bricks		710			
	C2084	Sundries		220			
				930	223		1 153

Week ending	Wages:															
	Bricklayers			Carpenters			Plumbers			Electricians			Decorators			Total
	Hrs.	Rate	£	Hrs.	Rate	£	Hrs.	Rate	£	Hrs.	Rate	£	Hrs.	Rate	£	£
	185	3.00	555	45	2.40	108	40	2.50	100	20	3.10	62	60	2.20	132	957
	Overheads: 50%															
			278			54			50			31			66	479

Date	Details	Invoice	Date	Details	Invoice
		£			£

Remarks

Summary	Estimate	Cost
	£	£
Materials:		
Direct purchases	910	930
Stores requisitions	218	223
Wages	939	957
Overheads	470	479
	2 537	2 589
Selling price	3 050	3 050
Profit	513	461
Loss		

Fig. 6.17 Question 5: a cost sheet

Workings:
Materials:

$$\frac{£780\,000}{120\,000} = £6.50 \text{ each. Reduction of } 6\% = \frac{£6.50}{100} \times 94 = £6.11 \text{ each}$$

Direct wages:

$$\frac{£360\,000}{120\,000} = £3.00. \text{ Increase of } 3\% = \frac{£3.00}{100} \times 103 = £3.09 \text{ each}$$

Other costs:

$$\frac{£380\,000 - £50\,000}{120\,000} = £2.75 \text{ variable}$$

Fixed cost = £50 000 + £15 000 = £65 000

8. Books of A. Subcontractor

Cost statement (job costs)

	A		B		C	
Units produced	10		25		50	
Direct materials:	£	£	£	£	£	£
Direct purchases	360		–		2 850	
Stores materials	740		1 350		950	
		1 100		1 350		3 800
Direct wages:						
Machining at £2 per hour	320		1 000		2 500	
Fitting at £1.75 per hour	140		525		525	
Painting and polishing at £1.50 per hour	60		225		375	
		520		1 750		3 400
Prime costs:		1 620		3 100		7 200
Works overhead:						
Machining at £10 per hour	1 600		5 000		12 500	
Fitting at £4 per hour	320		1 200		1 200	
Painting and polishing at £7 per hour	280		1 050		1 750	
		2 200		7 250		15 450
Works cost:		3 820		10 350		22 650
Administration cost		810		1 550		3 600
Total cost:		4 630		11 900		26 250
Selling price (cost + 25%)		5 788		14 875		32 812
Profit at 20% of selling price		1 158		2 975		6 562

9. Books of B. Construction Ltd

(a)

Contract Account for construction of office block (3 January to 31 October 19 . 8)

		£			£
Materials issued		161 000	Materials returned		14 000
Wages paid		68 000	Materials on site	c/d	24 000
Plant at cost		96 000	Plant at written-down value	c/d	86 000
Hire of plant and scaffolding		72 000	Cost of work not yet completed	c/d	40 000
Supervisory staff: direct		11 000			
indirect		12 000			
Head office charges		63 000			164 000
Wages accrued	c/d	2 000			
		485 000	Cost of work certified (to Profit and Loss A/c as cost of sales)		321 000
		£485 000			£485 000
		£			£
Materials on site	b/d	24 000	Wages accrued	b/d	2 000
Plant at written-down value	b/d	86 000			
Cost of work not yet completed	b/d	40 000			

(b)

Profit and Loss Account for year ending 31 December 19 . 8

19 . 8	£	19.8	£
Cost of sales	321 000	Turnover (work certified)	400 000
Profit reserved	35 550		
Profit taken	43 450		
	£400 000		£400 000

Balance Sheet as at 31 December 19 . 8 (extract only)

Assets

Balance on Contract A/c £148 000

Debtor (balance to pay) £70 000 (Amount recoverable on contract)

Liabilities

Profit Reserved Account £35 550

Appropriation Account (profit taken) £43 450

Notional profit = Value of work certified − Cost of work certified
= £400 000 − (£485 000 − £164 000)
= £400 000 − £321 000 = £79 000

$$\text{Profit taken} = \tfrac{2}{3} \times \text{Notional profit} \times \frac{\text{Cash received}}{\text{Work certified}}$$

$$= \tfrac{2}{3} \times £79\,000 \times \frac{£330\,000}{£400\,000}$$

$$= £43\,450$$

Profit reserved = £79 000 − £43 450 = £35 550

10.

Contract Account
February 19 . 7 to 30 September 19 . 7

		£			£
Materials delivered to site		67 620	Materials to other contract sites		1 320
Wages paid		48 180	Plant returned to yard at valuation		5 700
Plant issued to site		27 000	Plant transferred to other sites at valuation		3 600
Materials from stores		10 200	Plant on site at valuation	c/d	16 200
Direct expenses		3 360	Materials on site	c/d	5 700
Overhead expenses		7 800	Cost of work done but not certified	c/d	7 200
Payments to sub-contractors		17 100			39 720
Materials transferred from other sites		3 900			
Sub-contract work not yet paid	c/d	720			
Wages accrued	c/d	840			
		186 720	Cost of work certified, transferred to Profit and Loss A/c as cost of sales		147 000
		£186 720			£186 720
Plant at valuation	b/d	16 200	Sub-contract work not yet paid	b/d	720
Materials on site	b/d	5 700	Wages accrued	b/d	840
Cost of work not yet certified	b/d	7 200			

Workings:

Cash received = 80% of value of work certified = £153 600

$$\text{Work certified} = \frac{100\%}{80\%} \times £153\,600 = £192\,000$$

Cost of work certified = £186 720 − £39 720 = £147 000
Notional profit = Value of work certified (turnover) − Cost of work certified
= £192 000 − £147 000 = £45 000 (cost of sales)

Profit to be taken as profit for the year

$$= \tfrac{2}{3} \times \text{Notional profit} \times \frac{\text{Cash received}}{\text{Value of work certified}}$$

$$= \tfrac{2}{3} \times £45\,000 \times \frac{£153\,600}{£192\,000} = £24\,000$$

Profit reserved = £45 000 − £24 000 = £21 000

		Balance Sheet	*Profit and Loss Account*
	(£'000)	(£'000)	(£'000)
Turnover			
Value of work certified (invoiced)	192		192
Cumulative payments on account	153.6		
Amounts recoverable on contracts	38.4	38.4	
Total cost to date (cost of sales)	147		
Transferred to cost of sales	(147)		(147)
Profit on contract to date			45
(Of which profit reserved)			21
Profit for year			24

11. *(a)*

Contract Account: underground car park

		£			£
Plant sent to site		111 250	Plant transferred		43 750
Materials sent by stores department		1 875	Plant at valuation	c/d	40 000
Direct purchases sent by suppliers		260 000	Materials on site	c/d	3 750
Wages paid		125 000			87 500
Site general expenses		4 750	Cost of work not yet certified	c/d	12 500
Transport charges		3 000			100 000
Head office overheads		37 875			
Wages accrued	c/d	6 250			
		550 000	Cost of sales transferred to Profit and Loss A/c		450 000
		£550 000			£550 000
		£			£
Plant at valuation	b/d	40 000	Wages accrued	b/d	6 250
Materials on site	b/d	3 750			
Cost of work not yet certified	b/d	12 500			

(b)

Profit and Loss Account
for year ending 31 December 19 . 9

	£		£
Cost of sales	450 000	Turnover on contract	590 000
Total profit to date	150 000	Extra work certified	10 000
	£600 000		£600 000
Profit Reserved A/c	61 500	Total profit to date	150 000
Profit taken	88 500		
	£150 000		£150 000
		Profit for year	88 500

$$\text{Profit taken} = \tfrac{2}{3} \times \text{Notional profit} \times \frac{\text{Cash received}}{\text{Value of work certified}}$$

$$= \tfrac{2}{3} \times £150\,000 \times \frac{£531\,000}{£600\,000}$$

$$= £88\,500$$

$$\text{Profit reserved} = £150\,000 - £88\,500$$
$$= £61\,500$$

Retention Money Account

		£
19 . 9		
31 Dec.	Work certified but retained	59 000

Profit Reserved Account

			£
	19 . 9		
	31 Dec.	Profit and Loss A/c	61 500

(c) **Balance Sheet items:**

Assets

Debtor £10 000 (amount recoverable on contract)
Retention Money £59 000 (amount recoverable on contract)
Balance on Contract A/c (net) £50 000

Liabilities

Profit Reserved £61 500
Profit Available £88 500

UNIT 7

Process costing

7.1 Suggested answers to exercises

1. Points to make:
   (a) (i) Treat as a credit to Profit and Loss Account *or*
   (ii) Treat as a reduction of the cost of the main product.
   (b) (i) Use market value as a sale.
   (ii) Fix standard costs.
   (iii) Use cost of similar or alternative material.
   (c) Use methods in *(b)* above, allowing for cost of further processing.

2.

	Process 1	*Process 2*
	£	£
Material input	24 441	47 044
Labour and overheads	23 500	51 000
	47 941	98 044
Less Scrap value	897	1 612
Value of good production	£47 044	£96 432
Output of good finished units:		
Process 1 good units	2 505	
Less Scrapped process 2	496	
Good units process 2	2 009	

Cost per unit of finished product passing inspection test

$$= \frac{£96\,432}{2\,009} = £48$$

3.

Process Account

	Units	£		Units	£
Materials: A and B	2 000	31 000	Normal loss	100	700
A		1 434	By-product		160
B		1 191	Transfer to Finished		
Wages: A and B		4 500	Stock Account:		
A		2 000	Product A	1 045	26 961
B		1 200	Product B	855	21 204
Overheads: A and B		4 500			
A		2 000			
B		1 200			
	2 000	£49 025		2 000	£49 025

Workings:

Common costs:

		£
2 000 units of material at £15.50		31 000
Wages		4 500
Overheads		4 500
		40 000
Less Normal loss (5% of 2 000) × £7.00		
=100 × £7.00	700	
By-product (£190 − £30)	160	
		860
Common costs (1 900 units)		£39 140

$$\text{Common costs per unit} = \frac{£39\,140}{1\,900} = £20.60$$

Apportionment:

	£
Product A = (55% of 1 900) × £20.60	
= 1 045 × £20.60 =	21 527
Product B = (45% of 1 900) × £20.60	
= 855 × £20.60 =	17 613
	£39 140

Cost of production:

Product A:

	£
Common costs	21 527
Materials	1 434
Wages	2 000
Overheads	2 000
Cost transferred to Finished Stock Account	£26 961

= 1 045 units at £25.80 per unit

Product B:

	£
Common costs	17 613
Materials	1 191
Wages	1 200
Overheads	1 200
Cost transferred to Finished Stock Account	£21 204

= 855 units at £24.80 per unit

4.

Process Account

	Units	Per unit	Value		Units	Per unit	Value
		£	£			£	£
Materials	3 800	4.75	18 050	Normal wastage	190	0.95	180.50
Direct wages			5 054	Transfer to Finished Stock A/c	3 630	8.45	30 673.50
Works overhead			7 581				
Abnormal gain	20	8.45	169				
	3 820		£30 854		3 820		£30 854.00

Normal Loss Account

	Units	Per unit	Value		Units	Per unit	Value
		£	£			£	£
Process A/c	190	0.95	180.50	Abnormal yield	20	0.95	19.00
				Debtor	170	0.95	161.50
	190		180.50		190		£180.50

Abnormal Gain Account

	Units	Per unit	Value		Units	Per unit	Value
		£	£			£	£
Normal Loss A/c	20	0.95	19.00	Process A/c	20	8.45	169.00
Profit and Loss A/c			150.00				
	20		£169.00		20		£169.00

Workings:

	Units
Charged to process	3 800
Normal wastage 5%	190
Normal yield	3 610
Production	3 630
Normal yield	3 610
Abnormal gain	20

$$\text{Cost per unit} = \frac{\text{Costs}}{\text{Normal yield}}$$

$$= \frac{£18\,050 + £5\,054 + £7\,581 - £180.50}{3\,610}$$

$$= \frac{£30\,504.50}{3\,610} = £8.45$$

5. *(a) Job costing* is a method of production related to specific orders or operations where the items manufactured are different. *Process costing* is the manufacture of identical items where the materials or units pass through a process in a continuous flow. After allowing for normal loss, sale of scrap, etc., the total cost represents the units produced and provides the cost per unit. Process costing is used in industries such as the manufacture of paper, paint, cement, rubber and petrochemicals, and electric power generation.

(b)

Process 1 Account

	Units (kg)	Cost per unit	Value		Units (kg)	Cost per unit	Value
		£	£			£	£
Material A	6 000	1.00	6 000	Normal loss	500	0.32	160
Material B	4 000	2.00	8 000	Abnormal loss	300	2.00	600
Mixing labour			1 720	Transfer to			
Overheads			3 440	Process 2	9 200	2.00	18 400
	10 000		£19 160		10 000		£19 160

Process 2 Account

	Units (kg)	Cost per unit £	Value £		Units (kg)	Cost per unit £	Value £
Process 1	9 200	2.00	18 400	Normal loss	1 000	–	–
Material C	6 600	2.50	16 500	Transfer to			
Material D	4 200	1.50	6 300	Packing			
Flavouring				Dept A/c	18 000	2.44	43 920
essence			600	Work in			
Mixing labour			1 480	process			
Overheads			2 960	carried			
				down:			
				Materials	1 000	2.20	2 200
				Labour		0.08	40
				Overheads		0.16	80
	20 000		£46 240		20 000		£46 240
Work in process b/d	1 000		2 320				

Abnormal Scrap Account

	Units (kg)	Cost per unit £	Value £		Units (kg)	Cost per unit £	Value £
Process 1	300	2.00	600	Debtor(s)	300	0.32	96
				Profit and Loss Account			504
	300		£600		300		£600

Packing Department Account

	Units (kg)	Cost per unit £	Value £
Process 2	18 000	2.44	43 920

Workings:

Process 1:

$$\text{Normal output} = \frac{95}{100} \times 10\,000 = \underline{\underline{9\,500 \text{ units}}} \quad (\text{Normal loss } 500)$$

$$\text{Cost per unit} = \frac{\text{Process cost } \textit{less} \text{ Sale of scrap}}{\text{Normal output}} = \frac{£19\,160 - £160}{9\,500}$$

$$= \underline{\underline{£2.00}}$$

$$\text{Abnormal loss} = \text{Normal output} - \text{Actual output}$$
$$= 9\,500 - 9\,200 = \underline{\underline{300 \text{ units}}}$$

$$\text{Overheads: Mixing labour hours} = 430 \text{ (Process 1)} + 370 \text{ (Process 2)}$$
$$= \underline{\underline{800}}$$

$$\text{Overhead per hour} = \frac{£6\,400}{800} = \underline{\underline{£8}}$$

$$\text{For Process 1} = 430 \times £8 = \underline{\underline{£3\,440}}$$

$$\text{For Process 2} = 370 \times £8 = \underline{\underline{£2\,960}}$$

Process 2:

$$\text{Normal loss} = 5\% \times (9\,200 + 6\,600 + 4\,200)$$
$$= 5\% \times 20\,000 = \underline{\underline{1\,000 \text{ kg}}}$$

$$\text{Output transferred} = 20\,000 - [1\,000 \text{ (normal loss)} + 1\,000 \text{ (work in process)}]$$
$$= \underline{\underline{18\,000 \text{ kg}}}$$

Valuation of work in process:

$$\text{Materials: Equivalent units} = 18\,000 + (100\% \text{ of } 1\,000) = \underline{\underline{19\,000 \text{ units}}}$$

$$\text{Cost per unit} = \frac{£18\,400 + £16\,500 + £6\,300 + £600}{19\,000}$$

$$= \frac{£41\,800}{19\,000} = \underline{\underline{£2.20 \text{ per unit}}}$$

$$\text{Work in process} = 1\,000 \times £2.20 = \underline{\underline{£2\,200}}$$

$$\text{Wages: Equivalent units} = 18\,000 + (50\% \text{ of } 1\,000) = \underline{\underline{18\,500 \text{ units}}}$$

$$\text{Cost per unit} = \frac{£1\,480}{18\,500} = \underline{\underline{£0.08 \text{ per unit}}}$$

$$\text{Work in process} = 500 \times £0.08 = \underline{\underline{£40}}$$

$$\text{Overheads: Equivalent units} = 18\,000 + (50\% \text{ of } 1\,000) = \underline{\underline{18\,500 \text{ units}}}$$

$$\text{Cost per unit} = \frac{£2\,960}{18\,500} = \underline{\underline{£0.16 \text{ per unit}}}$$

Work in process = 500 × £0.16 = £80

Value of goods transferred to packing
= Total costs − Work in process
= £46 240 − £2 320
= £43 920

$$\text{Cost per unit} = \frac{£43\,920}{18\,000}$$

= £2.44

6. *(a)* and *(b)* See Unit 7.6.

(c) **Books of JP Manufacturing Co. Ltd**

(i)

Statement of estimated profit or loss
(assuming all products processed to post-separation stage)

Product	X	Y	Z	Total
Output	2 500 kg	1 000 kg	1 500 kg	5 000 kg
	£	£	£	£
Final sales price per kg	5	10	20	
Final sales income	12 500	10 000	30 000	52 500
Pre-separation costs	10 000	4 000	6 000	20 000
Post-separation costs	10 000	5 000	15 000	30 000
Total cost	20 000	9 000	21 000	50 000
Final profit/(loss)	(7 500)	1 000	9 000	2 500

(ii)

Statement of profit or loss on extra processing

Product	X	Y	Z	Total
	£	£	£	£
Extra sales income per unit	2	6	14	—
Extra sales income	5 000	6 000	21 000	32 000
Post-separation costs	10 000	5 000	15 000	30 000
Profit (Loss)	(5 000)	1 000	6 000	2 000

X loses £5 000 on extra processing and £2 500 at pre-separation stage. Y gains £1 000 on extra processing and nil at pre-separation stage. Z gains £6 000 on extra processing and £3 000 at pre-separation stage. Thus only Y and Z gain by extra processing.

To maximise profits:		£
Sell product X at separation point: 2 500 kg at £3.00	=	7 500
Sell product Y after further processing: 1 000 kg at £10.00	=	10 000
Sell product Z after further processing: 1 500 kg at £20.00	=	30 000
		47 500

	£	£
Less Costs: pre-separation	20 000	
post-separation (£5 000 Y + £15 000 Z)	20 000	
		40 000
Profit		£7 500

7.

Cost analysis statement

Process 1:

Elements of cost	Units finished and transferred	Equivalent units c/f	Total equivalent units	Total cost £	Cost per unit £	Transferred to process 2 £	Cost carried forward £
Materials	30 000	10 000	40 000	10 000	0.250 00	7 500	2 500
Wages	30 000	5 000	35 000	8 000	0.228 57	6 857	1 143
Overheads	30 000	5 000	35 000	12 000	0.342 86	10 286	1 714
Totals				30 000	–	24 643	5 357

Process 2:

Elements of cost	Units finished and transferred	Equivalent units c/f	Total equivalent units	Total cost £	Cost per unit £	Transferred to Finished Stock £	Cost carried forward £
Process 1	28 000	1 800	29 800	24 643	0.826 95	23 154	1 489
Materials	28 000	–	28 000	4 000	0.142 86	4 000	–
Wages	28 000	450	28 450	3 500	0.123 02	3 445	55
Overheads	28 000	450	28 450	4 500	0.158 17	4 429	71
Totals				36 643	–	35 028	1 615

Note: There were 200 units of normal loss.

Workings:

Process 1:

Equivalent units

		Materials		Direct wages	Factory overhead	Total
Transferred to Process 2		30 000		30 000	30 000	
Work in process	100%	10 000	50%	5 000	5 000	
		40 000		35 000	35 000	
Cost per equivalent unit		£10 000		£8 000	£12 000	
		40 000		35 000	35 000	
Cost per unit		£0.250 00		£0.228 57	£0.342 86	
Finished units		£7 500		£6 857	£10 286	£24 643
Closing work in process		£2 500		£1 143	£1 714	£5 357
		£10 000		£8 000	£12 000	£30 000

Process 2:

Equivalent units		Materials Process 1	Materials Process 2		Direct wages		Factory overhead	Total
Transferred to Finished Stock		28 000	28 000		28 000		28 000	
Work in process	100%	1 800	–	25%	450	25%	450	
		29 800	28 000		28 450		28 450	
Cost per equivalent unit		£24 643 / 29 800	£4 000 / 28 000		£3 500 / 28 450		£4 500 / 28 450	
Cost per unit		£0.826 95	£0.142 86		£0.123 02		£0.158 17	
Finished stock (transfer)		£23 154	£4 000		£3 445		£4 429	£35 028
Closing work in process		£1 489	–		£55		£71	£1 615
		£24 643	£4 000		£3 500		£4 500	£36 643

Unit = 28 000 (finished) + 1 800 (work in process) + 200 (normal loss)

8. *(a)*

Foundry costs

Yield	50% Tonnes	Price £	Value £	60% Tonnes	Price £	Value £	70% Tonnes	Price £	Value £
Copper	70	450	31 500						
Zinc	30	120	3 600						
Cost of metal melted	100	351	35 100						
Melting loss	10	–	–						
Melting costs	90	50	4 500						
Cost of metal poured	90	440	39 600	90	440	39 600	90	440	39 600
Less Scrap	45	351	15 795	36	351	12 636	27	351	9 477
Cost of good castings	45	£529	£23 805	54	£499	£26 964	63	£478	£30 123

(b) The use of the scrap will make no difference to these costs, since the metal content of the scrap is in the same ratio as that of the original charge, and is valued at the same price.

9.

Normal period costs

Output (sales):		£	£
Product A	500 tonnes at	100	50 000
By-product Y	70 tonnes at	20	1 400
By-product Z	80 tonnes	–	–
			51 400
Input (costs):		£	
Direct materials		21 000	
Direct wages		8 000	
Variable overheads (50% of direct wages)		4 000	
Contractor (clearance of by-product Z)		400	
		33 400	
Fixed overheads		8 000	
Total cost			41 400
Profit			£10 000

Process cost and profit after further treatment

By-product Y:			
Output (sales):			£
100 tonnes product M at £40 per tonne			4 000
Less Income from normal period sales			1 400
			2 600
Input (costs):		£	
Direct materials		600	
Direct wages		800	
Variable overheads (50% of direct wages)		400	
			1 800
Additional profit			800
By-product Z:			
Output (sales):			
100 tonnes product P at £24 per tonne		2 400	
Input (costs):	£		
Direct materials	800		
Direct wages	600		
Variable overheads (50% of direct wages)	300		
	1 700		
Less Contractor's charge for cartage	400		
		1 300	
Additional profit			1 100
Total additional profit			£1 900

Cost and sales (processing of product A and by-products M and P)

Output (sales):		£	£
Product A	500 tonnes at	100	50 000
Product M	100 tonnes at	40	4 000
Product P	100 tonnes at	24	2 400
			56 400
Input (costs):			
Direct materials		22 400	
Direct wages		9 400	
Variable overheads (50% of direct wages)		4 700	
Fixed overheads		8 000	
			44 500
Profit			£11 900

Advice to management

Sales value can be increased by £5 000 for an extra expenditure of £3 100. This would produce an additional profit of £1 900, increasing the profit to sales from 19.5 per cent to 21.1 per cent. As the existing facilities can be used and there is to be no increase in fixed costs, it would be advisable to proceed with the proposition. This is provided that the sales of the main product A are not disturbed in any way by withdrawing the sales of product Y and by selling product M and product P.

10. *(a)*

Production overhead analysis and apportionment sheet

Overhead	Bases of apportionment	Annual cost	Production processes A	B	Service departments Stores	Canteen
		£	£	£	£	£
Indirect wages	Direct	95 000	25 000	40 000	20 000	10 000
Indirect materials	Direct	119 750	51 510	58 505	1 310	8 425
Rent and rates	Area	450 000	150 000	75 000	150 000	75 000
Depreciation on plant	Book value of plant	140 000	100 000	20 000	15 000	5 000
Power	HP of plant	50 000	40 000	10 000		
Fire insurance	Area	3 750	1 250	625	1 250	625
Compensation insurance	2% of total wages	12 000	6 100	5 300	400	200
Heat and light	Area	4 500	1 500	750	1 500	750
		875 000	375 360	210 180	189 460	100 000
Canteen	No. of employees		50 000	37 500	12 500	(100 000)
Stores	No. of stores issues		134 640	67 320	(201 960)	
		875 000	560 000	315 000	–	–

(b)

Overhead recovery rate

	Process A	Process B
Labour hours	70 000	45 000
Production overhead cost per hour	£8	£7

(c)

Product costs

			X		Y
			£		£
Direct materials:	P	37		93	
	Q	2		48	
	R	4		15	
			43		156
Direct wages:	A	8		16	
	B	5		15	
			13		31
Production overhead:	Process A	16		32	
	Process B	7		21	
			23		53
Royalty			1		–
Commission			5		15
Packing materials			1		4
Transport			2		5
Advertising			2		6
Total cost			90		270

(d)

	X	*Y*
Product	£	£
Selling price	100	300
Total cost	90	270
Profit	10	30

UNIT 8

Marginal costing

8.1 Suggested answers to exercises

1. *(a)* *Workings for Fig. 8.10* *(see p. 458)*

			£
(i)	Selling price		80 000
	Less Fixed costs	10 000	
	Variable cost	64 000	
			74 000
	Profit		6 000

Contribution = Fixed cost + Profit
= £10 000 + £6 000 = £16 000 = (£2 per unit)

$$\text{Break-even point} = \frac{\text{Fixed cost}}{\text{Contribution per unit}}$$

$$= \frac{£10\,000}{£2} = 5\,000 \text{ units}$$

(ii) The advantages of a break-even chart are that it gives a simple, pictorial representation of the profitability of the activity concerned, which pinpoints where the activity will break even and profits will start to accrue. It shows what the margin of safety is, so that we can see the effects of possible competition.

The disadvantages are that the picture is over-simplified. Cost behaviour is the response of cost to a variety of influences besides volume, and there are limitations to break-even charts. When working out a cost–contribution–sales analysis we must take into account any factors which may have an effect on the results. The break-even graph is only a pictorial expression which relates costs and profit to activity. Costs and revenues are shown as straight lines, but selling prices are not necessarily fixed. The revenue may change depending on the quantities of goods sold direct, sold through agents and sold at a discount. Fixed costs do not always remain constant during the period of activity. Variable costs may not be proportional to volume because of overtime working, or reductions in price of materials when bulk discounts are given.

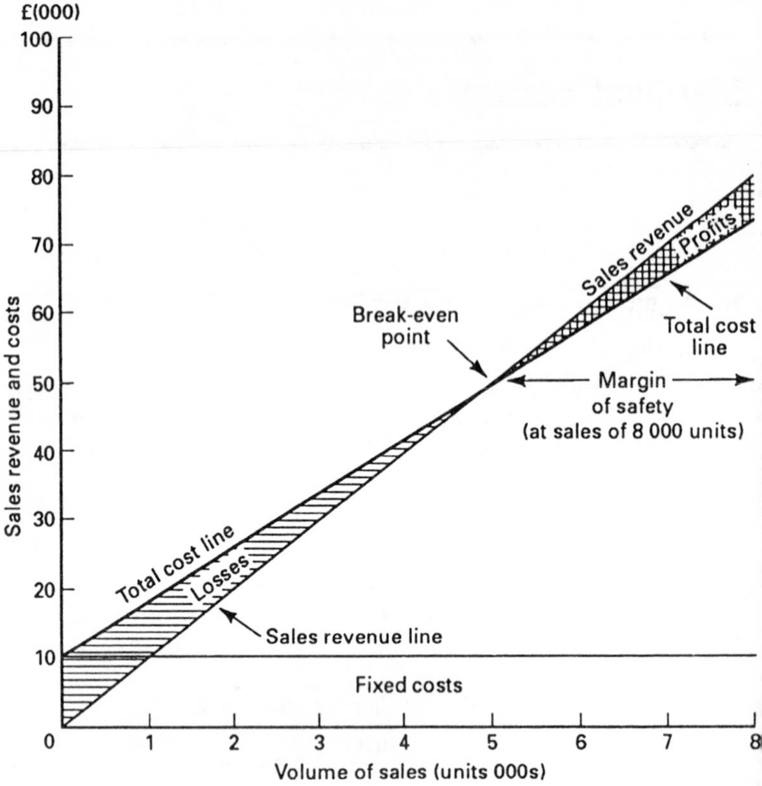

Fig. 8.10 Question 1(a)(i): break-even chart (George Williams)

(b) (i) **Output and sales increased from 8 000 units to 9 000 units.**

The break-even point remains at 5 000 units.
The budgeted profit of £6 000 is increased by £2 000 to £8 000

(9 000 units *less* 8 000 units × Contribution of £2 per unit = £2 000

(ii) **Selling price reduced from £10 per unit to £9.60 per unit.**

$$\text{Break-even point} = \frac{\text{Fixed cost}}{\text{Contribution per unit}} = \frac{£10\,000}{£1.60} = 6\,250 \text{ units}$$

The budgeted profit is reduced from £6 000 to £2 800.

(The reduction is 8 000 units × £0.40 = £3 200.)

(iii) **An increase in variable cost per unit from £8.00 to £8.50.**
The break-even point increases from 5 000 units to 6 666.6 units as the contribution is reduced from £2 to £1.50 per unit.

$$\text{Break-even point} = \frac{\text{Fixed cost}}{\text{Contribution per unit}} = \frac{£10\,000}{£1.50} = \underline{\underline{6\,666.6 \text{ units}}}$$

Profit is reduced from £6 000 to £2 000.

(Profit = Sales £80 000 − [Fixed costs £10 000 + Variable costs £68 000]
= £80 000 − £78 000 = £2 000)

(iv) **Reduction in fixed costs from £10 000 to £8 000.**
The break-even point moves from 5 000 units to 4 000 units.

$$\text{Break-even point} = \frac{\text{Fixed cost}}{\text{Contribution per unit}} = \frac{£8\,000}{£2} = \underline{\underline{4\,000 \text{ units}}}$$

The budgeted profit increases by £2 000 to £8 000.

(Profit = Sales £80 000 − [Fixed costs £8 000 + Variable costs £64 000]
= £80 000 − £72 000 = £8 000)

2. *(a)* See Unit 8.1 (v) and the notes to Fig. 8.1 (viii) and Fig. 8.2.
(b) See Units 8.5, 8.6 and 8.7.

3.

Trading and Profit and Loss Account: Gadgets (Camside) Ltd

		First quarter			*Second quarter*		
	Per unit	Units	£	£	Units	£	£
Sales	5.00	59 000		295 000	62 000		310 000
Cost of production:							
Variable	1.50	69 000	103 500		59 000	88 500	
Add Opening stock	1.50	–	–		10 000	15 000	
		69 000	103 500		69 000	103 500	
Less Closing stock	1.50	10 000	15 000		7 000	10 500	
Marginal cost of sales		59 000	88 500	88 500	62 000	93 000	93 000
Contribution				206 500			217 000
Fixed costs:							
Production			130 000			130 000	
Selling and administration			16 250	146 250		16 250	146 250
Profit				£60 250			£70 750

4. *(a) Calculation of variable cost per unit:*

	Units produced	Monthly increase in units	Overhead expenses £	Monthly increase in overheads £	Variable cost per unit £
October	9 000	–	62 500	–	
November	10 500	1 500	66 250	3 750	2.50
December	13 500	3 000	73 750	7 500	2.50

Calculation of fixed overheads:

For October: Overhead expenses *less* Variable overhead (9 000 units × £2.50)
= £62 500 *less* £22 500 = £40.000

Proof:

For November: £66 250 *less* (10 500 × £2.50)
= £66 250 *less* £26 250 = £40 000

For December: £73 750 *less* (13 500 × £2.50)
= £73 750 *less* £33 750 = £40 000

Variable overhead costs as shown: £22 500; £26 250; £33 750.

Prime costs = $\frac{£67\,500}{9\,000}$ = £7.50 per unit (October), also £7.50 for November and December.

(b)

Cost statement: 12 000 units

	Units	Per unit	£
Prime cost	12 000	£7.50	90 000
Variable overheads	12 000	£2.50	30 000
Variable costs			120 000
Fixed overheads			40 000
			£160 000

(c) The diagrams should resemble curves (i), (ii) and (viii) in Fig. 8.1.

5. *(a)*

Statement of sales, costs and profit or loss

Process A:

Production	Fixed cost £	Variable cost £	Total cost £	Selling price £	Profit/(Loss) £
8 000 units	35 000	64 000	99 000	96 000	(3 000)
9 000 units	35 000	72 000	107 000	108 000	1 000
11 000 units	35 000	88 000	123 000	132 000	9 000
Process B:					
13 000 units	60 000	104 000	164 000	156 000	(8 000)
14 000 units	60 000	112 000	172 000	168 000	(4 000)
15 000 units	60 000	120 000	180 000	180 000	–

(b)

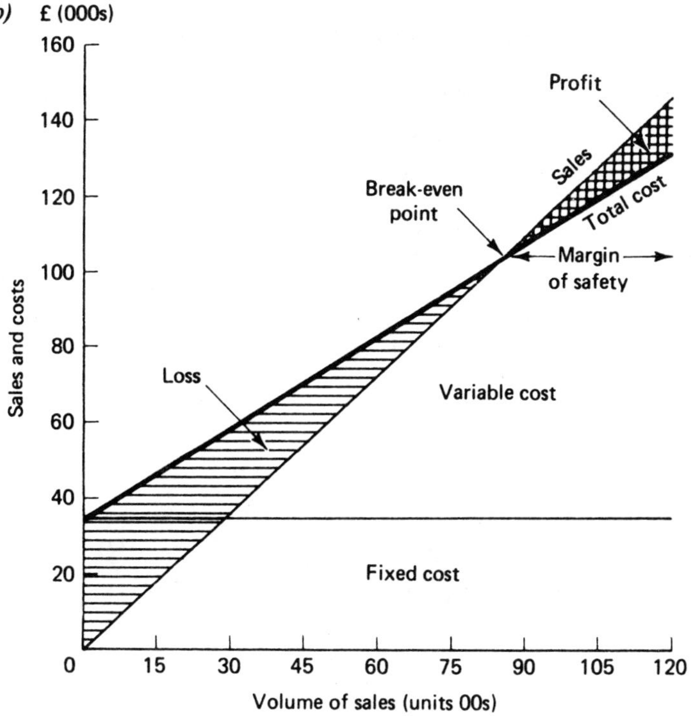

Fig. 8.11 Question 5(b): break-even chart (process A)

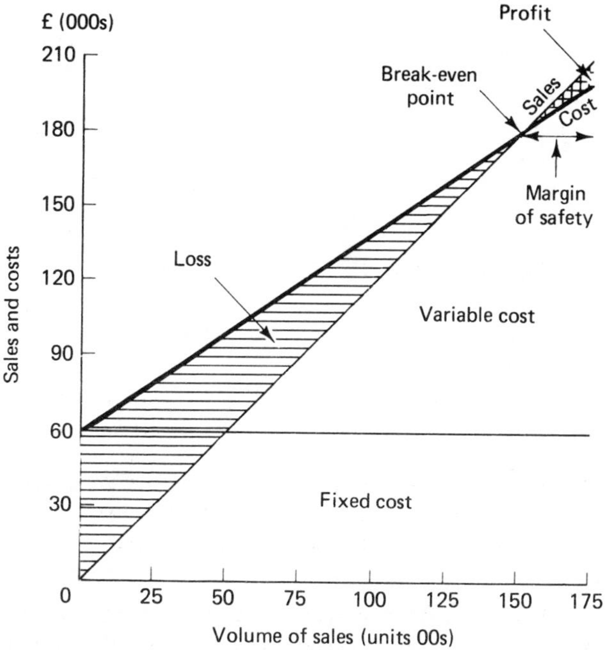

Fig. 8.12 Question 5(b): break-even chart (process B)

(c) The contribution/sales ratio is:

$$\frac{\text{Contribution}}{\text{Sales}} \times 100 = \frac{£4}{£12} \times 100 = 33\tfrac{1}{3}\%$$

The break-even point of process B is at sales of 15 000 units for £180 000. For process B to secure a profit of £9 000 (as at 11 000 units in process A) the number of units that must be sold

$$= \text{Sales at break-even point} + \frac{\text{Profit}}{\text{Contribution}}$$

$$= 15\,000 + \frac{£9\,000}{£4}$$

$$= 15\,000 + 2\,250 = 17\,250 \text{ units}$$

This is an increase in sales of 2 250 units at £12 each, a total of £27 000.

This figure can alternatively be obtained by using the contribution/sales ratio, as the profit per unit is a certain percentage of invoices value.

$$\frac{\text{Profit}}{\text{Contribution/Sales ratio}} = \frac{£9\,000}{33\tfrac{1}{3}\%} = \frac{£9\,000}{100} \times 300 = £27\,000$$

The recommendation is to the effect that operations should proceed as at present with the hope that sales will reach 11 000 units or above. The change to process B should only take place if there is a very good chance of sales exceeding 17 250 units on a fairly regular basis. The higher fixed costs are a burden which should not be carried unless there is a real chance of much higher profits in the future.

6. If the gross profit is 60 per cent, the cost of sales must be 40 per cent of sales.

	%	
Cost of sales	40	
Variable expenses	20	
Marginal cost	60	(Variable cost)
Contribution	40	(C/S ratio 40%)
Sales	100	

$$\text{Break-even point} = \frac{\text{Fixed cost}}{\text{C/S ratio}}$$

$$= \frac{£18\,000}{40} \times 100 = \underline{\underline{£45\,000}}$$

Sales revenue selected for break-even chart = $\underline{\underline{£90\,000}}$

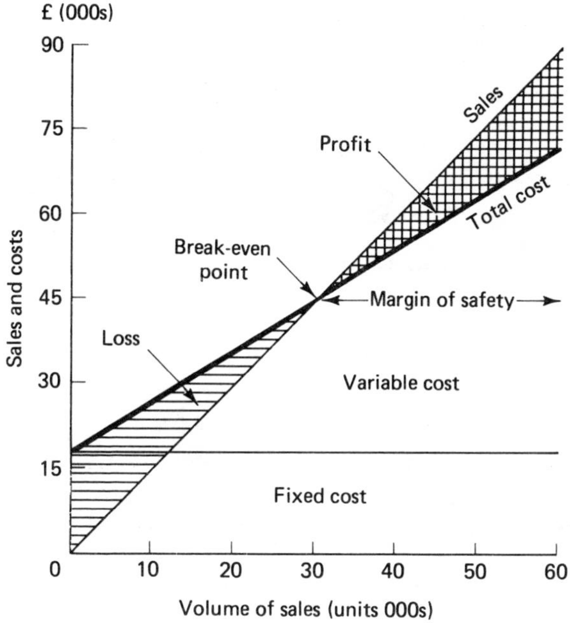

Fig. 8.13 Question 6: break-even chart

7. See Unit 8.9.

8. Books of A and B

(a) Fixed cost:

	£
Interest on loan at 15%	4 500
Rent	15 000
Rates	2 500
Insurance	500
Depreciation (15% of £50 000)	7 500
	£30 000

(b) Total return required:

	£	
Capital A	60 000	
Capital B	42 000	
$33\frac{1}{3}$% of	£102 000	= £34 000

(c) Contribution/sales ratio:
If Selling price = 250%, Material cost = 100%

and Material cost as a percentage of sales = $\frac{100}{250} \times 100 = 40\%$:

	% of sales
Material cost	40
Other variable costs	20
Marginal cost	60
C/S ratio	40

Contribution:

	£
Fixed cost	30 000
Return required	34 000
Contribution	£64 000 (40%)

(d) Total sales:

$$\text{Total sales} = \frac{\text{Contribution required}}{\text{C/S ratio}}$$

$$= \frac{£64\,000}{40} \times 100 = £160\,000$$

Sales at break-even point:

$$\text{Sales at break-even point} = \frac{\text{Fixed cost}}{\text{C/S ratio}}$$

$$= \frac{£30\,000}{40} \times 100 = £75\,000$$

(e) Total cost:
Total cost = Sales *less* Return required
= £160 000 − £34 000 = £126 000

or

Total cost = Marginal cost + Fixed cost
Marginal cost = 60% of Total sales

		£
	= 60% of £160 000 =	96 000
Add Fixed cost	=	30 000
		£126 000

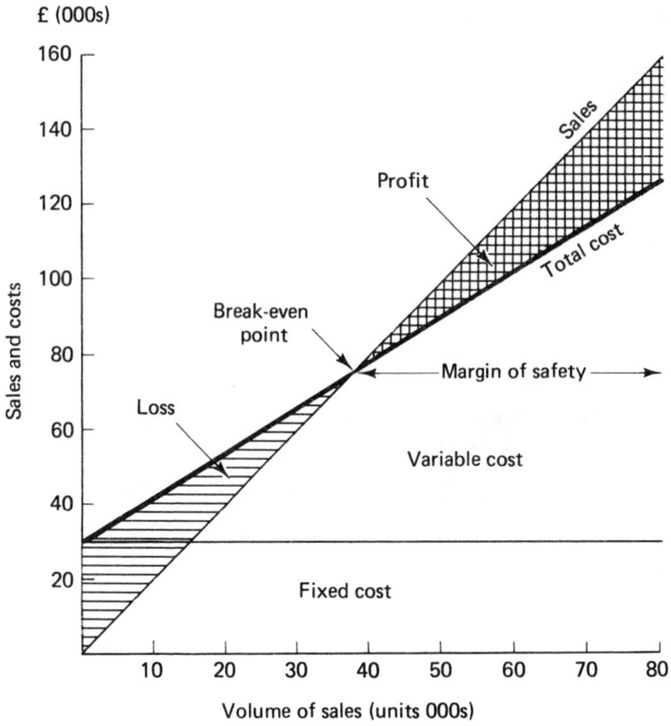

Fig. 8.14 Question 8: break-even chart (partnership of A and B)

9. *(a)*

Statement of present and proposed activities

		Present			*Proposed*
(i)	Unit sales		90 000		160 000
		£	£	£	£
(ii)	Sales value		900 000		1 600 000
	Materials	200 000		310 000	
	Wages and variable overhead	400 000		490 000	
(iii)	Marginal cost		600 000		800 000
(iv)	Contribution		300 000		800 000
	Less Fixed cost		200 000		400 000
(v)	Profit		100 000		400 000

(vi) Contribution/Sales ratio

$$= \frac{\text{Contribution}}{\text{Sales}} \times 100 \qquad \frac{£300\,000}{£900\,000} \times 100 \qquad \frac{£800\,000}{£1\,600\,000} \times 100$$

$$= 33\tfrac{1}{3}\% \qquad = 50\%$$

(vii) Sales at break-even point

$$= \frac{\text{Fixed cost}}{\text{C/S ratio}} \qquad \frac{£200\,000}{33\frac{1}{3}} \times 100 \qquad \frac{£400\,000}{50} \times 100$$

$$= £600\,000 \qquad = £800\,000$$

Workings:

Proposed activities:

Materials	£200 000	Wages and variable overhead	£400 000
Additional	£110 000	Additional	£90 000
	£310 000		£490 000

	£	
Fixed cost	200 000	
Depreciation:		
Buildings	30 000	(5% of £600 000)
Equipment	90 000	(10% of £900 000)
Other fixed	80 000	
	£400 000	

(b) See Fig. 8.15.

10. Books of XY Ltd

(a) Marginal costs for the 60 per cent level of activity are found by calculating the difference between those for the 70 per cent and the 80 per cent levels (a difference of 10 per cent) and then multiplying by 6 – i.e., the change in activity represents the marginal cost. For instance, using variable overheads as the example:

Overheads at 80% =	£49 600
Overheads at 70% =	£45 400
10% change	£4 200

Then marginal costs at the 60% level are:

	£		£
Direct materials:	10 500 × 6	=	63 000
Direct wages:	6 300 × 6	=	37 800
Variable overhead:	4 200 × 6	=	25 200

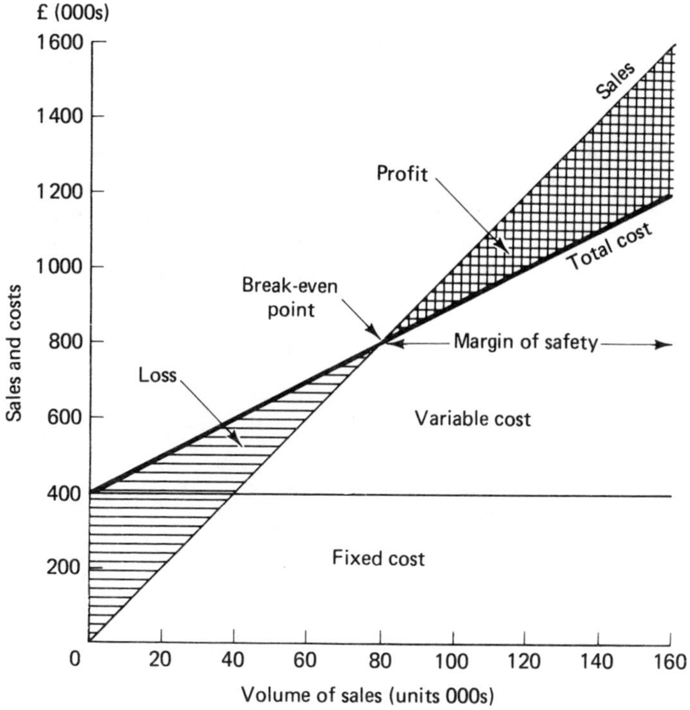

Fig. 8.15 Question 9: break-even chart for first stage of expansion

We can also calculate the fixed overhead costs:

Overhead at 70% level	=	£45 400	
Less Variable overheads	=	£29 400	(£4 200 × 7)
		£16 000	

Now we can construct a forecast statement of marginal costs and contribution at 60 per cent activity:

			£
Sales (£196 000 × $\frac{6}{7}$)			168 000
Less Marginal costs:	£		
Direct materials	63 000		
Direct wages	37 800		
Variable overheads	25 200		
			126 000
		Contribution	£42 000

(b) See Units 8.1, 8.6 and 8.7 and Figs. 8.6 and 8.7.

11. *(a)* Points to make:

(i) *Fixed costs:* costs for the period that are unaffected by variations in the volume of output.

(ii) *Variable cost:* a cost that varies directly with the variations in the volume of output.

(iii) Fixed costs are normally shared between the *estimated units* (that is, all the units expected to be produced). When fixed costs are shared among the actual units produced, the fixed costs *per unit* fall as production rises: fixed costs per unit vary inversely with the variations in the volume of output.

(b)

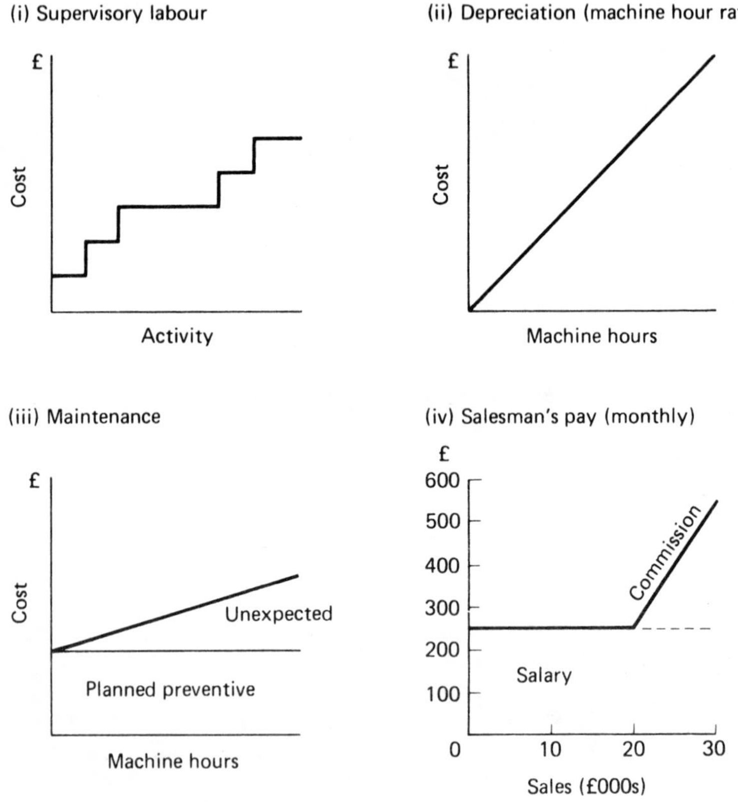

Fig. 8.16 Question 11(b): expense graphs

12. *(a)* and *(b)*

Trading and Profit and Loss Accounts

Marginal cost (March):

	£'000	£'000
Sales (10 000 at £50)		500
Less Variable cost		
Direct materials (12 000 at £18)	216	
Direct labour (12 000 at £4)	48	
Variable overhead (12 000 at £3)	36	
	300	
Less Closing stock (2 000 at £25)	50	
Variable cost of sales (production)	250	
Variable selling expenses (10% of £500 000)	50	
Less Marginal cost		300
Contribution		200
Less		
Fixed production expenses	99	
Fixed selling expenses	14	
Fixed administration expenses	26	
		139
Net profit		61

Absorption cost (March):

	£'000	£'000
Sales		500
Less Cost of production		
Direct materials	216	
Direct labour	48	
Overhead		
$12\,000 \times \left(£3 + \frac{£99\,000}{11\,000}\right)$	144	
	408	
Less Closing stock (2 000 at £34)	68	
Cost of sales		340
Gross profit		160
Less Variable selling expenses	50	
Fixed selling expenses	14	
Fixed administration expenses	26	
		90
		70
Add Overheads over-absorbed £144 *less* (12 × 3 + 99)		9
Net profit		79

Marginal cost (April):

	£'000	£'000
Sales (12 000 at £50)		600
Less Variable cost		
Direct materials (10 000 at £18)	180	
Direct labour (10 000 at £4)	40	
Variable overhead (10 000 at £3)	30	
	250	
Add Opening stock	50	

Absorption cost (April):

	£'000	£'000
Sales		600
Less Cost of production:		
Direct materials	180	
Direct labour	40	
Overhead (10 000 at £12)	120	
	340	
Add Opening stock	68	
Cost of sales		408

	b/d	600
Variable cost of sales (production)	300	
Add Variable selling expenses	60	
Less Marginal cost		360
Contribution		240
Less Fixed production expenses	99	
Fixed selling expenses	14	
Fixed administration expenses	26	
		139
Net profit		£101

	£'000	£'000
Gross profit		192
Less Variable selling expenses	60	
Fixed selling expenses	14	
Fixed administration expenses	26	
Under-absorbed overheads (£120 *less* £10 × 3 + 99)	9	
		109
Net profit		£83

Note: There is no opening stock in March and no closing stock in April, therefore the total profit should be the same for both methods (£61 + £101 = £162 and £79 + £83 = £162). The difference of 18 at the end of March (absorption 79 *less* marginal 61) has arisen because under the absorption method 'fixed production overhead' is included in the value of closing stock.

13. *(a)*

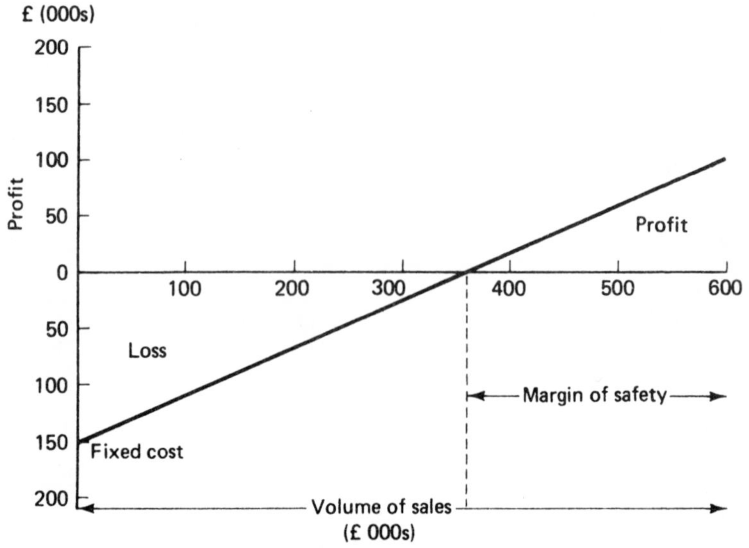

Fig. 8.17 Question 13(a): a contribution/sales graph

$$\text{Break-even point} = \text{Fixed cost} \times \frac{\text{Sales}}{\text{Contribution}}$$

$$= £150\,000 \times \frac{£600\,000}{£250\,000} = \underline{\underline{£360\,000}}$$

or

$$\text{Break-even point} = \frac{\text{Fixed cost}}{\text{Contribution}} \times 100 = \frac{£150\,000}{£250\,000} \times 100$$

$$= \underline{\underline{60\% \text{ of sales}}}$$

$$\text{Margin of safety} = \text{Sales} - \text{Sales at break-even point}$$
$$= 100\% - 60\% = 40\% \text{ or } \underline{\underline{£240\,000}}$$

(b) Points to make:

(i) It is constructed on the assumption that the product mix is the same at all volumes of production.

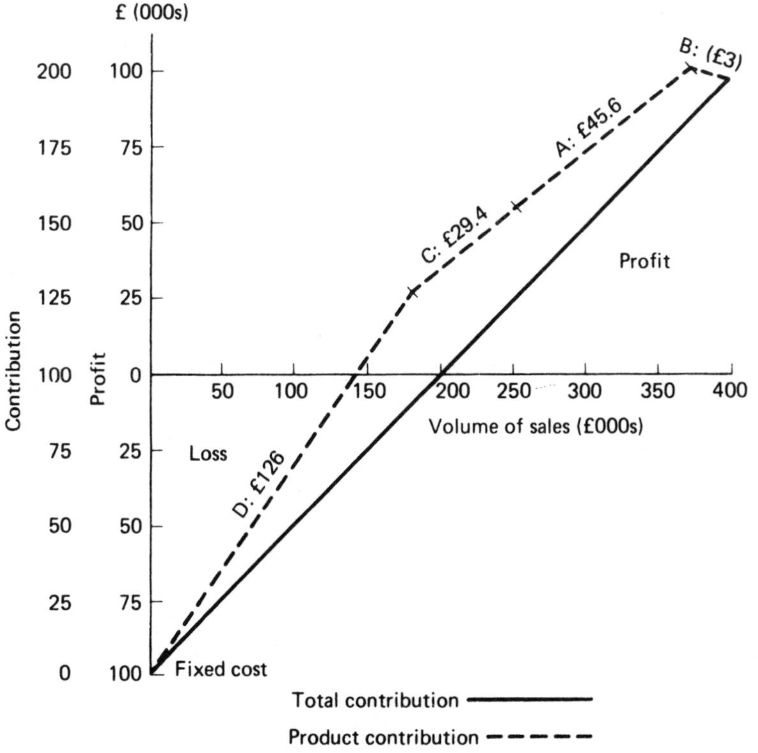

Fig. 8.18 Question 14: a cumulative contribution/sales graph

(ii) It does not show the relationship between cost and income.
(iii) No account is taken of the amount of capital employed in differing situations.
(iv) There is a presumption that there is a direct (linear) relationship in the items involved, including fixed and variable costs, volume and sales.

14. See Fig. 8.18, p. 471.

Workings:

Product	Sales	C/S ratio	Contribution	Cumulative sales	Cumulative contribution
	£	%	£	£	£
D	180 000	70	126 000	180 000	126 000
C	70 000	42	29 400	250 000	155 400
A	120 000	38	45 600	370 000	201 000
B	30 000	(10)	(3 000)	400 000	198 000
	£400 000	$49\frac{1}{2}$	£198 000		
		Less Fixed cost	100 000		
		Profit	£98 000		

UNIT 9

Variance accounting (standard costing)

9.1 Suggested answers to exercises

1. Points to make:

Historical costing:

(i) Actual cost adjustment is delayed until after the completion of the operation and there is no indication of efficient or inefficient performance.

(ii) The time-lag in reporting costs delays the introduction of corrective action.

(iii) The necessary investigation is time-consuming.

Standard costing:

(i) Standard costing is a system which introduces cost control and cost reduction.

(ii) Standard costs are carefully prepared estimates of the cost of operations, carried out under specified working conditions.

(iii) Management is motivated and employees are given an incentive. A yard-stick is provided to measure performance.

(iv) Only variances are investigated by use of the principle of exceptions.

(v) Corrective action can be taken at an early stage.

2. *(a)* See Unit 9.13.
(b) See Unit 9.14.
(c) See Unit 9.18.
(d) See Unit 9.18.

3. See Unit 9.3.

4. See Units 9.5, 9.6, 9.12 and 9.13.

5. *(a)*

Direct material total variance
= (Standard units × Standard price) − (Actual units × Actual price)
= (34 000 × £1.50) − (34 500 × £1.60)
= £51 000 − £55 200
= £4 200 (A)

Direct material price variance
= (Actual material used × Standard price) − (Actual cost of material used)
= (34 500 × £1.50) − (34 500 × £1.60)

= £51 750 − £55 200
= £3 450 (A)

Direct material usage variance
= (Standard quantity of material specified for actual production × Standard price) − (Actual material used × Standard price)
= (34 000 × £1.50) − (34 500 × £1.50)
= £51 000 − £51 750
= £750 (A)

(b)

Direct labour total variance
= (Standard hours of actual production × Standard direct labour rate) − (Actual hours worked × Actual hourly rate)
= (21 250 × £4) − (22 600 × £4.10)
= £85 000 − £92 660
= £7 660 (A)

Direct labour rate variance
= (Actual hours worked × Standard direct labour rate) − (Actual hours worked × Actual hourly rate)
= (22 600 × £4) − (22 600 × £4.10)
= £90 400 − £92 660
= £2 260 (A)

Direct labour efficiency variance
= (Standard hours of actual production × Standard direct labour rate) − (Actual direct hours worked × Standard direct labour rate)
= (21 250 × £4) − (22 600 × £4)
= £85 000 − £90 400
= £5 400 (A)

6. *Overhead expenditure:* as per budget (8 000 units)

	Rate per unit	Rate per standard hour
	£	£
Department F	17.50	2.50
Department M	39.00	3.25

Workings:

$$\frac{£140\,000}{8\,000} = £17.50 \quad \frac{£17.50}{7} = £2.50$$

$$\frac{£312\,000}{8\,000} = £39.00 \quad \frac{£39.00}{12} = £3.25$$

$$\frac{\text{Standard hours of production}}{\text{Standard hours allowed}} = \frac{152\,000}{19} = 8\,000 \text{ units (budget)}$$

(a) Standard overhead cost per unit of Z = £17.50 + £39.00 = £56.50

(b) Standard overhead cost for each department:
(i) Department F = 750 units × £17.50 = £13 125

(ii) Department M = 750 units × £39.00 = £29 250

(c) Overhead variance for the month for each department:
(i) Department F = Standard overhead cost for the production achieved *less* Actual cost
= £13 125 *less* £13 005 = £120 (F)

(ii) Department M = £29 250 *less* £29 405 = £155 (A)

7.

Budget statement

Overhead	Budget			Actual	Variance	
	Fixed	Variable	Total		Adverse	Favourable
	£	£	£	£	£	£
Management	30 000	–	30 000	30 000	–	–
Shift premium	–	3 600	3 600	4 000	400	
National insurance	6 000	7 920	13 920	15 000	1 080	
Inspection	20 000	9 000	29 000	28 000		1 000
Supplies	6 000	6 480	12 480	12 700	220	
Power	–	7 200	7 200	7 800	600	
Light and heat	4 000	–	4 000	4 200	200	
Rates	9 000	–	9 000	9 000		
Repairs	8 000	5 400	13 400	15 100	1 700	
Materials handling	10 000	10 800	20 800	21 400	600	
Depreciation	15 000	–	15 000	15 000		
Administration	12 000	–	12 000	11 500		500
Idle time	–	–	–	1 600	1 600	
Totals	120 000	50 400	170 400	175 300	6 400	1 500
					(4 900)	

8. *(a) Material variances:*

Direct material total variance
= (Standard quantity of material specified for actual production units × Standard price) – (Actual units × Actual price)
= (1 020 × £8.30) – (1 000 × £8.56)
= £8 466 – £8 560
= £94 (A)

Direct material price variance
= (Actual quantity × Standard price) − (Actual quantity × Actual price)
= (1 000 × £8.30) − (1 000 × £8.56)
= £8 300 − £8 560
= £260 (A)

Direct material usage variance
= (Standard quantity × Standard price) − (Actual quantity × Standard price)
= (1 020 × £8.30) − (1 000 × £8.30)
= £8 466 − £8 300
= £166 (F)

∴ Net variance = −£260 (A) + £166 (F) = £94 (A)

(b) Labour variances:

Direct labour total variance:
= (Standard direct labour hours produced × Standard rate per hour) − (Actual direct labour hours × Actual rate per hour)
= (136 × £3.60) − (170 × £3.90)
= £489.60 − £663.00
= £173.40 (A)

Workings:
Standard hours produced = 1 020 articles at 8 minutes per article
= 8 160 minutes
= 136 hours

Direct labour rate variance:
= (Actual hours worked × Standard rate) − (Actual hours worked × Actual rate)
= (170 × £3.60) − (170 × £3.90)
= £612 − £663
= £51 (A)

Direct labour efficiency variance:
= (Standard hours produced × Standard rate) − (Actual hours worked × Standard rate)
= (136 × £3.60) − (170 × £3.60)
= £489.60 − £612
= £122.40 (A)

9. *(a) Material variances:*

Direct material total variance:
(Standard units × Standard price) – (Actual units × Actual price)
= (780 × £4.20) – (800 × £4)
= £3 276 – £3 200
= £76 (F)

Note: 'Standard units' means units actually produced and 'actual units' means actual units issued.

Direct material price variance:
= (Actual quantity × Standard price) – (Actual quantity × Actual price)
= (800 × £4.20) – (800 × £4)
= £3 360 – £3 200
= £160 (F)

Direct material usage variance:
= (Standard quantity × Standard price) – (Actual quantity × Standard price)
= (780 × £4.20) – (800 × £4.20)
= £3 276 – £3 360
= £84 (A)

(b) Labour variances:

Direct labour total variance:
= (Standard hours of actual production × Standard rate per hour) – (Actual direct labour hours × Actual rate per hour)
= (208 × £3.80) – (195 × £3.70)
= £790.40 – £721.50
= £68.90 (F)

Direct labour rate variance:
= (Actual hours worked × Standard direct labour rate) – (Actual hours worked × Actual hourly rate)
= (195 × £3.80) – (195 × £3.70)
= £741.00 – £721.50
= £19.50 (F)

Direct labour efficiency variance:
= (Standard hours produced × Standard direct labour rate) – (Actual hours worked × Standard direct rate)
= (208 × £3.80) – (195 × £3.80)
= £790.40 – £741.00
= £49.40 (F)

Workings:

Standard hours produced = 780 articles at 16 minutes per article
= 12 480 minutes
= 208 hours

10. *Overhead absorption rates (OAR):*

$$\text{Fixed overhead absorption rate} = \frac{£88\,000}{22\,000} = £4.00 \text{ per hour}$$

$$\text{Variable overhead absorption rate} = \frac{£55\,000}{22\,000} = £2.50 \text{ per hour}$$

$$\text{Standard hours per unit} = \frac{22\,000}{2\,750} = 8 \text{ hours}$$

Standard hours of production achieved = 2 700 × 8 = 21 600 hours

(a) Overhead total variance:

= (Standard variable overhead for the production achieved + Standard fixed overhead for the production achieved) − (Actual variable overhead + Actual fixed overhead)
= (£54 000 + £86 400) − (£58 000 + £90 000)
= £140 400 − £148 000
= £7 600 (A)

Workings:

Production achieved = 21 600 hrs
Overheads: Variable: 21 600 × £2.50 = £54 000
Fixed: 21 600 × £4.00 = £86 400

(b) Fixed overhead total variance:

= Standard fixed overhead for production achieved − Actual fixed overhead
= (21 600 × £4) − £90 000
= £86 400 − £90 000
= £3 600 (A)

(c) Variable overhead total variance:

= Standard variable overhead for production achieved − Actual variable overhead
= (£21 600 × £2.50) − £58 000
= £54 000 − £58 000
= £4 000 (A)

(d) Fixed production overhead expenditure variance:

= Budgeted fixed overhead − Actual fixed overhead
= £88 000 − £90 000
= £2 000 (A)

(e) Fixed production overhead volume variance:

= Standard absorbed cost for actual production achieved − Budgeted fixed production overhead
= (21 600 × £4) − £88 000
= £86 400 − £88 000
= £1 600 (A)

(f) Variable production overhead expenditure variance:

= (Actual hours × Standard variable rate) − Actual variable overhead
= (21 500 × £2.50) − £58 000
= £53 750 − £58 000
= £4 250 (A)

(g) Variable production overhead efficiency variance:

= Standard variable production overhead for production achieved − (Actual hours taken × Standard variable rate)
= (21 600 × £2.50) − (21 500 × £2.50)
= £54 000 − £53 750
= £250 (F)

Summary:
Overhead total variance = £7 600 (A)

Made up of:		
Fixed overhead expenditure variance	£2 000 (A)	
Fixed overhead volume variance	£1 600 (A)	
Fixed overhead total variance		£3 600 (A)
Variable overhead expenditure variance	£4 250 (A)	
Variable overhead efficiency variance	£ 250 (F)	
Variable overhead total variance		£4 000 (A)
		£7 600 (A)

11. *Overhead absorption rates (OAR):*

$$\text{Fixed overhead absorption rate} = \frac{£126\,000}{25\,200} = £5.00 \text{ per hour}$$

$$\text{Variable overhead absorption rate} = \frac{£88\,200}{25\,200} = \underline{\underline{£3.50 \text{ per hour}}}$$

$$\text{Standard hours per unit} = \frac{25\,200}{8\,400} = \underline{\underline{3 \text{ hours}}}$$

Standard hours of production achieved = 8 200 × 3 = 24 600 hours

(a) Overhead total variance:

= Standard overhead cost (both fixed and variable) for the production achieved − Actual overhead cost (both fixed and variable)
= (24 600 × £8.50) − (£130 000 + £90 000)
= £209 100 − £220 000
= 10 900 (A)

(b) Fixed overhead variances:

(i) Total variance = Standard fixed overhead for production achieved − Actual fixed overhead
= (24 600 × £5) − £130 000
= £123 000 − £130 000
= £7 000 (A)

(ii) Expenditure variance = Budgeted fixed overhead − Actual fixed overhead
= £126 000 − £130 000
= £4 000 (A)

(iii) Volume variance = Standard absorbed cost for production achieved − Budgeted fixed overhead
= (24 600 × £5) − £126 000
= £123 000 − £126 000
= £3 000 (A)

(c) Variable overhead variances:

(i) Total variance = Standard variable overhead for production achieved − Actual variable overhead
= (24 600 × £3.50) − £90 000
= £86 100 − £90 000
= £3 900 (A)

(ii) Expenditure variance = (Actual hours × Standard variable rate) − Actual variable overhead
= (26 000 × £3.50) − £90 000
= £91 000 − £90 000
= £1 000 (F)

(iii) Efficiency variance = Standard variable overhead for production achieved – (Actual hours × Standard variable rate)
= (24 600 × £3.50) – (26 000 × £3.50)
= £86 100 – £91 000
= £4 900 (A)

Summary:

Overhead total variance		= £10 900 (A)
Made up of:		
Fixed overhead expenditure variance	£4 000 (A)	
Fixed overhead volume variance	£3 000 (A)	
Total fixed overhead variance		£ 7 000 (A)
Variable expenditure variance	£1 000 (F)	
Variable efficiency variance	£4 900 (A)	
Total variable overhead variance		£ 3 900 (A)
		£10 900 (A)

12. *(a)* (i) See Units 9.5 and 9.6.
(ii) See Fig. 9.1 and Units 9.12 and 9.13.

(b)

Variance statement for direct material and direct labour for week ending 12 November 19..

Direct material total variance:
= (Standard units × Standard price) – (Actual units × Actual price)
= [(240 × 12) × £18] – £52 800
= £51 840 – £52 800
= £960 (A)

Direct material price variance:
= (Actual quantity × Standard price) – Actual cost of material used
= (2 640 × £18) – £52 800
= £47 520 – £52 800
= £5 280 (A)

Direct material usage variance:
= (Standard quantity × Standard price) – (Actual quantity × Standard price)
= (2 880 × £18) – (2 640 × £18)
= £51 840 – £47 520
= £4 320 (F)

∴ Net material variance = £4 320 – £5 280 = £960 (A)

Direct labour total variance:

= (Standard hours of actual production × Standard rate per hour) − (Actual direct labour hours × Actual rate per hour)
= [(240 × 10) × £4] − (2 520 × £4.40)
= £9 600 − £11 088
= £1 488 (A)

Direct labour rate variance:

= (Actual hours worked × Standard direct labour rate) − (Actual hours worked × Actual rate)
= (2 520 × £4) − (2 520 × £4.40)
= £10 080 − £11 088
= £1 008 (A)

Note: Actual rate = $\frac{\text{Wages paid}}{\text{Hours worked}}$

$= \frac{\pounds 11\,088}{2\,520}$

= £4.40

Direct labour efficiency variance:

= (Standard hours produced × Standard rate) − (Actual hours worked × Standard rate)
= (2 400 × £4) − (2 520 × £4)
= £9 600 − £10 080
= £480 (A)

∴ Total labour variance = £1 008 + £480 = £1 488 (A)

Copies of this statement would be sent to the general manager, works manager, purchasing officer, personnel manager and other persons responsible for setting standards and controlling manufacturing processes.

13. *(a) Overhead total variance:*

= Standard overhead cost (both fixed and variable) for the production achieved − Actual overhead (both fixed and variable)
= [(180 × 20) × £6.25] − £19 400
= (3 600 × £6.25) − £19 400
= £22 500 − £19 400
= £3 100 (F)

(b) *Fixed overhead total variance:*

= Fixed overhead cost for production achieved − Actual fixed production overhead
= (3 600 × £4) − £12 000
= £14 400 − £12 000
= £2 400 (F)

(c) *Variable overhead total variance:*

= Standard overhead cost for the production achieved − Actual variable overhead
= (3 600 × £2.25) − £7 400
= £8 100 − £7 400
= £700 (F)

Check: Net effect = £2 400 (F) + £700 (F)
= £3 100 (F) overhead total variance

(d) *Fixed overhead expenditure variance:*

= Budgeted fixed overhead − Actual fixed overhead
= (4 000 × £4) − £12 000
= £16 000 − £12 000
= £4 000 (F)

(e) *Fixed overhead volume variance:*

= Standard absorbed cost for production achieved − Budgeted fixed overhead
= (3 600 × £4) − (4 000 × £4)
= £14 400 − £16 000
= £1 600 (A)

Check: Net effect = £4 000 (F) − £1 600 (A)
= £2 400 (F) fixed overhead total variance

(f) *Variable overhead expenditure variance:*

= (Actual hours × Standard variable rate) − Actual variable overhead
= (4 050 × £2.25) − £7 400
= £9 112.50 − £7 400
= £1 712.50 (F)

(g) Variable overhead efficiency variance:

= Standard variable overhead for the production achieved − (Actual hours × Standard variable rate)
= (3 600 × £2.25) − (4 050 × £2.25)
= £8 100 − £9 112.50
= £1 012.50 (A)

Check: Net effect = £1 712.50 (F) − £1 012.50 (A)
= £700 (F) variable overhead total variance

14. *(a)* (i) *Sales volume variance:*

= (Budgeted meals × Standard profit) − (Actual meals × Standard profit)
= (1 240 × £1.80) − (1 260 × £1.80)
= −(20 × £1.80)
= £36.00 (F)

(ii) *Ingredient price variances:*

= (Actual price − Standard price) × Actual usage
For ingredient A:
= (£3.58 − £3.48) × 300 kg
= £0.10 × 300 kg
= £30.00 (A)

For ingredient B:
= (£7.20 − £7.44) × 150 kg
= −£0.24 × 150 kg
= £36.00 (F)

(iii) *Ingredient usage variance:*

= (Actual quantity − Standard quantity) × Standard price
For ingredient A:
= (300 kg − 315 kg) × £3.48
= −15 kg × £3.48
= £52.20 (F)

For ingredient B:
= (150 kg − 157$\frac{1}{2}$ kg) × £7.44
= −7$\frac{1}{2}$ kg × £7.44
= £55.80 (F)

(b)

	£	£
Budgeted gross profit		2 232.00
Add Favourable variances:		
Sales volume variance	36.00	
Price:		
Ingredient B	36.00	
Usage:		
Ingredient A	52.20	
Ingredient B	55.80	
		180.00
		2 412.00
Less Adverse variance:		
Price:		
Ingredient A		30.00
Actual gross profit		£2 382.00

(c) There is a small increase in sales volume which accounts for the sales volume variance of £36.

Ingredient A shows an *adverse price variance* of £30 and this requires investigation to establish the reason for the variance of 10 pence per kg. If this is an increase of a permanent nature it will be necessary to adjust the standard price in due course.

Ingredient B has a *favourable price variance* of 24 pence per kg, which may be the result of a special purchase. The purchasing department will be able to state whether advantage can be taken of this price in the future.

The *favourable usage variances* of ingredients A and B (£52.20 and £55.80 respectively) may be the result of efficency or possibly an error in the fixing of the quantity standard.

It is assumed that there are no clerical errors in the information that was supplied by the staff.

UNIT 10

Budgetary control

10.1 Suggested answers to exercises

1. *(a)*

Cash budget for the six months July to December 19 . 1

	July	August	September	October	November	December	Totals
	£	£	£	£	£	£	£
Balance b/f	25 000	25 850	27 400	22 850	25 300	28 950	25 000 (July)
Receipts							
Bank loan	30 000						30 000
Capital	20 000						20 000
Sales	12 600	12 600	15 500	15 500	15 500	19 300	91 000
	£87 600	£38 450	£42 900	£38 350	£40 800	£48 250	166 000
Payments							
Purchases	6 800	6 800	6 800	6 800	7 600	7 600	42 400
Wages and salaries	2 500	2 500	2 500	2 500	2 500	2 500	15 000
Rent			7 000			7 000	14 000
Light and heat	200	200	200	200	200	200	1 200
Office expenses	500	500	500	500	500	500	3 000
Loan interest	450	450	450	450	450	450	2 700
Rates			2 000	2 000			4 000
Consultancy fee	700						700
Advertising	200	200	200	200	200	200	1 200
Machinery	50 000						50 000
Drawings	400	400	400	400	400	400	2400
	£61 750	£11 050	£20 050	£13 050	£11 850	£18 850	136 600
Balance c/f	£25 850	£27 400	£22 850	£25 300	£28 950	£29 400	29 400

(b)

Forecast profit calculation for six months to December 19 . 1

	£	£		£
Purchases	42 400		Sales	91 000
Less Stock	3 000			
		39 400		
Wages and salaries		15 000		
Rent		14 000		
Light and heat		1 200		
Office expenses		3 000		
Loan interest		2 700		
Rates		4 000		
Consultancy fee		700		
Advertising		1 200		
Cost of sales		81 200		
Estimate profit		9 800		
		£91 000		£91 000

2. *(a)* Points to make:
   (i) size and structure of the budget committee;
   (ii) establishing and charting levels of responsibility and authority throughout the organisation;
   (iii) the types of budget to be prepared for each area, the frequency of reports, and the information which is to be given to management;
   (iv) the need to explain the purpose and objects of the budgetary control system in order to obtain the co-operation and interest of staff and to avoid the resistance to change which may occur;
   (v) preparation of a timetable for introducing the various aspects of the new system and, for accounting purposes, the division of the year into calendar months, weekly or four-weekly periods, etc.;
   (vi) design of forms, ordering of stationery and training of staff to operate the system.

   (b) (i) decision on the composition of the committee so that the heads of the main departments are represented, as well as other officials with special responsibilities;
   (ii) defining the functions of the committee and formulating a declaration of the policy of the company in respect of sales quantities, types of product and price ranges;
   (iii) a statement on the service and production facilities available or to be made available in respect of labour, direct labour hours,

machines and machine hours, also estimates on the future costs of materials, wages and overheads;

(iv) provision of working capital to meet the proposed programme;

(v) determination of the key factor, which is the level of demand for the products or services of the undertaking, or a shortage of one of the productive resources – skilled labour, for instance.

3. *(a)*

Statement of costs and profit for a four-week period

	Budget (units) 10 000	Per unit	Flexible budget (units 6 200	Actual (units) 6 200	Variance
	£	£	£	£	£
Direct costs:					
Materials	130 000	13.00	80 600	83 018	2 418(A)
Wages	65 000	6.50	40 300	44 330	4 030(A)
	195 000	19.50	120 900	127 348	6 448(A)
Overheads:					
Variable	13 000	1.30	8 060	8 060	–
	208 000	20.80	128 960	135 408	6 448
Fixed	117 000	11.70	117 000	117 000	–
	325 000	32.50	245 960	252 408	6 448
Profit	85 000	8.50	8 240	1 792	(6 448)
Selling price	£410 000	£41.00	£254 200	£254 200	–

(b) There is an operation profit variance of £83 208 (£85 000 – £1 792). This variance is due to the low volume of activity, which is 3 800 units below the budget figure of 10 000 units, and to the increases in the cost of materials and wages. The total variance consists of:

	£	
Sales volume (3 800 × £8.50)	32 300	
Fixed production overhead volume variance (3 800 × £11.70)	44 460	
	76 760	
Direct materials price variance	2 418	(3% of £80 600)
Direct wages rate variance	4 030	(10% of £40 300)
	£83 208	

4.

Statement of budgeted, actual and absorbed overhead
for year ended 31 December 19..

Production department	Hours worked	Absorption rate	Budget	Actual	Absorbed	(Under-)/ over-absorbed
		£	£'000	£'000	£'000	£'000
A	185 000	3.00	554	539	555	16
A	200 000	2.00	390	399	400	1
			944	938	955	17

Workings:

	Budget	Actual
	£	£
Production department A	280 000	290 000
Service department: X($\frac{3}{4}$)	72 000	78 000
Y($\frac{3}{5}$)	90 000	75 000
Z($\frac{2}{3}$)	112 000	96 000
	£554 000	£539 000

Overhead absorbed for
production achieved = 185 000 hours @ £3.00 = £555 000

	Budget	Actual
	£	£
Production department B	250 000	275 000
Service department: X($\frac{1}{4}$)	24 000	26 000
Y($\frac{2}{5}$)	60 000	50 000
Z($\frac{1}{3}$)	56 000	48 000
	£390 000	£399 000

Overhead absorbed for
production achieved = 200 000 hours @ £2.00 = £400 000

5.

Flexible budget (monthly)

Hours of work	3 000	4 000	*Fixed* 4 500	5 000
Expense:	£	£	£	£
Supervision	2 000	2 480	2 720	2 960
Indirect wages	1 920	2 560	2 880	3 200
Consumable materials	3 000	4 000	4 500	5 000
Rent and rates	1 480	1 480	1 480	1 480
Heat and light	400	400	500	500
Power	2 640	3 520	3 960	4 380
Cleaning	240	240	300	300
Repairs	800	1 000	1 100	1 260
Depreciation	3 000	3 000	3 800	3 800
	15 480	18 680	21 240	22 880

Departmental standard rate: £4.72

6.

Cash budget for quarter ending 31 December 19..

	October	November	December
	£	£	£
Balance brought forward	3 600	(7 970)	(16 850)
Receipts:			
Sales	27 500	31 000	36 500
	31 100	23 030	19 650
Payments:			
Purchases	24 000	25 000	14 000
Rates	1 920		
Gas and electricity	430		
Wages	9 600	12 000	12 000
Overheads	3 120	2 880	3 260
	39 070	39 880	29 260
Balance carried forward	(£7 970)	(£16 850)	(£9 610)

Workings:

Sales

	October	November	December
	£	£	£
	28 000	32 000	38 000
Less 25% credit	7 000	8 000	9 500
	21 000	24 000	28 500
Add Previous month's credit sales	6 500	7 000	8 000
	27 500	31 000	36 500

Purchases

August: £24 000 (paid October)
September: £25 000 (paid November)
October: £14 000 (paid December)

Overheads

	October		November		December	
		£		£		£
		3 600		3 400		3 800
Less Gas and electricity	160		200		220	
Rates	320		320		320	
		480		520		540
		3 120		2 880		3 260

7. See p. 492.

8. See Unit 10.2.

9. See Units 10.4 to 10.13 inclusive.

7.

Monthly sales report
Month ended 30 June 19..

Product	Actual sales		Actual sales at standard prices		Budgeted sales at standard prices		Variances:		
	Quantity	Value	Price	Value	Quantity	Value	Total	Price	Volume
		£	£	£		£	£	£	£
A	1 800	198 000	100	180 000	1 200	120 000	78 000 (F)	18 000 (F)	60 000 (F)
B	300	9 000	25	7 500	400	10 000	1 000 (A)	1 500 (F)	2 500 (A)
C	1 020	86 700	80	81 600	960	76 800	9 900 (F)	5 100 (F)	4 800 (F)
D	120	7 200	50	6 000	240	12 000	4 800 (A)	1 200 (F)	6 000 (A)
E	1 100	36 300	30	33 000	850	25 500	10 800 (F)	3 300 (F)	7 500 (F)
Totals		337 200		308 100		244 300	92 900 (F)	29 100 (F)	63 800 (F)

10. *(c)*

(ii) Direct wages

	Rate per hour	Quarter ending 31 Mar.		30 June		30 Sept.		31 Dec.		*Totals*	
	£	Hours	£	Hours	£	Hours	£	Hours	£	Hours	£
Department 1											
Product: A	1.50	2 300	3 450	2 000	3 000	1 800	2 700	2 700	4 050	8 800	13 200
B	1.50	2 400	3 600	2 160	3 240	1 440	2 160	2 040	3 060	8 040	12 060
		4 700	7 050	4 160	6 240	3 240	4 860	4 740	7 110	16 840	25 260
Department 2											
Product: A	2.00	1 840	3 680	1 600	3 200	1 440	2 880	2 160	4 320	7 040	14 080
B	2.00	2 120	4 240	1 908	3 816	1 272	2 544	1 802	3 604	7 102	14 204
		3 960	7 920	3 508	7 016	2 712	5 424	3 962	7 924	14 142	28 284
Totals		8 660	£14 970	7 668	£13 256	5 952	£10 284	8 702	£15 034	30 982	£53 544

10. *(a)*

Quarterly sales budget for period ending 31 December 19 . 9

	Quarter ending				
	31 Mar.	30 June	30 Sept.	31 Dec.	*Totals*
	£	£	£	£	£
Area P					
Product: A	16 900	20 280	15 210	23 660	76 050
B	16 240	12 180	12 180	20 300	60 900
	33 140	32 460	27 390	43 960	136 950
Area Q					
Product: A	8 450	6 760	5 070	10 140	30 420
B	14 210	12 180	8 120	10 150	44 660
	22 660	18 940	13 190	20 290	75 080
Area R					
Product: A	13 520	6 760	10 140	11 830	42 250
B	10 150	12 180	4 060	4 060	30 450
	23 670	18 940	14 200	15 890	72 700
Totals	£79 470	£70 340	£54 780	£80 140	£284 730

(b)

Quarterly production budget for period ending 31 December 19 . 9

	Quarter ending									
	31 Mar.		30 June		30 Sept.		31 Dec.		Total	
	M/cs	Hours	M/cs	Hours	M/cs	Hours	M/cs	Hours	M/cs	Hours
Department 1										
Product: A	23	2 300	20	2 000	18	1 800	27	2 700	88	8 800
B	20	2 400	18	2 160	12	1 440	17	2 040	67	8 040
	43	4 700	38	4 160	30	3 240	44	4 740	155	16 840
Department 2										
Product: A	23	1 840	20	1 600	18	1 440	27	2 160	88	7 040
B	20	2 120	18	1 908	12	1 272	17	1 802	67	7 102
	43	3 960	38	3 508	30	2 712	44	3 962	155	14 142
Totals	43	8 660	38	7 668	30	5 952	44	8 702	155	30 982

(c)

Quarterly production cost budget for period ending 31 December 19 . 9
(i) Direct materials

	Cost per machine	Quarter ending 31 Mar.	30 June	30 Sept.	31 Dec.	*Totals*
	£	£	£	£	£	£
Materials: Group X						
Product: A	150	3 450	3 000	2 700	4 050	13 200
B	200	4 000	3 600	2 400	3 400	13 400
	350	7 450	6 600	5 100	7 450	26 600
Materials: Group Y						
Product: A	87	2 001	1 740	1 566	2 349	7 656
B	61	1 220	1 098	732	1 037	4 087
	148	3 221	2 838	2 298	3 386	11 743
Totals		£10 671	£9 438	£7 398	£10 836	£38 343

(ii) See p. 493.

(iii) Factory overhead (absorbed)

	% on direct wages	Quarter ending 31 Mar.	30 June	30 Sept.	31 Dec.	*Totals*
		£	£	£	£	£
Department 1						
Product: A	150	5 175	4 500	4 050	6 075	19 800
B	150	5 400	4 860	3 240	4 590	18 090
		10 575	9 360	7 290	10 665	37 890
Department 2						
Product: A	75	2 760	2 400	2 160	3 240	10 560
B	75	3 180	2 862	1 908	2 703	10 653
		5 940	5 262	4 068	5 943	21 213
Totals		£16 515	£14 622	£11 358	£16 608	£59 103

(d)

Quarterly factory overhead cost budget for period ending 31 December 19 . 9

	Quarter ending 31 Mar.	30 June	30 Sept.	31 Dec.	*Totals*
Department 1					
	£	£	£	£	£
Indirect material	1 064	887	709	886	3 546
Fuel and lighting	396	330	265	331	1 322
Repairs to machines	414	345	276	345	1 380
Indirect wages	4 390	3 658	2 927	3 658	14 633
Factory expenses	3 429	2 857	2 286	2 857	11 429
Depreciation					
Machinery and plant	1 674	1 395	1 116	1 395	5 580
	£11 367	£9 472	£7 579	£9 472	£37 890
Department 2	£	£	£	£	£
Indirect material	709	591	473	591	2 364
Fuel and lighting	265	221	176	220	882
Repairs to machines	276	230	184	230	920
Indirect wages	2 927	2 439	1 951	2 439	9 756
Factory expenses	1 071	893	714	893	3 571
Depreciation					
Machinery and plant	1 116	930	744	930	3 720
	£6 364	£5 304	£4 242	£5 303	£21 213
Totals	£17 731	£14 776	£11 821	£14 775	£59 103

$$\text{Absorption rate} = \frac{\text{Budgeted overhead}}{\text{Budgeted direct wages}} \times 100$$

$$\text{For Department 1: } \frac{£37\,890}{£25\,260} \times 100 = \underline{\underline{150\%}}$$

$$\text{For Department 2: } \frac{£21\,213}{£28\,284} \times 100 = \underline{\underline{75\%}}$$

(e)

Quarterly administration overhead budget for period ending 31 December 19.9

	Quarter ending 31 Mar.	30 June	30 Sept.	31 Dec.	*Totals*
	£	£	£	£	£
Office expenses	7 872	6 560	5 248	6 560	26 240
Salaries	4 074	4 074	4 074	4 074	16 296
Directors' fees	1 250	1 250	1 250	1 250	5 000
Training levy	1 375	1 375	1 375	1 375	5 500
Depreciation					
Office furniture	127	127	127	127	508
Totals	£14 698	£13 386	£12 074	£13 386	£53 544

(f)

Quarterly selling expenses budget for period ending 31 December 19.9

	Quarter ending 31 Mar.	30 June	30 Sept.	31 Dec.	*Totals*
	£	£	£	£	£
Travellers' salaries	3 143	3 143	3 144	3 144	12 574
Advertising	780	650	520	650	2 600
Motor expenses	2 048	1 707	1 365	1 706	6 826
Depreciation					
Motor vehicles	312	312	313	313	1 250
	£6 283	£5 812	£5 342	£5 813	£23 250

Absorption rates:

Administration overhead rate (as percentage on direct wages)

$$= \frac{\text{Administration overhead}}{\text{Direct wages}} \times 100$$

$$= \frac{£53\,544}{£53\,544} \times 100 = \underline{\underline{100\%}}$$

$$\text{Selling overhead rate} = \frac{\text{Selling overhead}}{\text{Machines sold}}$$

$$= \frac{£23\,250}{155} = \underline{\underline{£150 \text{ per machine}}}$$

(g)

Quarterly cash budget for period ending 31 December 19 . 9

	Quarter ending			
	31 Mar.	30 June	30 Sept.	31 Dec.
	£	£	£	£
Balance brought forward	9 220	25 836	(9 437)	2 900
Receipts				
Sales	84 502	70 418	56 335	70 419
	93 722	96 254	46 898	73 319
Payments				
Direct and indirect materials	15 388	12 823	10 259	12 823
Wages: direct and indirect	23 230	19 358	15 487	19 358
Fuel and lighting	661	551	441	551
Repairs to machines	690	575	460	575
Factory expenses	4 500	3 750	3 000	3 750
Office expenses	7 872	6 560	5 248	6 560
Salaries: Administration	4 074	4 074	4 074	4 074
Travellers	3 143	3 143	3 144	3 144
Directors' fees		2 500		2 500
Training levy	5 500			
Advertising	780	650	520	650
Motor expenses	2 048	1 707	1 365	1 706
Freehold property		50 000		
	£67 886	£105 691	£43 998	£55 691
Balance carried forward	25 836	(9 437)	2 900	17 628

(h)

Forecast product costs for period ending 31 December 19 . 9

		Product A			*Product B*	
		£	£		£	£
Material:						
Group X		150			200	
Y		87			61	
			237			261
Direct labour:	Hours			Hours		
Department 1	100	150		120	180	
2	80	160		106	212	
	180		310	226		392
			547			653
Factory overhead:	%			%		
Department 1	150	225		150	270	
2	75	120		75	159	
			345			429
			892			1 082
	%					
Administration overhead:	100		310			392
			1 202			1 474
Selling overhead:			150			150
			1 352			1 624
Profit (20% on selling price):			338			406
Selling price:			1 690			2 030

Budgeted profit:

	£
88 machines @ £338 =	29 744
67 machines @ £406 =	27 202
	£56 946

(i)

Master budget
Forecasted Profit and Loss Account for year ending 31 December 19 . 9

	£	£		%
Sales		284 730		100
Production costs				
Direct materials		38 343		
Direct labour		53 544		
Factory overhead		59 103		
Cost of sales		150 990		53
Gross profit		133 740		47
Less Administration costs	53 544		18.8	
Selling expenses	23 250		8.2	
		76 794		27.0
Profit before taxation		56 946		20.0
Less Corporation tax		28 000		9.8
Profit after taxation		28 946		10.2
Appropriation of profits				
Balance brought forward		7 000		
Profit available for distribution		35 946		
General reserve	5 000			
Preference dividend 8%	8 000			
Proposed ordinary dividend 8%	10 000			
		23 000		
Balance (carried forward)		12 946		

Workings:

		£
Stock of materials:	Opening stock	41 280
	Purchases	41 383
		82 663
	Less Quantity used	38 343
	Closing stock	£44 320

Budgeted Balance Sheet as at 31 December 19 . 9

	Cost	*Depreciation*	*Net*
Assets employed	£	£	£
Freehold premises	200 000		200 000
Plant and machinery	90 000	39 300	50 700
Motor vehicles	20 000	11 250	8 750
Office furniture	8 000	3 008	4 992
	£318 000	£53 558	264 442
Investments (market value £10 550)			10 000
Current assets			
Stock		44 320	
Debtors		18 056	
Cash at bank and in hand		17 628	
		80 004	
Less Current liabilities:			
Creditors	28 000		
Wages due	2 500		
Preference dividend	8 000		
Ordinary dividend	10 000		
		48 500	
Working capital			31 504
			£305 946

Financed by

	Authorised	Issued
Ordinary shareholders' interest in the company	£	£
125 000 ordinary shares of £1 each, fully paid	125 000	125 000
Reserves		
General reserve	40 000	
Profit and Loss Account	12 946	
		52 946
Ordinary shareholders' equity		177 946
Preference shareholders' interest in the company	Authorised	
100 000 8% preference shares of £1 fully paid	100 000	100 000
Deferred taxation		28 000
		£305 946

Workings:

Fixed assets:

Freehold premises: £150 000 + £50 000 (cash budget, June) = £200 000

Plant and machinery: Depreciation £30 000 + £5 580 (department 1) + £3 720 (department 2) = £39 300

Motor vehicles: Depreciation £10 000 + £1 250 (selling expenses budget) = £11 250

Office furniture: Depreciation £2 500 + £508 (administration expenses budget) = £3 008

Stock: see p. 500.

Debtors:

	£
Receipts from sales (cash budget)	84 502
	70 418
	56 335
	70 419
	281 674
Less Debtors (Balance Sheet 19 . 8)	15 000
	266 674
Sales (sales budget)	284 730
Debtors at 31 December 19 . 9	£ 18 056

Creditors:	£	£
Creditors (balance sheet 19 . 8)		32 000
Add Purchases (direct and indirect materials)		47 293
		79 293
	£	
Less Payments (cash budget)	15 388	
	12 823	
	10 259	
	12 823	
		51 293
Creditors at 31 December 19 . 9		£28 000

Wages:

		£
Direct (production cost budget)		53 544
Indirect: Department 1 (factory overhead budget)		14 633
2 (factory overhead budget)		9 756
		77 933
Add Wages due at 31 December 19 . 8 (Balance Sheet)		2 000
		79 933
Less Payments: (cash budget)	23 230	
	19 358	
	15 487	
	19 358	
		77 433
Wages due at 31 December 19 . 9		£2 500

General reserve: £35 000 + £5 000 (appropriation) = £40 000

UNIT 11

Integrated and non-integrated accounts

11.1 Suggested answers to exercises

1. *(a)* Points to make:

(i) The various documents recording costs, such as purchases, wages, overheads, etc., are recorded by double entry in various subsidiary ledgers, the general rule being that expenses are debited in the cost accounts and credited in the Financial Ledger Control Account (which really represents all the creditors', cash and bank payments in the financial accounts). The Cost Ledger is the principal ledger in the cost department and it contains Control Accounts which record the details shown in the subsidiary ledgers, in summarised form.

(ii) There are also other accounts which deal with under- or over-absorbed overheads, capital expenditure and cost of sales, as well as a costing Profit and Loss Account.

(iii) The Cost Ledger is made self-balancing by the use of a Financial Ledger Control Account and this enables a Trial Balance to be extracted.

(iv) The detailed costs in the subsidiary ledgers are analysed in order to obtain the separate amounts chargeable to the cost centres and Control Accounts.

(b)

(i) Integrated accounts are accounts in an integrated system in the Financial Ledger. This avoids the duplication of records which occurs when the cost department has a separate set of books.

(ii) Interlocking accounts are a system in which a link between the Financial Ledger and the Cost Ledger is made by keeping a Memorandum Account in the Financial Ledger. This is the Cost Ledger Control Account, which usually has identical entries to those in the Financial Ledger Control Account in the Cost Ledger, but appearing on the opposite side of the account. The interlocking accounts are continuously in agreement or are readily reconcilable.

(iii) A Control Account is an account in the principal ledger and its purpose is to control the entries in the subsidiary ledger. The subsidiary ledger has transactions which are recorded in detail in individual accounts and these are entered in total or summary form in the Control Account. At the end of the period the total of the balances in the accounts in the subsidiary ledger should equal the balance in the Control Account.

2. *(a)* The items which are responsible for the difference in profit are disclosed in a reconciliation statement.

(b) Items which may appear in the Financial Ledger but not in the Cost Ledger are:

(i) charitable donations;
(ii) dividends and interest received or paid;
(iii) bad debts;
(iv) expenses written off;
(v) legal charges;
(vi) rent receivable;
(vii) penalties and damages payable;
(viii) reserves or provisions;
(ix) depreciation calculated on a different basis;
(x) profit or loss on investments and fixed assets.

Items in the Cost Ledger which may differ from those shown in the Financial Ledger are:

(i) variations in the value of stocks;
(ii) work-in-progress – there may be anticipated losses and provisions against these in the financial accounts. In some circumstances interest on borrowed money may be included in the cost but will be excluded from the valuation in the final accounts. Work-in-progress value in the financial accounts will be in accordance with the standard accounting practice and may well differ from the cost shown in the Cost Ledger.

3.

Financial Ledger Control A/c

	£'000		£'000
Costing Profit and Loss A/c (sales)	1 600	Balance b/d	154
Balance c/d	175	*Purchases*	
		Stores Ledger Control A/c	260
		Work-in-progress Ledger Control A/c	23
		Wages Ledger Control A/c	1 050
		Expenses	
		Works	60
		Administration	110
		Selling and Distribution	50
		Costing Profit and Loss A/c	68
	£1 775		£1 775
		Balance b/d	175

Stores Ledger Control A/c

	£'000		£'000
Balance b/d	49	Work-in-progress Ledger Control A/c	267
Financial Ledger Control A/c (purchases)	260	Balance c/d	42
	£309		£309
Balance b/d	42		

Wages Ledger Control A/c

	£'000		£'000
Financial Ledger Control A/c	1 050	Work-in-progress Ledger Control A/c	800
		Production Overhead Control A/c	250
	£1 050		£1 050

Production Overhead Control A/c

	£'000		£'000
Stores Ledger Control A/c	27	Work-in-progress Ledger Control A/c	302
Wages Ledger Control A/c	250	Overhead Adjustment A/c	35
Financial Ledger Control A/c (expenses)	60		
	£337		£337

Administration Overhead Control A/c

	£'000		£'000
Financial Ledger Control A/c	110	Finished Goods Stock Ledger Control A/c	110
	£110		£110

Selling and Distribution Overhead Control A/c

	£'000		£'000
Financial Ledger Control A/c (expenses)	50	Cost of Sales A/c	50
	£50		£50

Work-in-progress Ledger Control A/c

	£'000		£'000
Balance b/d	70	Finished Goods Stock Ledger Control A/c	1 337
Financial Ledger Control A/c (purchases)	23	Balance c/d	98
Stores Ledger Control A/c	240		
Wages Ledger Control A/c	800		
Production Overhead Control A/c	302		
	£1 435		£1 435
Balance b/d	98		

Finished Goods Stock Ledger Control A/c

	£'000		£'000
Balance b/d	35	Cost of Sales A/c	1 447
Work-in-progress Ledger Control A/c	1 337	Balance c/d	35
Administration Overhead Control A/c	110		
	£1 482		£1 482
Balance b/d	35		

Cost of Sales A/c

	£'000		£'000
Finished Goods Stock Ledger Control A/c	1 447	Costing Profit and Loss A/c	1 497
Selling and Distribution Overhead Control A/c	50		
	£1 497		£1 497

Overhead Adjustment A/c

	£'000		£'000
Production Overhead Control A/c	35	Costing Profit and Loss A/c	35
	£35		£35

Costing Profit and Loss A/c

	£'000		£'000
Cost of Sales A/c	1 497	Financial Ledger Control	
Overhead Adjustment A/c	35	A/c (sales)	1 600
Financial Ledger			
Control A/c	68		
	£1 600		£1 600

Trial Balance as at 31 December 19 . 7

	£'000	£'000
Financial Ledger Control A/c		175
Stores Ledger Control A/c	42	
Work-in-progress Ledger Control A/c	98	
Finished Goods Stock Ledger Control A/c	35	
	£175	£175

4.

Financial Ledger Control A/c

	£		£	£
Capital		Balance		640 648
Expenditure A/c	12 793	*Purchases*		
Costing Profit		Stores Ledger		
and Loss A/c		Control A/c	371 926	
(sales)	993 494	Production		
Balance c/d	784 236	Overhead		
		Control A/c	32 484	
		Work-in-		
		Progress		
		Ledger Control		
		A/c	46 591	
		Administration		
		Overhead		
		Control A/c	1 342	
		Selling and		
		Distribution		
		Overhead		
		Control A/c	2 917	
				455 260
		Wages Ledger		
		Control A/c		408 439
		Salaries Ledger		
		Control A/c		149 379

	£		£	£
		Expenses		
		Production Overhead Control A/c	4 209	
		Administration Overhead Control A/c	3 876	
		Selling and Distribution Overhead Control A/c	5 843	
				13 928
		Costing Profit and Loss A/c (profit)		122 869
	£1 790 523			£1 790 523
		Balance b/d		784 236

Stores Ledger Control A/c

	£		£
Balance b/d	224 209	Work-in-progress Ledger Control A/c	392 246
Financial Ledger Control A/c (purchases)	371 926	Production Overhead Control A/c	15 498
Work-in-progress Ledger Control A/c	72 785	Administration Overhead Control A/c	397
Material returns	2 106	Selling and Distribution Overhead Control A/c	1 024
		Stock Discrepancy A/c	234
		Balance c/d	261 627
	£671 026		£671 026
Balance b/d	261 627		

Wages Ledger Control A/c

	£		£
Financial Ledger Control A/c	408 439	Work-in-progress Ledger Control A/c	348 976
		Production Overhead Control A/c	59 463
	£408 439		£408 439

Salaries Ledger Control A/c

	£		£
Financial Ledger Control A/c	149 379	Production Overhead Control A/c	21 862
		Administration Overhead Control A/c	87 654
		Selling and Distribution Overhead Control A/c	39 863
	£149 379		£149 379

Production Overhead Control A/c

	£		£
Financial Ledger Control A/c (purchases)	32 484	Work-in-progress Ledger Control A/c	133 841
Stores Ledger Control A/c	15 498		
Wages Ledger Control A/c	59 463		
Salaries Ledger Control A/c	21 862		
Financial Ledger Control A/c (expenses)	4 209		
Overhead Adjustment A/c	325		
	£133 841		£133 841

Administration Overhead Control A/c

	£		£
Stores Ledger Control A/c	397	Overheads Adjustment A/c	298
Salaries Ledger Control A/c	87 654	Finished Goods Stock Ledger Control A/c	92 971
Financial Ledger Control A/c (purchases)	1 342		
Financial Ledger Control A/c (expenses)	3 876		
	£93 269		£93 269

Selling and Distribution Overhead Control A/c

	£		£
Stores Ledger Control A/c	1 024	Overheads Adjustment A/c	304
Salaries Ledger Control A/c	39 863	Cost of Sales A/c	49 343
Financial Ledger Control A/c (purchases)	2 917		
Financial Ledger Control A/c (expenses)	5 843		
	£49 647		£49 647

Work-in-progress Ledger Control A/c

	£		£
Balance b/d	197 375	Capital Expenditure A/c	12 793
Financial Ledger Control A/c (purchases)	46 591	Stores Ledger Control A/c	
		Manufactured parts	72 785
Stores Ledger Control A/c	392 246	Material returns	2 106
Wages Ledger Control A/c	348 976	Finished Goods Stock Ledger Control A/c	806 790
Production Overhead Control A/c	133 841	Balance c/d	224 555
	£1 119 029		£1 119 029
Balance b/d	224 555		

Capital Expenditure A/c

	£		£
Work-in-progress Ledger Control A/c	12 793	Financial Ledger Control A/c	12 793
	£12 793		£12 793

Finished Goods Stock Ledger Control A/c

	£		£
Balance b/d	219 064	Cost of Sales A/c	820 771
Work-in-progress Ledger Control A/c	806 790	Balance c/d	298 054
Administration Overhead Control A/c	92 971		
	£1 118 825		£1 118 825

Cost of Sales A/c

	£		£
Finished Goods Stock Ledger Control A/c	820 771	Costing Profit and Loss A/c	870 114
Selling and Distribution Overhead Control A/c	49 343		
	£870 114		£870 114

Overheads Adjustment A/c

	£		£
Administration Overhead Control A/c	298	Production Overhead Control A/c	325
Selling and Distribution Overhead Control A/c	304	Costing Profit and Loss A/c	277
	£602		£602

Stock Discrepancy A/c

	£		£
Stores Ledger Control A/c (abnormal loss)	234	Costing Profit and Loss A/c	234
	£234		£234

Costing Profit and Loss A/c

	£		£
Cost of Sales A/c	870 114	Financial Ledger Control A/c (sales)	993 494
Overhead Adjustment A/c	277		
Stock Discrepancy A/c	234		
Financial Ledger Control A/c (profit)	122 869		
	£993 494		£993 494

Trial Balance as at 31 December 19 . 8

	£	£
Financial Ledger Control A/c		784 236
Stores Ledger Control A/c	261 627	
Work-in-progress Ledger Control A/c	224 555	
Finished Goods Stock Ledger Control A/c	298 054	
	£784 236	£784 236

5. *(a)* The object of opening the following accounts is as follows:

(i) **Work-in-progress Account.** This is an account or cost sheet in a subsidiary ledger, which takes the form of printed cards or sheets. These are contained in the Work-in-progress Ledger and each account represents a production order for materials, components, contracts or products. The object is to show in detail the prime costs and absorbed overheads and the value of the work-in-progress for each order. The orders are in various stages of completion, transactions are recorded in detail and the values are controlled by the Work-in-progress Ledger Control Account in the principal ledger. On completion the account is withdrawn from the ledger and is transferred to the finished goods ledger.

(ii) **Finished Goods Stock Ledger Control Account.** Control Accounts appear in the principal ledger and the object of this account is to control the values of the finished goods stock shown in the subsidiary ledger. The total of the balances on the individual accounts should always equal the value of the balance in the control account. There are debits for the opening balance, for amounts transferred from the Work-in-progress Ledger Control Account and for the administration overhead. When goods are sold the account is credited and the value is transferred to the Cost of Sales Account.

(iii) **Overhead Adjustment Account.** Overheads are included in the cost of specific products or saleable services and are charged to these items by means of absorption rates, which are based on estimates. This may lead to an over- or under-absorption of overhead expenses, and at the end of an accounting period the difference or balance on each overhead Control Account is transferred to the Overhead Adjustment Account. The object is to dispose of under- or over-absorptions by transferring them to an adjustment account, which is closed by transferring the balance of the account to the Costing Profit and Loss Account.

(iv) **Cost of Sales Account.** The cost of the finished goods which are sold are debited to this account together with the selling overhead expenses which apply to the sales. The balance of the account is transferred to the Costing Profit and Loss Account. The object of this account is to deal with the total cost of production, administration and marketing which applies to the goods sold, and to transfer this to the Costing Profit and Loss Account.

(b) When there is a difference between the profit shown in the financial accounts and that shown in the Costing Profit and Loss Account it is necessary to reconcile these by preparing a Memorandum Reconciliation Statement. This can be undertaken by checking the items shown in the Control Accounts with the same items in the financial books and then by making a note of the items which appear in one set of accounts only. This will reveal items which have different values and items which are related to the type of accounts produced.

The reason for such items is that different methods of accounting may be used in the cost or financial accounts. In the financial accounts there may be items which are not related to manufacturing operations, such as investment income and donations to charities, and there may be provisions for bad debts and other items. The cost accounts may include items which are not relevant to the financial accounts, such as notional rent and the interest which is sometimes charged to contract accounts. Timing differences are sometimes responsible for costs which vary, and this may be due to the fact that in one set of accounts the expenses may cover a slightly different period.

The reconciliation statement when in vertical form will commence with the profit as shown in the cost ledger, and there will be additions or subtractions to this figure until it reaches the profit shown in the financial accounts. If the reconciliation statement is in horizontal or account form, the financial profit is shown on the left-hand side and costing profit is on the right.

Entries and additions are made to the financial profit for those items which do not appear in the cost accounts but which have reduced the financial profit, and additions are made to the costing profit for the items which have increased the financial profit. Items which have appeared only in the Cost Ledger and which have increased the costing profit are entered and added to the financial profit, and any items which may have reduced the costing profit are added to that profit. If all the variations are accounted for the totals on each side of the statement will agree.

6.

Memorandum Reconciliation Statement

	£		£
Profit in Financial Ledger	122 982	Profit in Cost Ledger	139 088
Loss on sale of computer	7 000	Dividend received	3 000
Payment to member of staff	25 000	Profit on sale of machinery	7 294
		Extra depreciation	5 000
		Variation in stock valuation	600
	£154 982		£154 982

Memorandum Reconciliation Statement

	£	£
Costing profit		139 088
Add Amounts debited in Cost Ledger:		
Cost of sales (difference in valuation of stores stock)	600	
Production overhead:		
Extra depreciation in cost accounts	5 000	
		5 600
		144 688
Add Amounts credited in Financial Ledger:		
Dividend received	3 000	
Profit on sale of machinery	7 294	
		10 294
		154 982
Less Amounts debited in Financial Ledger:		
Loss on sale of computer	7 000	
Payment to member of staff	25 000	
		32 000
Profit as per financial accounts		£122 982

Workings:
Stock valuation

	Financial accounts £	Cost accounts £	Difference £	Effect on profit
Opening stock	93 964	99 252	5 288	–
Closing stock	107 542	112 230	4 688	+
Reduction in cost	– 13 578	– 12 978	– 600	–

Financial profit is £600 above that in the cost accounts.

In the Cost Ledger opening stock increases costs by £5 288 and closing stock reduces cost by £4 688, a difference of £600, representing extra cost of sales, and lower profit.

Ascertaining the profit in the Cost Ledger
This is the balancing figure in a statement in account form or the last total in a vertical statement which commences with the financial profit. Otherwise it can be found by taking the financial profit and adding or subtracting the difference between the adjustments to financial profit and the adjustments to the costing profit.

	Additions to financial profit £		Additions to costing profit £		Difference £
	7 000		3 000		
	25 000		7 294		
			5 000		
			600		
	32 000	–	15 894	=	16 106
Financial profit					122 982
Costing profit					£139 088

7. *(a) Layout in account form:*

Reconciliation Statement

	£		£
Profit in financial ledger	57 000	Profit in cost ledger	1 000
Debenture interest	2 000	Interest received	1 000
Discount allowed	8 000	Discount received	3 000
Stock valuation		*Stock valuation*	
Work-in-progress	1 000	Raw materials	23 000
Finished stock	1 000	Interest on capital	30 000
Over-absorbed overheads		Notional rent	20 000
Administration	10 000	*Under-absorbed overheads*	
Selling and distribution	14 000	Production	15 000
	£93 000		£93 000

Alternative layout in vertical form:

Reconciliation Statement

	£'000	£'000
Costing profit		1
Add Items not credited in cost accounts:		
Interest received	1	
Discount received	3	
		4
		5
Less Items excluded from the cost accounts:		
Debenture interest	2	
Discount allowed	8	
		10
		(5)
Add Items included only in the cost accounts:		
Interest on capital	30	
Notional rent	20	
		50
		45
Less Overhead adjustments shown only in the cost accounts:		
Administration over-absorbed	10	
Selling and distribution over-absorbed	14	
	24	
Add Production overhead under-absorbed	15	
		9
		36
Add Net increase in stock values shown in financial accounts:		
Raw materials	23	
Work-in-progress	(1)	
Finished stock	(1)	
		21
Profit in financial accounts		£57

(b) Interest on capital and notional rent are imputed or notional costs; that is, they are assumed or hypothetical costs charged to the

accounts in order that the figures produced should be comparable with those of other organisations where these expenses are actual costs. It is suggested by some, although not generally accepted, that these costs should be included because capital in the form of materials and other assets should return an income.

The following arguments are put forward in favour of:

(i) **interest on capital.**

(1) There should be a return on capital invested in contracts of long duration and those on which no progress payments are received. Whether the cash comes from company funds or from other sources, it should earn interest. Interest is payable when there is a loan or overdraft which is related to the expenditure on the contract.

(2) Materials which are held in stock until they mature (timber, tobacco, wine and spirits) incur costs in the form of rent for the storage space and interest on the capital invested.

(3) Credit should be taken for the use of the capital provided by the firm because it is borrowed or used on behalf of the customer and interest has to be paid when money is borrowed.

(4) When different methods of production are used or when production is financed in different ways it is essential to include interest, otherwise a proper comparison cannot be made between these methods or procedures.

(5) In economic terms interest is the reward of capital and profit is not indicated until interest is included in costs.

(ii) **notional rent.**

(1) If a comparison is to be made of the manufacturing and trading results of factories or firms, and premises are owned by one factory or organisation but not by others, then it is necessary to include a charge for rent.

(2) Different profit is shown when one organisation only includes depreciation for the premises used and another charges the rent payable.

8.

	£	£
Costing profit		249 005
Less Amounts only included in the financial accounts:		
Discount allowed	6 799	
Debenture interest	4 625	
Loss caused by fire	3 025	
		14 449
		234 556

	£	£
Add Income included only in financial accounts:		
Discount received	8 127	
Dividend received	1 516	
		9 643
		244 199
Add Additional depreciation included in cost accounts		1 229
		245 428
Less Items only included in the cost accounts:		
Notional rent	12 750	
Interest on capital	18 500	
		31 250
		214 178
Less Income arising from stock valuation:		
Stores stock	(85)	
Work-in-progress	(225)	
Finished stock	3 213	
		2 903
Profit in financial accounts		£211 275

Workings:

Income arising from stock valuation:

		Cost accounts		
	Stores stock	Work-in-progress	Finished stock	
	£	£	£	£
Opening stock	8 860	37 260	51 282	
Closing stock	8 325	39 285	57 645	
Income	(535)	2 025	6 363	
		Financial accounts		
	£	£	£	
Opening stock	8 550	37 800	52 200	
Closing stock	8 100	40 050	55 350	
Income	(450)	2 250	3 150	4 950
Less Income in cost accounts	(535)	2 025	6 363	7 853
Difference	(85)	(225)	3 213	2 903

9. See Unit 11.8.
Points to make:
Advantages of an integrated system
(i) Elimination of a principal ledger.
(ii) Saving of time and effort.
(iii) Reconciliation statement unnecessary.
(iv) It assists the auditor (reduction in time spent on explanations).
(v) Stocks and valuations only apply to one set of accounts.
(vi) Reduction in errors which may occur when two systems are used.
(vii) No need for a Memorandum Cost Ledger Control Account.
(viii) Avoidance of duplication of accounting records.

Disadvantages
(i) In particular cases the loss of independence by those engaged on the costing function may be considered a disadvantage.
(ii) The accountant responsible for costing may be hampered or feel that the system restricts his or her freedom of action.
(iii) Accounting information is required in greater detail for purposes of costing and problems may arise when there is reliance on the financial accounting system for information.

These disadvantages may be imagined rather than real, but generally the success of a single system will depend on the efficiency of the organisation.

10. *(a)*

Figures in £'000s

Capital Account

		Balance b/d	500

Reserves Accounts

		Balance b/d	100

Creditors Accounts

Materials returned	20	Balance b/d	75
Bank	448	Materials purchased	495
Discount received	12	Carriage inwards	22
Balance c/d	112		
	592		592
		Balance b/d	112

Expense Creditors Accounts

Bank	365	Balance b/d	10
		Production overhead	160
		Administration overhead	130
		Selling and distribution overhead	60
		Balance c/d	5
	365		365
Balance b/d	5		

Freehold Buildings Account

At cost b/d	250		

Plant and Machinery Account

At cost b/d	150		

Provision for Depreciation of Plant and Machinery Account

Balance c/d	75	Balance b/d	50
		Production overheads	25
	75		75
		Balance b/d	75

Raw Materials Stock Account

Balance b/d	110	Creditors (returns)	20
Creditors	495	Work-in-progress	425
Creditors (carriage)	22	Price variance	18
		Balance c/d	164
	627		627
Balance b/d	164		

Bank Account

Balance b/d	75	Wages and salaries	212
Debtors	1 175	Creditors	448
		Expense creditors	365
		Balance c/d	225
	1 250		1 250
Balance b/d	225		

Wages and Salaries Account

Bank	212	Work-in-progress	125
Deductions	25	Production overhead	30
Wage rate variance	8	Administration overhead	50
		Selling and distribution overhead	40
	245		245

Sundry Deductions Account

		Wages and salaries	25

Cost of Sales Account

Selling and distribution overheads	105	Profit and Loss Account	1 105
Finished goods	1 000		
	1 105		1 105

Sales Account

Profit and Loss Account	1 250	Debtors	1 250

Variances Account

Material (price)	18	Material (usage)	10
Production overhead (expense)	12	Wages (rate)	8
Administration overhead	9	Labour (efficiency)	15
Profit and Loss Account	28	Production overhead (efficiency)	20
		Production overhead (capacity)	9
		Selling and distribution	5
	67		67

Discounts Allowed Account

Debtors	18	Administration overhead	18

Discounts Received Account

Administration overheads	12	Creditors	12

Bad Debts Account

Debtors	13	Administration overhead	13

Work-in-progress Account

Balance b/d	20	Finished goods	800
Raw materials	425	Balance c/d	27
Wages	125		
Production overheads	212		
Usage variance	10		
Labour efficiency variance	15		
Production overhead efficiency variance	20		
	827		827
Balance b/d	27		

Finished Goods Account

Balance b/d	30	Cost of sales	1 000
Work-in-progress	800	Balance c/d	20
Administration overheads	190		
	1 020		1 020
Balance b/d	20		

Production Overheads Account

Salaries	30	Work-in-progress	212
Expense creditors	160	Expense variance	12
Depreciation	25		
Capacity variance	9		
	224		224

Administration Overheads Account

Salaries	50	Finished goods	190
Expense creditors	130	Discounts received	12
Discounts allowed	18	Variance (under-absorption)	9
Bad debts	13		
	211		211

Selling and Distribution Overheads Account

Salaries	40	Cost of sales	105
Expense creditors	60		
Variance (over-absorption)	5		
	105		105

Debtors Accounts

Balance b/d	100	Bank	1 175
Sales	1 250	Discount allowed	18
		Bad debt written off	13
		Balance c/d	144
	1 350		1 350
Balance b/d	144		

(b)

Trial Balance

	£	£
Capital Account		500
Reserves		100
Creditors		112
Expense Creditors	5	
Freehold Buildings	250	
Plant and Machinery	150	
Provision for Depreciation of Plant and Machinery		75
Raw Materials Stock	164	
Bank Account	225	
Sundry Deductions		25
Cost of Sales Account	1 105	
Sales Account		1 250
Variances Account		28
Work-in-progress	27	
Finished Goods	20	
Debtors	144	
	2 090	2 090

UNIT 12

The computerisation of management accounting

12.1 Suggested answers to exercises

1. See Units 12.3 and 12.8.

2. See Units 12.3 and 12.8.

3. The schedule should include:

(i) customer details, including name, address, telephone number, credit rating, terms of trading (if special), order details, etc.;

(ii) internal customer details (i.e. departments entitled to initiate production orders), who has the authority, production order details, etc.;

(iii) estimate system, standard costs of production, selling costs, materials specifications, component costs, grades of labour, etc.;

(iv) procedures for recording costs, waste, re-operations, etc., from all departments;

(v) procedures for recording overheads and absorbing them on to particular jobs.

4. This requires a description of the system illustrated in Fig. 12.2 and discussed in Unit 12.4.

5. Points to include:

(i) The cost accounts and the financial accounts will be prepared from the same input of data and the duplication of work inherent in traditional management accounting systems will be avoided.

(ii) The use of networked terminals will enable data to be fed in as they arise as each job or process is carried out, without the need for detailed paper records.

(iii) Records will be updated faster and give earlier awareness of problems and of opportunities to correct adverse trends or take account of favourable changes in the business environment. This improved information may enable more efficient estimation and more competitive tendering.

(iv) Detailed analysis of costs and expenditures will help the budgetary control process by signalling exceeded budgets and initiating controls and corrective actions.

(v) Routine data collection and analysis of paper records will cease, leaving management free to take positive action in the planning and implementation of policies. Changes in production schedules made necessary by trends in sales, costs, etc., can be implemented.

(vi) The ability of the computer to analyse routine entries gives an improved set of information to management, which is made fully aware of the true situation in all critical areas, such as the order book, cash flow, work-in-progress, stock inventories, personnel and profitability positions. Adverse movements in prices will generate variance reports to alert management to problem areas.

6. *(a)* The functional budgets include the following:

a sales budget;
a production budget;
a manufacturing budget (direct materials, direct wages, factory overhead);
administration, selling and distribution cost budgets;
a purchases budget;
a cash budget;
a plant utilisation budget;
a capital expenditure budget.

(b) Problems likely to be encountered are as follows:

(i) The structure of the existing budgetary control arrangements would need to be known, including the chief personalities in the field, the budget officer and the budgetary committee and those responsible for the functional budgets listed above.

(ii) The policy of the company will set the framework for the budget, and the current general picture needs to be known as a background for the budgets to be developed.

(iii) Each functional budget needs to be examined in detail to find out what are the pre-conditions for setting up the budget (for example, production cannot be planned until sales have been forecast and have set out the level of production required to reach the planned sales figure). Then the setting up of standards for each aspect of activity has to be developed. From this can be developed a system of information about expenditures, sales, payments and profitability.

(iv) Sub-systems will need to be developed in all areas. For example; systems in the production management field will involve cost estimation, the scheduling of production, materials inventory control, work-in-progress control and finished inventory control.

UNIT 13

Other aspects of management accounting

13.1 Suggested answers to exercises

1. (*a*) and (*b*) See Unit 13.1.

2. See Unit 13.2.

3. Points to make:

(*a*) An investigation by technical experts into the availability of plant to replace the existing equipment is needed. There should also be a provisional examination of the problems associated with the introduction of automation principles, especially in regard to structural changes in premises, provision of plant and equipment, staffing, training and working capital requirements.

(*b*) Quotations must be obtained and costs estimated for all expenditure expected in connection with the possible change to automation.

(*c*) An estimate of the life of the projects and the forecast of cash flows must be made.

(*d*) Rates for the cost of capital and the internal rate of return desired by management must be established.

(*e*) A statement must be provided which discounts net cash flows and provides information on (i) pay-back period, (ii) average annual rate of return on investment, (iii) average annual rate of return on average investment, (iv) net present value and (v) internal rate of return.

4. See Unit 13.3.

5. (*a*) **Pay-back period**

	Project A			*Project B*		
Year	*Cash flow inwards* £	*Total cash flow* £	*Amount outstanding* £	*Cash flow inwards* £	*Total cash flow* £	*Amount outstanding* £
0	–	–	200 000	–	–	250 000
1	90 000	90 000	110 000	60 000	60 000	190 000
2	80 000	170 000	30 000	80 000	140 000	110 000
3	70 000	240 000	–	100 000	240 000	10 000
4	60 000	300 000	–	120 000	360 000	–

Project A:

$$\text{Period} = 2 + \frac{30\,000}{70\,000} = \underline{\underline{2.4 \text{ years}}}$$

Project B:

$$\text{Period} = 3 + \frac{10\,000}{120\,000} = \underline{\underline{3.1 \text{ years}}}$$

(b) **Average annual return on investment**

	Project A	*Project B*
	£	£
Total cash flow	300 000	360 000
Less Depreciation	200 000	250 000
Net return	100 000	110 000
Average annual return	£25 000	£27 500

$$\text{Rate of return} = \frac{\text{Average profit}}{\text{Capital invested}}$$

$$= \frac{£25\,000}{£200\,000} \times 100 \qquad \frac{£27\,500}{£250\,000} \times 100$$

$$= 12\tfrac{1}{2}\% \qquad 11\%$$

(c) **Average annual return on average investment**

Project A = 25% Project B = 22%

that is, twice the above figures in *(b)* because the average investment is half the total investment.

Project A:

$$\frac{\text{Average profit}}{\text{Average investment}} \times 100 = \frac{£25\,000}{£100\,000} \times 100 = 25\%$$

Project B:

$$\frac{\text{Average profit}}{\text{Average investment}} \times 100 = \frac{£27\,500}{£125\,000} \times 100 = 22\%$$

6. Net present value method

	Project A			*Project B*		
Year	*Cash flow inwards*	*Present value factor*	*Discounted cash flows*	*Cash flow inwards*	*Present value factor*	*Discounted cash flows*
	£	20%	£	£	20%	£
1	90 000	0.833	74 970	60 000	0.833	49 980
2	80 000	0.694	55 520	80 000	0.694	55 520
3	70 000	0.579	40 530	100 000	0.579	57 900
4	60 000	0.482	28 920	120 000	0.482	57 840
	£300 000		£199 940	£360 000		£221 240
Less Cost of capital at beginning of year 1			£200 000			£250 000
Net present value			(£60)			(£28 760)

Project A produces greater receipts at the beginning whereas Project B has greater receipts in the latter years when the present value of cash flows is much smaller. The net present value of Project A is almost zero and this indicates that the internal rate of return is close to 20 per cent. Project B has a far larger negative net present value and therefore the internal rate of return for this project is much lower than 20 per cent.

7. Internal rate of return

Year	*Cash flow* £	*Present value factor* 20%	*Discounted cash flow* £	*Present value factor* 25%	*Discounted cash flow* £
1	100 000	0.833	83 300	0.800	80 000
2	120 000	0.694	83 280	0.640	76 800
3	80 000	0.579	46 320	0.512	40 960
4	60 000	0.482	28 920	0.410	24 600
5	30 000	0.402	12 060	0.328	9 840
Totals	£390 000		£253 880		£232 200
Less Cost of capital			£235 000		£235 000
Net present value			£18 880		(£2 800)

$$\text{Internal rate of return} = \text{Present value \% at lower rate} + \frac{(\text{Net present value at low rate} \times \text{Range \%})}{(\text{Difference in DCFs})}$$

$$= 20\% + \frac{£18\,880}{£21\,680} \times 5\%$$

$$= 20\% + 4.4\%$$

$$= \underline{\underline{24.4\%}}$$

8. See Unit 13.4

9. See Unit 13.4.

10. (*a*), (*b*), (*c*) and (*d*) See Unit 13.7.

Index